AF606058

Zen Buddhist Landscape Arts of Early Muromachi Japan (1336–1573)

SUNY series in Buddhist Studies
Matthew Kapstein, editor

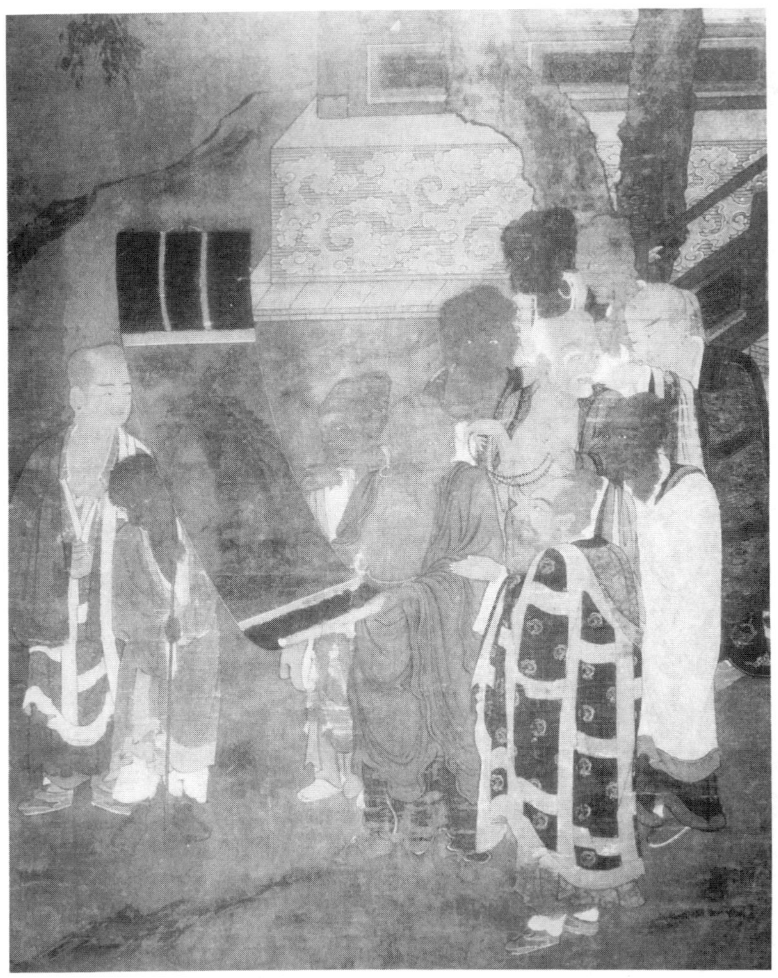

Frontispiece. *Arhats Viewing Landscape Painting*. Minchō (1351–1431). One of forty-five hanging scrolls of *Five Hundred Arhats*. Ink with color on silk. 173.6 x 89.4 cm. Important Cultural Property. Late fourteenth or early fifteenth century. Tōfuku-ji, Kyoto. Detail.

ZEN BUDDHIST LANDSCAPE ARTS OF EARLY MUROMACHI JAPAN (1336–1573)

Joseph D. Parker

STATE UNIVERSITY OF NEW YORK PRESS

Published by
State University of New York Press, Albany

Printed in the United States of America

For information, address State University of New York Press, State University Plaza, Albany, N.Y., 12246

Production by Cathleen Collins
Marketing by Patrick Durocher

Library of Congress Cataloging in Publication Data

Parker, Joseph D., 1956–
Zen Buddhist landscape arts of early Muromachi Japan (1336–1573) / Joseph D. Parker.
p. cm. — (SUNY series in Buddhist studies)
Includes bibliographical references and index.
ISBN 0-7914-3909-7 (alk. paper). — ISBN 0-7914-3910-0 (pbk. : alk. paper)
1. Arts, Zen—Japan. 2. Arts, Japanese—Kamakura-Momoyama periods, 1185–1600. 3. Landscape painting, Japanese—Kamakura-Momoyama period, 1185–1600. 4. Zen literature—Japan—History and criticism. 5. Arts, Buddhist—Japan. 6. Buddhism and the arts—Japan. I. Title. II. Series.
NX676.3.Z45P36 1998
700′.42′0882943—dc21 97-52581
CIP

10 9 8 7 6 5 4 3 2 1

Contents

Illustrations

Preface

Over two decades ago some curiosity about medieval Japanese and Chinese landscape paintings led me to investigate whether they were understood to be Zen paintings by the Buddhist monks who produced them. In this attempt I settled on the Muromachi period Japanese monk-painters Shūbun and Sesshū, and was singularly unsuccessful. All I could decipher was that for some reason a few historians and the authors of an enormous popular literature seemed absolutely convinced that their art was of the deepest religious significance, yet scholars didn't seem to know very much about the painters, little or no writings by the artists seemed to exist, and most historians thought that Zen art was really only an obscure branch of secular culture. About a decade after leaving this contradictory and dissatisfying project behind I found myself in a Ph.D. program searching for a dissertation topic. I wished to study an aspect of Buddhist art that had a substantial premodern commentary literature, so that I could work with information about how the art objects were understood by the artist's contemporaries. The objects that were recommended to me by the art historian John M. Rosenfield, a member of my dissertation committee, were landscape paintings of a genre that included the extensive inscriptions by Japanese Zen monks discussed in the present study, a number of whose visual images by chance were attributed to the very same painter Shūbun that I had studied years earlier.

When I began my work on this topic, Five Mountains Zen literature was not commonly studied in Japan or abroad because much of it is written in very poor Chinese by Japanese, a difficult situation compounded by frequent allusions to Chinese literary and historical texts that had not been explicated in annotated editions and modern translations. I was cautioned by my advisors that such work would require many years of language and literary training, and indeed it did. After years of language study I traveled to Japan for advice from specialists, and discovered several senior scholars training a new generation of younger students of Five Mountains Zen literature, history, and art. As I began to make my many journeys up the flank of Mt. Hiei to have my translations reviewed with one scholar, Iriya Yoshitaka, I observed drafts of entries being reviewed for the book Professor Iriya edited with Shimada Shūjirō, now published as *Zenrin gasan: Chūsei suibokuga or yomu* or *Painting Inscriptions of the Zen Forest: Reading Medieval Ink Paintings*. The publication of this book, together with scholarship by other younger scholars, has revolutionized the field of Japanese Five Mountains Zen studies, making it now more accessible to postwar students with some acquaintance with classical Chinese and modern Japanese than it was to such pioneers as Kageki Hideo, Marion Ury, David Pollack, and Burton Watson. Now the study of Zen textual and cultural history may beneft from the work of art historians and students of literary history as much as from Buddhist doctrinal and textual scholars.

When I was finally able to read the Five Mountains Zen texts themselves, an entire new world of Japanese intellectual life and learning opened up before me. Rather than finding devout Buddhists of a sectarian sort, I found monks highly syncretic in their study and their writing, in this manner reflecting the intellectual conditions of the mainland. Yet in their broad reading and intellectual range the Five Mountains monks contradicted virtually every assumption I held about how clear distinctions could be drawn between different schools of Buddhism; between Buddhism, Taoism, Confucianism; and even more between "religious" schools and an entire range of "secular" movements in political theory, intellectual history, poetic and prose styles, aesthetic theories, and more. While I had been trained to understand Japanese landscape arts as centered on the traditions of Japanese *waka* poetry and poetics, these monks seemed much more interested in the landscape poetry and prose writings of Six Dynasties and Sung dynasty China. And while I had expected to find Zen monks living in solitary mountain retreats, as apparently depicted in the paintings, the inscriptions consistently indicated that the monks were engaging in lives in the capitals of Kyoto and Kamakura that could only be described as highly social and greatly interested in current affairs of the day. Here I encountered an entire intellectual and social tradition supported by the massive institutional base of the Five Mountains Zen temples, an intellectual tradition that is yet to be fully integrated into the history of Japanese aesthetics and culture.

When I was attempting to select individuals and themes on which I could center my analysis, two topics were recommended to me by a very well-respected art historian, Shimada Shūjirō, yet they seemed initially to have little to do with Buddhism: artistic illusion and playfulness. On returning to read through the painting inscriptions, I quickly came to see how the Five Mountains monks understood them to be Buddhist, if I could only allow my own preconceptions of Buddhism to give way to the arguments and textual references they presented. This process led me to conceive of Zen Buddhism and of Muromachi Japanese religious and intellectual history in the broader and more complex ways I have tried to represent here.

Reading histories, one often learns more about the authors through their choices than one does about the putative subjects of their studies. When reading the history of medieval Japanese culture I had always wondered why the Zen monks most mentioned, such as Eihei Dōgen or Shūhō Myōchō (also Daitō Kokushi), were only minor figures when viewed in terms of their institutional importance. True, both founded important temples, but so did many other Zen monks and nuns during the same periods. Partially in response to this overemphasis on Dōgen and Daitō I have written a monograph to introduce some of the leading individuals and themes in the Zen Buddhism that dominated mainstream elite society during the early Muromachi Japan: the Zen of the Five Mountains temples. Moreover, I now think that answering this question about the importance of Dōgen and Daitō will take me into an investigation of Edo, Meiji, and postwar Zen and other aspects of Japanese intellectual history that could not be incorporated into the present study.

Through much of this project I have assumed that if I just translated the interpretive inscriptions on the paintings, then I would understand what the relation was between the paintings and Zen religious beliefs in the views of the Japanese Five Mountains Zen monks. However, I no longer hold the assumption informing the early stages of this work that a twentieth-century Euro-American can somehow objectively understand the interpretive categories of fourteenth-century Japanese. And this is not due to the cultural nationalism of the belief that only Japanese people can understand Japanese art and culture, nor is it due to the essentialist assumption that the differences of racial groups or of the "east" and "west" are fixed and somehow support essentially different cultural patterns. Still I would say that indeed I do now have a fairly good sense of the Muromachi period significance of the paintings, although that became possible only when buttressed by a good deal of social, literary, and institutional history.

Yet as I complete this study I do not believe that I have gotten to the bottom of the unsettling contradiction that I found in the investigation into Zen art with which I began. Rather than untangle this seeming contradiction here, I can only say at this point that it will take an entirely new type of project to uncover why it is that postwar historians' views, affected as they were by the industrialization of Japan and by the Pacific War itself, differ so significantly from the idealized views of Zen art that still have such a grip on popular conceptions both in Japan and overseas in North America, Europe, and elsewhere. It now seems to me that understanding how such deep and widespread pre- and postwar interest in the Zen landscape arts could persevere and indeed flourish in the face of opposed views held by much of the academy and other institutions requires much more than the publication of further historical data about Muromachi Japanese and Sung Chinese culture. Instead I have become increasingly aware of how important to the twentieth-century understanding of Zen Buddhism are the events and beliefs of the present century, including both mass culture and the history of the different national academies, as well as of the social mechanisms and institutions that produce and distribute knowledge of history and of contemporary events. For now I must return to some of these issues in the epilogue, and in future studies.

Below I list conventions used in the text. Romanization used is the standard modified Hepburn system for Japanese, and a modified Wade-Giles for Chinese. Because many of the texts I discuss are written in Chinese by Japanese monks, I have generally given Chinese transliterations for most terms, but where it seemed useful I have also given Japanese or, in the case of some Buddhist terms, Sanskrit readings. Western names have been given with surname last, and Chinese and Japanese names with surname first, following ordinary practice. Where characters for names are missing, I so indicate with a filled-in square. For abbreviated references I have generally used the surname, and for Buddhist monks I have generally used the *dōgo*. Occasional exceptions are those monks and artists who have come to be known by their *hōki* rather than by their *dōgō*, for example, I refer to Gidō Shūshin as Gidō and Yüan-wu K'o-ch'in as Yüan-wu, but to Gyokuen Bompō as Bompō and Chüeh-fan Hui-hung as Hui-hung.

I have listed Chinese characters in a glossary for all premodern terms and personal names, except names of paintings and titles of books and essays. Unless otherwise noted, Japanese language books have been published in Tokyo and English language publications in New York.

Acknowledgments

This work would never have been accomplished without the inspiration and guidance of Iriya Yoshitaka, Shimada Shūjirō, Kohara Hironobu, John Rosenfield, and Masatoshi Nagatomi. Professors Rosenfield and Nagatomi supervised the writing of an earlier version of this manuscript in its form as a doctoral dissertation. My one wish would be that Professor Shimada could have seen this book in print before he passed away.

Numerous others have been helpful along the long road leading from graduate school research to publication. Masatoshi Nagatomi, John Rosenfield, Griff Foulk, and anonymous reviewers for the Kuroda Institute and SUNY Press read the entire manuscript and made numerous comments useful for revisions. I am indebted to scholarship by Susan Bush and Tamamura Takeji in ways that cannot be fully acknowledged in citations. Other individuals who contributed in signficant ways include: Akazawa Eiji, Chu Chieh, Chris Cleary, Bruce Coats, Martin Collcutt, Edwin Cranston, Bill Deal, Robert Easley, Ebine Toshio, Ron Egan, Michael Fuller, Haga Kōshirō, Earl Jackson, Franklyn Josselyn, Kageki Hideo, Kanazawa Hiroshi, Kinugawa Kenji, Liz Lillehoj, Valerie Malenfer, Sam Morse, Cuong Nguyen, Ann Nishimura-Morse, Sharalyn Orbaugh, Stephen Owen, Edith Sarra, Sasaki Jōhei, Adele Schlombs, Bob Sharf, Shimao Arata, Shimizu Yoshiaki, Robert Singer, Sugahara Hisao, Takahashi Noriko, Tamura Yoshirō, Tu Wei-ming, Yanagida Seizan, and Louise Yuhas. Michael Honer and Elizabeth Lillehoj generously took photographs of the illustrations. For help with word processing and other manuscript work in the last stages of the process, I am also grateful to Ibby Ambrose and Gennane Zeller. Of course, any mistakes that remain are my own.

Financial support for the research and writing of the manuscript was provided by the Fulbright-Hays Doctoral Dissertation Research Abroad Program, the Japan Foundation, the Metropolitan Center for Far Eastern Art Study, Bucknell University, and Pitzer College's Summer Research Fellowships in the Humanities. Institutional affiliation with Kyoto University and Hanazono University made library and archival research possible, and the reading of materials was aided by participation in reading groups in Zen Buddhist texts given by Iriya Yoshitaka and Yanagida Seizan. A semester sabbatical from Pitzer College allowed me to complete some final research and revisions, and research travel during that sabbatical was supported by the Northeast Asia Council of the Association of Asian Studies. Pitzer College also provided a small publication grant to support the final stages of manuscript preparation.

The following museums, foundations, and temples allowed me to view relevant paintings in their collections: Masaki Museum, Konchi-in, Kyoto National Museum, Tokiwayama Bunko, Tokyo National Museum, Nezu Museum, and Umezawa Kinenkan. I am grateful to the following institutions for permission to publish art works from their collections: Agency for Cultural Affairs, Tokyo; the Art Institute of Chicago; Chōfuku-ji, Kyoto; Cleveland Museum of Art; Denshū-an, Engaku-ji, Kamakura; Fujita Musuem of Art, Osaka; Fukuoka Art Museum, Fukuoka Prefecture; the Gotoh Museum, Tokyo; Idemitsu Museum of Arts; Jishi-in, Nanzen-ji; Jōtenkaku Museum, Shōkoku-ji, Kyoto; Konchi-in, Kyoto; Masaki Museum, Osaka; National Palace Museum, Republic of China; Nezu Institute of Fine Arts, Tokyo; the Art Museum, Princeton University; Reiun-in, Kyoto; The Seikadō Bunka Art Museum, Tokyo; Sunritz Hattori Museum of Arts, Nagano Prefecture; Taizō-in, Kyoto; Tōfuku-ji, Kyoto; Tokiwayama Bunko, Kanagawa Prefecture; Tokyo National Museum; Umezawa Kinenkan, Tokyo; the Museum Yamato Bunkakan, Nara. I would also like to thank the following journals and university press for permission to publish here materials that they had published previously: *The Journal of Japanese Studies*, for permission to publish research that appeared in volume 21, number 1 (1995) as "The Hermit at Court: Reclusion in Early Fifteenth-Century Japanese Zen Buddhism"; *Monumenta Nipponica* volume 52, number 2, which published "Attaining Landscapes in the Mind: Nature Poetry and Painting in Gozan Zen" in their summer 1997 issue; and Princeton University Press, which published an entry titled "Contested Orthodoxies in Five Mountains Zen Buddhism" in George Tanabe, Jr., editor, *Religions of Japan in Practice*, copyright © 1998 by Princeton University Press; reprinted by permission of Princeton University Press.

Finally, I would like to express my deepest appreciation to Benjamin Kiyoshi Miyamoto, who over the past three years exchanged a wondrous sense of life and discovery for many hours stolen for final revisions, and to Jeannette Kyoko Miyamoto, who through the past decade of research and writing contributed suggestions for clarity, sense, and conciseness, and who helped make the entire journey meaningful in so many other ways.

Introduction

> The era's major [Zen] monasteries were not forbidden cloisters but grand and open public institutions. The leading Ch'an [Zen] figures of the day enjoyed eminence not only within clerical circles but also at court and among the secular elite.
>
> —Robert M. Gimello, "Mārga and Culture: Learning, Letters, and Liberation in Northern Sung [Chinese] Ch'an [Zen]"

> "Truth" about a place . . . was not discovered, but produced as a result of specific social and imaginative relationships. . . . But places are not only the result of such complex social processes; they also help to organize them and give them coherence.
>
> —Peter Bishop, *The Myth of Shangri-La*

In the year 1410 a Zen Buddhist monk from Nanzen-ji, a large temple complex in the Japanese capital of Kyoto, wrote out a landscape poem and had a painting done of the scene described by the poem. Then, following the prevailing custom of his day, he gathered responses to the images by asking prominent fellow monks and government officials to inscribe it, thereby creating a *shigajiku* poem and painting scroll. Such scrolls emerged as a preeminent form of elite Japanese culture in the last two decades of the fourteenth century, a golden age in the phenomenon now known as Japanese Zen culture. Since this painting still exists, entitled *Plantain in Evening Rain* (fig. I.1), we know that some fifteen individuals responded, including abbots of important Zen temples, a powerful daimyo official in the government, and even a Korean emissary sent to commemorate the appointment of the new Japanese shogun, Ashikaga Yoshimochi (1386–1428). All the individuals wrote their poems out in Chinese, the language of international cultural, social, political, and economic exchange of the day.[1] However, two Zen prelates were given special honor, Taihaku Shingen (1358–1415) and Chūhō En'i (1355–1413), and asked to write prose prefaces defining the Zen religious value of this social appreciation of the landscape arts.

The subject of this interdisciplinary study is the views of these two monks and their contemporaries on the Zen Buddhist significance of the landscape arts of

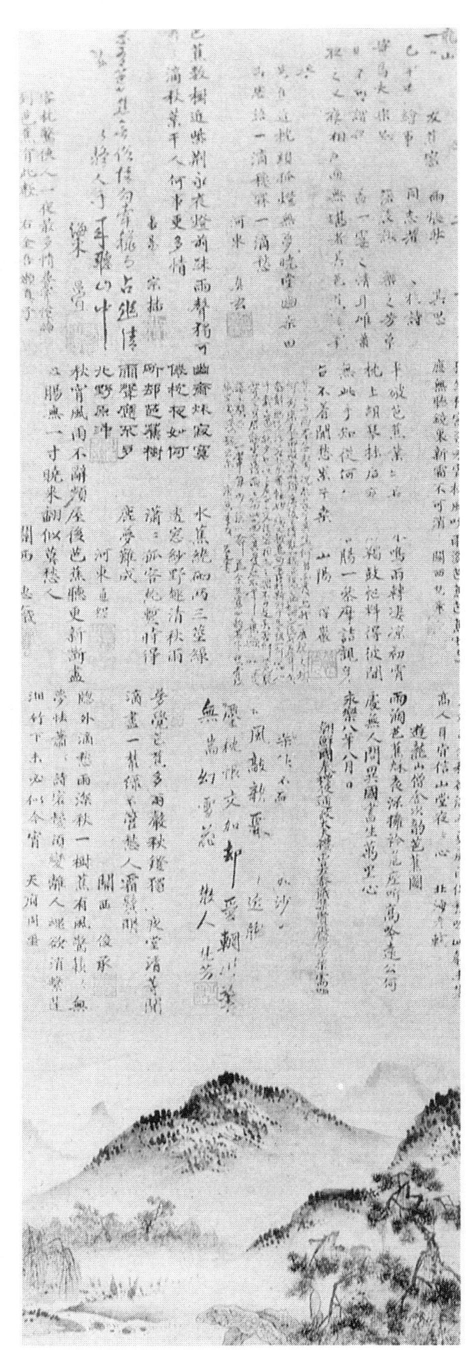

Fig. I.1. *Plantain in Evening Rain.* Inscribed by Taihaku Shingen (1358–1415) and thirteen others, with separate preface by Chūhō En'i (1355–1413). 1410. Hand scroll mounted as hanging scroll. Ink on paper. 96.2 x 31.0 cm. Important Cultural Property. Agency for Cultural Affairs, Tokyo.

painting, poetry, prose, and rock gardens. These Zen monks understood culture to be a valid mode for the production of religious value, just as they saw the Zen meditation hall as a place for the deepening of Buddhist insight. Early Muromachi period (1336–1573) documents such as this and other scrolls and related texts demonstrate that these Zen monks found the landscape arts to carry deep religious significance. The present study of these documents explores the general question of how religion is related to culture and society as it was formulated and answered by early Muromachi Japanese Zen monks at the highest levels of social status and prestige. I will show that elite Japense Zen monks in this period understood religion to be woven into ordinary social experience, such as the gathering shown in the frontispiece, rather than transcendent to society. They also saw Buddhism as discoverable through and encountered in cultural training and practice rather than separated out from culture in some separate and distinct sphere of "the religious." As we will see, in their views on this topic the Japanese Zen monks followed closely the central role of literature and culture in the general understanding and articulation of religious, moral, and philosophical truths that characterized certain important if still not well understood strands of Chinese religion, thought, and aesthetics.

In this study I investigate the location of the boundaries of the sphere of the religious through the specific conceptual theme of the Buddhist significance of the landscape arts for the early Muromachi Japanese Zen monks. We will see that prominent Japanese Zen teachers like Taihaku and Chūhō grounded their thinking on the religious significance of the landscape arts in the classical Chinese Mahayana Buddhist teaching of affirming the importance of enlightened practice in the mundane world of delusion and suffering. In the Zen tradition this teaching was given a distinctive emphasis on realizing enlightenment through lived experience that, for Taihaku and Chūhō living in the large monasteries of the *gozan* or Five Mountains Zen temple system, included frequent participation in such social occasions as that which produced the *Plantain in Evening Rain* scroll. In their socially engaged reading of the landscape arts the Muromachi Japanese Zen monks redefine the very distinction between nature and culture as it is conventionally defined both in medieval East Asian culture and in twentieth-century Japanese and Euro-American culture. In interpreting the religious significance of such social and cultural activities, we will find that the Japanese Five Mountains monks synthesized Zen and other Buddhist conceptions of religious practice and aesthetic value with those from other important Chinese intellectual traditions, including literati or *wen-jen* (J. *bunjin*) culture, the Ancient Civilization or *ku-wen* movement, early Taoism and Confucianism, and Neo-Confucianism. They did so in a manner inherited from theologians, thinkers, and aestheticians active in Sung (960–1279) and Yüan (1279–1367) dynasty China, the heyday of Chinese syncretism, without losing their sense of Zen Buddhism as their home tradition.[2] Yet ultimately these documents show how the Five Mountains monks developed a distinctively

Buddhist vision of the landscape arts through exploration of the two related themes of the illusory character of reality and the playful expression of enlightened beings.

These and other prominent Japanese Zen monks took the lead in elite cultural affairs during a period of relative stability around the turn of the fifteenth century during what was otherwise a time of great transformation in late medieval society. Domestically tensions continued in the ongoing struggle between aristocrats and newly powerful warriors for preeminence in administrative authority and prestige, land rights, and taxation. Women's social autonomy as well as property and inheritance rights at the elite levels of society were appropriated increasingly by men as male warrior influence was increasingly consolidated at the elite levels of government. Money-based trade in rapidly expanding markets intensified during the fourteenth and fifteenth centuries and, with such fundamental changes in the production and distribution of wealth, competition and social tensions brewed. Through much of the fourteenth century the military government and its aristocratic allies fought to reunite the divided Northern and Southern branches of the imperial court while peasants campaigned against estate managers through violent struggle and protest petitions, auguring the sixteenth-century spread of violent uprisings. Simultaneously a surprising number of social groups and cultural genres vaulted from lowly origins to positions of great prominence: an itinerant theater troupe with the shogun's patronage founded the elegant Nō theater; popular poetic forms were transformed into the courtly art of *renga* or linked verse, the ancestor of *haikai* or haiku poetry; and the lowly *dōbōshū* became art connoisseurs and formalized the popular art of tea into a ceremony. After the shogun Ashikaga Yoshimitsu (1358–1408) succeeded in centralizing authority late in the fourteenth century, he shifted tensions to a new arena by violating custom through attempts to outshine even the emperor not in political authority and wealth alone, but also in splendor and cultural prestige. After Yoshimitsu's death, however, the delicate balance he established of centralized shogunal authority and local warrior hunger for power lasted only a few decades before collapsing in the flames of the burning capital during the Ōnin War (1467–77).

The great metropolitan Zen temple monasteries were deeply entangled in these struggles both domestically and overseas. By the beginning of the Muromachi period Nanzen-ji and other major Zen monastic complexes had been organized by the political authorities into an administrative system known as the *gozan* (also *gosan*) or Five Mountains temples,[3] and dominant Five Mountains temples soon became active players in contemporary political struggles. Through educating Japanese monks in Chinese, they prepared representatives for visits to the continent as pilgrims, foreign emissaries, and even merchants, and these monks returned with what were for their patrons a major source of cultural capital in the form of objects and trained individuals. The temples also were places of learning as well as a site for establishing control over the latest mainland news of historical developments, bureaucratic structures, and political theories; technology and samples of material culture; architectural, printing, and cultural forms; and more. Monks from Zen monasteries competed against Buddhist monks from other major schools for political sway over the shogun, such as Yoshimitsu's nephew the Daigo-ji Shingon monk Manzai Jugō (1378–1435), whose influence and wealth became so great he was known as the "black-robed prime minister." Since the twelfth century, nunneries of the Zen and Ritsu or Vinaya sects were increasing exponentially in number and size, and this expansion was just peaking in the late fourteenth century. Resentment by rival schools of growing Zen wealth and influence at both the imperial and shogunal courts even led to attacks by armed monks from both the Zen and the previously dominant Tendai schools of Buddhism in the streets of the capital, killing monks and novices in the 1360s. During these decades the great Zen temple complexes also competed for access to land and income with the military government, with temples of other Buddhist schools, and with strengthening and proliferating *za* or guilds. The struggle continued into the fifteenth century as the military government attempted to wrest away from Zen and other temples and shrines the authority to adjudicate legal disputes, regulate rights to monopoly markets, and collect taxes. In these and many other ways, as we shall see below, the Zen temples were much more than havens for meditation, spiritual cultivation, and cultural production.[4]

In these turbulent times Zen monks strove to apply Buddhist philosophy and practice to their everyday lives in the bustling, dusty world of the temple complexes of the Five Mountains system of large metropolitan Zen temples. Certainly they experienced tensions between their religious calling and the social and political demands made on them in their busy schedules. Yet in their lives in these monasteries, the monks of the Five Mountains monasteries saw themselves as fulfilling the greatest challenge Zen Buddhism offered to its practitioners: the difficult practice of realizing enlightened insight while active in the mundane world of samsaric suffering and delusion. It was in the largest of these Five Mountains temples, such as Nanzen-ji in the eastern hills of Kyoto, where virtually all of the known poem-and-painting landscape scrolls were produced.

As we can ascertain from the various individuals who inscribed the *Plantain in Evening Rain* scroll, Five Mountains Zen was a type of Zen Buddhism whose practitioners were very much active at the highest levels in domestic and overseas elite politics and society. Close involvement with political and social leaders at the levels of both local and imperial or other central authorities' courts was nothing new to Buddhist monks from the Zen or other schools. Wherever Buddhism found a home it did so in large part due to patronage and other support from political and socioeconomic elites, from King Aśoka in India to Prince Shōtoku (574–622) in Japan. This is no less true of the Zen tradition of Buddhism throughout its history in East, Central, and Southeast Asia and beyond, whether we speak of imperial Chinese support of the important early Zen Northern school monks Shen-hsiu (606?–706) and P'u-chi (651–739)[5] and the T'ang monk Tsung-mi (780–841),[6] the role of Zen at the Tibetan Council of Lhasa,[7] or the relations of early Korean Zen monks to the Korean imperial family and of the Vietnamese emperor and Zen theologian Trần Thài Tông (r. 1225–58).[8] While the Japanese Five Mountains Zen monks joined in this tradition, they modeled their own lifestyles and religious thought more directly on Chinese Zen monks who had close relations with political elites during the Sung, Yüan, and early Ming (1368–1661) dynasties. Virtually all major Chinese monks from these periods engaged in such relations. Ta-hui Tsung-kao (1089–1163), to take perhaps the most important individual Zen master of the Sung dynasty, developed extensive contacts with powerful lay followers and patrons, as did the Yüan dynasty teacher Chung-feng Ming-pen (1263–1323), who was so highly regarded by the Japanese Five Mountains monks.[9] Japanese Five Mountains Zen may be distinctive in the systematic relationship of monks to elites of both centralized and regional governmental structures, though historians have yet to agree on the extent to which a comparable Sung or Yüan temple system may have existed.[10] Yet documents produced by the Japanese Five Mountains monks provide an important historical source for understanding the sociopolitical and particularly the cultural dimension of Zen Buddhist history.

In the present study I explore the cultural dimension to Zen Buddhist religious practice, an aspect that has received relatively little attention in historical scholarship, by selecting for in-depth study the theme of the natural landscape so popular in contemporary Five Mountains culture. My specific method is to study how the Japanese monks conceptualized the relation of the landscape arts to religious insight. My general objective is to show how these monks worked to remain true to Buddhist insight while building social and cultural relationships both with fellow Five Mountains monks and with nonordained social and political elites. Of course, as senior ecclesiastical officers in the Five Mountains temple administrative system, these monks also forged sociopolitical alliances and rivalries, promoted the economic interests of their monastic complexes, enjoyed the privileges of considerable wealth, education, and other manifestations of great social influence and prestige, and otherwise remained active in the elite circles of mundane Japanese society in the capital. However, I leave extended discussion of the political processes and socioeconomic consequences of Five Mountains Zen participation in elite secular social relations to future studies.[11] By basing my study on textual sources and focusing on doctrinal, conceptual, and terminological issues, I here follow long-standing scholarly tradition in the field of Buddhist and East Asian studies, and hope to contribute to this still poorly understood aspect of Zen Buddhist history and thought.[12]

Being culturally active both within and outside their monastic walls, the Five Mountains monks quickly became conversant in a wide range of cultural and religious traditions not limited to Zen Buddhism. This has led some religious, institutional, and cultural historians in the twentieth century to label these monks "*bunjinsō*" or "literati monks," emphasizing the deep learning of many Five

Mountains monks in Chinese *bunjin* or literati culture. Many of these scholars have then questioned the degree to which "literati monks" remained faithful to what they consider to be a rigorous Zen monastic tradition, often narrowly defined in terms of intensive meditation practice, and suggesting, in the words of one influential historian, that "cultural avocations and secular interests . . . [by the fifteenth century] weakened the religious spirit" of the Five Mountains monks.[13] Many Five Mountains Zen monks of the early Muromachi period contradicted the views of these postwar historians, for they saw culture not as an avocation but as a central part of their religious practice. They also participated in what are termed by these twentieth-century scholars as "secular" activities, such as public ceremonies, administrative duties, literary gatherings, political happenings, and social events. Yet again the views of the early Muromachi monks contrast strongly with those of postwar scholars, for the monks saw these activities not as secular interests outside the pale of their religious calling but as work at the very center of their lives as fully enlightened beings engaging in the daily business of their roles as leaders of large monastic institutions. According to the late-fourteenth- and early-fifteenth-century documents we will examine, the social and political aspects to their lives were defined by the Five Mountains monks not as secular but as integral to their religious practice. Whether writing poetry with friends, joining the shogun at a social occasion, or administering their temples, these Japanese Zen monks saw their successful completion of these activities at a high level of religious insight as a challenge to their Buddhist training to which they rose readily. They openly caution each other about the allures and dangers of lives filled with activity in the mundane world of deluded, attached, and suffering beings, which in the twentieth century we may term secular but which they saw as a realm of suffering to which any enlightened person must in compassion respond.

The larger question here is one of syncretism in both intellectual issues and social roles. In their social roles the monks clearly do combine several roles that were kept largely distinct on the continent: while choosing lives as religious leaders they also functioned as intellectual elites in a manner loosely comparable more to that of Chinese scholar-officials than to their Chinese Zen monk contemporaries. Having made the distinction, we must recall that, as we shall see, Chinese Zen monks also can be termed intellectual elites in a general sense, since they often syncretically integrated the Buddhist sectarian tradition with Taoist and Confucian or Neo-Confucian ideals as well as those of literary culture more broadly defined. However, in combining these social roles the Japanese monks often worked to master the intellectual traditions of several groups, including the Buddhist, literati, and other schools that flourished in the Sung and later dynasties: *ku-wen* or Ancient Civilization, Neo-Confucianism, and others.

For our present considerations it is important to differentiate this syncretism both in Japan and on the mainland from simple eclecticism and, more importantly, from hypocritical manipulation of ideas and beliefs for corrupt political or economic benefit.[14] In their integration of these several religious, intellectual or spiritual, and cultural traditions, the Japanese Five Mountains monks that we will read about below were on the whole quite successful in maintaining a clearly defined "home tradition," which for the monks we study is without question Zen Buddhism. The Five Mountains monks we will be reading discuss the character of their "Unity of the Three Creeds" teachings, and consistently follow a conventional pattern in their prose writings, in which they begin by presenting an array of references to several non-Buddhist traditions, and then present an argument for how the terms or individuals they mentioned may best be understood in Buddhist terms. In their syncretism they follow quite consciously the examples of their Zen Buddhist predecessors on the continent, to whom the Japanese monks looked as their teachers and the definers of their own identities. We will introduce the character of this aspect of Chinese Zen culture in our next chapter.

Understanding this aspect of Five Mountains Zen is complicated by the vexed general problem of the relation between culture and religion. Literati culture, to take the most obvious example among the mainland traditions just mentioned, is generally defined by twentieth-century literary and art historians as in its essence a cultural tradition, in a manner comparable to the way in which until recently Confucianism and Neo-Confucianism were defined by cultural historians as philosophical or political and not religious traditions. Yet both of these characterizations have come into question recently, and scholars are just now beginning to explore their religious dimensions.[15] Whatever twentieth-century cultural historians may conclude, the Muromachi Five Mountains monks were deeply impressed by the theories of spiritual and moral cultivation in continental literati culture, and were particularly conscious of the roots of Sung literati theories and practices in the contemporary *ku-wen* or Ancient Civilization movement, which they also interpreted in religious terms. Through their interests in this array of what we might define as religious, philosophical, and cultural movements, the Japanese Zen monks followed their Chinese predecessors in developing a syncretic vision of religious life as they knew it both within and beyond the confines of the Five Mountains monasteries.

Activity in the midst of ordinary sociopolitical relationships is one outcome of an important teaching common to most Mahayana Buddhist schools in the Chinese cultural sphere, including much of southeast and northeast Asia: the positive association or, to use a popular Muromachi term, the "nondualism" of the phenomenal world of suffering with the absolute realm of Buddhist wisdom.[16] This nondualism of the conventional world and the absolute realm affirms the soteriological and ontological value of both realms, and in this way joins in the important tendency in Chinese Mahayana Buddhism of attributing positive qualities to both the absolute and to the mundane. This affirmative tradition in Chinese Mahayana Buddhism should be contrasted with the tradition of apophatic denial of ultimate and mundane reality found at the historical and intellectual foundation of the

Mahayana schools in India, identified most importantly with the *prajñāpāramitā* or Perfection of Wisdom texts and the philosophy of *śūnyatā* or emptiness developed by Nāgārjuna (c. 150–250). This philosophy was modified and even challenged in a number of Mahayana Buddhist schools throughout Asia, but perhaps particularly so in China, leading to the development of conceptions of not only the religious existence of ultimate reality but also of the central role of ordinary, mundane reality in realizing religious truth.[17]

These positive assertions may best be seen in arguments asserting that the Buddha Nature exists in all beings, known more technically as the Tathāgatagarbha (J. *nyoraizō*) tradition, and its elaborations in theories of innate enlightenment (C. *pen-hsüeh*; J. *hongaku*), also referred to as absolute phenomenalism.[18] By attributing positive qualities to the absolute and asserting that the absolute was accessible or even intrinsic to humans, Buddhist philosophers began to explore the ways in which the absolute might be available to perception in various aspects of human experience before, during, and after enlightenment. Rather than negating the ordinary world of experience for the enlightened and also the unenlightened, schools of Chinese Mahayana Buddhism affirmed its soteriological and hermeneutic value, perhaps in its most sophisticated theological form in the Hua-yen school. In numerous passages translated below we will observe that the Japanese Zen monks of the Five Mountains temples were deeply committed to this tradition.

The Mahayana affirmation of mundane reality received its own distinctive interpretation in many Zen Buddhist lineages through an emphasis on the realization of insight through the most ordinary activities of everyday experience. The realization of enlightenment in mundane experience is often associated in Zen with the concept developed by the important T'ang dynasty (618–907) monk Ma-tsu Tao-i (709–88) of "ordinary mind," but was commonly found in the writings of successive generations. To return again to the influential Sung dynasty monk Ta-hui, for example, we find him writing,

> Once enlightenment is right, then throughout the twenty-four hours of your daily activities, when seeing form, hearing sounds, smelling scents, tasting flavors, feeling sensations, or knowing mental objects, whether walking, standing, sitting, or lying down, whether speaking or silent, active or still, there's nothing that is not clear.[19]

Zen masters (and twentieth-century scholars) have tended to divide, however, on the extent to which this teaching encouraged Zen monks to venture forth from their monastic cloisters, after completing extensive Buddhist practice, to the realm of ordinary social relations.[20] Other thinkers, historians, and social commentators have disagreed about whether religious organizations should become socially involved, and about whether policies of different social groups, particularly the state, should support social inequities or practice imperialism and militarism.[21] On this topic the Five Mountains Zen monks clearly aligned themselves with those in the Zen tradition who felt that the most challenging and most rewarding path of Zen practice was to be found in extensive participation in the challenging world of political, economic, and social relations.

The Zen of the Japanese Five Mountains temples might be termed the "mainstream" Zen of the day, for the Five Mountains Zen monks were powerful players in elite religious, philosophical, literary, artistic, aesthetic, social, and even political circles of Kyoto and Kamakura during the fourteenth and fifteenth centuries. While Japanese Zen had its early beginnings in the eighth and ninth centuries, it began to flourish institutionally with the success at the Kyoto court of such monks as Dainichi Nōnin (d. 1195 or 1196), Myōan Eisai (also Yōsai; 1141–1215), and Enni Ben'en (1202–80) and the arrival in Kamakura of the Chinese monks Lan-ch'i Tao-lung (1213–78) and Wu-hsüeh Tsu-yüan (1226–86). Thanks to the patronage of powerful officials both at the imperial court and in the warrior governments, both Zen monasteries and nunneries grew rapidly in size, number, and influence during the late thirteenth and through the fourteenth centuries.[22]

With the political struggles at the end of the Kamakura period, first Emperor Go-Daigo (1288–1339) and then the early Ashikaga shoguns began to systematize the largest Zen monasteries and nunneries into hierarchally ranked groupings for administrative and other purposes. During these decades they quickly came to rival and eventually to overshadow even the long-established and powerful Buddhist monastic complexes and syncretist multiplexes located near the capital of Kyoto, on Mt. Hiei north of Kyoto, and in the old, southern capital of Nara. As a system of temples that may have been modelled on a similar Chinese system, the Five Mountains temples grew rapidly during the fourteenth century to include a large number of temples in many provinces in addition to the major urban temple complexes located in and around the Japanese capitals of Kamakura and Kyoto. The term Five Mountains actually refers to ten temples, of which five were officially designated in Kyoto, the Muromachi capital near present-day Osaka, and five more in Kamakura, a former capital during the Kamakura period (1185–1333) located south of the current Japanese capital of Tokyo.[23] This temple system also included, by one estimate for the mid-fifteenth century, some sixty *jissatsu*-rank temples and over two hundred *shozan*-level temples with some five thousand branch temples. By the late fourteenth century, leading monks in these temples had been given the responsibility for administering this enormous system, appointing officers, collecting fees, ranking monasteries, and maintaining monastic regulations, while they also officiated at court ceremonies, lectured on Chinese religion and culture, tutored the shoguns, mediated political disputes, and drafted documents for overseas political relations and trade.[24] Such were the duties and conditions in which the Five Mountains monks worked and lived, circumstances far from the idyllic stereotype of the Zen monastery as a peaceful mountain refuge from ordinary social and political life.

At different points in their histories the Five Mountains temples also faced competition for patronage and authority from rival Zen monks and other Zen temples, such as Eihei Dōgen (1200–53), who was ultimately unsuccessful in his pursuit of patronage in the capital; National Teacher Daitō (or Shūhō Myōchō; 1282–1337), who founded the powerful temple of Daitoku-ji that now dominates Japanese Zen; and the eccentric Daitoku-ji monk and critic of Five Mountains Zen Ikkyū Sōjun (1394–1481).[25] From the mid-fourteenth century until late in the fifteenth century, however, the Zen of the Five Mountains temples thrived as the political and economic prosperity of the Ashikaga shogunate continued unabated.

Despite their historical importance the religious views of monks from the Japanese Five Mountains monasteries and their cultural heritage have until the past decade been comparatively little studied, despite an abundance of source materials.[26] This situation derives largely from twentieth-century conceptions of Zen in Japan and Euro-America. The Japanese Five Mountains temples were not active during the T'ang dynasty in China, which was to be canonized as the "classical" period of Zen in Sung and later Chinese histories and much twentieth-century historical scholarship. Nor were they the institutions of choice for Japanese masters celebrated in nineteenth- and twentieth-century Japanese cultural nationalism and its derivative, Euro-American popular conceptions of Zen.

These canonical judgments and their attendant simplifications of Zen history and thought have been subjected to critique during the past decade by a group of younger scholars active largely in North America, particularly assumptions of a "pure" form of Zen reaching from T'ang Chinese masters through Dōgen and Daitō to modern Japanese monastic training.[27] These conceptions may be familiar to readers in the form of a set collection of stock phrases popularly said to represent the unique character of Zen from the time of its founding: "a special transmission outside of doctrine" that "does not rely on the written word" but instead through "directly pointing to the mind" enables practitioners "to see the nature and fulfill Buddhahood."[28] The North American historians, many of them trained under the Japanese scholar Yanagida Seizan, have questioned the broad application of these phrases and such other characterizations of Zen as being radical and iconoclastic in character; antiritualist, antitextual, and antinomian in orientation; and having a special emphasis on direct intuitive, nonlinguistically based mystical insight through a neo-Hegelian merging of subject and object. I would suggest that such preconceptions have precluded the investigation of a Zen tradition like that of Japanese Five Mountains Zen, which diverges from this stereotype in several ways: it was not radical socially, since it took the form virtually of a state religion; it was clearly not iconolastic in its reverence for the sages of several Zen lineages as well as of Chinese poetry and painting; it emphasized textual and literary study; and it practiced a highly allusive and indirect mode of producing meaning. In part the present volume is an attempt to correct the neglect of the Buddhist teachings and cultural history of Five Mountains Zen that has resulted from these preconceptions, and that has also prevented other scholars from devoting a full-length study to the religious beliefs of the Five Mountains Zen monks that the present volume represents.

The present exploration of Five Mountains Zen Buddhism emphasizes precisely these cultural and social dimensions to Muromachi Japanese Zen history. Literary gatherings and other cultural events were important venues for participation by the monks of the Five Mountains temples in elite social circles, in addition of course to being appointed to abbacies and other high ecclesiastical offices and to being consulted on religious matters. In this they followed a pattern for Zen monks first established in eighth- and ninth-century China by which they gained acceptance in mainstream society through cultural means.[29] Certainly by the mid-Sung dynasty, Zen had been fully accepted into elite Chinese culture as a major intellectual and cultural tradition. With this acceptance the Chinese Zen school no longer needed to insist on its claims to Buddhist authority independent of other Buddhist schools, as it had in earlier centuries through such important self-characterizations as "the teaching outside of tradition" (*chiao-wai pieh-ch'uan*) and "not relying on words" (*pu-li mo-tzu*).[30] A number of historians have argued that the study of Buddhist texts from a wide variety of schools had been common practice in Zen from its origins.[31] By the Sung dynasty, literary practice seems to have became a central component of Zen monastic experience at leading monasteries, although certainly the objectives of such study and practice continued to be a subject of debate.[32] Japanese monks traveling to the mainland were often trained during their visits in this aspect of Zen practice, and usually returned to the islands with some competence in Chinese language, calligraphy, court and vernacular literary genres, formal document and informal literary styles, and other aspects of Chinese cultural practice. In turn those Japanese masters who had visited the mainland joined with Chinese masters teaching in Japan during the thirteenth and fourteenth centuries to reproduce this tradition in the Japanese Five Mountains temples and other monasteries. From this fount flowed not only the voluminous literature by Five Mountains Zen and other monks, but also writings on aesthetics and reflection on the appropriate role of literature and other arts in Zen practice that played a prestigious and increasingly central role in the development of indigenous literary writings, public documents, and aesthetics. Indeed, textual and literary study itself was a central image in the paintings and writings we will study, taking the visual form of the monk's studio or *shosai* where he (and less often she) read, wrote, and met with his (or her) ordained and lay associates. Through readings of their written reflections on this theme we will see how the monks worked out their sense of self and the significance of this aspect to their lives. Since the entire body of Five Mountains Zen writings is too varied to survey in the present study, I have emphasized the aspects of their writings that provide evidence for their relations with the continental traditions of literati culture and other mainstream aesthetics, thought, religion, and philosophy. This tradition of Zen dialogue with non-Buddhist culture, aesthetics, philosophy, and religion both on the mainland and in Japan produced a very large and important body of texts that is still very little studied and poorly understood, and historians have only begun to surmise the considerable extent of relations between Buddhist and non-Buddhist elites that this corpus represents.

The present study concentrates on the high point of Five Mountains literature during the decades just before and after the turn of the fifteenth century, rather than comprehensively surveying Muromachi Five Mountains literature or other landscape arts. Focusing on this period will allow us to study in depth a well-defined group of monks, rather than surveying the enormous corpus of available Five Mountains literary and other documents. These same decades are particularly important for our topic of the landscape arts, for the period in which they were active was when the natural landscape peaks in popularity as a subject in Japanese Five Mountains Zen culture, particularly in painting. As a result, the religious documents translated and discussed below from this period provide an important source for understanding Zen monks' thinking about landscape when it was squarely at the center of contemporary elite Japanese culture. The turn of the fifteenth century also seems to have been when the monk's study becomes a major theme in Japanese landscape painting, and this topos represents what will be an important strand in our consideration of the Five Mountains monks' thinking about the value of studying literary and religious texts.

This period has been chosen also for its importance as a time of Ashikaga efflorescence, dominated by the shogun Ashikaga Yoshimitsu and his successor Ashikaga Yoshimochi. Due to the period's association with Yoshimitsu, these decades have been canonized by traditional cultural historians as the Kitayama period, after the North Hills of Kyoto where Yoshimitsu built his villa, the Kinkaku-ji or Golden Pavilion, which served as the center of Muromachi elite culture. It was during these decades, too, that many of the new cultural forms now associated with the Muromachi period first came to prominence in the elite society of the Japanese imperial and shogunal courts: the *michi* or Way of *renga* or linked verse, through the efforts of the aristocrat Nijō Yoshimoto (1320–88) and the instruction in linked verse of later generations by the Five Mountains Zen monk *waka* poet Shōtetsu (1381–1459); the Nō theater of the actors, aestheticians, and playwrights Kan'ami (1332 or 1355–1384 or 1406) and his son Zeami (1363–1443) with Yoshimitsu's patronage; the ink landscape painters and Five Mountains Zen monks Shūbun (active c. 1423–60) and Minchō (1351–1431); and the formal tea ceremony developed by Nōami (1397–1471) and other members of the shōgun's new group of *dōbōshū* connoisseurs of Chinese art objects. As we will see, the Zen monks of the Five Mountains temples were important players in these and other aspects of Yoshimitsu and Yoshimochi's network of cultural and social relationships.

Finally, these five or so decades also span the mature periods of perhaps the two most renowned authors of Five Mountains Zen literature, the poet Zekkai

Chūshin (1336–1405) and the prose master Gidō Shūshin (1325–88). This study centers its analysis on the writings of these two individual Zen monks, with more emphasis on Gidō than Zekkai, together with three of their disciples and students, Taihaku and Chūhō mentioned above, and Kiyō Hōshū (1361–1424), with reference also to Gyokuen Bompō (1348–after 1420) and Ishō Tokugan (d. 1437). My objective here is not to establish the originality of an individual monk, the Romantic original genius working in splendid isolation, that has been the traditional interest of postwar New Critical approaches to texts. Rather, I look more fully at the social interaction through which the *shigajiku* poem-and-painting scrolls were completed at poetry meetings, through serial correspondence, and in other aspects of life in the Muromachi literary salons. The preservation of oral conversations is one of the most distinctive hallmarks of Zen literature, as seen in the collected sayings literature (C. *yü-lu*; J. *goroku*), and also characterizes such other aspects of Chinese and Japanese culture as the Pure Conversation (*ch'ing-t'an*) of Six Dynasties Chinese Taoism and the Kamakura period Japanese poetry meeting (*utaawase*).[33] The Japanese Five Mountains records are composed in classical Chinese that presumably does not reflect actual colloquial speech, unlike some Chinese Zen textual traditions. Yet by listening in on the conversations and arguments between these monks and their teachers, associates, and patrons, we can still discern the social processes of constructing meaning for the landscape and other prominent subjects.

These monks have been chosen primarily because of the respect given them by their contemporaries for their views on the landscape arts. We know that these seven monks were highly regarded both from the large quantity of their prose inscriptions on extant landscape scrolls, and by the great privilege it was among their contemporaries to be asked to write the preface or postface on a landscape painting. The honor of composing a prose inscription was generally given to the individual held in the highest esteem by other members of the group. These prose pieces were not only discourses on religious meaning and aesthetic theory, they were also finely crafted literary creations, often with rhymed passages interwoven through them culminating in a final poem. The reasons for this honor were simple: the preface not only provided the viewer of the scroll with the greatest knowledge of the circumstances leading to its creation, but also expounded on the significance of the landscape subject of the painting and poems on the scroll; in other words, the preface defined the sum and spiritual significance of the scroll.

These seven monks were also the Five Mountains monks most esteemed from this period among their contemporaries on the mainland in the case of Zekkai and among later generations of Japanese Zen monks, nuns, and laymen and laywomen for their learning, their insight, and their mastery of literary expression. Gidō and Kiyō were most highly respected for the depth of their knowledge of Zen Buddhist texts. Taihaku, Chūhō, and Ishō together with Gidō were renowned for their skills at prose composition, which, as we shall see below, meant much more than mere verbal dexterity. Chūhō and Kiyō gained high repute for their insight into Neo-Confucian theories of self-cultivation and ethics, while Taihaku and Chūhō commanded a most sophisticated knowledge of Chinese artistic theory and Chūhō was respected for his knowledge of *ku-wen* or Ancient Civilization theories of the spiritual significance of literature. Finally, Zekkai's skill at poetry was unsurpassed among the Five Mountains Japanese monks and Bompō was revered for his skill at painting flower subjects. In the areas of Buddhist learning, literary accomplishment, philosophy, aesthetics, and artistic skill, then, these monks were highly accomplished in the judgment of their contemporaries.

Ultimately, however, the importance of all of these monks extended well beyond the confines of the abbots' quarters, libraries, meditation halls, and art collections of the Five Mountains monasteries. As we will see below, Zekkai and Gidō were important political advisors and religious and cultural tutors to the shoguns Yoshimitsu, as was Kiyō for Yoshimochi. Gidō is known to have worked very closely on continental aesthetics and culture with the important founder of the court art of linked verse, the aristocrat Nijō Yoshimoto.[34] Kiyō was also one of only two Zen monks known to have had contact with the influential Nō playwright and aesthetician Zeami,[35] and also tutored the important political figure and Neo-Confucian and Shinto thinker Ichijo Kaneyoshi (also Kanera; 1402–81). Of course, we have only very limited information about the precise character of these relationships, and I am here not asserting influences of these monks over the cultural creations of their lay associates but only their central roles in contemporary elite cultural circles.

What interaction of the seven Five Mountains monks we can find with this impressive collection of influential politicians, poets, dramatists, aetheticians, scholars, and religious thinkers is perhaps less important than their indirect importance for the period. As leading figures of the Five Mountains temples during such a formative period for these and other traditions of Japanese culture, study of their views provides insight into the general values and ethos of early Muromachi Zen culture generally and its modes of interaction with elite lay society and culture. This is particularly important since the Five Mountains cultural documents are widely available, and their study may contribute to a deeper understanding of Muromachi literary and artistic history and theory that is often written about based on little or no familiarity with Five Mountains Zen religious aesthetics.

The central documents for this study are taken directly from the *shigajiku* poem-and-painting scrolls much like the Nanzen-ji scroll, *Plantain in Evening Rain*, with which we began. Many of the poems, prefaces, and related documents we will examine are not from extant paintings but from the extensive corpus of collected works of Five Mountains monks, many of which are available in modern printed editions. These documents reveal that the extant paintings represent only a tiny fraction of what was certainly a thriving and extensive network of individuals both within and without the Five Mountains monasteries who produced a quite substantial number of poetry collections, painting scrolls, rock gardens, and a variety of other cultural objects on landscape subjects. These scrolls, and particularly their prose prefaces, are a rich resource for the study of the religious values and aesthetic judgments produced, discussed, and propagated through a variety of public and private social forums for interaction between groups of the Japanese Five Mountains monks and, on occasion, the monks with their lay patrons, who often doubled as political authorities, fellow writers, artists, and other unordained peers.

These documents show that in these social situations the Kitayama monks worked to uncover the Buddhist significance of seemingly secular circumstances, ideals, and aesthetics, as opposed to the interest of earlier Zen texts in what seem to be, to twentieth-century conceptions, religiously oriented methods of inducing enlightenment and other master-disciple interactions. This study thus supplements our knowledge of the important master-disciple dimensions of Zen Buddhism with exploration of the interactions of mature monks with their peers, generally other mature Zen masters and their lay associates, through debate and cultural creation. This interaction occurred both in informal social forums in the monastic complexes such as poetry meetings and in more public occasions such as that which led to the production of the *Plantain in Evening Rain* scroll discussed above. These documents may be compared to Zen "encounter literature" in that they were read as a record of spiritual insight, as we shall see, and both were anthologized for use in both religious practice and in literary or linguistic study. They tell twentieth-century readers that the Zen monks of the Five Mountains monasteries lived lives of considerable social interaction and debate about the meaning of Zen Buddhism, of artistic and literary study and practice, of social relations and political theory, and of the natural landscape and its applicability to their lifestyles in the busy capitals.

In the twentieth century, scholars have generally held that Zen Buddhism was central to Muromachi period aesthetics, yet the voluminous writings by Zen monks on aesthetics from this period have not received much attention from historians. Zen aesthetics has certainly gained popularity both in Japan and abroad from the writings of Japanese scholars and philosophers such as D. T. Suzuki or Hisamatsu Shin'ichi and such Euro-American thinkers and popularizers as Alan Watts. However, for various reasons outside the purview of this study,[36] the tendency has been either to develop abstract characterizations of Zen art, to examine the iconography of particular painting or literary subjects, or to attempt to understand the motives and aesthetic values of the artists themselves in isolation from context. Such abstract characterizations have proven popular among readers searching for an introductory sketch to the vast and complex subject of Zen culture, but may seem unsatisfactory to those interested in more complexly historicized and less essentialist interpretations.

Each of these approaches to the study of Zen art is problematic. When abstract values taken from T'ang dynasty Chinese masters or twentieth-century aestheticized images of Asia are used to discuss the subject, they have little direct relevance to fourteenth- or fifteenth-century Zen religious ideals. The limitations of the iconographic approach have been well expressed by one art historian, who lamented that

"One cannot escape the impression that the philosophical content of Ch'an painting increases as the symbolism becomes less specific, particularly near the indistinct borderline between religious and secular painting."[37] And interest in the views of individual artists is often frustrated by a lack of sources, for unfortunately few writings exist by many of the most important individuals, such as the monk-painters Shūbun and Sesshū Tōyō (1420–1506), the largely unknown early Zen garden masters, and the early tea masters Nōami and Murata Jukō (1422–1502). When the views of a particular Japanese Zen monk are introduced into discussions of aesthetics, however, it most often is Dōgen who, while central to twentieth-century Japanese Buddhist philosophy, was almost completely unknown in the imperial and shogunal courts of the fourteenth and fifteenth centuries.[38]

Here we will take a different tack, by examining the complex linkages between religious and aesthetic values and conventions of an interpretive community whose members moved freely back and forth across the social boundaries of the ordained and the nonordained or across the symbolic lines between the religious and the secular. Understanding these linkages will do more than introduce the arcane jottings of bookish Japanese monks writing about art in Chinese, it will help us understand the assumptions and common vocabulary of much of elite Muromachi culture, thought, and religion. As Arthur Waley once observed about the Kitayama period, "It was in the language of Zen that poetry and painting were discussed,"[39] while the early historian George Sansom remarked about the Nō theater, "The indirect influence of Zen . . . cannot be exaggerated, [since] the producers and the actors worked primarily for an audience whose aesthetic standards were those of Zen."[40] By reading and analyzing Japanese Five Mountains Zen aesthetics, we can discover what these Zen standards were and how the Five Mountains monks understood them to be related to their Buddhist religion.

The Muromachi period in Japanese cultural history has also become widely known in the twentieth century as the fount of the Zen *michi* or Ways of such arts as ink painting, the Nō theater, linked verse, Zen gardens, and the tea ceremony. The *michi* or Ways are generally said to have begun in the late Heian period (794–1185) and flourished with the rise of Zen aesthetics in the fourteenth and fifteenth centuries. When we examine the actual writings of the Zen monks active in court cultural circles, however, their extensive knowledge of the continental masters of religion, culture, and aesthetics introduces a new world of aesthetic value to the ways in which the *michi* have generally been understood. As a result, readers already familiar with the terms traditionally associated with such so-called Zen arts, such as archaic simplicity, *wabi*, and *sabi*, will find that the Five Mountains Zen monks preferred different terms, making their aesthetic and intellectual world a dramatically different and highly sinified one. In the discussion below, for example, will be found scattered references to such Chinese aesthetic terms as *p'ing-t'an* or even and bland, *t'ien-chen* or natural instinct, and *kao-ku* or lofty and ancient, which clearly overlap in usage, content, and value to what have come to be known as the "tea" values of archaic simplicity, *wabi*, and *sabi* and may have provided important historical origins.

Yet other terms popularly associated with the *michi* and the Zen arts, such as mystery, suggestion, and natural simplicity, are clearly contradicted by the writings of Five Mountains Zen monks: their writings might better be described as highly allusive and complex texts which assume a common knowledge of a broad range of intellectual, religious, and aesthetic treatises. Contrary to views of Zen as somehow resisting linguistic expression and interpretation in its insistence on immediacy of expression,[41] the Five Mountains Zen monks clearly participated in cultural circles in which textual allusions and subtle, written or verbal appreciation of Zen art was very much the norm. The allusive character of Five Mountains literature has proved an obstacle to postwar scholarly study, partially explaining why most discussions of the so-called Zen arts have ignored this rich interpretive resource.[42] Yet the same trait makes reading these Zen texts an immensely rich and rewarding exploration of the associated aesthetic and religious traditions and images that Muromachi Zen monks used in their artistic interpretations.

The aesthetics of Zen and of the *michi* or Zen arts have often been associated in twentieth-century scholarship with the topic of the natural world. Many of the reasons for this association have less to do with Japanese cultural history than with late-nineteenth- and twentieth-century relations of Euro-America with the various countries of Asia.[43] Yet Muromachi Japanese poets, painters, monks, dramatists, and gardeners were clearly interested in the natural world, and the late fourteenth century witnessed a dramatic rise in the popularity of landscape themes in poetry, prose, and painting from the Five Mountains Zen temples. Indeed, the first extant poem-and-painting or *shigajiku* scrolls are dominated by landscape subjects.

In much East Asian elite culture the landscape was traditionally an image of spiritual freedom, religious power, moral purity, and a political position transcendent to or outside of the ambitions and avarice of ordinary life. By applying the landscape to their lives in the busy world of the capital, the Japanese Five Mountains monks laid claim to that spiritual value and consequently religious authority for themselves. By doing so largely through allusions to Chinese cultural sources, they reminded their readers of their preeminence in contemporary knowledge of mainland culture for the Japanese islanders. In this manner they produced for themselves a locus of symbolic value and cultural capital independent of other major institutions in the capital, including the imperial and shogunal courts and other Buddhist, Shinto, and syncretist centers. In addition to the obvious political advantages such a resource would have for any institution, it also provided these Zen monks with an implicit critique of these rival institutions through the implication that, by not being associated with the transcendent purity, their rivals were part of the spiritual degeneration, religious corruption, and immorality at times associated with powerful institutions. This same critique was also used to question the spiritual insight and moral development of their own colleagues in the

Five Mountains institutions when needed, since as a powerful institution in its own right monks in the Five Mountains temples certainly confronted these same problems. Through applying the landscape to the Five Mountains temples, they developed a mode of participating in ordinary society that preserved in their view a transcendent spiritual goal without forcing them to retreat from the samsaric realm of political and social affairs.

The Kitayama monks applied the landscape to their lives in a variety of ways, but one of the most important to them in painting inscriptions was through the theme of "the hermit at court" or the "hermit in the marketplace." This theme played a minor role in early and medieval Chinese cultural history, and became important only in the Yüan dynasty, when it was closely related to the image of the scholar's study that also came to prominence in the Yüan as a central motif in literati and other social spheres. The images yoked together by the phrase "hermit at court" may at first seem contradictory, since they combine the hermit, who is conventionally understood to have rejected human culture, with the capital, a location traditionally taken in elite sectors of society to be the very center of human culture at the imperial or shogunal court. Yet in Chinese and Japanese elite cultural history, interpretations of the landscape and of hermits were often highly cultural exercises. In the classical literary traditions of East Asia the natural world was read historically or mythologically as a landscape inhabited by various well-known poets, as the residences of particular spirits and deities, or as the location of particular important historical events. This is true from the early Chinese landscape literature of T'ao Ch'ien (365–427) and Hsieh Ling-yün (385–433) through the T'ang landscape poet Wang Wei (699?–761) or the eccentric Zen layman Han-shan and on to the Sung poets Su Shih (1037–1101) and Yang Wan-li (1127–1206). A similar statement can be made about the early images of the Japanese islands in the *chōka* or long songs of Kakimoto no Hitomarō (active late seventh century) or the medieval *waka* poetry of Saigyō (1118–90) and the early modern diaries and *haikai* of Matsuo Bashō (1644–94).[44] It is in this intellectual and cultural context that envisions the natural landscape in terms highly determined by cultural tradition that the Kitayama monks' writings on landscape may best be understood.

Indeed, the Five Mountains Zen monks renegotiate and at times even reject the very distinction between nature and culture on which any apparent contradiction in a twentieth-century characterization of the "recluse at court" might be grounded. In their writings they ask us to rethink this boundary line as it is conventionally drawn, as they did their Muromachi period contemporaries within and without the monastery walls. We will see that their application of the landscape to busy lives in the capital through this theme was very useful in coming to terms with the inevitable tensions in elite urban life between religious and moral imperatives of a well-considered life and the political and economic opportunities that may await members of a privileged social group.[45] Similar tensions await many in the twentieth century, and the Kitayama monks may contribute in some way to current reconsiderations of the relation of nature and culture in our own times; I develop this theme in chapter 4 below.[46]

Finally, the Japanese *michi* have been traditionally interpreted in terms that ignore Chinese aesthetics and exclusively emphasize Japanese culture, much as Matsuo Bashō (1644–94) seemed to do when he associated his own view of nature and poetry with those of the *waka* poet Saigyō, the linked-verse poet Sōgi (1421–1502), the painter Sesshū, and the tea master Sen no Rikyū (1521–91). However, Bashō himself was introduced to Zen aesthetics through the literature and commentaries of the Japanese Five Mountains Zen monks, and is known to have studied Chinese religion, poetry, and aesthetics, particularly the Taoist text *Chuang-tzu* and the T'ang dynasty poet Tu Fu (712–70). The reasons twentieth-century Japanese and Western scholars have followed this Edo tradition are complex and worthy of further investigation, but are tangled up in Japanese cultural nationalism, leading to stringent separations of Japanese and non-Japanese cultures of East Asia, and its impact on disciplinary divisions in the academy. Until recent work by Murai Shōsuke, Amino Yoshihiko, and others, few scholars in Japan and abroad had explored the relations between Chinese or Korean and Japanese aesthetics, and such divisions were faithfully observed except by independent-minded Japanese scholars such as Konishi Jin'ichi and the North American cultural historians Timothy Wixted, David Pollack, and Arthur Thornhill.[47] By following the lead of the Japanese Five Mountains monks in emphasizing the highly sinified and internationalized character of Japanese aesthetics and spirituality, I will introduce not only important mainland precedents to Japanese island culture but also explore the highly cosmopolitan character of late medieval Japanese culture and society.

So what meaning will be found for the landscape arts in the views discussed below of the Five Mountains monks and their lives in the bustling urban monasteries? As already stated, in reading their inscriptions we find they participate in the Chinese Mahayana Buddhist tradition of affirming the positive role the world of ordinary experience plays in realizing enlightenment, and the traditional Zen interest in the daily, mundane affairs of elite life in the capital. These Japanese Zen monks chose to carry this ideal out primarily through activities in the social and cultural realm, in addition to their administrative and spiritual advising duties as abbots of the large metropolitan temples of the Five Mountains Zen system. Chapters 1 and 2 will lay out the Japanese historical context and Chinese religious and aesthetic background to the development of Five Mountains Zen culture in Japan, with particular attention to the understanding of the landscape arts. We will see that the Japanese monks' artistic interpretations of landscape art centered on the mind in aesthetic and epistemological theories that were, however, integrated into syncretic theories taken primarily from Chinese sources of spiritual self-cultivation through the arts. Their focus on the mind is not surprising, since the mind had been at the center both of Buddhist conceptions of spiritual practice and of Japanese artistic theory for some centuries.

The early Muromachi monks to be studied developed conceptions of Zen culture that forced themselves and both their ordained and lay companions to confront the pitfalls of attachment and the various attractions of power, wealth, and prestige to be found in elite Japanese social circles. To this end they drew on Chinese poetics and painting theory together with recluse poetry for a critique of life at the center of Chinese elite society, and integrated this critique into conceptualizations of their own lifestyles even while active in the Five Mountains monasteries located on the busy thoroughfares of the capital. We will explore the theme of enlightened action in the mundane world in Zen and Mahayana Buddhism as applied to the cultural practices of the Japanese Five Mountains monks in chapter 3, and then examine in chapter 4 how they found such action in the landscape arts.

The Five Mountains Japanese monks drew heavily both on Buddhist and on Sung and Yüan dynasty Chinese literati, Ancient Civilization, and Confucian aesthetics as applied to the landscape arts. In their interest in Buddhist ideals and mainland aesthetics they followed the precedent set by previous Japanese writers on literary theory, but they did so to an unusual extent. They developed their own vision of the landscape arts most distinctively through exploration of two classic Mahayana Buddhist themes: the illusory and dreamlike character of reality and of art, artist, and audience; and the unimpeded play of the enlightened being roaming free of attachment in the realm of the nondualism of the conditioned and the unconditioned. Both illusion and playfulness are fundamentally Buddhist in that they provide, in the words of one scholar of Mahayana Buddhism, "no sedative dwelling place for the mind."[48] By refusing in their very constitution the production of a stable world that might provide the basis for delusion and attachment, these twin themes were ideal for Five Mountains heuristic and soteriological purposes.

The Japanese Five Mountains monks defined textual and artistic study and practice as activities occurring in a world characterized as illusory. The consequences of this are twofold: this conception undermines other value conceptions of the arts and of landscape that were prevalent in elite Japanese society of the day, while simultaneously establishing a clearly Buddhist framework for interpreting the landscape arts. The Buddhist theories of illusion in turn free these monks to enjoy a state of enlightenment known as "the samadhi of playfulness" or lusory roaming free of causal determination, their primary mode of activity as fully enlightened beings active in the mundane world of causation and suffering. This is a type of Buddhist insight that can draw syncretically on a variety of aesthetic and spiritual traditions without being attached to any particular theory, and that may proceed among the multifarious entanglements of the world in a liberatory and unimpeded fashion. These twin themes of illusion and playfulness as found in the landscape arts provide the subject of the final two chapters.

Chapter 1

The Chinese Religious and Cultural Context

How expansive is your heart,
Hills and rivers cool themselves inside. . . .
A river village with few houses,
A misty hamlet with clusters of old trees.
I know you [Sung Ti] have hidden thoughts,
I examine closely to find them.

—Su Shih

All the enlightened ones and ancestral teachers take this one true thing very seriously. . . . If this matter were in words, then it should be definable in a single statement, with no further change. Why should there be thousands and thousands of sayings imparted by enlightened adepts, with no end to them? From this we know that it is not within words, but we need to use words to illustrate this matter. Sharp-spirited people should directly comprehend this idea.

—Yüan-wu K'o-ch'in

We begin where the Kitayama Japanese monks began their training and education: with Chinese religious and cultural tradition. Members of elite Muromachi Japanese society were, like their predecessors in the Nara (710–784) and Kamakura (1185–1333) periods, fascinated with the mainland. The Five Mountains monks themselves were sinophiles, if nothing else, in their lifestyle in the urban monasteries, in their institutional basis, in their thinking and writing, and in their acculturation. In order to understand the Five Mountains interpretations of the landscape arts we must become acquainted with some of the mainland religious and intellectual traditions in which they were educated and to which they turned as their religious, intellectual, and linguistic resources.

For the present purposes I will briefly introduce two large traditions from Chinese elite culture on which the Japanese Five Mountains monks relied, Zen

Buddhism and the culture of educated scholar-officials, with an emphasis on the Sung and Yüan periods. In these centuries Chinese Zen monks and the literati shared an abiding interest in the role of textual study in spiritual and moral cultivation, but debated vigorously the nature of the best methods, the most appropriate texts, and the role of literary study, as they did the significance of the natural landscape. Many monks and nonordained elites developed syncretic integrations that accommodated and responded to each other's implicit assumptions and explicit views. These Sung and Yüan views, as we shall see in this and subsequent chapters, were in turn crucial to the Japanese Five Mountains Zen understanding of artistic practice and of the landscape.

Views in the Chinese Zen school of textual study or literary and artistic practice have varied over the centuries and among different lineages. The study of canonical Buddhist texts, such as the *Perfection of Wisdom*, the *Vimalakīrti Sutra*, and the *Perfect Enlightenment Sutra*, seems to have been important in some or even all of the earliest Zen schools during the seventh and into the eighth centuries.[1] However, the soteriological value of canonical study was at times questioned pointedly by some teachers of Zen, often when the writings or recorded sayings of the same teacher revealed a familiarity with the canonical tradition. It may suffice here to say that certainly there was some tension in the early Zen tradition with the canonical tradition, perhaps due to the struggle of the newly developing school to establish independence of rival Buddhist schools.[2]

By the ninth century, however, we find a clear statement of the importance of studying Buddhist canonical texts in the writings of Tsung-mi (780–841), who argues in his important *Zen Preface* (C. *Ch'an-yüan chu-chüan-chi tu-hsü*) that canonical writings were not only complementary to Zen enlightenment but that they were necessary to validate Zen insight.[3] While Tsung-mi's views were not directly influential in later generations, as his line of Zen died out soon after his death, they were of interest to later generations of Zen teachers, including, as we shall see below, the Japanese Five Mountains monk Kiyō Hōshū. More generally, Tsang-mi's views represent the type of Zen that was congruent with the values of elite Chinese (and Japanese) culture in the high esteem for textual study. This attracted the interest even during his lifetime of such well-known literati as Po Chü-i (772–846) and Liu Yü-hsi (772–842), a close associate of both the famous poet Han Yü (768–824) and the landscape poet and important essayist Liu Tsung-yüan (773–819).[4] All of these writers and government officials were involved in one or another of different literary movements seeking through various styles and means to return moral and philosophical value to literary practice, known variously as *fu-ku* or "Return to Antiquity" and *ku-wen* or "Ancient Civilization." This common interest in the religious value of texts helped bring Zen monks who valued textual study such as Tsung-mi together with educated literati elites interested in the spiritual and philosophical dimension to literary practice and other textual study and expression. This development, perhaps first seen in the mid-T'ang, would recur again and again in Zen history, and represents the same trend in Zen history to which the Japanese Five Mountains monks belong.

Zen monks were becoming known for their poetry in the southeast and in the northern capital already in eighth century on the continent, including Ling-yi (727–62), Chiao-jan (734–c. 792), and Ling-ch'e (746–816).[5] These monks represent an early strand of Zen that accepted the importance of studying not only Buddhist texts but also the religious, intellectual, and literary writings of non-Buddhists, and participated actively and extensively in regional elite and imperial court cultural circles. Later T'ang Zen artists are relatively well known in twentieth-century Zen studies, such as the Zen lay poet Han-shan (active late eighth to early ninth centuries) and the monk-painter, poet, and calligrapher Kuan-hsiu (832–912). We find in the former's work cultural styles that, unlike those of his predecessors, were outside of the elite tradition and that were virtually ignored by most contemporary artists. Yet we also see that the work of these artists shared a common interest in landscape themes in art with their mid-T'ang predecessors, as well as with earlier monks and lay devotees associated with other Buddhist schools, such as Hui-yüan (344–416/7), and his lay disciples, the landscape poet Hsieh Ling-yün (385–433) and the aesthetician Tsung Ping (375–443).[6] With Kuan-hsiu and Han-shan we encounter what has come to represent the first independent tradition of Zen art in the popular twentieth-century conception of Zen. However, while appreciating Han-shan's poetry many of the Kitayama Japanese Five Mountains monks, like their Yüan and early Ming Chinese monk-poet contemporaries, seem to trace the origins of their own poetic activities back to pre-T'ang Buddhists such as Hui-yüan and the mid-T'ang Zen poetic heritage more closely associated with mainstream elite Chinese culture.

The T'ang is traditionally known among cultural and religious historians as the classical age and high point of Chinese Zen, in contrast with the Zen of the Sung and later dynasties in China and many Japanese schools. The Zen of these later periods is said in this devolutionary narrative to violate the T'ang Zen spirit by advocating study of canonical and *kōan* (C. *kung-an*) texts, being syncretic or overly emphasizing poetry, and generally possessing inferior insight.[7] In this historical accounting the common characteristic of post-T'ang Zen, sometimes dubbed "secular" Zen, when contrasted with earlier or "pure" Zen, is often involvement with mainstream Chinese elite, metropolitan culture broadly understood. The differences between "pure" and "secular" Zen are generally described by most Japanese historians in two ways: distinctions of "pure" Zen from either the "eclectic" Zen teachings that incorporate elements of the Esoteric and other Buddhist schools or syncretic beliefs combining Zen ideals with those of Confucianism and Taoism; and those distinguishing "pure" Zen from forms of Zen involving literary or artistic study and practice.[8]

Recently Robert Buswell has reconsidered this narrative of Zen development, which he indicates derives from Sung historical texts but which has also been influential in twentieth-century historical scholarship, particularly from Japan and Euro-American scholars who have studied in Japan. He argues that Sung rather than T'ang dynasty Zen should be seen as the climax of a complex, gradual development of meditation practices, religious language and rhetoric, soteriology, and pedagogical styles. The character of the Zen of this period has been shown by Chün-fang Yü to be based in textual study and a sophisticated pedagogical program that included both Buddhist and non-Buddhist texts. Yü has argued that

> Like Chu Hsi and Ch'eng I, [Ch'an or Zen masters in the Sung] liked to quote from the Classics and talk about the ancient sages as exemplary models. I was struck time and again by the Ch'an masters' ecumenical openness toward the classical Confucian and Taoist traditions . . . [for which] we can detect the same kind of loving reverence as expressed by the Neo-Confucian masters. I suggest that both Ch'an and Neo-Confucian masters regarded the classical tradition as their own heritage.[9]

This historical narrative more closely accords with the understanding of Zen history held by the Muromachi Japanese Five Mountains monks, so I have adopted it here.

By the Sung dynasty, Zen had been fully accepted into the mainstream of Chinese elite culture. Many historians believe that as a consequence in the Northern Sung (960–1126) Zen monks and laymen began to compile histories and anthologize Zen anecdotes or "encounter literature" and public cases now known popularly as *kōan*. Such Sung Zen monks as Fen-yang Shan-chao (947–1024) and Hsüeh-tou Ch'ung-hsien (980–1052) also composed poetry on various social occasions, including poems as a form of commentary for these collections. As their poems became known in other Zen temples and in elite social and cultural circles, this movement became known as "literary Zen" (C. *wen-tzu* Ch'an; J. *monji* Zen).[10] The best-known Sung dynasty monks in this movement were both active at the end of the Northern Sung, Chüeh-fan Hui-hung (1071–1128), a younger contemporary and student of influential poet-official Su Shih, and the Tsao-tung (J. Sōtō) school monk Hung-chih Cheng-chüeh (1091–1157), whose verses would be immortalized as the core of the 1224 *kōan* collection *Record of Serenity* (C. *Tsung-jung lu*; J. *Shōyōroku*). The former provided the Japanese Five Mountains Zen monks with an important model for Zen literary practice.

With these changes the nature of the relationship between literary practice and the development of Zen insight became a subject of debate within the Sung Zen schools. The response best known in twentieth-century historical scholarship is that of Yüan-wu K'o-ch'in (1063–1135), who compiled the popular *Blue Cliff Records* based on Hsueh-tou's verse collection, and his enormously influential disciple, Ta-hui Tsung-kao. For different reasons both agreed that the Zen literature tradition of *kōan* collections and verse commentaries should be studied as an aid in realizing one's own enlightenment for the way in which they reveal the mind of enlightenment of the monk who wrote or whose speech was recorded in the text.[11] The mind of enlightenment and insight could be found, Yüan-wu and Ta-hui agreed, in passages that were "live" (C. *huo-chu*) with this state of mind, and hence pointed the reader directly to the innate, enlightened mind of the author.[12] This emphasis on the mind in the Zen textual hermeneutic tradition closely approximates the textual hermeutic of contemporary literati and Neo-Confucians, as we shall see shortly. In an important development, however, Ta-hui also attacked the "literary Zen" of Hui-hung and the "silent meditation" method of Hung-chih in promoting his "live words" hermeneutical tradition as the basis for what would soon become a very widely influential *k'an-hua* or "observing the phrase" meditation method. His attack on these two poet-monks helped to discredit them in the eyes of some later Lin-chi school monks, and has had continuing effects down to the present day. By way of contrast, however, Ta-hui and Yüan-wu did not oppose the study of other canonical Buddhist texts as subjects of textual study.[13]

In the Southern Sung (1127–1279) and later dynasties Chinese Zen monks quite commonly studied texts and composed poetry in different schools and throughout subsequent centuries despite this attack, just as they also continued to study canonical texts. While we may attribute this continued interest to particular soteriological positions or pedagogical methods, it was also certainly encouraged through the continued social relationships of Zen monks with highly literate, nonordained elite social groups. Indeed, from the late Northern Sung it was commonplace for Chinese Zen monks at leading monasteries not only to compose poetry but also to practice other arts conventionally associated with the literati, such as calligraphy, as well as to read widely in canonical Buddhist texts and in the non-Buddhist Chinese canonical traditions.

It was under these conditions that the early Japanese independent Zen monastic institutions first developed through the efforts of monks from both Japan and the mainland. Many of the Chinese teachers of Zen who wielded a formative influence on the Japanese Five Mountains Zen institution were active during the last half of the Southern Sung dynasty; perhaps the most important monk was Ching-sou (also Pei-chien) Chü-chien (1164–1246), whose extensive writings were collected and read widely in the Japanese monasteries. This was when numerous Japanese visitors came to the mainland in search of the teachings of the Zen sect during the last decades of the twelfth century and in the early thirteenth century. It was also at this same time that the first Chinese teachers of Zen who traveled to Japan received their training.[14]

The Southern Sung relationship of textual study and poetic practice to religious insight can be summarized by examining the writings of two prominent members of the Zen community in Southern Sung China, Wu-chun Shih-fan (1177–1249) and Hsu-t'ang Chih-yu (1185–1269), who were quite important for the development of the Japanese Zen tradition. Wu-chun's importance for the

Japanese tradition can be seen from his having taught[15] virtually all of the most highly respected early Chinese masters to come to Japan, including Wu-hsüeh Tsu-yüan (J. Mugaku Sogen), Wu-an Pu-ning (J. Gottan Funei) (1197–1276), and Lan-ch'i (also Lau-hsi) Tao-lung (J. Rankei Dōryū), as well as one of the earliest and most important Japanese monks to study the Zen sect in China, Enni Ben'en.[16] Enni used texts such as the *Tsung-ching lu* (J. *Sugyōroku*)[17] that argue for the unity of Zen and the teaching schools, as did his fellow disciples from the mainland. Wu-hsueh, for example, used the *Perfect Enlightenment Sutra* (C. *Yüan-chueh ching*; J. *Engakukyō*) and the *Śūraṅgama Sutra* or *Ta-fo-ting Ching* (J. *Daibutchōkyō*) for the same general purposes that Enni used the *Tsung-ching lu*: to develop a basis for Zen teachings in terms taken from other Buddhist sects.[18] As we shall see below, these same texts were the subjects of lectures by the leading early Japanese Five Mountains to the shoguns themselves, and in this sense the Muromachi monks inherited the legacy of the Southern Sung dynasty continental Zen tradition.

Their shared interest in these texts also constitutes an important similarity with the teachings of Wu-chun himself, who advocated not only the use of the *Perfect Enlightenment Sutra* but also a syncretism of Buddhism, Confucianism, and Taoism, known as the Unity of the Three Creeds (J. *sankyō itchi*).[19] Another Chinese disciple of Wu-chun who played an important, formative role in the development of Japanese Zen, the monk Lan-ch'i Tao-lung, likewise taught in a manner based on three teachings syncretism. We can see that Lan-ch'i studied widely in a number of different textual traditions from his use of Confucian teachings in his relationship with the shogun Hōjō Tokiyori (1227–63).[20] Lan-ch'i and Wu-hsüeh both also showed awareness of the recent developments in Neo-Confucian thinking represented by the very important work of Chu Hsi (1130–1200). This awareness is reflected primarily in their study of the *Doctrine of the Mean* and *The Great Learning*, two texts that were raised from positions of little importance to the status of canonical texts by Chu Hsi, as well as in their knowledge of the Neo-Confucian writings of Chou Tun-i (1017–73).[21] The Zen of both these Chinese masters and their Japanese disciples seems to be founded in a syncretism that did not establish a clear distinction between Zen and other teachings.

With regard to relations with literati elites, Wu-chun, Enni, and Wu-hsüeh all shared a fundamentally accommodating attitude, seen in the willingness of all three to accept the patronage of the highest secular powers in society. Wu-chun accepted the support of Emperor Li-tsung (r. 1225–74), as Enni and Wu-hsüeh accepted the support and patronage of Japanese political leaders in Kyoto and Kamakura respectively.[22] Such patronage relationships not only involved financial and institutional support, but certainly led to increased social interchange between Wu-chun and his followers, with consequent pressures to participate in cultural and religious circles at court. Wu-chun's willingness to participate in court life certainly had practical benefits, but it also shows that he felt his integrity as a Buddhist leader would not be compromised by such activity in the "secular" world of court society.

An important example of the close relationship in this period on the continent between literature and Zen is that of Hsü-t'ang Chih-yü, another monk who was also patronized by the Chinese emperor Li-tsung and whose disciples likewise became central to the development of Japanese Zen. Hsü-t'ang's key role is often summarized by historians through his teaching of the Japanese monk Nampo Jōmyō (also Jōmin; 1235–1308), who returned to Japan where he founded the line of Zen known for the rigorous preservation of what is termed "pure" Zen.[23] If we inquire into the character of Hsü-t'ang's Zen, however, we find that it is often characterized by a strong interest in the composition of poetry,[24] one of the characteristics associated with secularized or "degenerate" Zen.[25] We also find among the Chinese monks who studied under Hsü-t'ang one monk who traveled to Japan, Wu-hsüeh Tsu-yüan, who we have also seen studied under Wu-chun. It is important to note that Wu-hsüeh described his own experience while studying under Hsü-t'ang in terms of achieving "verse samadhi" (*chü-yü san-mei*), a term that indicates his own literary inclinations but also those of the years he spent under Hsü-t'ang's tutelage. In their interest in achieving a Buddhist state of samadhi through writing, Wü-hsüeh and Hsü-t'ang were drawing on a Zen tradition that stretched back at least to Ta-hui in the Northern Sung. We know, for example, that Ta-hui commented on Su Shih's writing that he "always loved to read Su Shih's prose [for] he is someone who is near to achieving the Way. Even though he has not attained the Way, his 'language samadhi' (*yen-yü san-mei*) is truly close to it."[26]

Hsü-t'ang's interest in poetry is important for understanding the character of Japanese Zen generally, and especially for the views held by the Kitayama monks, for he was a major, early proponent of poetry meetings and their commemoration in poem scrolls, which we shall see were crucial to the early Muromachi Japanese *shigajiku* poem-and-painting scrolls. We see Hsü-t'ang's interest in poetry composition in his relationship with Nampo himself, for Hsü-t'ang chose to express his farewell to Nampo on his return to Japan by assembling one of these poem scrolls. Hsü-t'ang wrote a verse that was to become famous in Japan, forty-one of his disciples wrote poems rhyming with their master's verse, and together these poems were made into a poem scroll and presented to Nampo.[27] Hsü-t'ang also participated in literary meetings with secular poets, and this mixing of monks and laymen on such social occasions itself became a subject of poetry and painting.[28] Tamamura finds that Hsü-t'ang's literary activities were only one important example of the popularity of poetry meetings during the 1260s and 1270s, a period that saw Chinese Zen literature flourish as never before. These literary meetings were widely popular among such disciples of Hsü-t'ang who traveled to Japan as Wu-hsüeh, Lan-ch'i, and Ta-hsiu Cheng-nien (1214–88) and in Japanese Five Mountains temples of both Kyoto and Kamakura throughout the fourteenth century.[29] As we shall see, literary meetings of monks and laity were also among the most important elements in the Japanese development of the poem scrolls of the late thirteenth and fourteenth centuries.

In accord with the popularity of the study and practice of literature among these formative period Chinese monks, we find that they recognized the value of textual study and linguistic expression as a source of religious insight without compromising their awareness of the dangers of overdependence on words and textual study. Many Five Mountains monks admonished their disciples against literary study at the same time that they were skilled in literary expression and obviously learned in the very traditions they seemed to be prohibiting their students from studying. Lan-ch'i wrote one of the most commonly mentioned such admonitions, as did Musō Soseki, whose statement ranked his disciples into three types, with the lowest ranking reserved for those "drunk with literature." Lan-ch'i's approach to textual study became widely influential at the Kamakura temple he founded, Kenchō-ji, which was seen as a model of continental Zen and so became associated with his teachings throughout Japan. Lan-ch'i cautioned his disciples against becoming enamored of textual study, in a vein similar to that of numerous Japanese monks, most importantly Musō Soseki, whose admonition later came to be recited in many of the Five Mountains temples. Lan-ch'i wrote, "For those who practice meditation and study the Way, do not [concentrate on] the parallel prose [writing style]; you should study the living intent of the patriarchs, and not think about their dead 'capping phrases' (C. *hua-t'ou*; J. *watō*)."[30] Lan-ch'i followed the typical emphasis placed by Yüan-wu and Ta-hui on reading for the "living intent" in a textual hermeneutic that is centered on the realization of Buddhist enlightenment. While some have interpreted this passage to prohibit all literary study, if read carefully we can see that Lan-ch'i was steering his disciples away from some modes of reading texts, that is, "dead phrases" in the Yüan-wu formulation, and away from some styles of writing, particularly parallel prose, and toward other interpretive approaches and styles. On reading the writings of Wu-hsüeh, we find that he shared with Lan-ch'i a comparable though distinctive view of the role of language in Zen religious practice. In a discussion of writing of verse, for example, Wu-hsüeh suggested that the Zen monk should "search out the path where there is no path, search out language where there is no language."[31] Wu-hsüeh here seems to suggest that the practitioner should use language only after having developed a nondualistic approach in which the value of language is not based on a dualistic need to use or to rely on language.

While these early monks and their Chinese teachers clearly affirmed the relevance of prose and poetic practice to Zen insight, most scholars agree that it is only with the next generation of teachers from both the mainland and Japan that the Japanese Five Mountains literary tradition truly flourishes.[32] During the first quarter of the fourteenth century numerous Japanese monks traveled to the mainland, and after their return in the 1310s and 1320s many of them wrote voluminously in poetry as well as in prose while demonstrating their proficiency in such other arts as calligraphy. This cultural tradition also flourished under guidance of more Chinese monks who made their way to Japan, with poetry receiving particular encouragement from the two monks Ch'ing-cho Cheng-ch'eng (1274–1339) and Chu-hsien Fan-hsien (1292–1348). Throughout we find such cautionary statements as those of Lan-ch'i and Musō, and we know that these approaches to textual hermeneutics continued into the Kitayama period from warnings to students to stay away from excessive poetic study.[33]

As we can see from the above discussion of Zen textual and literary hermeneutics, the boundaries between literary study and religious practice were not as clear-cut as we might assume. This also held true in Sung dynasty Chinese traditions that to some may appear to be largely secular in orientation: poetry, prose composition, artistic expression, and even the study of history and government. As in the Zen tradition, the philosophical, moral, and religious value of the study of texts was also a hotly debated topic among literati, officials, and philosophers in Northern Sung China, most of whom took up more than one of these social roles. The Sung experienced a broad revival of interest in how to achieve the Tao or Way of past sages, and this Way was available in the view of most primarily through such texts as histories, philosophical treatises, and even poetry and poetic or artistic commentary. The general view of many in this period might be summarized in the words of an early Neo-Confucian thinker, Chou Tun-i:

> Literature is that by which one carries the Way. . . . Artful (*wen*) language is a skill; the Way and virtue are realities. When someone devoted to these realities and skilled writes down [the Way], if it is beautiful, then people will love it, and it will be passed on.[34]

Similar views were expressed by the Northern Sung literatus and close friend of Su Shih, Huang T'ing-chien (1045–1105): "In his breast there are myriad volumes, and from his brush [comes] not a speck of common spirit."[35] Through internalizing Chinese culture as preserved in written texts, the Sung Neo-Confucians and literati believed they could attain great spiritual heights, and we shall see later how important these views were for the Kitayama Japanese monks.

The different Sung schools of thought on how to achieve the sagely Way diverged on how to achieve their goal: what texts to read, what interpretive approaches to use, and what to do with the knowledge gained: serve in government, express oneself in prose or poetry, or teach. In the twentieth century the Sung has become known primarily for the Confucian revival sometimes called Neo-Confucianism and associated with Chu Hsi, yet these Confucian thinkers made up only one of several groups active and they did not come to dominate Chinese philosophy and state policy until later. Other movements were what might be termed Sung Learning,[36] which would include those involved in the broad Confucian revival without limiting it to the orthodox lineage of Neo-Confucian thinkers established by Chu Hsi; the *ku-wen* or Ancient Civilization movement, led by the literati official Ou-yang Hsiu (1007–72) and his influential student Su Shih; and the newly defined literati movement among officials and amateur artists, poets, and calligraphers, for whom Su Shih and members of his circle are the primary spokespersons. Although there was overlap in memberships among these here very broadly defined movements, each can be distinguished fairly clearly in their values and practices.

While generally agreed on the importance of textual study generally, one issue on which these Sung groups divided is the spiritual and moral value of literary practice, which was largely opposed by the Neo-Confucians and many members of Sung Learning but generally supported by proponents of the Ancient Civilization and literati groups. Because of later success by the Neo-Confucians in establishing a state orthodoxy, the views of the other movements on this topic have been somewhat obscured in the scholarship.[37] As a result, the Sung Learning and Ancient Civilization movements have been neglected, while the literati movement has been treated by historians not as a literary, intellectual, or philosophic tradition but primarily as a movement of painters and calligraphers. As Peter Bol has pointed out, however, cultural accomplishment was central in the Northern Sung and later dynasties to social prestige, education, and advancement in political office, and it was also held by Ancient Civilization and literati thinkers to be a deeply meaningful means of realizing the Way of the universe.[38] As we might expect, what was at stake in these debates over the best way to realize the Way was much more than the role of literature narrowly defined: textual study and cultural practice were the most common means of linking learning, values, and social practice. In this way culture was very much entangled with the establishment of moral authority, access to political and especially governmental power, and the believability of truth claims by those who could argue they best represented the prestige of the vaunted past. While the views of Ou-yang Hsiu and Su Shih may have ultimately lost in these debates on the continent, the Japanese Five Mountains monks found such conceptions of literature in many ways the most congenial for their own interests and purposes as they negotiated their way through the tangled relations of culture with morality, power, and spiritual truth. Because these views laid important groundwork for the early Muromachi Five Mountains monks, I here introduce some of their central features.

The most important criterion for judging the value of literary expression for members of the Ancient Civilization movement was not the mastery of a particular style or the ability to make appropriate allusions, but the degree to which it expressed the Way (C. *Tao*) of the ancients.[39] Moral cultivation of the writer led to an understanding of this Way, which in turn was manifested in an individual's literary expression. Many Sung proponents of the Way in literature followed Liu K'ai's (947–1000) lead in arguing that in literature, as in morality, the inner character and spiritual self-cultivation of the writer were the most important elements.[40]

For Ou-yang Hsiu, the Way of the ancients was pursued through both the study of the classics, study that led to moral self-cultivation, and the development of a good writing style. This process, Ou-yang wrote, centered on the individual's ability when reading the classics to understand the intention or ideas (*i*), and the effect this process had on the individual's mind:

> Those who learn ought to make the classics their teacher. To make the classics their teacher they must first uncover their ideas. When the ideas are apprehended the mind will be settled. When the mind is settled their Way will be pure. When the Way is pure then what will fill [them] up inside will be real; when what is filling them up inside is real then what is expressed as *wen* [literature or culture] will be dazzling.[41]

Ou-yang Hsiu's theory of self-cultivation also stressed the inner state of mind as the basis for spiritual insight:

> When something is reflected in water, if the water is agitated the image will be blurred. But if the water remains still then the smallest detail will be discernible. As for men, who rely upon their ears to hear and their eyes to see, . . . [i]f a person can keep his senses from being dazzled and agitated by external things, then his mind will remain still, and if his mind remains still, then his understanding will be clear. Thereafter, as he praises what is right and finds fault with what is wrong, he will be correct in everything he does.[42]

Judgment depends on one's inner state, Ou-yang argued, specifically on the achievement of mental quietude. Once this state is reached, then moral judgment will be perfected, and the Way of the ancients will be realized in all activity.

Ou-yang's theory of reading was also a theory of writing: when the student discovered the ideas of the ancients in the texts he read, his own mind would become settled, and so his inner self would be expressed through writing (*wen*) in a worthy manner. Like the study of the classics, for Ou-yang Hsiu the reading and writing of poetry centered on the author's idea (*i*) in the literary work as it expressed the mind (*hsin*). Some indication of his views on this subject can be gathered from a discussion of meaning in poetry with his good friend, the poet Mei Yao-ch'en (1002–60). Of the two criteria Mei held to be necessary for the best poetry, Ou-yang seems most interested in the "inexhaustible meaning which exists beyond words."

> [Mei Yao-ch'en] once said to me [Ou-yang Hsiu], "Though the poet may emphasize intention (*i*), it is difficult to choose the proper diction. . . . He must be able to depict a scene that is difficult to describe in such a way that it seems to be right before the eyes of the readers and to express inexhaustible meaning which exists beyond the words—only then can he be regarded as great. . . ." I said, "But what poems illustrate 'depicting a scene that is difficult to describe' and 'expressing inexhaustible meaning'?" [Mei Yao-ch'en] replied, "The author achieves it in his mind (*te yu hsin*) and the reader understands it through the intention."[43]

Mei emphasized that it was the mind where the poet must grasp what he wanted to express in his poetry if he was to express it well in writing, and the reader must in turn understand the meaning for himself by engaging with (C. *hui*) the intent of the author. We will see in chapter 3 a similar theory of poetic interpretation in the writings of the Japanese monks.

When considering the importance of Ancient Civilization theories for the Kitayama Japanese, it is important to note that Ou-yang's conception of literature centered on the classics and on prose, and not primarily on the composition of poetry. As opposed to the widely accepted moral and social worth of public prose, the value of poetry was a disputed topic in Northern Sung theories of literary interpretation.[44] In reaction against the writings of the Hsi-k'un school of poetry, many of the early Sung Ancient Civilization writers conceived of prose as the appropriate vehicle for expression of the Way, turning to poetry rarely or only in their less serious moments.[45] A clear distinction in Ou-yang's conception of literature can be seen between those prose genres associated with government or other activity in the public domain and poetry, together with informal prose genres such as the preface (C. *hsü*) and the account (C. *chi*).[46] These more personal and informal types of literature were precisely those that most interested the Kitayama Japanese in the documents we are to consider, however, and we must examine the reasons for this.

The poetry of the Northern Sung is often characterized in terms of a lyricism that tended not to themes of sorrow, but to a transcendent joy and carefree simplicity.[47] For Ou-yang Hsiu, poetry and other personal literature were often written at times of exile from government, when Ou-yang found a source of value outside the structured, hierarchical world of society, society being the proper realm for the Confucian enactment of the Way.[48] Ou-yang complained of those poets who lamented their distance from the capital and the moral fulfillment of government service,[49] and instead transformed through his writings this lifestyle into a source of pleasure and fulfillment. In these lyrical writings, such as his well-known "Record of the Old Drunkard's Pavilion," Ou-yang reveled in his dissolute life in exile, a dissolution that, however, was still grounded in Confucian theories of the happiness of the minister for his subjects.[50]

With the writings of Ou-yang's student, Su Shih, we encounter a conception of transcendence in both his poetry and prose freed from conditions of exile or government service. As Su wrote in his famous "Record of the Pavilion of Transcendence," written during his banishment to remote Mi-chou, "Where could I go where I would not be happy?"[51] Unlike Ou-yang Hsiu, Su carried this transcendent attitude not only from the capital into exile, but on his return to government from the hinterlands of the empire.[52] In his lyrical prose as well as in his poetry we see Su reveling in the playful transcendence of an individual freed from the burdens of the world. As we might imagine, this unobstructed and playful attitude held much appeal for Chinese Zen masters, and this was also the poetry of Su that the Kitayama monks found most appealing, appearing again and again in their inscriptions on paintings.

Of more general significance was Su's development of transcendent value without dependence on government service, always under threat of banishment or exile, combining spiritual cultivation with cultural practice and political involvement. As Peter Bol has pointed out, this model provided individuals in later dynasties a philosophy for participating in a political system while maintaining their own moral integrity and independence, and a powerful means of coming to terms with the inevitable tensions between political power and moral authority.[53] Moreover, the literary study and practice of Su and other poet-officials from earlier dynasties, such as T'ao Ch'ien and Po Chü-i, provided later literati scholars and poets with a philosophy for establishing the moral, spiritual, and other enduring value of their own identity without being forced to rely solely on the traditional means for members of elite social strata of government service. This became in turn a central value underlying Chin and Yüan dynasty changes in the social role of the literati, as we will see below. The Japanese Five Mountains monks looked to Su, the earlier poet-officials, and the Yüan literati in supporting their own conceptions of the central role of culture in the practice and propagation of enduring religious value outside of their roles in the meditation hall and master-disciple encounters. The general importance of cultural study and practice suggests that we in the twentieth century might recognize the important place in East Asian culture of this period of culture as much more than a decorative art, but as a major venue for the learning, discovery, and perpetuation of deeply important personal and universal values and meaning.

One of the most important literary genres in which the spiritual value of cultural practice is seen is in the development of a new genre of literature, the painting inscription. Su Shih, together with his close friend Huang T'ing-chien, was also a central figure in the establishment of painting inscriptions as an acceptable poetic subgenre in court literature. Many of Su and Huang's inscriptions were poems rather than prose, and the subgenre came to be known as "poems on paintings" (C. *t'i-hua shih*; J. *daigashi*).[54] In these poetic inscriptions Su and Huang together developed an argument for the value of painting equal to that of poetry. The substance of this argument reveals a number of assumptions about how both poetry and painting were valued and interpreted in the Northern Sung, assumptions that were to form the basis for the interpretation of paintings through later centuries on the mainland as well as for the establishment of the *shigajiku* scrolls in Japan.

In eleventh-century mainland theories of painting are found arguments for changing the status of painting as an art from that of a craft done by professionals to that of an art suitable for literati and equal in status to poetry and calligraphy. Su Shih and Huang T'ing-chien effected this change to a status close to that of poetry largely through borrowings from poetic theory.[55] For the present purposes I can summarize Su and Huang's argument for the new value of painting in terms of two central points: an attack on painting by professionals as not really being "true" painting;[56] and the assertion that "true" painting consisted in art that upheld the same values as poetry and, most often, was in fact done by amateur poet-painters.[57] Since we can uncover in this discussion a number of assumptions underlying the combination of poetry with painting in the Kitayama Japanese poem-and-painting scrolls, let us examine them briefly.

A common way that Su Shih characterizes the "true" painter was in terms of a poet who also painted, and for Su the best painting since the time of the ancients was also by poets. We see this view in a poem he inscribed on a painting by Li Kung-lin (1049–c. 1105):

> Since ancient times, painters have not been common men,
> Their miraculous visualizations of reality are produced the same way as
> poetry.
> The retired scholar Dragon Vision [Li Kung-lin] is originally a poet,
> And caused thunderbolts to crash on Dragon Pond.[58]

The verse alludes to a Tu Fu poem that recorded that thunder, a sign of excellence, was heard at the imperial Dragon Pond when a painter painted a favorite horse. The conceptions of art in Su's evaluation of painting were shared by Ou-yang Hsiu and other Ancient Civilization practitioners' conceptions of literature as a means of self-cultivation: the interest in replicating the cultural activities of the ancients; the moral character of the artist; and the interest in reality in literature. For Su Shih the prime example of a great poet who was also an accomplished painter was Wang Wei (701–61), who was known in the Sung and in Kitayama Japan for his landscape paintings in addition to the poetry that Su admired so much. Su's comments on the work of Wang Wei identifying his painting with his poetry was to be referred to again and again by later generations:

> Savoring Mo-chieh's poems,
> one finds paintings in them;
> Contemplating Mo-chieh's paintings,
> one finds poems in them.[59]

A similar notion is found in the popular expressions, originating most likely with Huang T'ing-chien, that associate poems and paintings, characterizing paintings as "poems without voices" (*wu-sheng shih*) and poems as "paintings with voices" (*yu-sheng hua*).[60] Through such explicit identification with poetry by these influential literati, calligraphers, and poets who themselves apparently dabbled in painting, painting began to take on a status equivalent to that of poetry and calligraphy in the artistic as well as spiritual practice of the scholar.

In later centuries this close relationship between painting and poetry led to the appearance in the Sung, Chin, and especially in the Yüan dynasty of paintings illustrating lines to well-known poems of ancient classics, such as the *Book of Poetry*, of T'ang masters of poetry like Tu Fu and Wang Wei, of Su Shih himself, and of early recluse poets such as T'ao Ch'ien[61] (fig. 1.1). Examples of these

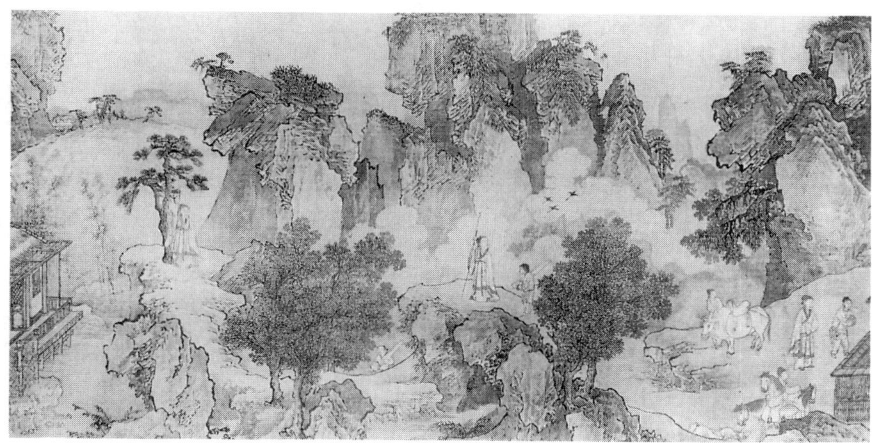

Fig. 1.1. *T'ao Ch'ien's "Homecoming."* Handscroll. Ink and light color on silk. 34.6 x 566.4 cm. 14th century. © Cleveland Museum of Art, 1996. Leonard C. Hanna Jr. Fund, 1982.152. Detail.

paintings are numerous, but it is important to note that the identification in the Northern Sung of painting with poetry contributed to the popularity of poetic subjects, as opposed to themes taken from history or the classics. This type of painting became popular in Japan during the years when the *shigajiku* poem-and-painting scrolls were first being created, and they signal a growth of interest in the identity between painting and poetry among the Japanese Five Mountains monks.

The interest of Su Shih and later literati in the enduring spiritual and moral value of cultural production helped determine their aesthetics and artistic interpretive approach. We can see this in their painting inscriptions, where their interpretations show an abiding interest in the moral character and personality of the artist.[62] If the reading of poetry had increasingly become centered around an interest in the inner character of the poet, the identification of painting with poetry aroused the interest of the viewer of a painting in the character of the painter. We see such an interest in an inscription by Su Shih on a landscape painting by Sung Ti (c. 1015–c. 1080):

> How expansive is your heart,
> Hills and rivers cool themselves inside. . . .
> A river village with few houses,
> A misty hamlet with clusters of old trees.
> I know you have hidden thoughts,
> I examine closely to find them.[63]

We can see a shift in the underlying approach to painting in Su's lack of interest in the rural images of the painting, an interest that Egan notes was characteristic of earlier poems on paintings.[64] Instead, in his careful examination of the painting Su was primarily interested in what the art object revealed about the mind or heart (*hsin*) and the innermost thought and character of the painter. Like Mei Yao-ch'en's reading of poetry and Ou-yang Hsiu's reading of the classics, we see that, as the locus of the moral character and innermost nature of the artist, the mind is again at the center of the interpretive act.

Another indication that conventions of painting interpretation closely follow the conventions of reading poetry and other texts discussed above is found in Su Shih's praise for the following comment by the landscapist Chu Hsiang-hsien (active c. 1094–1100), "I write to express my mind and paint to send forth my ideas, that is all."[65] Here Su Shih approved of Chu's explicit correlation of the importance of mind in literature with an emphasis on idea (*i*) in painting. As we saw above in the literary theory of Ou-yang Hsiu, Mei Yao-ch'en, and Su Shih, writing and reading centered on the expression and interpretation of the author's mind behind the meaning of the text. In the Muromachi Zen painting inscriptions, we will find closely comparable language, assumptions, and interests as seen in these Sung passages.

Su developed his emphasis on the mind and idea or intention and applied it specifically to art in a manner not seen in earlier Ancient Civilization writers.[66] The deeply spiritual and philosophical significance of this emphasis can be seen in his description of the process leading to the "lodging of his mind" (*yü-i*) in an art object. For the artist to do so, according to Su, he or she must attain a high level of concentration through immersion in creative activity that allows the artist to achieve a high level of freedom and spontaneity.[67] Significantly, this state of mind is described in terms of the sages who have mastered the Way taken from Taoist and Buddhist religious texts.[68] In one passage describing a friend's study, the Drunk on Ink Pavilion, Su quotes the *Chuang-tzu* to describe this state: "You say you find 'supreme happiness' in doing calligraphy / It makes you feel you are "rambling free and easy' / You've built a hall and named it 'Drunk on Ink.'" . . .[69] "Supreme joy" and "rambling free and easy" are important concepts in the *Chuang-tzu* to be discussed in the final chapter of the present work, and their usage here in a response to a friend's study is very much like the practice of the Japanese Five Mountains monks. We can see Su's specific reference to Buddhism when he encourages a monk friend of his to keep up his calligraphy practice for its ability to help release Buddhist wisdom in him.[70]

Similar theories of artistic interpretation were held by a number of painters and theorists whose views were to be influential in Kitayama Japan. Mi Fu (1052–1107), a painter and calligrapher friend of Su, praised his son Mi Yu-jen's (1086–1165) painting as having "grasped the idea" (*te ch'i i*). This quality, Mi argued, made his son's art better than that of a T'ang dynasty minister, who was reputed to be good at painting the intention of clouded mountains.[71] The inner, subjective significance of art, including the landscape arts, lay at the center of Sung literati interpretations of painting, as it did in their textual hermeneutic.

The subjective significance of art was often associated in Sung theories of art with the character of the painter as it was expressed in painting, as we saw in Su's inscription on Sung Ti's landscape. One influential statement of this principle is found in the aesthetic writings of Kuo Jo-hsu (dates unknown [d.u.]), a late-eleventh-century contemporary of Su Shih:

> I have . . . observed that the majority of the rare works of the past have been done by high officials, talented worthies, superior scholars or [recluses living in] cliffs and caves. . . . Their elevated and refined feelings have all been lodged in their paintings. Since their personal quality was already lofty, their "spirit consonance" (*ch'i-yun*) could not but be lofty.[72]

The painter lodges his feelings in the painting, and this expression of the painter is what the viewer looks for in interpreting the significance of the artwork.

This emphasis on spiritual development and the moral character of the artist in Sung interpretations of painting can be seen also in a growing aversion to formal representation in painting.[73] As Ronald Egan has shown, the model established by Su and Huang for treatment of painting in verse inscriptions was less concerned with the relationship of the painted image to reality than with the relationship of painterly representation to art history and to poetry. This distinguishes their views from those of Tu Fu, the only major literary figure to have written many inscriptions on paintings before the eleventh century.[74] Su's views on formal likeness in painting again makes explicit the parallel of painting with poetry:

> If anyone discusses painting in terms of formal likeness,
> His understanding is close to that of a child. . . .
> There is one fundamental rule in poetry and painting:
> Innate genius and fresh originality.[75]

Stated in such strong terms, Su's interest in the expression of the artist beyond formal likeness was to influence centuries of painting theory both on the continent and abroad in Japan and elsewhere.

We see this influence in an important Zen monk in the "literary Zen" movement who was acquainted with Su Shih and was known to the Japanese Five Mountains monks: Hui-hung. Hui-hung quoted this poem above after noting that Su said, "The skillful painter paints intention (*i*) and does not paint form (*hsing*); the skillful poem speaks intention and does not speak the name."[76] In my discussion in chapter 5 on the Kitayama monks' views of artistic illusion, we will find how important these views of Su and Hui-hung were in the Southern Sung, particularly in the writings of the poet Ch'en Yü-i (1090–1138), and how the Japanese monks adapted them to their own purposes. Here it is sufficient to note that the aversion to formal representation in painting of Su and later writers, including Zen monks, is closely associated with the interest in artistic interpretation in discovering the state of mind, moral character, or intention (*i*) of the artist as it enacts a potentially high state of religious insight. These same developments can be found in the origins during this same period of new subjects in Zen and literati painting such as the plum and bamboo, subjects that became important precisely because of their emphasis on moral character and the internal state of mind. It is important to note that, for example, the subject of the plum originated in interactions of Zen monks, in particular the monk Chung-jen and also Hui-hung, with literati fleeing the political turbulence of the late Northern Sung dynasty, showing the centrality of exchange between Zen monks and nonordained literati in the development of Sung culture.[77]

The Sung emphasis on the artistic expression of the painter's mind or inner intent at the expense of formal likeness should not be misunderstood as betraying a solipsistic or subjectivistic orientation.[78] The expression of a painter's personality in eleventh-century Chinese painting was, in contrast with a Romantic emphasis on private feelings, more a matter of personal character, encompassing both sentiments and the moral maturity whose development was central to the process of self-cultivation touched on above. Character and sentiments were conceived of not as unrelated to the outside world or unavailable to others, however, but as fundamentally connected to the external world and available to the perception of others in important ways.

For the Sung literati and Zen theorists of painting, then, an interest in the expression of inner truths in painting did not conflict with the expression of the truth of the object depicted. Su Shih's famous comments on Wen T'ung's (1019–79) bamboo is just such a statement of the relationship of inner moral truth with the truth of the objective world:

> The artisans of the world may be able to create the forms perfectly, but when it comes to principle (*li*), unless one is a superior man of outstanding talent one cannot achieve it. In bamboos and rocks, and withered trees, [Wen T'ung] can truly be said to have grasped their principle. . . . In the roots and stems, joints and leaves, in what is sharp and pointed or veined and striated, there are innumerable changes and transformations never once repeated; yet each part fits in its place, and is in harmony with divine creation and accords with men's conceptions. Is it not because of what the accomplished scholar has lodged in it?[79]

The highest accomplishment in art for Su captures the principle of its subject in a way that expresses not only man's intention but also accords with universal creative processes. Such art is possible only for men of the highest moral cultivation, for not only must they have progressed to an understanding of the principle of things, they must also be able to act it out in creative expression.

When expressed in art, the inner state of the individual and the inner perception of objective truths of his subject were not only "lodged" in the art object, Sung and later critics believed, but were also apparent to their audience in the act of interpretation. The assumption in these interpretive theories that an artist's inner state is available to others in creative expression is a long-standing assumption of Chinese artistic theory.[80] We have seen this assumption also in Sung theories of self-cultivation, for example, in the belief central to the Ancient Civilization movement that the classics could provide the basis for an understanding of the intent (*i*) or mind (*hsin*) of the ancients. As in textual study, the appreciation of an art object provided a means to acquire knowledge of the innermost moral and spiritual states of their contemporaries and also a means to realizing an understanding of the heights of religious self-cultivation achieved by the sages of ancient times.

This sense of deep interpersonal understanding provided not only a basis for the importance of tradition and the writings of the ancients, it also established the human community as an essential social basis for generalized claims to understanding universal truths common to all human experience.[81] Establishing a human community that bridged the centuries was the foundation for the abiding interest in recovering the Way of the ancients common to the different intellectual movements of the Sung, for the Way was found in the actions and writings of the ancient sages. Textual study was of course central to this project for the Neo-Confucians and members of the Sung Learning movement. Like proponents of the Ancient Civilization and literati positions, for the Neo-Confucians the mind was central to the process of understanding the texts of the ancients and so also to the building of human relations across the centuries and within one's own community. Chu Hsi comments on how to proceed in the study of the texts of sages:

> Responding to things, handling affairs, and so on, are similar to studying literature. If we drill and polish ourselves in the principles of things and studies, our minds will naturally be penetrating. [In] reading, for example, . . . even after a great deal of thought, we cannot see through to the real meaning. . . . In a case like this . . . repeated effort will find a way to go through. To go through means that the mind penetrates.[82]

By honing the mind to recognize the principle (*li*) so important to Neo-Confucian ontology and morality and expressed by the ancients in textual study, the individual may reach the highest level of spiritual achievement and also truly understand the mind of the sages of the Way.

The importance of a community of understanding also formed the basis for social gatherings that were at the center of Northern Sung culture, and that we will see were at the center of Kitayama Five Mountains society as well. In literati culture Su and Huang were the central members of a large group of poets, calligraphers, painters, politicians, and Buddhist monks who met occasionally to enjoy each other's company and to work jointly on creative projects. One such gathering, which may have occurred in 1087 in Kaifeng and was well known to later generations, was often depicted in paintings showing many of the most prominent scholar-officials, including Su Shih, Mi Fu, Huang T'ing-chien, and Li Kung-lin, together with the Zen monk Fa Hsiu (1027–90), the Taoist calligrapher Ch'en Ching-yüan, and the imperial prince Wang Shen (1036–after 1089) (fig. 1.2).[83] These gatherings were not a new phenomenon in Chinese culture, for the Northern Sung literati looked back to such groups as the Seven Sages of the Bamboo Grove, the group that met at the Orchid Pavilion when the calligrapher Wang Hsi-chih (c. 307–365) composed his famous preface, and the group that formed around the influential politician Huan Hsuan (369–404) and included the famous recluse poet T'ao Ch'ien and the important painter Ku K'ai-chih (344–c. 406).

The occasions for meetings of these groups varied from poetry composition gatherings to the departure of a member of the circle of friends, and the artistic objects produced at these meetings served as models for a number of other groups. One such gathering became a popular painting subject in later centuries, a literary meeting convened on the occasion of the departure of a friend of Li Kung-lin, a member of Su Shih's circle, with poems based on lines from a poem by Wang Wei contributed by Su Shih, his brother, and Huang T'ing-chien.[84] In Yüan dynasty painting and calligraphy, the poetry gathering itself became an important theme, and these paintings reveal the idealization of past gatherings of members of Su's circle, as well as other groups of poets, painters, calligraphers, and officials. These meetings are important in that they also served as important examples for the literary meetings among Zen monks and of Zen monks with literati in the Southern Sung as well as for Japanese Five Mountains Zen culture and society.

Another important dimension to the Kitayama Japanese interpretation of artistic images of landscape is the underlying assumptions concerning the significance of landscape. While of course indigenous conceptions of the landscape were available to the Kitayama Five Mountains monks, their assumptions seem to have been largely determined by their predecessors in China. Landscape had been an important subject in Northern Sung painting by both literati and professional painters, yet it declined in popularity only to revive and again dominate ink painting during the Yüan dynasty. In the Yüan period, landscape subjects retained the associations with transcendence of society and the purity and joy of retreat or exile from government service that they had held in the Sung.[85] However, the natural world as seen in these paintings was not simply the realm of the Taoist recluse, but had also come to be associated with a number of themes taken from the lifestyle of the Confucian scholar. It is this conception of the landscape, which falls somewhere between Taoist reclusion and Confucian service, that was most important to the Kitayama Japanese interpretation of the landscape arts, and also to Yüan intellectual history.

This change in the significance of landscape reflects some important developments in conceptions of the role of the poet and of the place of the Confucian

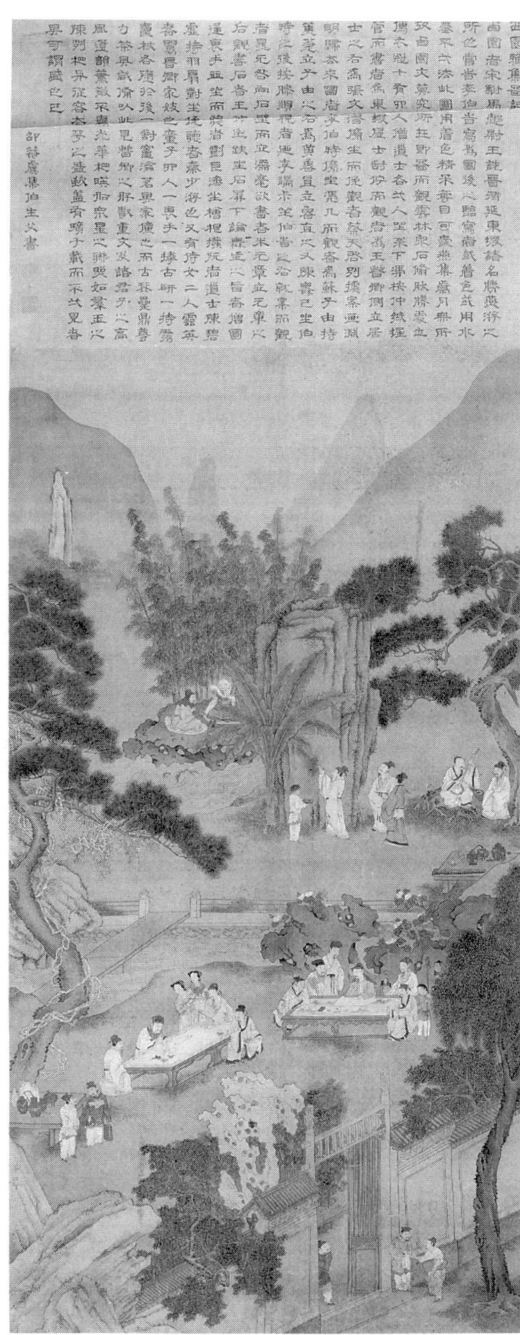

Fig. 1.2. *Elegant Gathering at West Garden*. Attributed to Chao Meng-fu (1254–1322). Yüan dynasty. Collection of the National Palace Museum, Taipei, Taiwan, Republic of China.

scholar in contemporary society. The fall of the Northern Sung and the rule of China by a non-Han Chinese people, whether the Jurchen in Northern China or the Mongols who conquered all of China, was cause for much discussion at the beginning of the Chin and Yüan dynasties respectively. Much debate ensued on the most appropriate roles in government and in reclusion for Confucian scholar-officials. In culture these debates also found expression; for example, painting saw the development of a number of themes that symbolically expressed the need to justify not serving in government. One of the best-known affirmations of the need to serve the Mongol government was that of Chao Meng-fu (1254–1322), himself a member of the Sung imperial family who went on to serve the Yüan government, but a number of scholars refused to serve in the government of a "foreign" people.

In the second half of the Yüan, the precedent of the refusal to serve in government during the early years of the dynasty combined with widespread unrest to lead to a new class of scholars who were ambivalent about the appropriateness of official service or felt no need to serve in government, and instead were active primarily in cultural circles, composing poetry and working independently as scholars.[86] In earlier ages only those literati who had retired, had fallen from official favor, or were traveling spent extended periods of time in the countryside and smaller towns, but in the Yüan this new social role led to an increase in the level of education and number of literati present in regions far from the capital. The two most prominent examples of this new class of literati were both to have significant impact on the Japanese monks who were active in the early years of the *shigajiku*: Kao Ch'i (1336–74) and Yang Wei-chen (1296–1370).[87] Japanese monks were to have contact with both of these literati during their travels on the continent,[88] and their writings were important for the Kitayama inscriptions in a number of ways. More crucially for a general understanding of the history of Chinese intellectuals is the establishment of a social basis for intellectuals who found their primary source of individual identity based on moral and spiritual value not in the government but in an independent social role and cultural institution, however informal.

The emergence of a new social role for Yüan intellectuals was entangled with the growth of a new significance of landscape imagery seen most clearly in landscape paintings depicting the scholar's studio, an image most closely associated in art history with the painter Wang Meng (c. 1301–85)[89] (fig. 1.3). The studio was a place of reclusion from society and of social gatherings with literary acquaintances, of escape from life as an official, and of meetings with other classically trained literati for the appreciation of the history, literature, and spiritual ideals of the ancients. We have seen something like this in the Sung dynasty, when Ou-yang Hsiu and Su Shih affirmed the transcendent value of the pleasure and leisure they enjoyed while holding minor office in exile. But in the Yüan this style of life became more than an interlude between offices, more than a period marking a hiatus from the always-longed-for life of Confucian service in society, and took on an independent status.

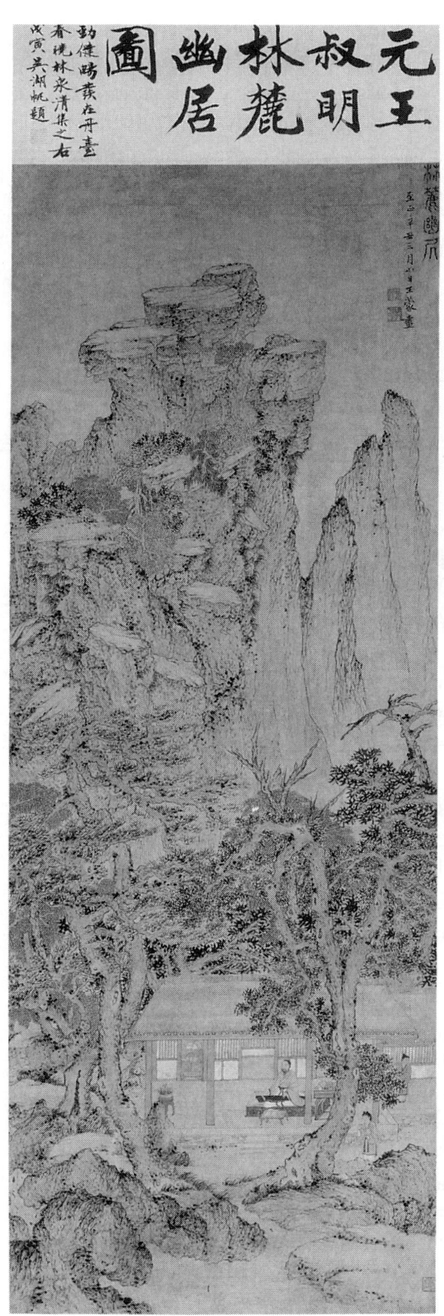

Fig. 1.3. *Quiet Life in a Wooded Glen.* In the manner of Wang Meng (c. 1301–85). Hanging scroll. Ink on paper. 177.8 x 64.2 cm. 1361(?). Kate S. Buckingham Collection, 1947.728.

One important support for the prestige of this new social role was the general spiritual value attributed to textual study that we have seen was widespread already in the Sung dynasty. This value was celebrated widely in poetry and painting on the topic of the scholar's study. In Yüan painting the scholar's retreat became the central theme of the landscape painting tradition and replaced the Sung conception of wandering through the landscape. While the motif was not new to Chinese painting, we find the scholar's study becomes a defining image in two of the four great Yün painters, Ni Tsan (1301–74) and Wang Meng.[90] These literati painters turned to landscape paintings in the T'ang and Sung for images of the recluse and scholar's hut in order to develop this theme in their own paintings.[91] In the early and mid-Yüan this topic was popular due to the large numbers of scholars who retreated into seclusion as a response to the non-Han Chinese rulers of the dynasty, but by the 1350s and 1360s, as social order deteriorated in southeastern China, many educated elites returned to metropolitan centers for refuge.[92]

In inscriptions on these paintings Wang Meng, Ni Tsan, and other literati explored the spiritual and religious dimensions to the life of the recluse and its implications for their own thinking about their art and other cultural production.[93] Yet this theme was not limited in appeal to the painting of literati, and is also found in the artwork of a number of Taoist painters and Zen monk painters of the day, as well as paintings by individuals living in urban centers and, most importantly for the style of the Kitayama Japanese paintings, professional painters in the Chekiang and Kiangsu areas.[94] Some of the most prominent Yüan Zen monks were also active in composing inscriptions and poetry in these cultural circles, such as Liao-an (also Nan-t'ang) Ch'ing-yü (1288–1363).[95] One example of a discourse on the theme of the Zen studio or retreat was inscribed by the prominent Zen master Ch'u-shih Fan-ch'i for his Japanese disciple, Muga Shōgo (1310–81).[96] Many of the Japanese Five Mountains monks who traveled to the continent practiced and studied with Nan-t'ang under his influential teacher Ku-lin Sei-mo (1262–1329), who had more Japanese disciples than any other Chinese monk, and then took up their cultural form of Zen on returning to the Japanese islands. Through these channels the theme of the scholar's studio and the value of reading texts made its way into Japanese Five Mountains Zen.

Often the Yüan literati activities in their studios were recorded through the production of cultural artifacts when visitors would drop by, such as a scroll of poems or a painting with prose and poetic inscriptions. These scrolls were then kept as a memento of the sentiments and ideas of the occasion. Events leading to the production of these scrolls, which are formally nearly identical to the Kitayama *shigajiku* poem-and-painting scrolls, took place as part of the free social interchange between literati, Zen and other Buddhist monks, court and academy painters, and influential public officials in the late Yüan and early Ming dynasties.[97] The cultural nature of these gatherings also led to an increase in the number of inscriptions on painting scrolls associated with literati beginning in the late Yüan, so that we come to see mainland painting scrolls with inscriptions in comparable numbers to those to be found in Kitayama Japan.[98] By the early Ming these group events included not only literati painters, but also painters working in the styles of the Southern Academy painters Ma Yüan (active before 1189–after 1224) and Hsia Kuei (active c. 1180–1224), as well as other artists influenced by the Northern Sung painters Fan Kuan (960–1030), Kuo Hsi (c. 1001–c. 1090), and Li Ch'eng (919–67), and painters such as Wang Fu (1362–1416), who worked in a variety of styles.[99] Most importantly for our purposes, Zen Buddhist monks were also active in these cultural circles and, as we shall see in the next chapter, Japanese monks traveling to the continent returned to ask painters in the Kitayama Five Mountains monasteries who were working in these same styles for paintings used in scrolls much like these.

We now turn to an important example of such a scroll whose author apparently provided a model for the Kitayama Five Mountains Japanese writers of the *shigajiku* inscriptions: a 1360 painting by Yao T'ing-mei (active c. 1325–65) in the Cleveland Museum, with a prose preface inscribed by the important Yüan literatus Yang Wei-chen entitled *Leisure Enough to Spare*[100] (fig. 1.4). Yang Wei-chen seems to have played a formative role for Kitayama period Japanese Five Mountains culture in a number of ways: his prefaces apparently provided a model for the standardized format of the Kitayama painting prefaces;[101] his poetic style was influential in Kitayama Five Mountains poetry;[102] through his importance as this new type of literati recluse; and in his theory of poetry discussed below. As a poet Yang was at the center of a number of literary groups,[103] groups that by Yang's day were central to the composition of literature both in Yüan China and contemporary Japanese culture. It was members of one such circle of fellow poets who put together the poem-and-painting scroll, *Leisure Enough to Spare*.

To develop some comparative perspective on the Muromachi Japanese poem-and-painting scrolls, we can first examine the process by which the painting and its inscriptions were mounted together on a single scroll, before turning to the spiritual values discussed in Yang Wei-chen's essay and the preface's underlying aesthetic. Wai-kam Ho has reconstructed the probable process of composition as follows: the artist and eight others first gathered in the winter of 1359, when they wrote poems and perhaps visited a place identified as Tu's (d.u.) hermitage, the hermitage that will serve as the subject of the scroll; later that same year, some fourteen other poems were written; and then perhaps about one year later Yao T'ing-mei was asked to complete a painting and the well-known literatus Yang Wei-chen was asked to compose a preface for the painting; all were then mounted together to form the scroll as it now exists, although some additional colophons and seals were added down into the present century.[104]

It is important to note that the painting itself is not central to the scroll as a whole, for it was completed quite late in the overall process, even though the painter seems to have written a poem at the first meeting. Rather, the final scroll is a product of poems composed at one or more literary gatherings, and the most

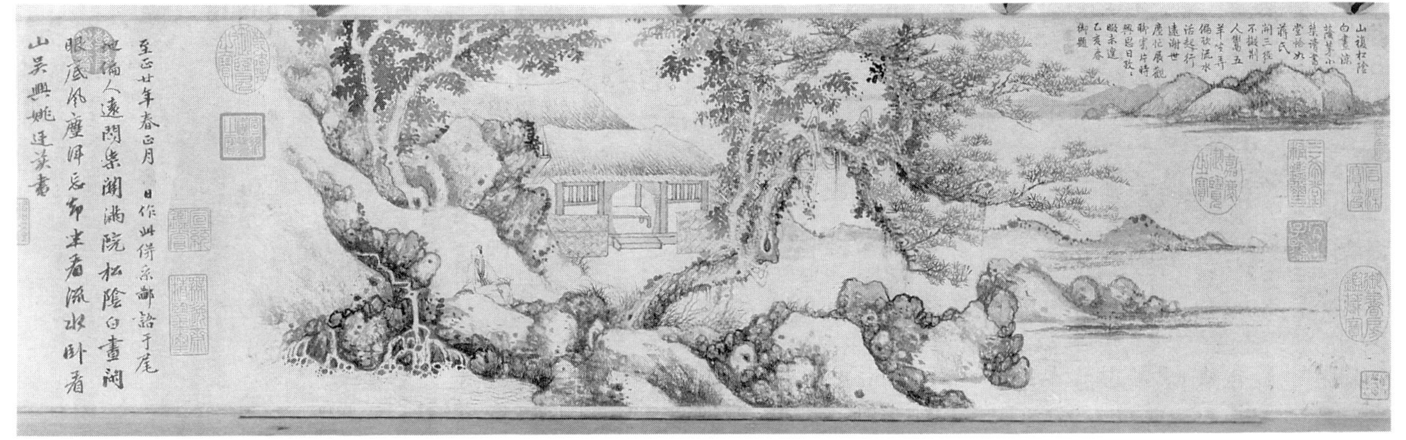

Fig. 1.4. *Leisure Enough to Spare*. By Yao T'ing-mei (active c. 1325–65). Artist's inscription with 23 others. Handscroll. Ink on paper. 23 x 84 cm. 1360. © Cleveland Museum of Art, 1996. Purchase from the John L. Severance Fund, 1954.791.

prominent person to complete an inscription is asked to write the preface. The complex process of accumulating such a large number of inscriptions, the addition of a painting late in the process to what otherwise could exist independently as a scroll of poems, and the importance of at least one and possibly two separate literary gatherings were all to also characterize the Japanese poem-and-painting scroll.[105]

The significance of the scroll to the artist, to the hermit Tu, and to the poets is defined in Yang Wei-chen's preface. Yang's prose essay is a discussion of the name of the painting, "Leisure Enough to Spare," which he applied to the lifestyle of the hermit. He began by quoting first Ou-yang Hsiu, Su Shih, and then an unidentified "man of late Sung" on methods of securing leisure time, but then rejected their methods as not leading to enough leisure to have any "to spare." He then turned to the hermit Tu, whom he described as living by the Sung River with fine children, diligent servants, and relatives and friends to watch out for him. He concluded his argument:

> Thus he has been able to live peacefully, and to eat heartily, and to pass his time in rest and play. Surely his leisure was not stolen from the few moments when he has company [like Ou-yang Hsiu]. It was not derived from illness [like Su Shih]. It was not jeopardized by extensive holdings of real estate [like the man of late Sung]. Could anyone question my word if I said this is truly abundant enough to spare?[106]

Yang then ended his essay by noting the reasons he came to write the preface for the painting: Tu had asked a mutual friend of theirs to request that Yang write the preface; Yang also observed that a number of others had composed poems to go together with the essay.

We can see from Yang's essay that the painting was valued together with the poetic inscriptions both as a record of a gathering of friends, and more importantly as an appreciation of Tu's reclusive lifestyle. Unlike the important role we have seen the painting play in Sung painting inscriptions, this painting is itself of little importance to the inscription writers; indeed, none of the poems even mention the painting, nor does Yang's essay. The minor role of the painting reflects the relatively minor role it plays in the overall social occasions that led to the final poem-and-painting scroll, which we will see again in Japanese Kitayama examples. Instead, the inscription writers seem mainly interested in the lifestyle and character of the individual who is the subject of the painting, and in discourse on the virtues and pleasures of the life of reclusion.[107] This lack of interest in the style and actual subject of the painting typifies the Sung emphasis on inner virtue in art as it did in Kitayama Japan.

Yang Wei-chen's own theory of art closely followed the interpretive theory of the Sung writers Ou-yang Hsiu, Su Shih, Kuo Jo-hsu, and Mi Fu in important respects. In a preface to Hsia Wen-yen's (1296–1370) history of painting, the *T'u-hui pao-chien* of 1365, Yang wrote:

> Although the traditional practice of calligraphy and painting has standard models, the characteristics of the inspired and excellent come from one's inner quality and cannot be obtained by the use of standard models. For this reason a painting's excellence or inferiority lies in the loftiness or baseness of an artist's character. . . . If they only have this inborn quality (C. *t'ien-chih*), they can be among the sages, able to excel in their own dynasty and be famous in later times. As for those who do not have it, they may be able to do some imitations and even come close to standard models, but none of them will have their minds expressed (C. *hsin-ch'uan*) and their thoughts transmitted (C. *i-ling*) in their own style.[108]

We saw the same focus on moral character as the most important criterion for judging art in Yang's preface to *Leisure with Time to Spare*. Moreover, the quality of the highest levels of artistic expression that distinguishes it from inferior art is identical to that of Ou-yang and Su Shih: that the artists have their "minds expressed and their thoughts transmitted."[109] In Yang's view the locus of moral character for the individual is in the mind, and it is through interpretation of art that the audience, whether the reader of poetry or the viewer of painting or calligraphy, can understand that character.

The important common thread that can be found in both Sung and Yüan inscriptions is the shared focus of artistic interpretation on moralistic or spiritual issues. If we read the poems together with the painting of *Leisure Enough to Spare* as clues to the significance of the painted image, we must conclude that for the painter and his contemporaries the painted image is not primarily a depiction of the locale where Tu lives with his family and servants, nor does it function as a representation of any other actual locale. Rather, the painting depicts the personality and moral accomplishment of a certain person: the lofty and pure character of their friend the hermit Tu. Yang finds this image of moral character not in any expressive quality of the brushwork of the painter, but in the significance of the subject of the painting itself.

In concluding I might suggest that for these Sung and Yüan Chinese audiences, the subjects of these scrolls of inscriptions with painting are not at all what modern viewers would call their subjects, that is, a branch of bamboo or a natural landscape. Nor was there a primary interest in the expressive qualities of painterly style and brushwork in this strand of Yüan painting theory. Instead, the significance of the paintings was found in the moral character of the individual connected with what is shown in the painting: in the case of the bamboo, the painter Wen T'ung; in the case of a landscape, for Su Shih it was Sung T'i, while for Yang Wei-chen it was his friend Tu. This same fundamental orientation to artistic interpretation is found in the Japanese landscape painting inscriptions, and it is to their development that I now turn.

Chapter 2

Japanese Five Mountains Zen and the Poem-and-Painting Scrolls

> I would say that as for [social] relations [in general], it is best to have tranquility in the mind. If [one's mind is] not tranquil then what good are relations?
>
> —Gyokuen Bompō

> Brocades are hung to the left and right, and paintings hung before and behind.
>
> —Taihaku Shingen description of a Five Mountains Zen monk's study

> The indirect influence of Zen [in Muromachi Japanese culture] . . . cannot be exaggerated, [since] the [artistic] producers and the [theater] actors worked primarily for an audience whose aesthetic standards were those of Zen.
>
> —George Sansom, *Japan: A Short Cultural History*

We now turn from Chinese models to introduce the early Muromachi Japanese Zen monks in their historical and cultural context. While the Five Mountains Zen monks looked up to their Chinese predecessors, their historical and intellectual circumstances differed in significant ways from those on the mainland. Understanding the Kitayama monks' writings on landscape is only possible after introducing briefly the history of Japanese Zen literature and culture, the changing early Muromachi fortunes of the landscape as an artistic subject, the history and early examples of the *shigajiku* poem-and-painting scrolls, together with the Kitayama monks most active in inscribing landscape paintings, whom we will study in our remaining chapters. Here as elsewhere I do not attempt to be comprehensive, but instead emphasize the aspects of these several broad areas of Muromachi cultural history that contributed most to the development of the central documents for this study: inscriptions on *shigajiku* poem-and-painting landscape scrolls. The earliest examples of the *shigajiku* scrolls will be surveyed in closing this chapter.

The general atmosphere and social circumstances under which the Kitayama Zen monks wrote about landscape are revealed by a preface to a no-longer-extant landscape poem-and-painting scroll by Chūhō En'i. Following contemporary convention, Chūhō describes for us early in his preface how the scroll was produced:

> The venerable Kengan Keieki [Genchū; d. 1421], in an overflow of the samadhi of playfulness, likes to give forth verses which astonish people. Even if he is compared to the three lofty monk[-poets Ch'iao-jan, Kuan-hsiu, and Ch'i-chi (active late ninth century)] of ancient [T'ang Chinese] times, he still does not give way very much to them. After composing a poem on "Snow Covered Plum Blossoms by a Bridge in the Wilderness," he had a professional painter paint the scene and together with a few others wrote inscriptions on it, all overpowering in the elegance of their writings. When it was mounted in final splendor, he presented it to the worthy one of the eastern mountains, Sekiho, and sent a message to me, En'i a man of Golden Flower Mountain, to write a preface at its head.[1]

Chūhō's record shows that a Zen monk of advanced practice who also was adept at poetry first composed a poem, in this case modeled on a poem on plum blossoms by the important Sung dynasty Zen monk Yüan-wu K'e-chin.[2] Then the monk requests that a painting be completed of the scene described in his poem by a professional painter, probably a monk in the atelier at the Five Mountains temple where he resided, perhaps Tōfuku-ji or Tenrū-ji where he served as abbot. With the painted scroll in hand he then gathers with his friends to compose inscriptions on blank space set aside on the scroll. Then as the last steps to the process he presented the scroll to a highly respected individual, in this case the venerable Sekiho, who may well be a powerful politician,[3] and finally asked another monk, in this case Chūhō, to compose the preface.

We may observe in this overall process close similarities to the Japanese scroll *Plantain in Evening Rain*, and the Yang Wei-chen–inscribed *Leisure Enough to Spare* scroll. The similarities include such features as the gathering in which the inscriptions are made and the leaving of the composition of the prose preface to the end, when a prominent author is asked to compose one. However, there is at least one important difference with its Chinese predecessor: rather than at the end of the process the Japanese painting is completed early on, although still subsequent to the composition of the initial poem. Since the scroll is no longer extant we must also surmise two other important differences with the Yang Wei-chen scroll: the participants were probably mostly or at times all monks rather than literati; and the format of the scroll was probably vertical and not horizontal, since that is the predominant format virtually without exception in this period in Japan.

The institutional context for this complex social and cultural process is defined by Chūhō's strong statement about the close relation between poetic practice and Japanese Zen. Poetry, and implicitly Kengan's entire production of the poetry-and-painting scroll, is defined as an expression of the state of advanced Buddhist insight, "the samadhi of playfulness," which we will investigate in the last chapter. Kengan is not merely a monk who writes poetry as an avocation or a good poet who happens to be a monk, in his friend Chūhō's eyes, but a person of high religious accomplishment. Moreover, through this poetic and artistic process Kengan equals the cultural accomplishments of highly respected T'ang Chinese predecessors, three Buddhist monks who wrote poetry popular in later centuries both on the mainland and in Japan. The Japanese Five Mountains temples were in this view an institution where the social relations with important political figures and the cultural production of Zen literature and other arts were of central importance.

From early in the history of Japanese Zen Buddhism, literature and other forms of cultural practice had been integrated in various ways into the institutions, monastic training, and even the qualifications for entering the newly established monasteries. The important Chinese teachers Lan-ch'i Tao-lung and Wu-hsüeh Tsu-yüan, who founded the first Chinese Zen–style monastic complexes in Japan, both frequently authored poetry, and a poem Wu-hsüeh composed as a young man was widely praised by contemporaries and such later literary illuminaries as one of the four great Yüan poets, Wu Chi (1272–1348).[4] Wu-hsüeh even referred to his period of study under the important master Hsü-t'ang Chih-yü as a time when he achieved a Buddhist state of mind he termed "verse samadhi" (C. *chü-yü san-mei*).[5] As a result of these individual and institutional influences, from early on many of the most influential Japanese Zen masters were adept at poetry composition. Even Dōgen Kigen seems to have become familiar with the poetry of T'ang Zen poets Han-shan and Kuan-hsiu together with the verse of the Sung literatus Su Shih during his stay in Southern Sung China, in addition to his lifelong interest in the poems of the T'ang court poet Po Chü-i, long popular in Japanese elite society.[6] These and other monks also practiced other cultural forms, including calligraphy and prose composition.

Following the formative period Japanese *gozan* poetry flourished in the early to mid-fourteenth century, and the poetic activities of Japanese monks in this period were to provide an important basis for the development of the poem-and-painting scrolls inscriptions at the end of the century. Literary activity among the *gozan* monks reached its first peak under the auspices of poetically inclined Chinese monks arriving in Japan during the late 1320s, particularly Ch'ing-cho Cheng-ch'eng and Chü-hsien Fan-hsien, and also of Japanese monks who returned after traveling widely on the continent in the 1310s and 1320s, including Jakushitsu Genkō (1290–1367), Betsugen Enshi (1294–1364), Sesson Yūbai (1290–1346), and Chūgan Engetsu (1300–75).[7] Both the Chinese and Japanese monks exercised their talents not only in Zen practice but also in a wide range of literary and cultural affairs.[8] Under the influence of these Chinese teachers and their Japanese contemporaries, who had often studied under the same masters in China, literary and cultural activities flourished among the Japanese Zen monasteries as never before.

One important institutional and social development occurred in the Five Mountains monasteries during the fourteenth century that would provide the basis to the highly social form of Zen found in the Kitayama period. This was the growth of the subtemple (*tatchū*) in the monasteries, and a subsequent change in the social relations and architectural surroundings of the Japanese Zen monks. The subtemple itself became an important part of Five Mountains temple life beginning in the late thirteenth century.[9] The subtemple, whose name *tatchū* means literally "the [master's] funerary monument," was seen initially by the monks as a place where a senior disciple might live as a gesture of respect after the death of his teacher, generally a former abbot of the large monastic complex on whose grounds the *tatchū* was built. As it became increasingly common to erect an abbot's quarters and living quarters near the grave of a particular master, small groups of former disciples of the deceased abbot also came to live and associate there together.[10] This new social unit in the monasteries also became a focus of economic support for the temples through donations of *shōen* estate rights by regional *shugo daimyō* and members of the local elites.[11] We see in Kitayama period paintings scenes depicting groups of monks studying together that perhaps represent contemporary practices in the Five Mountains temples (fig. 2.1). As a place of honor for past masters, as a popular site for study, religious practice, and cultural and social gatherings, and as a center of economic power, the *tatchū* subtemple became a major component of the large, metropolitan monasteries. In this institutional development we see a divergence from the traditional center of Chinese Zen monastic life in the monks' hall.

The increase in subtemples was also significant in a number of other ways, for they provided a central locus for the social groups and gatherings that produced a variety of group cultural objects, including poem scrolls to be discussed shortly and ultimately the poem-and-painting scrolls themselves. Again evidence is found in contemporary paintings which may depict gatherings of monks to appreciate art objects (frontispiece). One such important social occasion was the parting of friends, when the poems for the scrolls were written in order to present the person departing with a memento of his friendships in the monastic community. Parting had long been a major social occasion in China and also Japan, but during the Sung and Yüan dynasties appeared the farewell paintings that also became popular in the decades during which the early Muromachi Japanese poem-and-painting scrolls were produced.[12] These social events in the Japanese *gozan* monasteries occasionally involved a large number of individuals, numbering in one instance three hundred, where each would inscribe a poem, and provided a major social basis for the poem and also poem-and-painting scrolls.

Another social occasion important to the Japanese Five Mountains Zen temple life and to the evolution of the poem-and-painting scrolls was the poetry meeting (*shikai*). Such meetings were a popular social and cultural form on the mainland from at least T'ang times onwards.[13] In Japanese literary history, poetry meetings are found from the earliest times.[14] By the twelfth century, poetry meetings (*uta no*

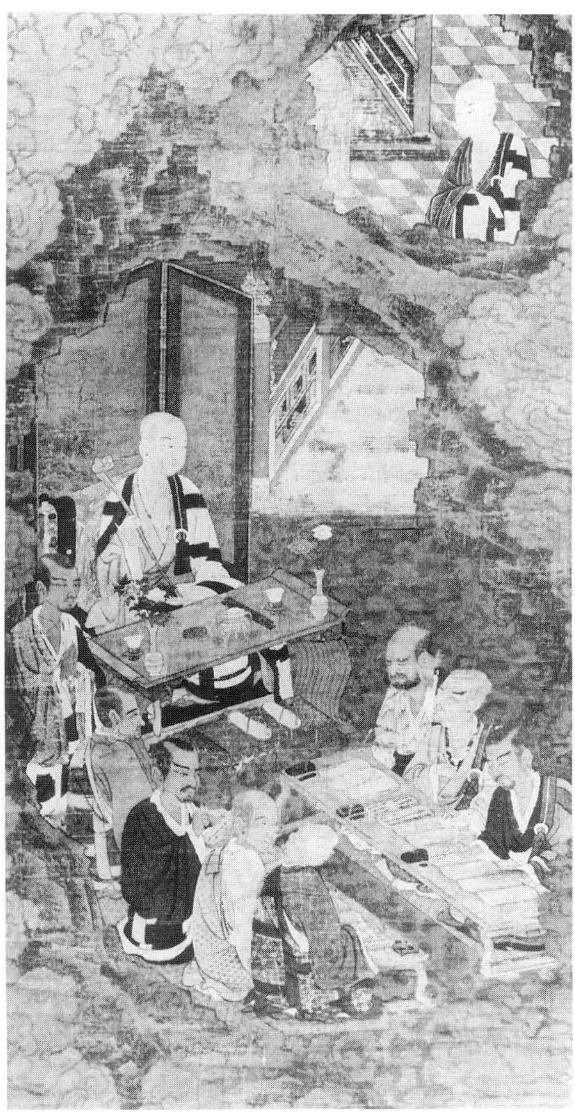

Fig. 2.1. *Arhats Studying Together*. Minchō (1351–1431). One of forty-five hanging scrolls of *Five Hundred Arhats*. Ink with color on silk. 173.6 x 89.4 cm. Important Cultural Property. Late fourteenth or early fifteenth century. Tōfuku-ji, Kyoto.

kai), poetry contests (*utaawase*), and poetry circles, sometimes including a large number of both lay and ordained poets, became an important part of court literature. During the fourteenth century, literary meetings were held for the composition of linked verse both at court and among circles including individuals from a variety of social classes. Some of these verse meetings produced verse links entirely in

Japanese, while others were compositions alternating links in Japanese and Chinese, and Five Mountains Zen monks were active participants in both types of meetings.[15] Poetry meetings were also held in the Five Mountains temples, where the participants included at times only monks and at other times both monks and influential laity.[16] These meetings provided the social occasions for the composition of poems that were to be assembled together in a single poem scroll, and often served the same function later for the creation of poem-and-painting scrolls.

The social group that created the *shijiku* poem scrolls, and eventually the poem-and-painting scrolls, was known as the *yūsha* or friends society, a salon of similar-minded monks and at times laity who were brought together for various reasons.[17] While there has been little study of the historical development of these groups,[18] we will see shortly that during the mid-fourteenth century they seem to have formed in individual Five Mountains temples in the capital, such as Tōfuku-ji, because of shared respect for an individual monk, such as Enni Ben'en or Daidō Ichii (1292–1370). Friends societies also arose among monks from different temples aligned along lines that reflect certain common interests or levels of skill in literature or in religious understanding.

Five Mountains Zen documents tell us that the Japanese friends society salons were formed based on Chinese models of such gatherings by monks and laity. As we shall see later, one early Chinese model for the fourteenth-century Japanese monks centered on the Six Dynasties monk Hui-yüan on Mt. Lu, whose group members included the aesthetician Tsung-ping and the important early landscape poet Hsieh Ling-yün. Literary gatherings of the Sung literati, including Su's circle of lay and ordained friends, were another important model, as were such Yüan gatherings as that recorded in the *Leisure Enough to Spare* scroll. By modeling their own activities on these Chinese gatherings, the Five Mountains monks associated themselves with the prestige and cultural authority of some of the best-respected figures in the continental cultural past.

Participation in the social institution of the friends society was, of course, one locus of daily life in the Five Mountains temples, and as such was a subject of religious and moral concern. Some scholars have criticized these societies and related gatherings in the *tatchū* as a source of privatization and factionalization in the monasteries, and certainly their growth did affect the Zen monks' lifestyle by increasingly dispersing them out of the central monks' hall (J. *sōdō*).[19] Yet these social changes do not themselves determine the ways in which the monks made sense of their lives, and many of the Five Mountains monks were fully aware of the spiritual and moral dangers of this social form. These monks criticized their contemporaries, when they felt it was necessary, for falling into narrow attachments to factional interests, and worked to develop positive models for friendships and other associations in the *tatchū* subtemples.

One important example for the Kitayama period of just such a positive model is found in an inscription by Gyokuen Bompō on an extant painting, *The Study of the Three Beneficial* [*Friends*].[20] Bompō begins by contrasting positive and negative forms of human relations:

> Relations in the world of humans take various forms: some are plain and relations go well; others are likeable and they fail; some preserve virtue and others scramble after influence; some gather together to sing and dance or to play *po* and *yi*[21] and others form cliques in history and letters. One by one individuals differ, with those cut and polished being few and those who speak glibly many. If you do not first choose [your friends] and then develop relations with them, then I fear you will invite criticism, and you cannot be imprudent. Consequently a *chun-tzu* of old [Confucius] established the teaching of the straightforward, the sincere, and the good listener,[22] and made it the model of a "friends society (*yūsha*)." Thereupon the holy one Ekyō Chūwa [d.u.] ordered a craftsman to paint a study under pines, bamboo, and plum trees, and the door placard [in the painting] read, "The Three Beneficials." Perhaps this is his aspiration.[23]

Bompō's friend's response to this social problem is, signficantly enough for our purposes, a cultural and also social one: to put together a *shigajiku* poem-and-painting scroll. By asking his friends to inscribe such a scroll, Ekyō is actively intervening in Five Mountains social relations and provoking discussion of his ideal of social interaction. Ekyō also used the triad of plants and trees, which had become associated with the "three virtues" or "three beneficial friends" by the later thirteenth and early fourteenth centuries among Chin (1115–1234) and early Yüan literati.[24] After an extended string of images of the pine, plum, and bamboo that interwove images of natural phenomena with terms of clearly high moral value, Bompō returns to his general point:

> Ah! Their nature and actions are not those which would bring shame to men, and how could I not praise them? I would say that as for [social] relations [in general], it is best to have tranquility in the mind. If not tranquil then what good are relations! Our Master [Eikyō] is pure and lofty, standing out from the group; in studying the ancients he never tires. Then with ceremony he summoned these three in under our eaves of centrality and harmony. Together enjoying the pleasures of friendship through the whole year, then did we not indeed have the good fortune of the three beneficial [friends]?[25]

In the complimentary literary form of the preface, Bompō of course praises his friend Eikyō, but like his early-fifteenth-century contemporaries we can also hear a clear message regarding the pitfalls and positive models of *tatchū* subtemple relations.

Group gatherings in the *tatchū* subtemples and elsewhere provided an important social basis for life in the Five Mountains monasteries. They also were the source of the most important specific cultural precedent that would provide a model for the poem-and-painting scroll inscriptions produced by the Japanese Five Mountains monks: a Chinese cultural form known in Japan as the *shijiku* or poem scroll. This form played an important role in the literary activities of the Chinese Zen monks who were the teachers and fellow practitioners of the Japanese Five Mountains monks both on the mainland and in Japan. Important evidence of the direct historical linkage between the Chinese and Japanese Zen poem scrolls can be found in a number of poem scrolls that were brought to Japan from the mainland by Japanese monks after having participated in poetry composition groups while studying under their Zen teachers in China. One such extant document actually shows the way this cultural form came to Japanese Zen temples through the complex process by which it was completed.[26] The scroll was initially put together in Yüan China by a number of monks to rhyme with two poems by the Japanese monk Muzō Jōshō (d. 1306), which he had written while training as a disciple in China of the important Southern Sung Chinese master Hsü-t'ang Chih-yü. However, the scroll was completed only after Muzō returned to Japan and asked a Chinese monk then residing in Japan, Ta-hsiu Cheng-nien, to write a preface for the scroll; only the preface is still extant (fig. 2.2). Through the process of gathering poetry and prose for this scroll by multiple authors both in China and in Japan, this document demonstrates by its very composition process the manner in which the poem scroll literary genre was brought from the mainland Zen temples to those in Japan.

These scrolls were often composed to record gatherings on particular social or religious occasions in the monasteries, including the conferment of an honorific name (J. *dōgō*), the promotion of a monk to an office in the temple hierarchy, the completion of an artwork, and other events.[27] These scrolls could reach considerable size, for in 1343 the monk Kempō Shidon (1285–1361) offered poems by over one hundred Tōfuku-ji line monks in memorial for the monastery's founder, Enni Ben'en, including poems by the Chinese monk Ch'ing-t'ang Chüeh-yüan (1244–1306) and the important Japanese scholar-monk Kokan Shiren (1278–1346). Other poem scrolls assembled to commemorate events in temple history include one put together in 1380 by nineteen monks celebrating the completion of a bridge on the temple grounds by rhyming poems with a verse by the most powerful single disciple of the enormously influential Five Mountains monk Musō Soseki (1275–1351), the monk Shun'oku Myōha (1311–88), and another on which several monks acknowledged the inclusion into the Buddhist canon of Kokan's history of Japanese Buddhism, the *Genkō shakusho*. Three scrolls from the same period that commemorated more personal events are associated with the monk Daidō Ichii, such as the death of a deer that Daidō had raised, a tree that he had loved, and a eulogy lamenting his death.[28] The personal character of this last group of poem scrolls was to prove central in the early poem-and-painting scrolls.

In addition to poems these mid-fourteenth-century scrolls often included a prose preface or postface, closely resembling the combination of literary genres

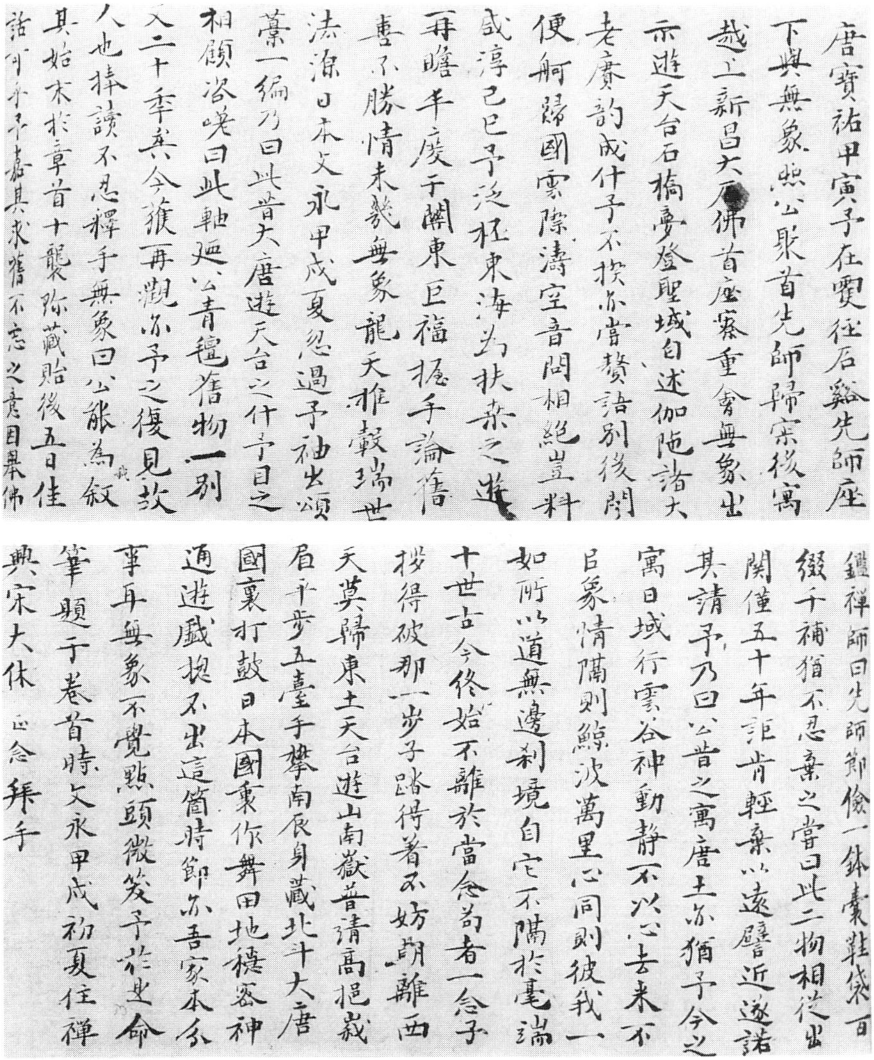

Fig. 2.2. Preface to *Mt. T'ien-t'ai Stone Bridge* Poem Scroll. By Ta-hsiu Cheng-nien (1214–88). Handscroll. Ink on paper. 32.5 x 109.8 cm. Important Cultural Property. 1274. The Gotoh Museum, Tokyo.

seen in the poem-and-painting scrolls that developed later in the century. Prose inscriptions were written both for scrolls assembled during events connected with temple life[29] and those completed in response to more personal concerns.[30] In Northern Sung China, prose prefaces were written on informal occasions, yet the fourteenth-century Japanese monks used them to record both private and public ones. The large numbers of prefaces and postfaces in the literary collections of the Chinese monks who came to teach in Japan[31] suggest that this genre was used widely in Chinese Zen monasteries by Southern Sung times. It is the prefaces and postfaces that provide twentieth-century readers with the most useful information about the levels and types of religious significance for the composers and audiences of the poem-and-painting scrolls.

We know that the *shijiku* poem scrolls continued in popularity down into the Kitayama period not only from documentary sources and the *shigajiku* scrolls, but also from other evidence. At times the literary meetings would be held to commemorate an event publicly, and afterwards the poems and prose composed at the meeting would apparently be posted publicly after having been carved into a wooden signboard. One extant example of such a "poem board" (*shiban*) is from a poetry meeting in 1418, and the participants included the Kitayama monks Gyokuen Bompō, Daigaku Shusū (1345–1423), and other of the most prominent Five Mountains monks of the day (fig. 2.3).[32] To summarize, then, we can see that by the middle of the fourteenth century an important element that was to become central to the poem-and-painting scrolls was already an important part of *gozan* Zen culture: long literary scrolls and other poem records put together by Zen monks gathering in poetry meetings that often included both poems and prose prefaces or postfaces.

Changing levels of interest in natural landscape themes were another factor in mid-century *gozan* culture that laid the foundation for the poem-and-painting scrolls. Landscape was the subject that would dominate the inscriptions on early poem-and-painting scrolls at the end of the century. Yet many scholars have noted the relative lack of popularity of landscape paintings among Japanese Zen monks during the fourteenth century, as compared to such subjects as figure paintings, Buddhist devotional subjects, *chinzō* (also *chinsō*) portraits, as well as bird and flower subjects.[33] Landscapes were a relatively minor subject in monochrome ink painting during the second half of the thirteenth and first half of the fourteenth centuries, although there were such popular subjects as the Four Seasons and the Eight Views of the Hsiao and Hsiang Rivers. Sources other than monochrome ink painting reveal a growing interest in landscape during this period: screen paintings in narrative scroll paintings from the early fourteenth century begin to show evidence of ink landscape paintings, as do screen paintings of non-Chinese scenery in the Yamato-e style. Landscape elements in ink paintings of Buddhist subjects, such as *Shakyamuni Leaving the Mountain* and the deity Kuan-yin, come to be emphasized by the middle of the century.[34] Literary collections of Zen monks also indicate the increasing importance of landscape imagery in poems and poem scrolls

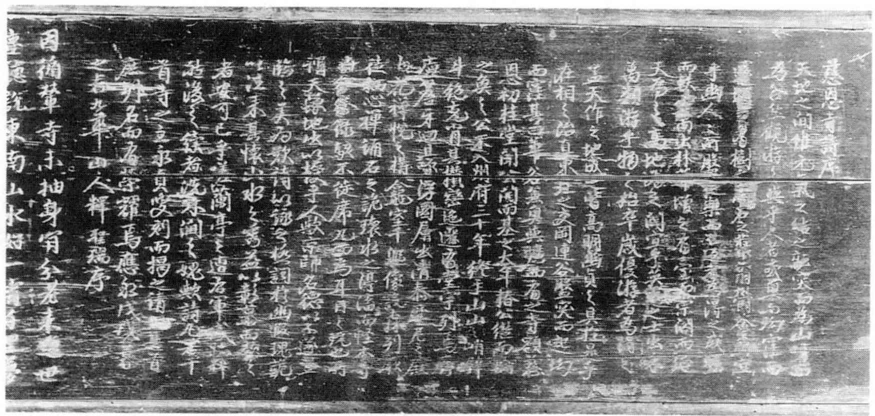

Fig. 2.3. Jion-ji Poem Board. Inscriptions by Ichidon Shōzui (active c. 1380–1423) and seventeen others. Wood. 28.7 x 308.5 cm. Muromachi Period. Denshū-an, Engaku-ji, Kamakura. Detail.

on the topics of landscape themes and parting during the first half of the century, while landscape elements in all types of poem scrolls increase after the middle of the century.[35]

The emergence of the practice of writing inscriptions directly on landscape paintings was a crucial link for the Kitayama monks in developing their views on the aesthetics and religious character of the landscape arts. As they began to write directly on paintings, they joined in a long and varied tradition of such a relationship between painting and literary texts over the history of Japanese culture. While the earliest poems on paintings in Japan seem to have been ninth-century Chinese verses written on Chinese-style paintings,[36] by the first decades of the tenth century it had become very popular to compose *waka* to be inscribed on Japanese-style screen paintings, at times composed on commission for the imperial family or influential aristocrats.[37] These screen poems flourished in the middle ages along with the poetry contests discussed above, while painting and text were also closely linked in the narrative scroll painting genre or *emakimono* and in illustrations of the thirty-six sages theme in Japanese poetry, the Sanjūrokkasen. Some art historians have argued that early paintings with literary inscriptions by Zen monks seem to follow these traditions, [38] including twelve poems that were inscribed by Musō Soseki and other Five Mountains monks and laity on a no longer extant landscape screen painting commissioned in 1344 by Ashikaga Takauji (1305–58)[39] and Josetsu's *Catfish and Gourd* (fig. 2.9) which was originally mounted on a small standing screen. There was ample precedent, then, in the Japanese artistic and literary traditions for a cultural phenomenon like that of the poem-and-painting scrolls.

Inscriptions are found on monochrome ink landscape paintings in formats other than screen paintings and associated with Japanese Zen temples from the earliest known examples, such as *Wild Geese Alighting on a Sandbar* attributed to Shitan (active late thirteenth to early fourteenth centuries) and inscribed by the Yüan monk I-shan I-ning (1247–1317) while in Japan. Landscape paintings that may have had inscriptions are also recorded in the extant literary collections of important early Japanese Five Mountains monks, including Shūkan Dōsen (1263–1323) and Sesson Yūbai.[40] In the decades after 1350 a small number of monks who were also painters of horizontal format landscapes were active, such as Tesshū Tokusai (fl. 1342–66), Mokuan Reien (d. 1345), Sōen Ōsei (active c. 1345–1418), and Gukei Ūe (fl. fourteenth century), discussed further below.[41] The documentary evidence and number of extant examples from the middle of the century suggest, however, that landscapes were not sufficiently popular to explain the explosive increase in the production of landscape paintings seen at the end of the century, with the beginning of the Kitayama period, and the reasons for this dramatic increase are still not fully understood.

To trace the development of Kitayama views of landscape as seen in painting inscriptions that will occupy us for the remainder of the book, I must first introduce the group of Japanese Zen monks that we will be studying. The monks all frequently wrote on the landscape arts and their names are: Gidō Shūshin, Zekkai Chūshin, Taihaku Shingen, Chūhō En'i, Gyokuen Bompō, Kiyō Hōshū, and Ishō Tokugan; Gidō, Taihaku, Chūhō, and Kiyō will receive more emphasis than the other three in the pages to come. The seven monks I have selected were all held in the highest esteem by their contemporaries for their writings on the landscape arts, as evidenced by the frequent occasions on which they were asked to write prose prefaces to the poem-and-painting landscape scrolls. Other monks may have been more prolific in writing poetic inscriptions quantitatively speaking,[42] but prose prefaces provide us with more carefully developed statements about the significance of the landscape arts than do the suggestive and at times even cryptic poems. These seven monks were linked by a network of two types of relationships over two generations: the formal relation of master and disciple; and, more commonly, the formal or informal social associations of teacher and student or of colleagues studying the subjects of Zen religion and Chinese cultural studies, and associations based on shared experiences participating together in many of the social and cultural group events that characterize the Five Mountains monasteries during the Kitayama period. Taken together these monks do not perhaps make up anything so well defined as a school or a movement, but they do share a common belief that the landscape arts held a deeply Buddhist significance. Their interpretations of the natural landscape views were certainly not shared by all Zen monks of the Five Mountains temples or other lineages, nor indeed were they shared by their ordained and lay contemporaries of different social classes; in fact, we will see that their views on this subject were questioned by friends and even attacked by other of their colleagues, attacks to which they attempted to respond. Methodologically speaking, by considering a group of monks rather than an individual in isolation I highlight the social relations that were at the center of Kitayama Five Mountains Zen life, and so hope to successfully listen in on the complex dialogue out of which their views on the landscape arts grew. Since such group social relations in Zen temples have been little studied in the twentieth century, it is difficult at this point to state definitively how typical such social groups were in Zen Buddhist history generally, but they clearly were the dominant form of social interaction in the Kitayama Five Mountains temples.

The two most senior and by some measures the most important monks of our group are Gidō Shūshin (fig. 2.4.) and Zekkai Chūshin. The two were close friends for decades, having studied together under the founder of the enormously influential Musō school, Musō Soseki. After Musō's death in 1351, both Gidō and Zekkai went to study under the Japanese monk Ryūzan Tokken (1284–1358), who had just returned from an extended stay on the continent of some forty-five years and whose accomplishment in Zen practice and Chinese culture was apparently unparalleled in his day among Japanese Five Mountains monks. Gidō and Zekkai also studied together with Hōgyū Kōrin (d. 1373), who had also recently returned from studying on the mainland with the rigorous master Chung-feng Ming-pen and with one of Ryūzan's teachers, the influential literary monk Ku-lin Sei-mo. Gidō and Zekkai were also active together in Kamakura in the mid-1360s, when Zekkai served as Gidō's attendant, and during the 1380s after Zekkai's return from his stay during the years 1368–76 in Ming China. Both monks became trusted advisors to the shogun Ashikaga Yoshimitsu, and took the premier position in the Five Mountains hierarchy both in administrative office and in contemporary influence. These two monks were also famed for their literary accomplishments, and became known to later generations in the Five Mountains monasteries as the two jewels of Five Mountains Zen literature.

Gidō's biography tells us of a deeply principled and widely learned man who rose quickly in the Five Mountains administrative ranks to wield considerable power culturally and politically in his last decade of life. His life and activities are better documented than perhaps any other early Muromachi monk, since he was a prolific author, lecturer, and anthologist and also kept a detailed diary for several decades;[43] for this reason he has been chosen as one of the monks whose views will be investigated in more depth. I here include a comparatively lengthy biography to give the reader a sense of the life course of a most successful Five Mountains monk.[44] In his life's work we see the stages of Five Mountains administrative duties typically taken by the Kitayama monks, which were at times for Gidō quite challenging politically and personally. Gidō also founded his own *tatchū* subtemple, a site for not only retirement and gatherings with friends and disciples but also for coordinating the numerous monks active in the Musō school. Finally, Gidō's biography shows clearly how cultural events were a key site for interaction of the Five Mountains Zen monks with political elites in both Kamakura and Kyoto.

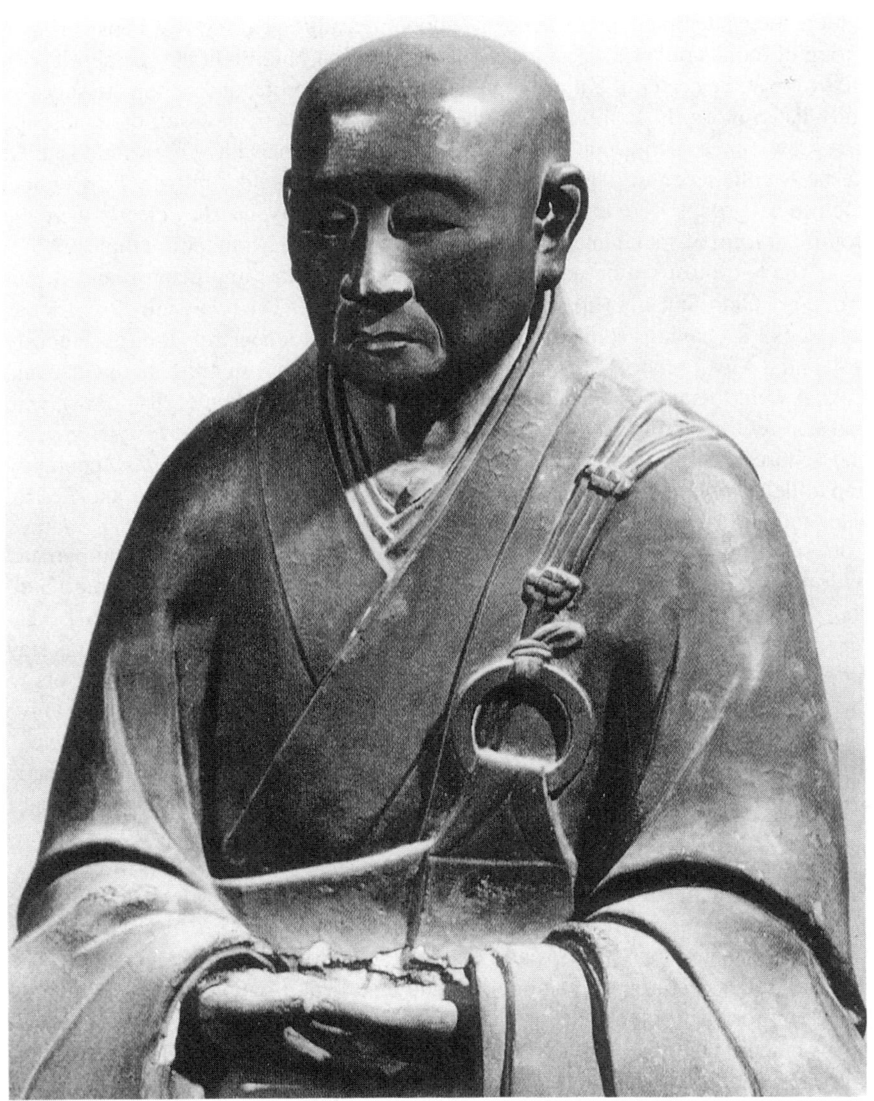

Fig. 2.4. Portrait of Gidō Shūshin (1325–88). Portrait sculpture. Dried lacquer. Muromachi Period. Jishi-in, Nanzen-ji, Kyoto. Detail.

Born to an aristocratic family in Tosa, Gidō's first education took place at both the village school, where he studied the central Mahayana Buddhist text *The Lotus Sutra* and Confucian classics, and at home, where he chanced upon and became enthralled by a book treasured by his father, the classic T'ang Zen classic *Record of Lin-chi*. Two years after being ordained at age fifteen into the Tendai school, he heard of the high repute of Musō Soseki, and journeyed to the capital to become a Zen disciple at Rinsen-ji, which was then the Musō school headquarters. When preparing to visit the Chinese mainland for Zen practice, he was discouraged from going by seasickness experienced on an ocean voyage and decided to give up his plans. By the mid-1340s he was giving satisfactory responses to Musō in public Zen encounters (*mondō*), and had begun compiling a collection of Sung and Yüan Zen verse, the *Jōwashū*, that would serve later generations of Five Mountains monks as a model literary collection. Eventually Gidō was accepted by Musō as his dharma heir, and invited to serve as his attendant but was unable to accept. With Musō's death in 1351, Gidō first went to learn from Ryūzan's vast knowledge of continental Zen and Zen culture, and then in 1357 became a disciple of Hōgyū Kōrin at the important Five Mountains temple Tenryū-ji. Gidō was still studying at Tenryū-ji in 1358, now under Ryūzan's direction, when the temple burned down, destroying his poetry collection manuscript. He returned to Tosa to help with fund-raising for rebuilding the temple when Ryūzan died the next year. After attending the funeral, he was sent to Kamakura by the head of the Musō school, Shun'oku Myōha, as leader of a delegation of Musō school monks to strengthen the school's influence in the Kantō area.

In Kamakura Gidō climbed quickly through the ranks at Engaku-ji during the late 1350s and 1360s, first serving as scribe (*shoki*) and then as head of the meditation hall. During the mid-1360s he also was gradually accepted as a full participant in poetry meetings with public officials, most importantly with the young Kantō Kanrei Ashikaga Motouji (1340–67), and by 1364 was an active member of formal poetry gatherings and had been appointed Motouji's tutor.[45] In 1366 Gidō was made official abbot of his first temple, a *shozan* temple, where Zekkai joined him as his attendant just before leaving for an extended period of study on the continent. Gidō then was briefly appointed head of the Ōbai-in *tatchū* of Engaku-ji, thus assuming the role of the formal head of the Kantō branch of the Musō school. Then he served as abbot of Zuisen-ji, where he presided over Ashikaga Motouji's funeral, and began solidifying relations with other powerful warriors. Kamakura Zen monks of Engaku-ji and its rival for supremacy Kenchō-ji had violently clashed in the mid-1370s, with part of Engaku-ji destroyed and numerous monks being killed in one fire set in 1374. In 1378 Gidō was appointed again as head of the Ōbai-in *tatchū*, and worked to rebuild the temple and restore good relations between the two temples and their patrons; this period was perhaps the most tense and painful of Gidō's life. During the late 1370s Gidō was also active at the center of a circle of monks who produced the first known *shigajiku* poem-

and-painting scrolls, and developed a relationship with another of the monks we will be studying, Taihaku Shingen.[46] Then, in 1379, Gidō took an active role in defeating the efforts in Kyoto of Ryūshū Shūtaku (1308–88), the leader of a rival faction of the Musō school. His success so impressed Shun'oku Myōha that he recalled Gidō to the capital.

On his return in 1379 to Kyoto Gidō began his last decade of life at the peak of power and influence. The learned and popular monk was given great deference by the young shogun Ashikaga Yoshimitsu, who was then only in his early twenties, and began instructing him in Zen meditation and cultural matters. Gidō also discussed with Yoshimitsu the Buddhist consequences of killing, a subject of some personal significance for the young shogun, who was deeply involved during these years in various armed conflicts as part of his efforts to reunify the divided imperial court. In the same year Yoshimitsu had taken control of the Five Mountains temples out of shogunal hands and placed them in the hands of Shun'oku and the Musō school. On his return Gidō was initially given his first abbacy of a Five Mountains temple, Kennin-ji, and then within a few months agreed to Yoshimitsu's request to become abbot of the Ashikaga family temple, Tōji-ji. During these years Gidō continued his lectures on an impressive range of texts, as he had done in Kamakura, from the *Perfect Enlightenment Sutra* to Zen collected sayings texts and the literary collections of Zen monks, as well as Neo-Confucian topics[47] and such non-Buddhist literary collections as the popular anthology of T'ang poetry *San-t'i shih* and an influential Chinese prose collection compiled in Japan by Kokan Shiren, the *Zengi gemonshū*. In 1386 Gidō was appointed to the abbacy of Nanzen-ji, an important Five Mountains temple and Musō school center, which later that year was given premier position above the entire Five Mountains system by Yoshimitsu at Gidō's recommendation. The same year Gidō was granted land on the Nanzen-ji grounds by Yoshimitsu to found a *tatchū* subtemple, which he named Jisshi-in, where his ashes would be interred. In these last years of his life Gidō developed close relationships with, among others, the powerful aristocrat and founder of *renga* linked verse as a court art, Nijō Yoshimoto, with whom Gidō participated frequently in poetry meetings and associated with nearly every day. Shortly after his appointment at Nanzen-ji, for example, Gidō hosted at Nanzen-ji a linked-verse party alternating verses in Chinese and Japanese (*wakan renku*) that was attended by Yoshimitsu, many other powerful officials, and a large number of Five Mountains monks.[48] By early in 1388, however, Gidō's health began to fail. After retiring from his administrative duties to travel to Arima Hot Springs for rest, recuperation, and a chance to make final revisions on his reconstructed *Jōwashū* poetry collection, he passed away in the third month.

Zekkai Chūshin, who was also from Tosa, studied as a boy at Tenryū-ji and Saihō-ji under Musō, eventually taking full ordination in 1352 and becoming a disciple of Shun'oku Myōha.[49] He then studied with Gidō under both Ryūzan Tokken and Hōgyū Kōrin, and in 1364 journeyed to Kamakura, where he studied under Gidō. Zekkai traveled to the mainland in 1368, the year of the founding of the Ming dynasty, where he practiced Zen under the important monk Chuan-shih Tsung-le (1318–91) among others, and traveled widely for eight years.[50] He met there with more official success culturally than any other Five Mountains Japanese monk, for his writing was praised by powerful literati official and author Sung Lien (1310–81), from whom he, following Sung and Yüan Zen convention, sought a prose piece for Musō's collected works. Zekkai was also given an audience with none other than the founding emperor, Ming T'ai-tsu (1368–88), an occasion on which they exchanged poems, and was honored by a preface to his own literary collection by the important official, literatus, and former monk Yao Kuang-hsiao (Buddhist name Tao-yen) (1325–1418).[51] While, unlike the other monks we will study, Zekkai did not hold high offices in the Five Mountains system or become active at court until the late 1380s, he was an important source for the Japanese *gozan* monks who sought out news and an opportunity to study with someone so familiar with recent developments in China.

Beginning in 1386 and increasingly after Gidō's death, however, Zekkai served as Yoshimitsu's trusted advisor in the role of abbot of the Ashikaga family temple Toji-ji and as abbot of the temple Shōkoku-ji, a complex founded by Yoshimitsu as his contribution to the expansion of the Five Mountains temple system. It was probably during his tenure at this temple that Zekkai gave a Buddhist name to Josetsu (also Nyosetsu) (fl. early fifteenth century), the important monochrome ink painter who headed Shōkoku-ji's painting atelier. Zekkai also filled the powerful administrative office of de facto *sōroku*, or head of the Five Mountains temple system, when appointed in 1399 as first head of the Rokuon-in subtemple built by Yoshimitsu on the grounds of Shōkoku-ji, which would later serve as Yoshimitsu's burial place.[52] During these years Zekkai lectured to the shogun on various Buddhist texts, such as the *Diamond Sutra*, the *Perfect Enlightenment Sutra*, and the *Śūraṅgama Sutra*, but also including the popular series of *Ten Oxherding Pictures* used to introduce the stages of Zen practice (discussed further in chapter 6). While Zekkai is now known primarily as a poet, he was also respected among his contemporaries as a Buddhist scholar and known for his views on Neo-Confucianism as well.[53] Significantly, Zekkai also enjoyed good relations with the future shogun, Yoshimitsu's son Yoshimochi, and was given the important role of designating different Buddhist names for him, including "Kenzan" or "Manifesting the Mountain," which will be discussed in chapter 4.[54] In addition to fulfilling these official duties Zekkai was also an active teacher during these years, and seems to have educated many of the next generation of Japanese Five Mountains monks in Chinese religion, continental culture, and the types of Chinese poetry and prose that were fully representative of early Ming Zen culture.

In the next generation the five monks we will examine all studied either with Gidō or Zekkai or under both of them, among their other teachers. All of these monks were important figures not only in the literary circles that were the source of the Ōei *shigajiku*, but also in the Five Mountains temple hierarchy, for they all served as abbots, often for only short periods of time,[55] at a number of the most important Five Mountains temples. Prominence in the Five Mountains temple system almost invariably meant some relationship with the shogun; in their generation this meant primarily contact with Yoshimochi. We will see that of these monks Bompō and Kiyō had the closest relationships with the shogun Yoshimochi, although monks whose writings we will not examine, including Guchū Shūkyū (1324–1409), Genchū Shūgaku (c. 1359–1428), and Daigaku Shūsū, were more influential politically in these years.[56] We find these monks conducted these relations not only individually but also together at social occasions, as seen in Taihaku and Chūhō having offered incense at a memorial ceremony commemorating the anniversary of the shogun's death in 1412.[57] All of these monks except Ishō were influential and respected enough by their Five Mountains peers and patrons in their time to be able to found their own subtemple late in life. In addition to their established credentials in the Zen temples, these monks were also very well respected in broader circles for various intellectual and cultural accomplishments. Chūhō and Kiyō were considered the two pillars of Confucian studies by their contemporaries, although as we shall see Kiyō's writings became significantly more important.[58] Later monks were to consider the parallel prose of Taihaku, Chūhō, and their younger contemporary Ishō, as the "three outstanding [prose writers]" (C. *san-shu*),[59] while a modern commentator has made the analogy that the superiority of Taihaku and Chūhō's prose compared to their contemporaries was like that of Gidō and Zekkai in their day.[60]

As we would expect from the importance of the friends societies in the Five Mountains temples, these monks knew each other and participated together in various religious and cultural events. To take an example of the cultural aspect of this social and cultural interaction, four of the five monks we will consider from this generation together inscribed the landscape scroll *Plantain in Evening Rain* with which I began the introduction to this volume. The frequent number of times these monks must have gathered or corresponded as part of cultural events is seen in the existence of five extant poem-and-painting scroll paintings on which at least three of this same group of five monks wrote inscriptions: *Catfish with a Gourd* from circa 1413, an ink plum by Motsugai in the Masaki Museum of 1413 (fig. 2.5), a figure painting from the same period known as *Noble-Minded Man Searching for Plum Blossoms*, the 1418 landscape *Study of the Three Friends* (fig. 2.18), and *Waiting for Blossoms Hut* from sometime before 1419 (fig. 2.19). We also know of another type of cultural event hosted by Chūhō: a linked-verse poetry meeting at a subtemple of Ima-Kumano shrine at which Zekkai, Taihaku, Ishō, and others were present.[61] This interlocking web of social relationships, shared teachers, communal literary activities, and the high respect held for these monks by their contemporaries and later generations demonstrate that the writings of this group of monks can give us a useful object for extended analysis in the pages to come.

The most senior of this generation is the monk Gyokuen Bompō (1348–after 1420).[62] Gyokuen is now probably best known as a painter of orchids, but he also inscribed prefaces on two of the earliest extant *shigajiku* and seems to have been a central monk in literary circles during the years after the death of Zekkai. Bompō studied in the 1360s with the Japanese monk-poet Jakushitsu Genkō, who had practiced Zen in Yüan China under Chung-feng Ming-pen. He then became an attendant to the powerful Shun'oku Myōha for over ten years, under whom he attained Buddhist enlightenment, before traveling to Kamakura, where he had contact in 1373 with Gidō. During the 1380s Bompō continued his relationship with Gidō, and advanced through the usual offices for monks of literary talent of sutra prefect (*zōsu*) and then scribe (*shoki*). The next steps in the conventional path of a Five Mountains monk were appointments as abbot to regional temples in the Five Mountains system, which he completed during the 1390s. By sometime late in the first decade of the fifteenth century he had advanced to the abbacy of a major Kyoto Five Mountains monastery, Kennin-ji, and became abbot of the highest-ranked temple, Nanzen-ji, in 1413. During this period Bompō was clearly one of the leading Zen monks in the capital, and was asked in 1410 to compose the preface to a scroll of responses to Yoshimochi's own name for his study in his new residence.[63] Before and after his abbacy at Nanzen-ji he had been closely affiliated with the temple, and he retired there to a subtemple he established. Unlike each of the other monks we will consider, none of Bompō's writings survive outside of poem-and-painting scroll inscriptions. However, these extant documents show that he relied more on the early Confucian classics than on the Neo-Confucian texts popular among other Kitayama monks, and used them as the basis for his critical thinking about contemporary social relations in the Five Mountains monasteries, as discussed further below. He is well known for his interest in Sung and Yüan literati themes as the orchids and bamboo, and in his prose writings shows a syncretic adaptation of these conceptions to a typically Buddhist hermeneutics.

While Taihaku Shingen (1358–1415) seems to have had the closest relation to Gidō and the early *shigajiku* poem-and-poetry scrolls among this group of monks, comparatively little is known of his biography.[64] The first we know of Taihaku is that he served as an attendant to a disciple of Sesson Yūbai, Taishin Sōi (1322–91), in the Unmon-an subtemple at Nanzen-ji, under whom he had a definitive enlightenment experience. Although Taishin never visited the mainland, he was a learned individual who had studied widely with the leading figures of his day, including not only Sesson but also Ryūzan Tokken, Kempō Shidon, Shōkai Reigen (1315–96), Ryūshū Shūtaku, and the Yüan Chinese monk Tung-ling Yung-hsing (d. 1365) who had come to Japan in 1351 and was abbot of a number of temples. It was perhaps during his period of study under Taishin that Taihaku took on the sobriquet, "Old Man of the Mountains at Dusk" (C. *mu-shan lao-jen*), which Keijō Shūrin (1440–1518) recorded in the *Inryōken Nichiroku* as having been taken from his hut named "Admiring the Mountain" (C. *mu-shan*) in respect for I-shan I-ning,

Sesson Yubai's (and hence Taishin's) teacher.[65] Taihaku studied under Gidō in the late 1370s, and during this period Gidō wrote an inscription for Taihaku on one of the earliest *shigajiku*, an image of *The Small Hermitage of Hidden Orchids* that dates from the early 1380s.[66] Taihaku also seems to have studied Chinese literature and composition under Zekkai perhaps during the 1380s in the capital. An examination of his writings and those of his contemporaries reveals that he was friends with many of the most active inscribers of paintings in the first decades of the fifteenth century, including Ishō Tokugan, with whom he was especially close from an early age,[67] Ichū Tsūjo (d. 1429), Chūhō En'i, Kiyō Hōshū, and Kōsei Ryūha (1375–1446).

There are no further records of Taihaku's activities until 1405, when, in an unusual appointment for a monk who had not yet held any significant *gozan* temple office, Taihaku became the head of the Nanzen-ji subtemple Unmon-an where he had studied under Taishin.[68] In the next year Taihaku began to ascend the *gozan* hierarchy, when he was appointed abbot of Hōrin-ji, a *shozan*-ranked temple in Harima, and then to the same office in the nearby *jissatsu* temple, Hōun-ji, in 1408. These two temples would also serve as important landmarks in the careers of two other of the monks we consider, Chūhō and Ishō, and indicate a close connection between this group of monks and the *shugo daimyō* Akamatsu family. In 1411 he attained the office of abbot in a *gozan* temple, Kennin-ji, just four years before his death. His tenure there was presumably brief, and he then retired to the Nanzen-ji subtemple Unmon-an, where he founded the Daidō-ken, and where he died in the eighth month of 1415.

Taihaku's extant writings, which include the literary collection *Gabi Ashūshu* and a *goroku* or collected sayings,[69] reveal wide learning in Buddhist and Neo-Confucian texts, as well as in *Yi Ching* studies and the aesthetic theories of the Sung and Yüan literati. In addition to citing the usual Zen *kōan* anthologies, he was well read in the poetry of two Northern Sung Zen monks who were both acquainted with Su Shih, Tao Chien (c. 1043–1106) and Chüeh-fan Hui-hung. He also showed particular interest in the role of the teacher and in study in the pursuit of the Way, an interest that characterized many of the Five Mountains monks of this period.[70] In the syncretism that underlay his wide-ranging reading, Taihaku developed an argument for the differences between Buddhist views on this subject and the well-known position of the T'ang proponent of the Ancient Civilization movement, Han Yü.

Finally, and most significantly for my purposes below, Taihaku's artistic theory was more sophisticated than even those found in Gido's prefaces and post-faces.[71] We see in his writings discussion of the artistic theory of Su Shih, which as Shimao Arata has noted is characteristic of many of the *shigajiku* inscription writers of this period.[72] In his own theory of literature, he argued for the expression of Buddhist wisdom in poetry, basing his position on the well-known Su Shih lines likening the origin of the sound of the mountain streams to the tongue of the

Buddha and mountainous forms to his body.[73] We will see some of the other ways that Taihaku, and also Chūhō, alluded to the writings and aesthetic theory of Su Shih in the coming chapters.

Chūhō En'i was Taihaku's senior by a few years, having been born in 1355.[74] He first took Buddhist orders at age of eight in the Echizen temple of Shōfuku-ji, then studied the Ritsu (or Vinaya) sect at Saidai-ji temple near the ancient capital of Nara. At some point he began practicing Zen under Nanrei Shietsu (1285–1363), whose dharma heir he became. Later he went to the important Five Mountains temple Tōfuku-ji, where he studied under Kempō Shidon, one of the most active monk-poets, and Yūzan Shisai (1302–70), who had studied on the continent for seventeen years and whose literary talents are evident in his having even been asked by Chinese contemporaries to inscribe paintings. In 1388 Chūhō's career took a sudden turn for the better when he received an official appointment by Yoshimitsu as scribe at the newly built Shōkoku-ji, but was soon forced to retire from the position due to illness. It may have been around this time that he studied Chinese prose with Zekkai, for he mastered the parallel prose style that Zekkai taught a number of members of Chūhō's generation. Other than news of an appointment at Tōfuku-ji, we do not know much of Chūhō's activities until 1402, when he assumed the abbacy at the same Hōun-ji temple in Harima where Taihaku had also been abbot. In 1407 Chūhō was appointed as abbot of Kōkaku-ji in Yamashiro to the south of the capital, and then in 1409 he became the eighty-first abbot of Kennin-ji. Like Taihaku and many other Five Mountains monks, then, Chūhō advanced through positions in regional Five Mountains system temples before taking his first position as abbot of a Five Mountains temple at Kennin-ji. At some unknown point between this appointment and his death in 1413, Chūhō also became the seventy-eighth abbot of Nanzen-ji, the most important of all the Five Mountains temples and an appointment of significant prestige suggesting good relations with the shogun. His importance as a leader respected for his Zen insight at Yoshimochi's court in 1409 or 1410 is clear from his having been asked to inscribe a preface for a poetry scroll on the Zen meditation room in Yoshimochi's new Sanjō residence.[75] Late in life Chūhō retired to a subtemple at Kennin-ji that he founded, Chōkei-in, where he died and his ashes were interred in the eighth month of 1413.

We may get a sense of Chūhō's relations with his contemporaries from his role in various cultural events of the day. We know of these activities from his inscriptions, for example, on an ink painting from 1413 by the painter Motsugai (d.u.) of plum blossoms in the Masaki museum[76] (fig. 2.5). On this painting we find that the preface, which is generally written by the most eminent monk in the group of inscribers, was written by Chūhō, while Taihaku and six other monks have only inscribed poems. A similar leading role was taken by Chūhō on a painting that has been lost, *Study Hall of the Lord of Ki*,[77] where Chūhō was asked by Taihaku to write the preface for a painting that Taihaku had painted. Taken together with our knowledge that Chūhō was the host of the linked-verse poetry meeting mentioned

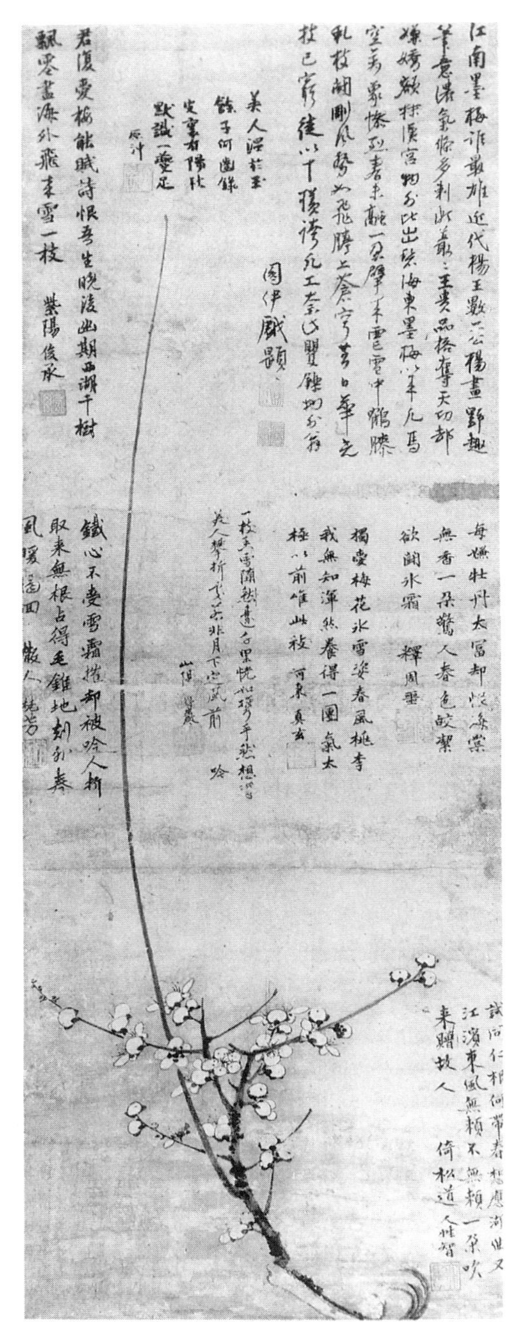

Fig. 2.5. *Ink Plum*. Motsugai (d.u.). Inscriptions by Chūhō En'i (1355–1413) and seven others. Hanging scroll. Ink on paper. 103.0 x 37.0 cm. 1413. Masaki Museum, Osaka.

above, the evidence suggests that Chūhō was more senior than Taihaku and the other monks we consider in such cultural contexts.

Among Chūhō's writings are two collected sayings, the *Chūhō Oshō goroku*[78] and the *Chōkei Oshō goroku*,[79] and a literary collection entitled the *Ranshitsu mankō*, which is only partially extant.[80] From these documents we can see that Chūhō studied a wide range of intellectual traditions, including Neo-Confucianism and Ancient Civilization (*ku-wen*) writings in addition to Buddhism. We know that Chūhō lectured on the *Ku-wen chen-pao*, a late Sung or Yüan collection of poetry and prose, which included both pre-Chin poetry as well as the poetry and prose of members of such Ancient Civilization writers as Han Yü, Ou-yang Hsiu, and Su Shih. His literary collection reveals an interest in the Ancient Civilization movement, particularly the role of textual study in self-cultivation and the centrality of mind in achieving the Way, which as we shall see are central to the Kitayama interpretations of landscape paintings.[81] As we might expect for a Zen monk so interested in Ancient Civilization theories of self-cultivation, Chūhō developed a theory of the call to government service that, as Ashikaga notes, had some precedent in Japanese Five Mountains Zen writings but was without parallel in its sophistication.[82]

Chūhō was also deeply interested in Neo-Confucian theories of self-cultivation, and seems to have read Chu Hsi's commentaries to the four books.[83] Chūhō was particularly influenced by the *Doctrine of the Mean*, following Chu Hsi's reading of this text closely while adding an exposition of Buddhist theories of the mean (*chung*). He also developed a theory of the relation of the mind (C. *hsin*; J. *shin*) and the nature (C. *hsing*; J. *shō*), arguing that while the nature is innate, it is lost by some individuals, and that recovering the Way means simply to follow this nature. However, Chūhō identified the practice of the mind and the nature with Zen, and his theory of self-cultivation may be understood in this sense as fundamentally Buddhist in orientation. As with his understanding of the *Doctrine of the Mean*, and as we shall see in the next chapters, while Chūhō believed that the three teachings were identical they ultimately orient his thinking squarely within Buddhist conceptions of the human individual and of religious practice.[84]

Chūhō's theory of poetry also shows wide reading in Sung materials. Like Taihaku and many other Kitayama monks, Chūhō was taken with the artistic theories of Su Shih, and quoted often from his writings. In his admiration for a preface by Ishō on a painting they thought was by Chao Meng-fu,[85] for example, he described Ishō's writing with Su Shih's famous description of his own as like a "ten thousand gallon spring."[86] Chūhō's writings as discussed in various passages in the chapters to come also reveal a more fully developed theory of the relation of poetry to Zen insight than do texts by most of his contemporaries, as well as an emphasis on the relation between religious insight and ordinary activity. Even in his artistic theory we can see that Chūhō's understanding of the writings of non-Buddhists was grounded both in a sense of commonality with practitioners of other branches of the

Way and in an ultimately Buddhist understanding of the importance of learning, poetry, and practice.

Kiyō Hōshū (1361–1424) is the most important of the monks from this generation for the history of Kitayama Japanese religion[87] (fig. 2.6). Kiyō differed in two respects from the three monks just discussed: he was slightly less prolific as an inscriber of *shigajiku* paintings; and he belonged to a group of monks who were a few years younger than Taihaku and Chūhō, seen in his inscribing paintings not in the years around 1410 but primarily just before 1420. Kiyō was born in 1360 in the city of Kotohira, modern Kagawa Prefecture, into the family of Saeki Kiyoyasu (d.u.). After his father fled during the fighting of the 1360s, Kiyō was taken to the capital by his mother and placed under the care of his maternal grandfather. When Kiyō was twelve his maternal grandfather died, however, and Kiyō was then taken by his mother to become a monk at the important Five Mountains temple Tōfuku-ji. We can see that shortly after becoming a monk Kiyō's talent was recognized, for he received a poem from the venerable Five Mountains monk Chūgan Engetsu and was able to study even in his youth under the influential Tōfuku-ji scholar-monk Mugan Soō (d. 1374), who would later also become one of Ishō's teachers[88] and also under his disciple Shoshitsu Tsūryō (d. 1409). Kiyō gradually worked his way up through a series of temple offices at Tōfuku-ji, Nanzen-ji, and other temples during his late teens. Kiyō also traveled to Jūfuku-ji in Kamakura in 1379, only to return to the capital shortly thereafter. It is during this period that Kiyō may have had some contact with Gidō, for Gidō wrote a preface describing Kiyō in terms filled with praise for his talent as a student.[89]

Around the turn of the century Kiyō studied Buddhist philosophy in the area near the ancient capital of Nara, including the Kusha and Kegon traditions, when he seems to have had substantial contact with monks from Ritsu or Vinaya and Kegon temples.[90] During this same period he was also acquiring a reputation for his learning in Neo-Confucian studies, a reputation already established by 1403.[91] We can tell that Kiyō was also continuing his studies of Buddhist texts, for when in the first years of the fifteenth century a group of Chinese monks came to visit Japan, Kiyō asked a number of questions of one of them and requested that Buddhist texts be sent back to him after they had returned to the continent. In these questions and requests Kiyō expressed a particular interest in the writings of Tsung-mi, a monk known as a patriarch of both the Kegon and Zen schools of Buddhism who argued for the importance of textual study in Zen.[92] This interest permeated the Buddhism found in Kiyō's extant writings, and we will see in the coming chapters that his work provides important clues as to the Buddhist context of many of the ideas found scattered through the painting inscriptions.

Kiyō was appointed to his first abbacy in 1403 at the *shozan*-rank temple Dōfuku-ji in his hometown of Kotohira, and then became the abbot of Fumon-ji, a *jissatsu* temple located in the capital near Tōfuku-ji in 1408. Kiyō attained the seat of abbot of a Five Mountains–rank temple for the first time in 1411, when he was

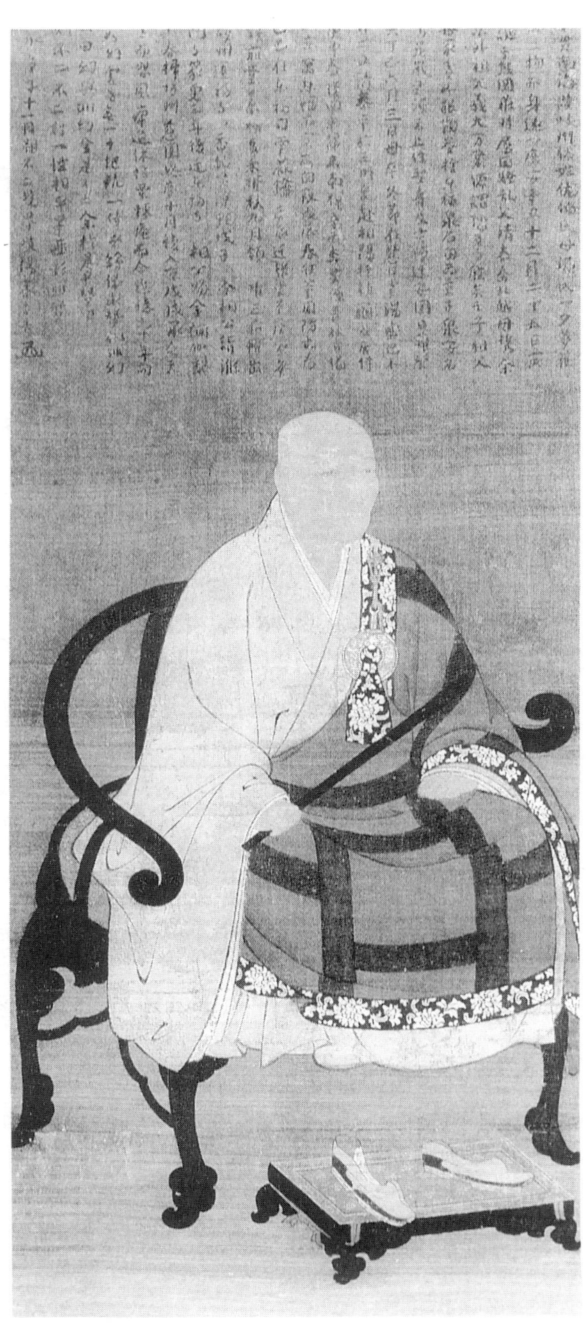

Fig. 2.6. Portrait of Kiyō Hōshū (1361–1424). Inscription by Kiyō Hōshū. Hanging scroll. Ink with color on silk. 102.5 x 39.7 cm. 1420. Reiun-in, Kyoto.

appointed abbot of Tōfuku-ji, and it was probably during these years that he developed a close relationship with the shogun Ashikaga Yoshimochi. Kiyō was then appointed abbot in 1418 of the important Musō school Five Mountains temple, Tenryū-ji. Shortly after this last appointment Kiyō retired to a position as head of the Rikkyoku-an subtemple of Tōfuku-ji, where he established a study named after his religious ideal of nondualism, the Funi-ken. Kiyō died in 1424 at the age of sixty-four, and his ashes were interred at Funi-ken.

Kiyo wrote prolifically, and his extant works include a literary collection, *Funi ikō*,[93] and a short historical work, the *Nihon sōhōden*;[94] several of his commentaries on Zen Buddhist and Neo-Confucian texts, and several poetry collections did not survive. At some time during his later years, when Kiyō had attained prominence as a Buddhist monk of broad learning, he became the teacher of several individuals who were to have a significant and lasting impact on Japanese cultural history. We can see Kiyō's close relationship with the shogun Ashikaga Yoshimitsu in Kiyo's inscription of two of Yoshimitsu's portraits dated to the year of Yoshimitsu's death in 1408,[95] as well as an inscription on a painting of Pu-tai (J. Hotei) by Yoshimitsu to be discussed in the next chapter.[96] Kiyō was also the teacher of Ichijō Kanera, the influential politician, cultural patron, and Shinto-Buddhist-Confucian syncretist. Moreover, as noted earlier, Kiyō was also a Zen monk who had documented contact with a favorite of Yoshimitsu, the important writer of Nō drama and dramatic theory Zeami Motokiyo. In this context Kiyō's heavy emphasis, compared to his Five Mountains colleagues, on the Way (C. Tao; J. Michi) of Buddhism takes on significance, for this emphasis accorded well with contemporary interest in the Way in Japanese aesthetic circles.

Kiyō is best known, however, not as a teacher but as a lecturer on texts in the Zen Buddhist and Neo-Confucian religious traditions. Kiyō wrote voluminously, and a number of his transcriptions of important texts were widely read in later generations. As for texts in the Zen Buddhist tradition Kiyō is still known for his perceptive commentary on the important Sung *kōan* anthology, the *Blue Cliff Record*, with unusually objective scholarly approach and detailed annotations of textual sources and allusions.[97] Kiyō also copied an extant text of the collected sayings of an important disciple in the line of Wu-chun Shih-fan, the Yüan monk Chung-feng Ming-pen.[98]

To later generations, Kiyō also became known as the first to spread the influence in Japan of Chu Hsi's commentaries on the Four Books, that is, the *Analects*, *Mencius*, *The Great Learning*, and *The Doctrine of the Mean*.[99] Kiyō's reputation rivaled that of Chūhō among their contemporaries, for they were both known as monks learned in the Neo-Confucian tradition, yet in the next centuries Kiyō's influence was to become much more important. As we might expect, Kiyō's views on study shared much the same orientation as Chūhō's, with a similar emphasis on textual study as a path to religious insight and showing a particular interest in the role of the mind in self-cultivation.[100] Kiyō's writings show a particu-

…inity with the Neo-Confucian emphasis on the innate virtue of the *Great …arning*, an innate virtue that Kiyō associated with the original nature of the …mind,[101] in contrast with Chūhō's interest in the *Doctrine of the Mean*. Like Gidō as well as the other Kitayama monks, Kiyō argued syncretically for the identity of Buddhism and Confucianism.[102]

The predominant view in Kiyō's writings, however, is the Mahayana Buddhist teaching of nondualism and the importance of this teaching for "entering the secular world."[103] Kiyō takes the theme of nondualism as his own name, and uses it to name the study where he retires in Tōfuku-ji as well as his writings on various topics. Here we see the importance of the canonical Buddhist tradition in Kiyō's personal identitification with this central Mahayana ontological notion. In this he may be compared to Tsung-mi, in whose writings as we saw above he showed an interest, for, like the great T'ang Zen and Kegon master, Kiyō was deeply learned in both Zen texts and those of the Kegon tradition, wrote for both scholarly Buddhist monks and the courtly elite, and was less interested in Buddhist conceptions of reality as illusion than he was in the affirmative innate enlightenment strand of Mahayana Buddhism.[104] Yet we will soon see how Kiyō used nondualism to pursue interests outside the realm of the Buddhist tradition narrowly defined without losing this type of Mahayana Buddhist orientation to his study, his practice, and his writing.

Our last monk, Ishō Tokugan (1359/1360–1437), is the most prolific of this generation and was active till much later than the other monks.[105] Born in either 1359 or 1360, Ishō was sent to a local temple after his father's death, and by 1375 had made his way to a subtemple of Nanzen-ji, Shōrin-an, with which he would be affiliated for the rest of his life. It is at this subtemple that he attains enlightenment while practicing Zen under the monk Sōdō Tokuhō (d.u.), who like Gidō and Zekkai had studied under Ryūzan Tokken but who in his youth had also been a disciple of the Chinese monk who had come to Japan, Ming-chi Ch'u-chün (1262–1336). It is probably during the early 1380s while living in the capital that he may have studied with Gidō and Zekkai, together with Mugan Soō, the well-known monk-scholar of Neo-Confucianism who had begun lecturing on this topic in 1369 and was also sought out as a teacher by Kiyō, Daigaku Shūsū, and other influential monks of the late Kitayama. In the mid-1380s he was practicing Zen at the Harima temple Hōun-ji where Taihaku and Chūhō were later active. He returned to Nanzen-ji in 1385, and shortly thereafter was sent to his first abbacy at a temple near modern Osaka. He returned again to Nanzen-ji to be head monk at the Shōrin-an, but traveled to study in Kamakura in 1390–93 only to return again to Nanzen-ji and attained his first Five Mountains abbacy of a *shozan* temple in 1404. Sometime during these years Ishō attended lectures given by the aristocrat Kōun on the Taoist text *Chuang-tzu* so popular among Chinese literati and Zen monks. By 1411, it seems, he was gaining a reputation as a scholar, for he was installed by Yoshimochi at Shōkoku-ji to conduct instruction in textual learning, and then was appointed abbot of the major temple Manjū-ji later that year. By 1421 Ishō had risen to become abbot of the important Musō school temple Tenryū-ji, and later that sa... year was appointed to the important position of abbot of Nanzen-ji. After holding this post for an unknown period, he remained at Nanzen-ji, retiring to a subtemple of the Shōrin-an where he spent his last years writing and lecturing.

Ishō Tokugan, together with Taihaku Shingen and Chūhō En'i, was known for his skill in the composition of prose, and we see in extant paintings and his extensive literary collection a number of prefaces to paintings. Ishō wrote voluminously, and his skill was admired by his contemporary Chūhō in a painting inscription. Chūhō described his writing by quoting Su Shih's famous description of literary creation as being like a "ten-thousand gallon spring" (C. *wan-hu ch'üan-yüan*).[106] Ishō is also important for the *shigajiku* poem-and-painting scrolls because, though he was a close contemporary of Chūhō and Taihaku, he remained active in the writing of painting inscriptions until near the end of the 1430s. Virtually all of the first generation of inscribers of extant paintings had died by the early 1420s, so Ishō together with Genchū Shūgaku (c. 1360–1428) and Daigu Shōchi (d. 1439) became the major figures through the end of the Ōei period in 1428 and on into the Eikyō period (1427–41).

Now that we are acquainted with the major players in Kitayama era Five Mountains Zen writings about landscape, we may turn to an introductory survey of the main primary documents we will be using: *shigajiku* poem-and-painting inscriptions on landscape subjects from this period.[107] The first extant Japanese *shigajiku* or poem-and-painting scrolls were produced in the *gozan* or Five Mountains Zen monasteries shortly in the first decades of the fifteenth century, although the first and now no longer extant Japanese poem-and-painting scrolls date from the late 1370s and early 1380s. As art objects integrating a visual, painted image of the natural landscape with the companion arts of calligraphy, poetry, and prose composition, the poem-and-painting scrolls present historians with the complex interpretive challenge of understanding how these multiple artistic traditions came together in the lives of the Five Mountains monks so as to be combined into a single art object. Moreover, extensive documentary sources from the extant writings of the Five Mountains monks who wrote the poem and prose inscriptions and other sources provide twentieth-century scholars with a unusually rich wealth of information regarding the circumstances in which these paintings first developed and were produced, used, and appreciated. To understand the evolution of this documentary form and the relation of the inscriptions to the art object, we may begin with a preliminary definition.

These scroll paintings were done in styles directly borrowed from Chinese painting using the Chinese materials of monochrome ink generally on paper at times highlighted with some light color. In this sense the Kitayama poem-and-painting landscape scrolls may be distinguished from so-called Yamato-e or Japanese–style painting scrolls, fans, album, and screen paintings of the same period, some of which likewise combined text with painted images. Yet even among ink landscapes in Chinese styles from this period, the poem-and-painting scrolls are distinctive for their format. Japanese art historians define the *shigajiku* or poem-and-painting scroll as an ink painting with two distinctive formal characteristics: first, a hanging scroll format and, second, the presence of a number of inscriptions generally written directly on the painting but at times inscribed on separate paper. It is impossible to tell from documentary sources what format most of the *shigajiku* scrolls from the late fourteenth century took. However, we do know that among landscape paintings with one known exception all of the earliest extant examples take the vertical format; the exceptional painting *Plantain in Evening Rain* (fig. I.1) seems to have been a horizontal scroll that was remounted into the hanging format at some unknown time.

The poem-and-painting scrolls may be distinguished from another common type of contemporary painting during the same period that was inscribed by only the painter or a single commentator. In contrast, the inscriptions on *shigajiku* poem-and-painting scrolls range in number from three or four to more than thirty, and included poetry and at times a prose preface (C. *hsü*; J. *jo*) or postface (C. *pa*; J. *batsu*). The presence of the comparatively large number of inscriptions underlines the importance of a social context for the production of these art objects, as well as the social and aesthetic context in which the visual object functioned and had meaning. The subjects of the poem-and-painting scroll paintings, including both those extant and those known from documentary sources, vary from landscape themes to flower subjects such as plum blossoms to figure paintings. However, the most important and common subject in the Kityama period is landscape and, in particular, the scholar or monk's studio or *shosaizu* shown in a mountain setting. Other themes popular in the Kitayama poem-and-painting scrolls include the very popular theme of paintings completed as mementos on occasions of parting from friends (*sōbetsuzu*), paintings illustrating lines from poetry (*shiizu*), and paintings done in memory of friends (*kaiyūzu*).[108]

Missing from this typology of the most common types of poem and painting scrolls is a category popular among many twentieth-century art historians, the *Zenkizu*, or paintings of incidents and encounters taken from the Zen textual tradition. The best-known extant example of this type is the Josetsu painting generally thought to illustrate the Zen *kōan* (C. *kung-an*) or public case of the *Catfish and Gourd*,[109] which was painted on shogunal command around 1410.[110] Until recently it was assumed that this painting had a direct relationship with the ideals and practices of the Zen sect, and clearly the object has many of the characteristics of the poem-and-painting scrolls genre. However, recent research has indicated convincingly that this is not the case, and that the painting subject is actually one taken from popular culture and thaumaturgy underlying but often not associated with Zen elite culture, based on stylistic, literary, and sociohistorical reasons.[111] Whatever our conclusions may be regarding the subject of the painting, it is not representative of the poem-and-painting scrolls we will be considering. In a variety of ways it differs from the poem-and-painting scroll genre: it was originally a screen painting and not a hanging scroll; and it was a public painting commissioned by the shogun and not a product of the personal relationships that were at the center of *gozan* temple life.

Recent research by Shimao Arata has uncovered the concrete historical origins of the *shigajiku* poem-and-painting scroll type. Several changes occurred early in the second half of the fourteenth century that, while building on such aspects of mid-fourteenth century *gozan* culture as the poem scroll and an interest in landscape, ultimately led to the appearance of the poem-and-painting scroll paintings. One of these developments is the sudden appearance of numerous scrolls in the hanging scroll format at the very end of the century. This development made possible the poem-and-painting scrolls when taken together with two other factors: the addition of a painting to the poem scroll and the rise in popularity of the image of a study or *shosaizu*.[112]

Historians are not yet certain as to the precise process by which painting scrolls came to be done in the vertical format. This format gives the painted image more prominence than it has in the horizontal scroll format. This development in Japan may of course have followed the increased popularity of the vertical format on the mainland during the late Yüan,[113] which one scholar has even suggested became popular as part of interest in representations of literary gatherings.[114] Another possible reason that vertical hanging paintings gained popularity was the growth of the subtemple (*tatchū*) in the Japanese Five Mountains Zen monasteries. The movement out of the central halls and into the subtemples during the fourteenth century brought changes in the lives of the monks crucial to the development of the poem-and-painting scrolls. Perhaps the most important such development was the appearance in the monks' study, following residential architectural styles, of a library alcove with a place to hang a Chinese-style painting and present offerings below it.[115]

Hanging paintings in monk's quarters certainly was not a new development, as we know from evidence of Chinese use of paintings such as Chuang Su, an early Yüan literatus, who noted that the popular Sung monk Mu Ch'i's (active mid-thirteenth century) paintings were fit only for decorations in monks' quarters.[116] However, the alcove was an important part of *shoin* private residential architecture, which eventually became the ever present *tokonoma*, and had an important effect on the history of Japanese ink painting: it provided a place for hanging vertical paintings, a format that by the end of the century was far and away the most important for the poem-and-painting scrolls, and led to the gradual decline in the fourteenth century of the use of horizontal scrolls.

We also find documentary evidence from the 1380s of monks using paintings to hang in their studies, as in the "Preface to Poems and a Painting of White Clouds and Cinnabar Chasms" written by Gidō Shūshin for Ichū Tsūjo.[117] In this preface Gidō notes that Ichū had a painter complete the painting and then he "hung it in on the wall of his room." Other similar passages describing this use of paintings appeared in prefaces in the first decades of the fifteenth century. Passages preserved in the extant writings of Taihaku Shingen[118] tell us of a fellow monk sitting at a desk surrounded by paintings and also of a scene where "brocades are hung to the left and right, and paintings hung before and behind." Indeed, in contemporary paintings we find examples of monks seated in a setting that shows the role such landscape scrolls and screens played in contemporary Five Mountains Zen life (fig. 2.7). Whether hanging scrolls or standing screens, we know from both documentary and visual evidence that landscape scrolls and screens were a common part of the Japanese Five Mountains monks' lives.

The *tatchū* subtemples were also the centers of the friends societies developing in the second half of the fourteenth century, which provided the social basis of relationships through which the poem-and-painting scrolls would came to be collected. It was also common for the prose inscriptions, the painting, as well as the several poems to be completed at different times, as the scroll was circulated from friend to friend. Shimao Arata has suggested that the usual process of assembling poem-and-painting scrolls was relatively informal. He contrasts this process with that of the painting *Catfish and Gourd*, in which a quite formalized and public process took place: the inscribers were given ahead of time not only the topic but even the type of poem they were to inscribe together at a large, formal meeting; the result of this process is an unusually orderly collection of inscriptions.[119] We even know of one instance in which a monk took a poem scroll that had been completed over twenty years earlier, recopied the poems, and mounted them together with a painting.[120] In scrolls with prose prefaces in particular, it seems that the painting was generally brought to the inscriber by a monk, who pulled the scroll out of his sleeve with many inscriptions and an illustration already completed on it, unrolled it to show to the potential inscriber, and then requested that he write a preface.

The subtemple was important for the poem-and-painting scrolls in one final and crucial way: the lifestyle in the subtemple came to be idealized, justified, and memorialized in the image of the scholar's study or *shosaizu*, often shown in a mountain setting. The subtemples were places of retreat from the busy life of the large, metropolitan monastery, where the monks could engage in religious practice, study Buddhist and non-Buddhist texts, and associate with learned friends and teachers. Unlike the hermit's mountain retreat, however, the Five Mountains subtemple was not secluded from the world but was very much a part of the monastery and of capital society at large. Through the image of the scholar's study, the Japanese Five Mountains monks attempted to maintain the spiritual quality of life in the subtemple, a life that was neither part of the life of the communal monks' hall that had been the center of Chinese Five Mountains monastic life, nor part of life in the solitude and contemplative quiet of the mountain retreat. In this idealization and adaptation of the scholar's study, the Japanese Five Mountains monks were following in the footsteps of the Yüan Chinese literati described above.

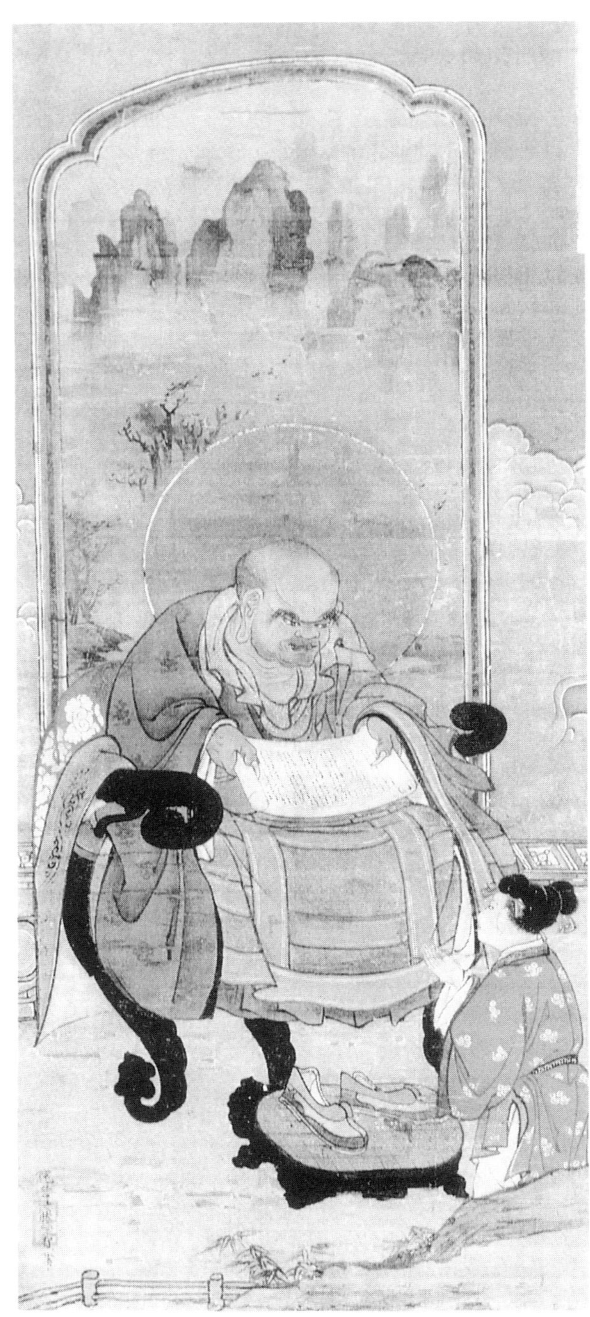

Fig. 2.7. Kanaka Bharadvāja (Third of the Sixteen Rakan). Takuma Eiga (active fourteenth century). Hanging Scroll. Important Cultural Property. Late fourteenth century. Fujita Museum of Art, Osaka.

Images of the scholar's study in a landscape setting are found increasingly in *gozan* Zen documentary sources beginning in the second half of the fourteenth century, as Akazawa Eiji has shown.[121] These early images were understood by the monks in a variety of ways, associated either with memories of friendship while living in a particular hut, with the virtues of various plants and trees, or with the residence of a well-known monk or non-Buddhist recluse.[122] In contrast with contemporary Chinese prefaces to paintings of scholars' huts, as Shimada has noted,[123] the Japanese were relatively uninterested in the actual location of the study and the nature of its surroundings; instead, these monks wished to associate their own lives with the virtues of the friend, the purity of the plum or other symbolic plants, or the sage of ancient times. It was the internal state of mind and the moral character of the resident and his style of life that most interested the Japanese monks about images of the scholar's study.

By focusing their discussions primarily on internal virtues and spiritual states, the Japanese monks were able to utilize a wide range of images associated with the natural landscape in understanding their own lives through the *shosaizu*. In this the Kitayama Japanese monks were following the example of their late Yüan literati predecessors and their Yüan Zen associates, who as we saw in the last chapter fled their mountain retreats for safety in urban centers during the social disorder and warfare of the 1350s and 1360s. These literati and monks had produced images of their retreats to which they longed to return while residing in the busy urban world, images that the Japanese Five Mountains monks easily adapted to their own circumstances. We see this process also in the rapid rise in interest in the image of the study and also in landscape imagery generally. By turning to the image of the study in a landscape setting the Kitayama Japanese Five Mountains monks seem to have been following the lead of their mainland literati and Zen Buddhist predecessors, as they did in so many other ways.

Another important factor in the dramatic increase in popularity of the *shosaizu* or study in the late fourteenth and early fifteenth centuries was the new influx of ideas and literary practices from the continent during this period. We can see that there was a distinct lull in the number of monks making the journey either to or from the continent between the early 1340s and the late 1360s, a period that coincides with when images of the scholar's study became so widespread on the mainland.[124] During these decades only two Japanese monks who were active inscribers of paintings in Japan do return: Shōkai Reigen, who went to China in 1343–51 and who inscribed a number of extant paintings, and Koken Myokai (d.u.), who went to China during the 1330s and returned in 1365. Koken's extant literary collection, the *Ryōgenshū*[125] includes prefaces to paintings in which he mentioned a number of poetry gatherings and poem scrolls. From the late 1360s to the mid-1370s and 1380s, however, a number of influential monks who were important to the early poem-and-painting scrolls returned to Japan from periods of stay on the continent, including Ikō Tokuken (c. 1314–1402), Zekkai Chūshin,

Gakuin Ekatsu (c. 1358–1425), and Joshin Chūjo (d. after 1411). These monks are likely sources for the increasing popularity of *shosai* imagery in the literature and painting seen in the last decades of the century.

Another important cause of the integration of painting into the Five Moutains cultural expression of the poetry meetings and other gatherings was the self-conscious effort of the Japanese monks to follow the artistic practices and aesthetic ideals of Su Shih and his circle of friends,[126] in particular the ideal of an identity of poetry and painting. Shimao Arata has shown that among the monks of the circle that produced the first poem-and-painting scrolls we find a conception of painting as equal in spiritual value to the other arts of the accomplished individual. Together, these arts formed the "four perfections"—poetry, painting, calligraphy, and prose.[127] The "four perfections" were understood as expressing the mind's level of spiritual accomplishment,[128] and this spiritual link between the four perfections is itself the subject of the earliest known poem-and-painting scrolls. Gidō and his fellow monks wished to include painting among poetry and other arts as part of their imitation of Su Shih and his circle.[129] The ideal social relationships of Su and his friends was for the Japanese monks more than a mode of friendship, however; it was also a means of enacting a shared community of religious insight through cultural activity. Such a spiritual community was the ideal for which Gidō and his contemporaries strived in their own lives, and was the underlying theme of the first poem-and-painting scroll landscapes.

The first known examples of the poem-and-painting scrolls in Japan were created in Kamakura during the late 1370s as products of the diverse cultural activities of a group of monks centering on Gidō Shūshin. With Gidō's move to the capital, the center of production of poem-and-painting scrolls also seems to have followed him to such Five Mountains temples as Tōfuku-ji, Kennin-ji, Nanzen-ji, and eventually to the soon to be established Shōkoku-ji. These temples are where the most active inscribers of poem-and-painting scrolls resided while in the capital, and where they participated in poetry meetings and other salon activities during the next several decades, when the first extant poem-and-painting scrolls were created.

Other monks active in Kamakura during the 1370s include Ikō Tokuken, who seems to have been at the center of the group that produced the first poem-and-painting scrolls.[130] Ikō had lived on the mainland for several decades, and returned to the Japanese capital in 1368 only to move to the Kantō region soon thereafter.[131] Unlike Gidō, Ikō seems to have been active not in the religious and administrative duties of high *gozan* temple office but primarily in literary circles. Ikō was at the center of many poetry meetings in the Kantō region during the 1370s, and took the head position writing the preface or postface in contemporary poem scrolls. Ikō also took the leading role in the composition of the oldest datable poem-and-painting scroll, *Verse Modelled on [Ch'u Yüan's 'Encountering] Sorrow' Written after a Poem of Longing for Venerable [Mannen] Kan.*[132] Other monks active in the composition of poem-and-painting scrolls under Gidō's leadership in the late 1370s are the monks Ichū Tsūjo, Kanchū Chūtai (1341–1406), and Taihaku Shingen, who has already been discussed.[133] It is in the activities of these monks that we can see most clearly the transition from such earlier cultural achievements as the *shijiku* poem scrolls to the *shigajiku* poem-and-painting scrolls.

While the earliest poem-and-painting scrolls are known only from documents, the earliest extant poem-and-painting scroll paintings are datable to the Ōei era (1394–1428), a period whose name Japanese art historians have used as a general designation for these paintings. Among the surviving Ōei poem-and-painting scrolls are found a broad range of subjects. This reflects the range of subject matter found in Kitayama period ink painting generally, which included paintings of Buddhist deities and other subjects, portraits and figure paintings, bird and flower subjects, and landscapes. Among the early extant poem-and-painting scrolls are figure paintings,[134] a number of paintings of flower and bird subjects,[135] and works difficult to categorize by subject, such as *Three Friends in Snow*, which often show trees with bamboo or birds and may be seen as depicting either a landscape or a bird and flower subject.[136] For the purposes of the present study we will not examine these paintings and their inscriptions, but instead focus primarily on landscape paintings.

By the early fifteenth century the social role of the artists who completed the first extant landscape scrolls had declined, with one important exception, to one of relatively low status, in contrast to the views of painters in the 1370s and 1380s in the circles surrounding Gidō in Kamakura and perhaps also Kyoto. As a result, we know relatively little about the monks who actually painted the early extant poem-and-painting scrolls, including the Five Mountains monks Minchō and Shūbun. We will see in some detail in later chapters how high was the esteem in which the painters were held who associated with Gidō in the 1370s and 1380s. However, in the earliest extant paintings from some forty years later this high level of respect for the painter is found in only one painting, *Small Cottage by a Mountain Stream.*

This painting seems to preserve a trace of late-fourteenth-century attitudes toward the painter, for he is discussed in Taihaku Shingen's prose preface as a "friend" of the author who has achieved deep spiritual understanding. In this painting we see that Taihaku referred to the painter as a "friend" of Junshi (d.u.), an important designation when the central social group in the *gozan* monasteries is the "friends society." Taihaku further defined the character of the painter's relationship with Junshi as "knowing his mind." This reflects an important characteristic of the social relations that were so central to the *gozan* temples and their literary circles: friendship was not a casual acquaintance but a process of understanding the mind of one's fellow monks.[137]

In considering the question of the position of painters in the Ōei Five Mountains temples, it is important to note that Taihaku referred to the painter himself as a full member of temple society, and not as someone in a subordinate role as a craftsman who was called to carry out some relatively unimportant task. What is also exceptional about this painting is that Taihaku recorded that the painter took it upon himself to paint the painting, rather than being ordered to do so as he was in many of Ōei period paintings, and even visited his fellow monks himself to request inscriptions.[138] In this case, the painter played a central role in not only the creation of the painting, but in the assembly of the entire scroll itself. This central role more closely approximates the role of the painters in Gidō's generation or of the Chinese literati who were active as amateur painters in Sung or Yüan China than the role of other painters active in Japan during the Ōei period or later in the fifteenth century. While this interest in the painter's moral and religious state seems to have been common among paintings that are no longer extant, it is exceptional when compared to inscriptions on other extant paintings, in which artistic practice seems to have been understood as religious in writing poetry, composing prose, making gardens, or appreciating paintings, but not in the art of painting.

The social prestige or value of the act of painting fluctuated both on the continent and in Japan. Some literati in the Yüan disagreed with Su Shih and others in rejecting the importance of painting as an act equivalent in moral and spiritual value to poetry, prose, and calligraphy. For these individuals the central act was one of composing the poetic or prose inscriptions, and a professional or even academic painter whose moral character or religious vision was secondary would suffice as the producer of the painted image. Importantly, one literati who held such views was Yang Wei-chen, who, as we saw in our last chapter, was very important to the Kitayama Five Mountains monks, and in the process of putting together the *Leisure Enough to Spare* scroll we might recall both that the inscriptions do not comment on the spiritual accomplishments of the painter and that the painting was added late in the process.[139]

An institutional aspect of the Five Mountains Zen temples may also have been important in the change in the painter's status, although this factor cannot explain why the change occurred after the turn of the century. Large Zen temples were divided administratively into two divisions, eastern and western, the monks in one of which centered on meditation and learning while the monks in the other conducted most of the other aspects of institutional life, including not just temple cleaning or repair, property and income management, and other administration, but also such crafts as painting. As a result, Zen monks would not necessarily need to complete their own paintings, but could rely on the services of monks in the atelier attached to their temple. We can see just this practice in inscriptions on the extant paintings. The inscriptions on many poem-and-painting scrolls from the Ōei period refer to the painter not as a cultured individual worthy of as much respect as a poet, however, but as a professional craftsman who is not named but described simply as someone "skilled at painting" (C. *hua-kung*; J. *gakō*).[140] By the end of the Kitayama period this social role is clearly predominant in the temples that produced the extant landscape scroll paintings.

The stylistic context in the late fourteenth century for the earliest extant Ōei Japanese ink *shigajiku* poem-and-poetry scroll landscapes can be seen from several extant Japanese paintings that are in other forms. The painter with most substantial group of extant landscape paintings from the second half of the fourteenth century is Gukei Ūe (active fourteenth century), a painter who as we will see below had significant ties to Gidō and his circle[141] (fig. 2.8). Another important indicator of landscape styles during the decades after Gukei seems to cease activity can be found in the extant works of the painter Sōen Ōsei, who was active during the last decades of the fourteenth century and the first two decades of the fifteenth century and also a painter associated with Gidō's circle.[142] While his extant works are primarily Kannon paintings and do not include any landscapes, this painter did paint some no longer extant pure landscapes, and we can gain some sense of the styles and techniques of the period from the landscape motifs in his Kannon paintings. We also have an extant landscape painting from sometime about 1402–5, *Searching for Mushrooms on Mt. Shang-shan* (Important Cultural Property) in the Kobayashi collection that, while not in the *shigajiku* poem-and-painting scroll format, is a useful example of landscape styles from right around the turn of the century.[143] Together with the landscape elements in other figure and Buddhist iconographic paintings by or attributed to Minchō, these paintings form the Japanese stylistic context for the earliest extant paintings.

The stylistic sources of the extant paintings to be discussed below have been the subject of extensive discussion among art historians, which I will only summarize briefly. While the stylistic complexities of these paintings are still being debated, we may say that they are traditionally divided stylistically into two rough groups: the "old style" (*koyō*) of the paintings loosely attributed to the Tōfuku-ji painter Minchō (1351–1431) and other, unknown painters; and the "new style" (*shin'yō*) paintings associated primarily with paintings loosely attributed to the Shōkoku-ji painter Tenshō Shūbun (active c. 1423–60). The "old style" is thought to derive from the tradition of the Northern Sung painters Fan K'uan, Kuo Hsi (c. 1020–90), and Li Ch'eng, painters whose styles were revived in the Chin and Yüan dynasties and then seem to have become influential in Korea and Japan. The "new style," so named because of the use of this term in the preface to *Catfish and Gourd*,[144] is largely derived from the Southern Sung painting academy styles of Ma Yüan and Hsia Kuei, which underwent a revival in the early Ming.[145]

In their subject matter many of the Yüan and early Ming Chinese painters working in these styles were also influenced by a different continental tradition: the important Yüan painters Ni Tsan and Wang Meng's depictions of the scholar's study in a landscape setting. Their paintings of these scholarly studies may have been formative in the production of the extant Ōei paintings either directly through observation by Japanese painters of imported examples of these works from the Chekiang and Kiangsu areas around Hangchou, Nanking, and Suchou, or indirectly through reports about these paintings by monks returning from the mainland.[146] In integrating Northern and Southern Sung styles with the subjects of Yüan dynasty literati paintings on the continent, the Japanese paintings may at first seem eclectic

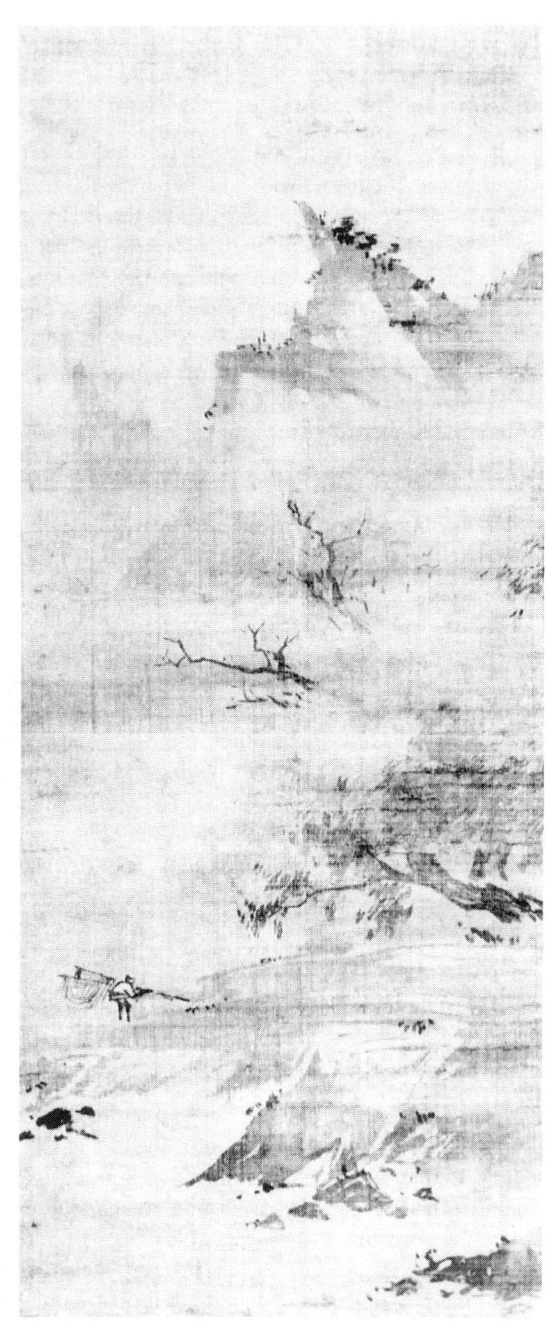

Fig. 2.8. *Landscape with a Fisherman*. By Ūe Gukei (active fourteenth century). One of a pair of hanging scrolls. Ink on silk. 98.6 x 40.3 cm. Second half of the fourteenth century. The Museum Yamato Bunkakan, Nara.

in nature, yet recent scholarship has shown that in late Yüan and early Ming continental painting circles there was a great deal of interaction between academy painters or other so-called professional painters and scholar or "amateur" painters. This suggests that we should not make too facile a distinction between professional and amateur painters in understanding the Japanese Kitayama landscape painting and its Chinese predecessors.[147] The complex styles and subjects resulting from this situation on the continent were apparently compounded by the importance for the Japanese painters of regional variations, as will be discussed below.

The Kitayama Japanese paintings themselves confirm that these disparate Sung, Yüan, and early Ming Chinese models were important for the different aspects of the poem-and-painting scrolls. We can find late Yüan and early Ming paintings that have the same subject, the scholar's study in a landscape, the same format combining a painted image with inscriptions, and many of the same basic compositional forms as the Ōei poem-and-painting scrolls. One such painting is *Farewell at Feng-ch'eng* (fig. 2.9) by Wang Fu (1362–1416), a literati scholar-painter who despite his social role worked not primarily in literati styles associated in twentieth-century scholarship with such Yüan painters as Ni Tsan and Wang Meng but in the Southern Sung academy styles of Ma Yüan and Hsia Kuei. This painting combines numerous inscriptions with an image of a scholarly gathering in a pavilion surrounded by towering mountains and silhouetted trees in a format closely comparable in a formal sense to a number of the Kitayama scrolls. Moreover, the mountains, trees, and other compositional elements are flattened and aligned vertically up one side of the painting in a manner developed in late Yüan China and closely paralleling several of the Shūbun-style Kitayama Japanese landscapes. Most importantly for our purposes, Wang Fu continued Wang Meng's interest in the scholar's study but argued in his writings that the styles of the Southern Sung academy masters "were in keeping with the literati advocacy of poetic and philosophical expression in painting."[148] When viewed in conjunction with their inscriptions and other documentation, we can see that the paintings show that the social role of the artist, visual themes, and sources of painterly styles were defined on the mainland in a manner very close and in some cases even identical to their definition in the early Kitayama Five Mountains poem-and-painting scrolls.

Having introduced the social, stylistic, and subject matter contexts for the Kitayama Five Mountains landscape poem-and-painting scrolls, we can now turn to a survey of the extant paintings that provide some of the central documents to be studied. All of these landscape scrolls seem to have been completed at a Five Mountains Zen temple in the Japanese capital during the Kitayama era, and they represent only a small fraction of the very large numbers of such landscape scrolls produced during the decades around the turn of the century, as we know from documentary sources.

When the poem-and-painting landscape scrolls are understood in the light of their inscriptions, they can be clearly distinguished by three types of subject: social

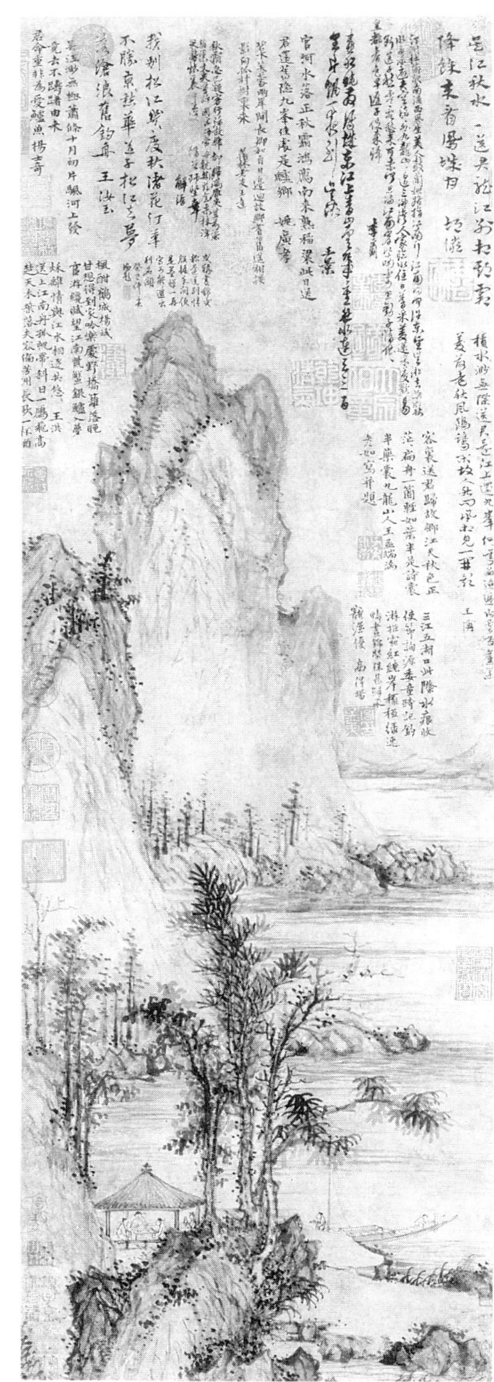

Fig. 2.9. *Farewell at Feng-ch'eng.* By Wang Fu (1362–1416). Inscriptions by Yang Shih-ch'i (1365–1444) and thirteen others. Hanging scroll. Ink on paper. 91.4 x 31.0 cm. Ming dynasty. National Palace Museum, Republic of China.

relations between monks, including parting and friendship; simple landscape; and the scholar's study, or *shosai*. The differences between these groups of poem-and-painting scrolls can be seen not only in their creation in different types of social contexts but also in the significantly different meaning they held for the Kitayama monks. In my survey below I will first discuss in some detail the earliest extant example of each of these three major types of paintings, and then note only significant characteristics of the other extant paintings of each type.[149] I will not explore here the stylistic issues that have already been discussed extensively by art historians, but only indicate those paintings that represent major stylistic developments.[150]

The social relations formed among members of literary circles are the subject of the earliest datable extant poem-and-painting scroll, *New Moon over a Brushwood Gate* of 1405 in the Fujita Museum (fig. 2.10). The biographies of six out of the eighteen monks who inscribed the painting are known, and all six had some connection with Nanzen-ji.[151] Nanzen-ji was the focal point of literary activities of the Zen monks during this period, perhaps because of Gidō's connection with the temple during his abbacy there beginning in 1385. Onishi has surmised that Ishō Tokugan, who occupied the office of head of the meditation hall at the time the painting was produced, may have been at the center of the process of gathering poem compositions and the painting, and then requesting that the senior Gidō disciple Gyokuen Bompō write the preface. As Bompō's preface indicates, the scroll was then sent to the monk Nankei Shū (d.u.), who is otherwise unknown. It is the reason for sending the monk Nankei the painting that provides us with the ultimate significance of the painting.

The overall conception underlying the assembly of the *New Moon over a Brushwood Gate* scroll can be uncovered in the inscriptions, which allude to two lines from a poem by the important T'ang dynasty poet Tu Fu,[152] "Neighbor to the South." The Tu Fu poem was composed to commemorate his friendship with a recluse known only as Chü Shan-jen (d.u.) who lived to the south of Tu Fu's residence in Cheng-tu, where he went to live in 760 after leaving the capital during the An-lu shan rebellion. The Japanese inscriptions noted that the illustration of the poem provided a "poem without a voice," while the poems are "paintings with a voice," following the classic formulation of the relation between poetry and painting developed by Su Shih and his circle, which we have seen also was a crucial factor in the rise of the earliest Japanese poem-and-painting scrolls around 1380. By taking this particular poem as the basis for the poem-and-painting scroll and illustrating it in the painting, however, the Nanzen-ji monks were choosing Tu Fu's relationship with the hermit Chü as an ideal for their relationship with the monk Nankei, to whom they sent the painting, and for the social relationships of the Japanese *gozan* monks more generally. Here we see the central importance of the *gozan* social relationships not only to the social process underlying the production of the poem-and-painting scrolls but also to the spiritual value of the painting and poems as it was understood in its fifteenth-century context.

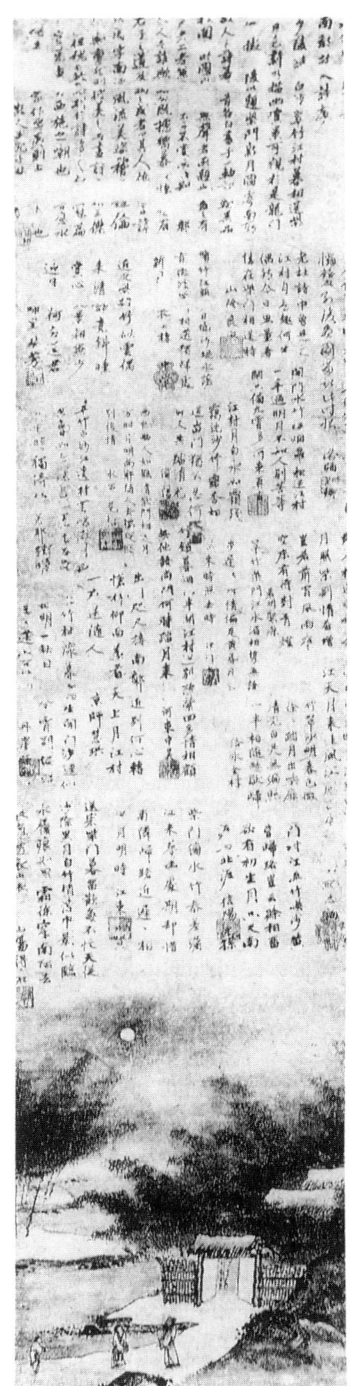

Fig. 2.10. *New Moon over a Brushwood Gate.* Inscriptions by Gyokuen Bompō (1348–after 1420) and sixteen others. Hanging scroll. Ink on paper. 129.2 x 31.0 cm. National Treasure. 1405. Fujita Museum of Art, Osaka.

The painting and inscriptions are in the Yüan Chinese tradition of "paintings of poetic ideas" (C. *shih-yi-t'u*; J. *shiizu*), for the scroll includes allusions to and an illustration of a poem by a famous Chinese poet. However, Bompō tells his audience in the preface that the scroll was not in his view primarily about the Tu Fu poem, but about a contemporary Japanese monk who was a friend of the inscribers. For these monks, then, the hermitage and its landscape setting depicted in the poems and the painting were defined neither in terms of Tu Fu's poem nor in more general terms of solitary life deep in the mountains or the scholar's life in his study. Bompō defines the image of the recluse through the Tu Fu poem as an image of friendship that accords well with the concrete conditions in which Bompō and his contemporaries were active in the large, metropolitan temple of Nanzen-ji. In this sense, this painting, which if it were judged from the visual image alone could possibly be seen as a landscape emphasizing the hermitage, is best understood in the context supplied to us by the inscriptions as an image of social relationship.[153]

A second aspect of social relations found among the earliest extant landscape scrolls is the common social theme of parting, a theme also central to the Japanese Five Mountains poem scrolls of the fourteenth century. This topic is the subject of the scroll *Returning Home Out of Filial Piety* in the Tokiwayama Bunko (fig. 2.11), a painting traditionally attributed to Shūbun from around the year 1417.[154] As a rare example among extant Kitayama paintings of this central subject in Five Mountains Zen culture, this painting is an important monument in understanding contemporary social relations in the subtemples. While the identity of the monk who is returning home to fulfill his filial duty is unknown, we can surmise from the identities of the inscribers that he was a monk who had studied at either Kennin-ji or Shōkoku-ji. This is significant in considering the centers of Five Mountains Zen culture outside of Nanzen-ji, for this scroll seems to be a product of a salon centering on monks from both Kennin-ji and Shōkoku-ji, two temples that would continue to be important for inscribed paintings through the fifteenth century.

In the inscriptions to this and other scrolls on the theme of parting, we find comparatively strong traces of a desire to leave the capital and go into retreat in the mountains in Kitayama Five Mountains Zen culture. In the case of this painting, most of the monks who write inscriptions express a longing to leave the bustling social environment of the capital through allusions to Chinese recluse poetry, as would be appropriate when sharing one's sentiments with a friend who is leaving. Significantly, however, the poet given the honor of the primary place among the inscriptions, Daigaku Shūsū, rejects this transcendental impulse in favor of the "great recluse" of the Chinese poet Po Chü-i, who resides at court.[155] We will return to this central theme in chapter 4.

Exact dates are not known for another extant Ōei painting about the theme of parting. *Blue Mountains and White Clouds*, a painting influenced by the Korean landscape tradition in a private collection and completed sometime before 1420 (fig. 2.12),[156] appears to be a simple landscape, but the inscriptions make it clear that

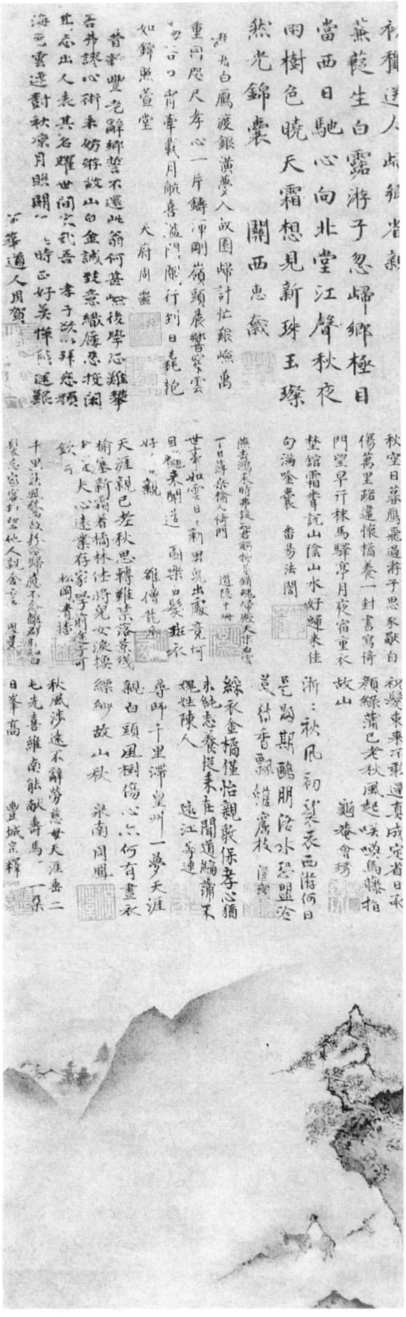

Fig. 2.11. *Returning Home Out of Filial Piety.* Attributed to Shūbun (active c. 1423–60). Inscriptions by Gakuin Ekatsu (1358–1425) and eleven others. Hanging scroll. Ink with color on paper. 83.9 x 25.7 cm. Important Cultural Property. C. 1417. Tokiwayama Bunko, Kanagawa Prefecture.

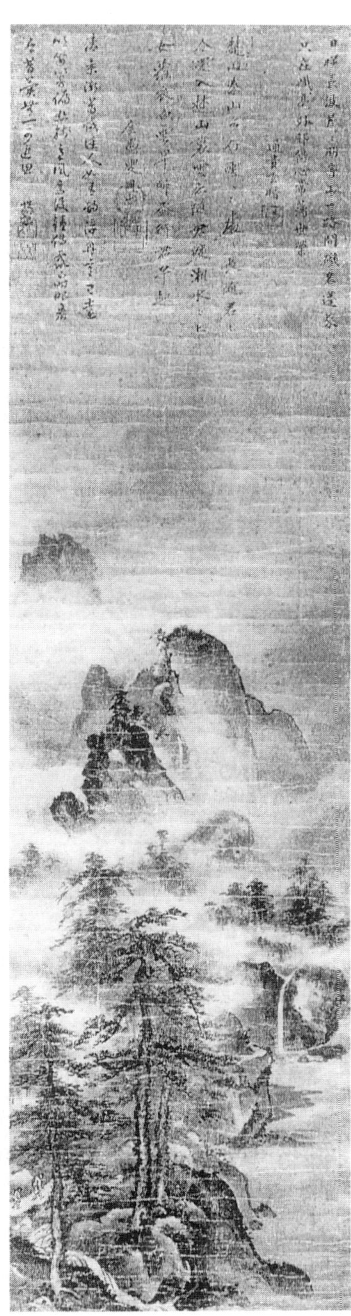

Fig. 2.12. *Blue Mountains and White Clouds.* Inscriptions by Minshuku Gensei (d. 1420) and two others. Hanging scroll. Ink on silk. 102.1 x 27.1 cm. Important Cultural Property. Before 1420. Sunritz Hattori Museum of Arts, Nagano Prefecture.

it was understood in terms of the well-known Li Po (701–62) poem of parting, "Song of the White Clouds."[157] The inscribers of this painting were representatives of a fourth major center of Kitayama Five Mountains Zen culture, the temple Tōfuku-ji, where the important Ōei painter Minchō, to whom this painting has often been attributed, was active. *Blue Mountains and White Clouds* is also an important early example, together with the Cleveland Museum *Towering above Wilderness Hall* painting (fig. 2.16) described below, of the decline in the number of inscriptions on poem-and-painting scrolls seen from the late 1420s and suddenly dropping significantly around 1440, a decline that certainly reflects changes in Five Mountains Zen society.[158]

The relatively little-known painting *Solitary Boat on a Watery Expanse* in a private collection (fig. 2.13), from around 1427 and showing elements of the Shūbun style, memorializes another dimension to personal relations among the Five Mountains monks: the longing while traveling or living in seclusion for life with fellow monks in the capital. In this sense this poem-and-painting scroll may be understood as intellectually representing the opposite sentiments of those seen in most of the inscriptions on the *Returning Home Out of Filial Piety* scroll, and more closely according with Daigaku's view. Stylistically, this painting is important as one example of a painting in the style attributed to Shūbun.

The earliest extant poem-and-painting scroll in the second major group of subjects I will discuss here is *Plantain in Evening Rain* in a private collection and dated 1410 (fig. I.1), a painting apparently showing influence from the Korean ink landscape tradition that was first discussed in our introduction. Unlike many other paintings from this period, this painting is not an appreciation of a poem by a famous Chinese poet but an appreciation of a poem by a Japanese monk, Ikka Kenbu (d.u.).[159] Many of the poem scrolls and poem-and-painting scrolls of the fourteenth century allude to lines by the sages of Chinese poetry, as did the extant painting already discussed, *New Moon over a Brushwood Gate*. Yet, as Akazawa Eiji has observed based on his survey of documentary sources, in the Ōei period there appeared a number of scrolls with inscriptions based on poems by Japanese monks.[160] In the case of this painting, the young Japanese poet seems to have been singled out as the subject of the scroll because of the promise he showed in his studies, and following the conventions of the occasion is praised highly in the inscriptions.

The inscriptions for this poem-and-painting scroll seem to follow the most common pattern, in that the inscriptions were apparently written at various times, perhaps with the scroll having been passed around from monk to monk to be inscribed at their leisure, based on the relatively irregular appearance of the inscriptions.[161] As was noted above, this scroll seems to be unique among the earliest extant *shigajiku* landscape paintings in its originally horizontal format, although it is now mounted in the more common vertical, hanging scroll form.

A second distinctive feature of this painting is the presence of an important guest who joined the Japanese monks in the appreciation of Ikka's poem, the

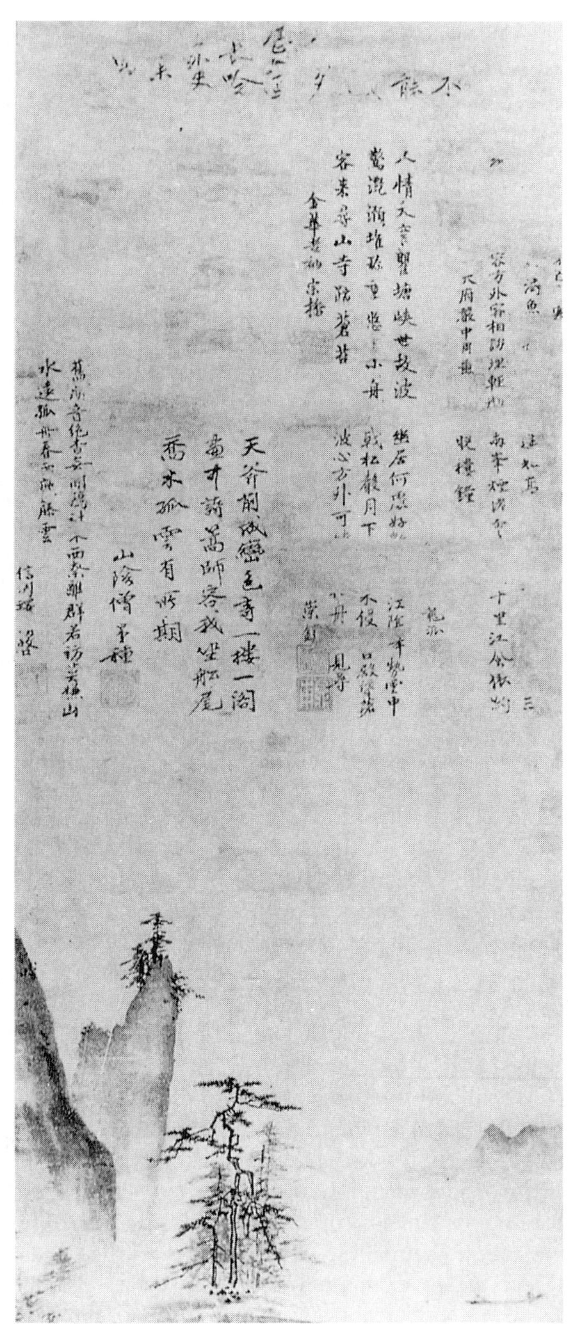

Fig. 2.13. *Solitary Boat on a Watery Expanse*. Attributed to Shūbun (active 1423–60). Inscriptions by Ishō Tokugan (d. 1437) and six others. Hanging scroll. Ink on paper. 93.0 x 37.6 cm. C. 1427. Idemitsu Museum of Arts.

Korean emissary Yang Su (d.u.),[162] who had been sent to Japan on the occasion of Ashikaga Yoshimochi's promotion to the rank of shogun. The importance of this event is suggested by the presence of prose inscriptions by all three of the monks who would be known to later generations as the most skilled in Chinese prose, Taihaku, Chūhō, and Ishō. This scroll was put together at the height of Taihaku and Chūhō's careers and during the period when they wrote many of their inscriptions, and it is important to note that both monks were asked to write prefaces for this painting, although both unfortunately are so badly damaged that they can no longer be read. That this inscription by a foreign dignitary held political implications is also seen in the inscription by the director of the shogunal office of military affairs, Yamana Tokihiro (1367–1435).[163] The painting memorialized the departure of the monk through the conventional association of the word "autumn" (C. *ch'iu*; J. *shū*) in the poem topic with the word "lament" (C. *ch'ou*; J. *shū*), an appropriate sentiment on the departure of a respected guest who has come from afar, together with the conventional association of raindrops with tears.[164] In asking the Korean emissary to join in the activities of their literary circle, the Nanzen-ji monks were welcoming him into their group of friends while at the same time taking the opportunity to wish him farewell. Their presence at this event marking the departure of such an honored foreign dignitary indicates the overlapping arenas of culture and politics in this age.

On one level this scroll is a "painting of a poetic idea" (*shiizu*), like the painting *New Moon over a Brushwood Gate*, since one subject of the painting and inscriptions is a poem. However, we find that the focus of interest in Ikka's poem for those who wrote inscriptions, including the Korean emissary, was not their own personal relationship with a fellow monk, as it was in *New Moon over a Brushwood Gate*. Rather, they commented again and again on the scene portrayed in the poem (and also in the painting) together with the sentiments and thoughts it aroused in themselves. Consequently, the subject of this scroll might be best described as neither the poem itself nor some personal relationship with another monk or even the poet, but the monks' response to the rainy, autumn landscape scene as it represents the character of the poet. This suggests that the poem-and-painting scroll *Plantain in Evening Rain* is not only a painting of a poetic idea (*shiizu*), but also a landscape painting (*sansuiga*), with the added note that the landscape is defined not primarily as an actual, physically existing location but as a literary conception developed in a poem. We might summarize the integration of these two layers of meaning to the poem-and-painting scrolls as an interest in the landscape mediated by the personal, literary medium of the poem.

In this emphasis on the inner, poetic aspect of the scene depicted, the Japanese Five Mountains Zen monks shared a fundamental orientation similar to that of Su Shih and other Sung and Yüan Chinese literati: they were reading both the poem and the painting not for what it represented about the world but for what it told the reader about inner human truths. These inner realities were both those of the poet, that is, his character and his level of spiritual accomplishment, and those of the readers, that is, the sentiments, poetic associations, and images, as well as the personal ideals that the rainy autumn evening brought to their minds. Since this painting is about both a poem and a landscape, then, it exemplifies both the dual character of the contemporary understanding of the painting, and the interpretive orientation of the Japanese Zen monks toward the inner significance of the painted image in their approach to the earliest extant poem-and-painting scrolls.

The next extant example of a landscape painting is the Nezu Museum painting from before 1419, *Distant Thoughts across Waters and Skies* (fig. 2.14). The subject of the painting at first seems to be the small hut in the foreground of the painting, but the inscriptions tell us that the monks were primarily interested not in the landscape itself but in the purity of a life, based on landscape imagery either far from their busy residences in the Five Mountains temples or right in the capital itself.[165] This painting is important in the history of Japanese ink painting as one of the very earliest examples of the style often attributed to the monk-painter Shūbun that was to dominate ink painting for the rest of the century.[166]

The remaining extant Ōei painting in the pure landscape category is the Masaki Museum *Landscape*, probably dating from before 1428[167] and inscribed by Genchū Shūgaku and four other monks (fig. 2.15). As in other of the landscapes we have seen, this painting is interpreted by the monks in terms alluding to the writings of a famous Chinese hermit, in this case the legend of Peach Blossom Spring in the writings of the Six Dynasties recluse-poet T'ao Ch'ien.

The earliest extant example from the final group of paintings I will consider, paintings of the scholar's study, is the 1413 painting attributed to Minchō now in the Nanzen-ji subtemple Konchi-in titled *Small Cottage by a Mountain Stream* (fig. 3.2).[168] This painting seems to center on monks with close association with Nanzen-ji, for all but one of the monks who wrote inscriptions were former abbots of that temple,[169] and they all were also students of either Zekkai or Gidō.

The hut shown in *Small Cottage by a Mountain Stream* is itself the focus of the poetic and prose inscriptions, unlike the many other Ōei paintings where the small hut of the recluse-scholar was not the actual focus of interest for the inscription writers. As Taihaku noted in his preface, a fellow monk from the Five Mountains monasteries by the name of Junshi Haku (d.u.) took as the name of his residence "Mountain Stream," and a "friend who knew his mind" made a painting of his residence while high-ranking priests wrote inscriptions for it. As on the other Japanese paintings of the scholar's study of this period, the poems join the preface in elaborating on the implications of the name of the hut for the religious self-cultivation, education, and moral accomplishment of the monk who made his residence there. Here we can see that the Japanese Five Mountains monks appreciated this painting in a manner comparable to the friends of Yang Wei-chen in Yüan dynasty China discussed above. However, by emphasizing the spiritual significance for their contemporaries of life in the scholar's study, the Ōei monks

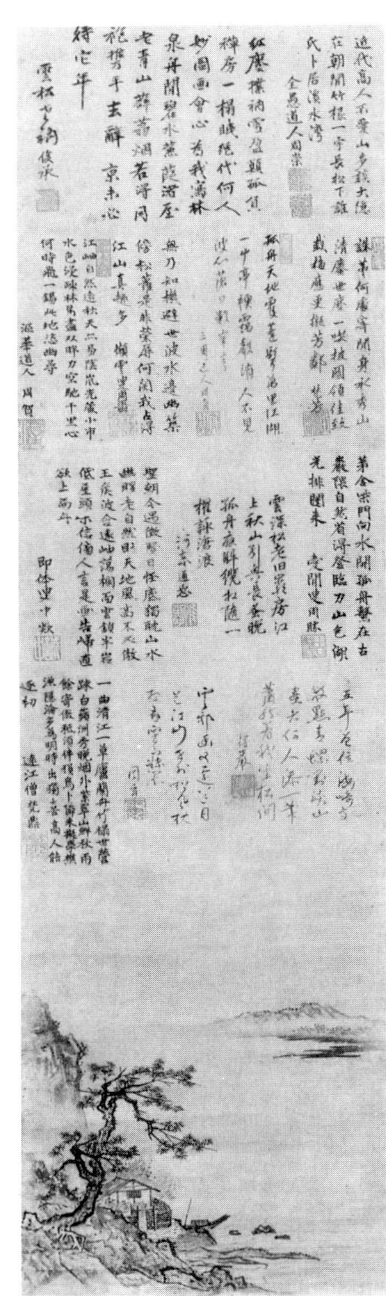

Fig. 2.14. *Distant Thoughts across Rivers and Skies*. Attributed to Shūbun (active c. 1423–60). Inscriptions by Daigaku Shūsū (1345–1423) and eleven others. Hanging scroll. Ink and color on paper. 103.6 x 33.9 cm. Important Cultural Property. Before 1419. Nezu Institute of Fine Arts, Tokyo.

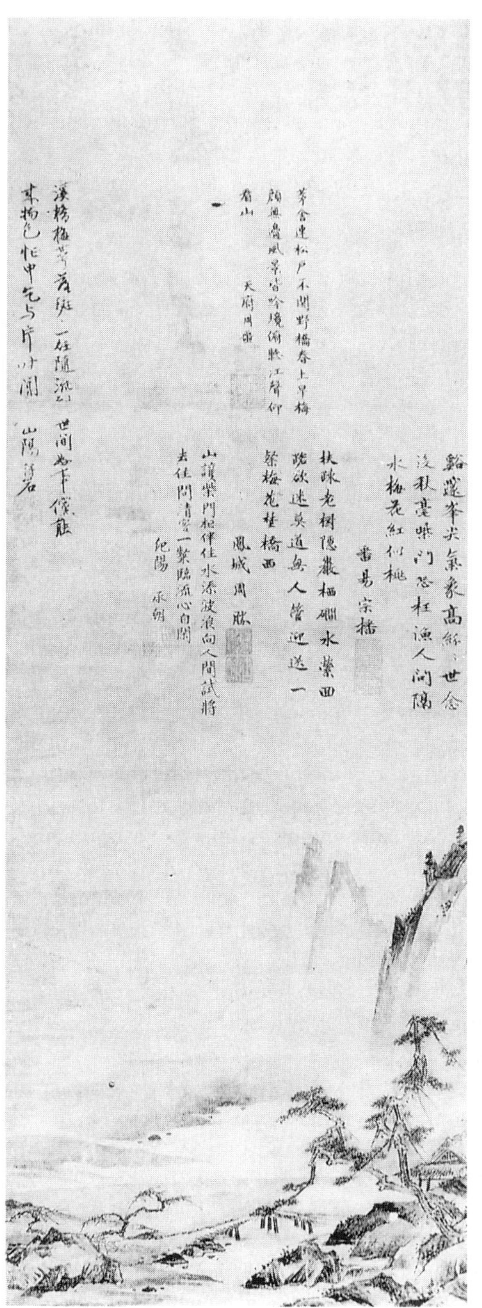

Fig. 2.15. *Landscape*. Inscriptions by Genchū Shūgaku (1359–1428) and four others. Hanging scroll. Ink with light color on paper. 108.8 x 36.3 cm. Before 1428. Masaki Museum, Osaka.

were actually describing an image of their own lives in the Five Mountains Zen subtemples. The painted and poetic images of the monk or scholar's study were in a certain sense images of the religious and moral dimensions to their lives in the Five Mountains temples, and for this reason are an important source for understanding the nature of Japanese Zen Buddhism during this period.

Another very early example of a landscape painting scroll depicting a scholar's study is a little-known painting with a preface by Seiin Shunjo (1358–1422) dated 1413, titled *Towering above Wilderness Hall*, which shows possible influence from Korean painting and has been recently purchased by the Cleveland Museum (fig. 2.16).[170] Allusions in the prefaces tell us that this hut was patterned after a residence of the important Northern Sung scholar official Ssu-ma Kuang (1019–86), who depicted it in his famous "Record of the Garden of Solitary Pleasures," which in turn was the subject of a Su Shih poem on Ssu-ma's "Record."[171]

Another very early yet not widely known example of this theme is the Masaki Museum painting from before 1415 titled *Mountain Villa* (fig. 2.17).[172] In the inscriptions, as in other paintings of scholars' studies, the hut is described in terms of the spiritual accomplishment of its resident, for it was associated both with the reclusive villa of the influential T'ang Chinese poet Wang Wei, who was so revered by Su Shih, and also with the Taoist sages who resided eternally on Mt. P'eng-lai.

One of the circumstances leading to the creation of this scroll important for our understanding of the Ōei poem-and-painting scrolls was the role played by the *shugo daimyō* Ōuchi Morimi (1377–1431). As Ōnishi Hiroshi has pointed out, the *shugo daimyō* were influential in the explosion in popularity of paintings of scholars' studies in the early fifteenth century first through increasing the importance of the Five Mountains subtemples through patronage, and then by requesting the paintings for their own studies in imitation of the Five Mountains Zen subtemple lifestyle.[173] Ōuchi, who was active in the literary circles surrounding Ashikaga Yoshimochi,[174] was a relative latecomer to the ranks of the most important *shugo daimyō*.[175] However, this painting and other evidence for his role in the circles that produced the Ōei poem-and-painting scrolls serve as important evidence of the cultural influence of these regional leaders in the early fifteenth century.[176]

Another important example of the scholar's studio painting is the *Study of the Three Friends* in the Seikadō collection (fig. 2.18), which was described by Gyokuen Bompō in his 1418 preface discussed above.[177] The final landscape poem-and-painting scroll is often closely associated with *Study of the Three Friends* in time and theme as well as in style and composition: the Idemitsu Museum painting of 1419, *Waiting for Blossoms Hut* (fig. 2.19).[178] The study in this painting is an image of the popular literary theme of waiting expectantly for the first blossoms of spring, with the scholar-monks' interest in textual study represented most explicitly in the neatly stacked books visible inside the hut. This painting and *Study of the Three Friends* were not only painted just one year apart, but they closely resemble each other visually in compositional structure, brushwork, architectural details, and

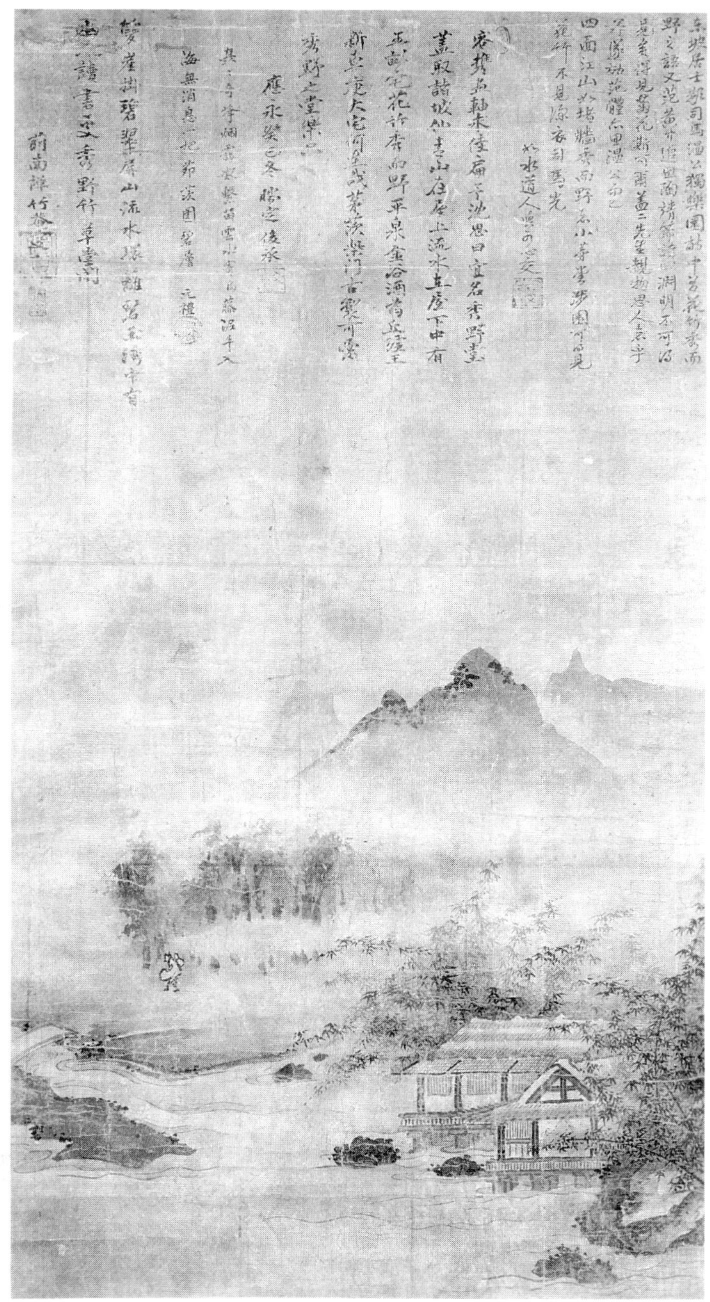

Fig. 2.16. *Towering above Wilderness Hall.* Inscriptions by Yoka Shinkō (d. 1437) and three others. Hanging scroll. Ink and light color on silk. 102.8 x 54.0 cm. 1413. © Cleveland Museum of Art, 1996, John L. Severance Fund, 1985.111.

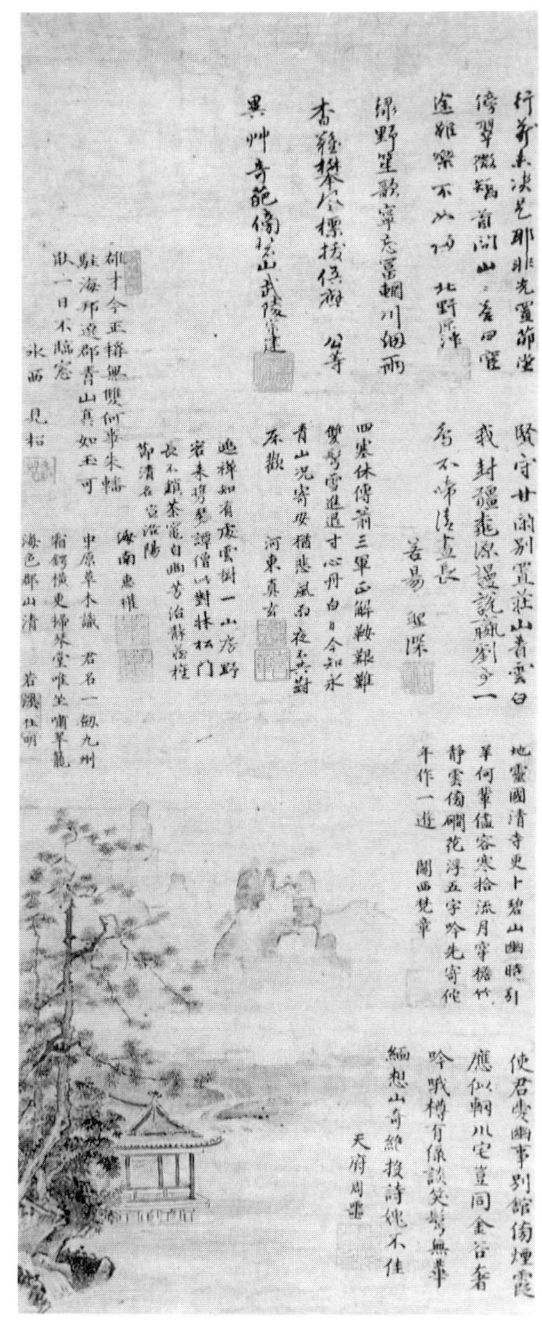

Fig. 2.17. *Mountain Villa.* Inscriptions by Kengan Genchū (d. 1421) and eight others. Hanging scroll. Ink and color on paper. 81.6 x 31.8 cm. Before 1415. Masaki Museum, Osaka.

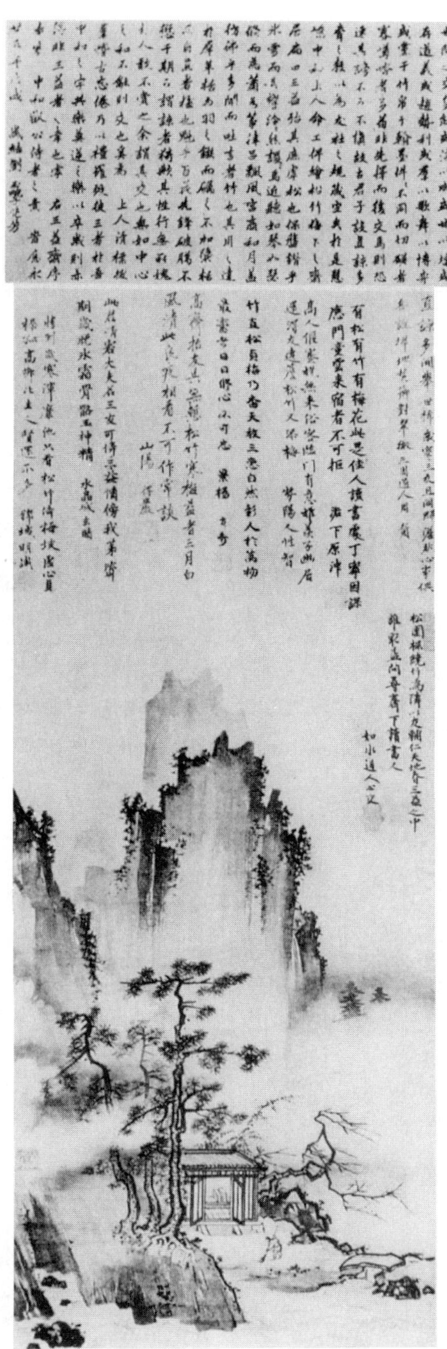

Fig. 2.18. *Study of the Three Friends.* Attributed to Shūbun (active c. 1423–60). Preface by Gyokuen Bompō (1348–after 1420) and inscriptions by eight others. Hanging scroll. Ink and light color on paper. 101.2 x 38.8 cm. Important Cultural Property. 1418. The Seikadō Bunka Art Museum, Tokyo.

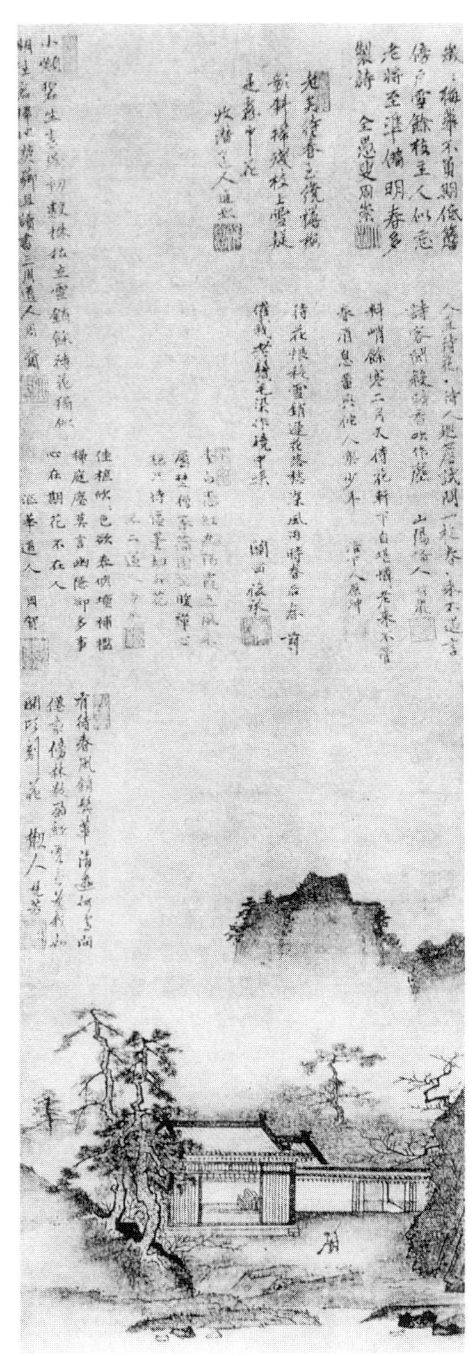

Fig. 2.19. *Waiting for Blossoms Hut.* Attributed to Shūbun (active c. 1423–60). Inscriptions by Daigaku Shusū (1345–1423) and eight others. Hanging scroll. Ink and light color on paper. 119.8 x 35.8 cm. Before 1419. Idemitsu Museum of Arts, Tokyo.

even the presence of a young attendant sweeping outside the study. These two paintings are also cited together by many art historians as important examples of the early style among those paintings attributed to Shūbun, seen especially in the one-corner composition, the axe-head brush technique, silhouetted pine trees, and the strong verticality so prominent in *Study of the Three Friends*.[179]

In surveying the various types of poem-and-painting scroll landscape paintings, we have seen that according to the Five Mountains Zen inscriptions that a central role is played by themes taken from Chinese court poetry and Chinese literati aesthetics and interpretive conventions. I would surmise that further study in the still undeveloped field of Sung, Yüan, and early Ming Zen culture will show that in this emphasis the Japanese Five Mountains monks were only following their mainland teachers and fellow monks. At any rate, studying the poem-and-painting scroll inscriptions aided us in understanding the paintings in ways differing significantly from study based only on stylistic evidence and from conclusions about the significance of certain images and motifs based on visual evidence alone. We have seen how the paintings functioned in the institutional context of the Five Mountains monasteries, including the *tatchū* subtemples, as well as in the social networks of the *yūsha* or friends societies. By grasping the earliest extant poem-and-painting scroll paintings in this complex historical and sociocultural context, we may begin to understand how these poem-and-painting scrolls were integrated into the social lives, religious practice, and Buddhist thinking of the early Muromachi period Japanese Five Mountains temples. It is to this Buddhist aspect of these poem-and-painting landscape scrolls that we now turn.

Chapter 3

The East Asian Religious Context for Cultural Practice

> Lettered Ch'an [Zen] . . . helped to bring Ch'an [Zen] into the mainstream of Chinese cultural life and also led to a fertile interchange between Ch'an [Zen] and secular belles lettres.
>
> —Robert Buswell, "The 'Short-Cut' Approach of K'an-hua Meditation"

As we have just seen, the Kitayama Five Mountains monks practiced their Buddhism through cultural means in addition to their meditation and other practices. The Zen monks who chose culture to express their enlightenment were well aware of the cultural tradition in Zen Buddhist and other East Asian religious traditions. In this chapter I briefly introduce the range of East Asian religious traditions from which the Kitayama monks drew in developing their theories and practice of the arts, and of the landscape arts in particular.

I begin with a Kitayama passage exemplifying the Buddhist basis for Five Mountains Zen interpretations of landscape images. In a landscape-painting inscription Kiyō Hōshū describes how he initially refused to compose the inscription on a painting of Sekidō mountain. After Kiyō explained his refusal by noting that he was too far in distance from the mountain and too far in time from a court poet associated with it, the guest who has brought him the painting then responds:

> How narrow your argument is! Didn't Tsao-pai [Ch'eng-kuan, 738–839] say, "In a boundless realm, self and other are separated by less than the tip of a fine autumn hair. In the ten realms of past and present, beginning and end diverge by less than an instant of thought."[1]

Kiyō acknowledges the wisdom of his visitor's remark, and after admonishing himself for neglecting his study of Buddhist philosophy due to his involvement in court society, assents to compose the inscription.

What may seem remarkable is the prominent role taken by a Chinese Hua-yen school Buddhist philosopher such as Ch'eng-kuan in a discussion of whether or not to write an inscription on a landscape painting some six centuries after his death. The linkage of Japanese landscape arts with Chinese Buddhist philosophy here is entangled with the several complex social and intellectual reasons for Kiyō's decision to assent to his guest's request, not the least of which would be social convention. Kiyō and his guest are demonstrating their learning, although at a none too technical level compared to the abstruse nature of much Hua-yen speculation, and then carefully recording it on the occasion of this social exchange. Yet this passage also demonstrates the implicit and in Kiyō's case explicit role of the Buddhist canonical and commentary tradition in generally supporting and, according to this narrative, even directly motivating the decision by a Kitayama Zen monk to inscribe a landscape painting. Certainly not all the Kitayama monks were as interested in Hua-yen philosophy as was Kiyō, who once sent a message to the mainland inquiring about the important Hua-yen philospher Tsung-mi's teachings, nor did they always choose to inscribe paintings for the same reasons. However, their writings do give us enough information to ascertain the nature of their Buddhist beliefs and the general relationship that these views had with the Kitayama Five Mountains interest in artistic practice and in landscape themes. We now turn to an exploration of these beliefs.

The Zen school is one of a number of schools belonging to the movement known as Mahayana Buddhism, first developing some two millennia ago in India and then in China, and now represented primarily in the Chinese cultural sphere in East and Southeast Asia. Generally speaking most Mahayana schools share first the ontology of *śūnyatā* or the illusory and ultimately empty nature of reality, not excepting the teaching of emptiness itself, and secondly the religious ideal of the bodhisattva, an enlightened being who works to relieve suffering in the samsaric world of sentient existence.[2] However, broadly speaking, Mahayana schools diverge on the relationship between emptiness and ordinary, conditioned reality, and the implication of this relationship for the soteriological methods necessary to realizing wisdom and becoming a bodhisattva, expressing wisdom, and other topics. The assertion of such a close relationship between the ultimate and the conditioned is grounded in the emptiness ontology seen in, for example, the famous line in the *Heart Sutra*, one of the *Perfection of Wisdom* texts, "Form is no different from emptiness, emptiness no different from form."[3] This teaching was widely known and recited in Zen temples throughout East Asia, and was given particular emphasis in both abstract theological speculation of the Hua-yen schools and in such texts as the *Vimalakīrti Sutra* that were read widely by both monastics and laymen and laywomen.

Simply put, two trends in Mahayana Buddhism may be identified: some schools view conventional reality as delusional and hence to be transcended, such as Candrakīrti-style Indian Madhyamika or certain strains of *Perfection of Wisdom* teaching; while others find conventional reality itself to manifest ultimate truth or reality, such as some lines of Yogācāra thought and much of the Tathāgatagarbha tradition. In the latter schools the relation between the realm of enlightenment and nirvana is closely associated and even identified with the samsaric world of form and passionate attachments. Consequently, among the latter schools the general need is often asserted for *upāya* (C. *fang-pien*; J. *hōben*) or expedient teachings of a provisional nature, adjusted to the circumstances and level of understanding of the audience. This has important implications for the usefulness of language in the Buddhist tradition, for those strands of Mahayana that accept the general importance of expedient means tend to also affirm the efficacy of language and other cultural mediums for realizing Buddhist wisdom. As we will see shortly, the Five Mountains Japanese Zen monks can best be understood as inheriting the latter Mahayana tradition of accepting expedient teachings.[4]

Among the various doctrinal formulations of the relation between ultimate truth or reality and conventional truth or reality, perhaps the best known in China was developed in the Tendai (C. T'ien-t'ai) school, which emphasized innate enlightenment and the inseparability of the Three Teachings of emptiness, provisional existence, and centrality. Numerous teachers in the Zen school took up this general conception and freely deployed it for their own ends. We find, for example, the influential Sung dynasty Chinese monk Yüan-wu identifying the Buddhist canonical source of this teaching and applying it to an important incident in early Zen lore in his important anthology, the *Pi-yen lü* (J. *Hekiganroku*) or *The Blue Cliff Record*. This passage, which is found in his commentary to the very first case in the anthology, reads:

> As it says in the Teachings, by the real truth we understand that it is not existent; by the conventional truth we understand that it is not non-existent. That the real truth and the conventional truth are not two is the highest meaning of the holy truths. This is the most esoteric, most abstruse point of the doctrinal schools. Hence the Emperor picked out this ultimate paradigm to ask Bodhidharma, "What is the highest meaning of the holy truths?" Bodhidharma answered, "Empty, without holiness." No monk in the world can leap clear of this. Bodhidharma gives them a single swordblow that cuts off everything. These days how people misunderstand! They go on giving play to their spirits, put a glare in their eyes and say, "Empty, without holiness!" Fortunately, this has nothing to do with it.[5]

This tradition was well known in the Japanese Five Mountains monasteries, and this text was even the subject of a commentary, still influential in the twentieth century, by one of the Kitayama monks we will be studying, Kiyō Hōshū.

Most Chinese Mahayana schools, including Zen, tended toward the affirmation of the heuristic and ontological value of ordinary, concrete lived experience, as seen for example in the continuing popularity of the sage Vimalakīrti in many different sectors of Chinese society. The Chinese Buddhist affirmation of ordinary experience and of innate enlightenment accorded well with influential indigenous conceptions of the appropriate place to find ultimate value, such as in government service and the family, and with theories of innate sagehood. This tendency in Chinese Buddhism can be seen in the deep interest held by many in Tathāgatagarbha attributions of positive qualities to the absolute, which were systematized in the *Ratnagotravibhāga* and popularized in such texts as the *Śrīmālā Sutra* and the Chinese apocryphal text, *Awakening of Faith.* Chinese Buddhists and others in the Chinese cultural sphere further developed this tradition through a popular teaching known as *pen-chüeh* (J. *hongaku*) or innate enlightenment, which suggests that delusion is only distorted vision that through practice can be corrected. This and similar views are found in the *Awakening of Faith* and several related Chinese apocryphal texts that, as we saw in the last chapter, were taught by Gidō and Zekkai in the Kitayama Five Mountains Zen temples, such as the *Perfect Enlightenment Sutra* and the *Śūraṅgama Sutra.* Soteriological practice in many of these schools then emphasized different methods useful to correct distorted vision and so allow the original, enlightened nature to be more fully manifested. This conception of a "true self" that is to be realized through religious practice is found in a wide variety of religious traditions.[6]

In the Zen school there is a comparatively strong tendency to focus on the particular and the concrete aspects of ordinary experience as the site for the recognition of the pervasive presence of ultimate reality and of the pervasive experience of enlightenment. Of course, various teachers emphasized different aspects. One dominant strand from the mid-T'ang onwards includes the dominant Ma-tsu lineage, whose teachers often underlined the importance of discovering what emptiness and illusion meant when applied to the all too concrete aspects of ordinary life, commonly characterized in terms of such basic actions as speaking and "the four postures" of sitting, standing, walking, and lying down. The interest in the realization of the originally enlightened mind is also seen in the Zen Buddhist philosophy of mind. Throughout the Zen tradition we find a struggle to apply original enlightenment to every aspect of human experience; the best-known resolution of this principle of Zen teaching was first articulated by Ma-tsu Tao-i in his widely influential identification of the "ordinary mind" (C. *p'ing-ch'ang hsin*) with Buddha nature.[7] This Zen ideal is one of the most thoroughgoing applications of the Mahayana doctrine of original enlightenment to ordinary reality and experience. The rejection of distinctions such as these that lay at the basis of conventional assumptions about morality and hierarchical order in society was an important consequence of the Buddhist philosophy of nondualism when joined to the notion of innate enlightenment.

Before becoming a teacher, disciples in this most influential lineage learned to recognize the ultimate reality in the most ordinary behavior without considering it to be anything special, and to embody this realization in their every deed. In the application of the state of nonduality to concrete experience, the practitioner moves freely in a realm that is at once both sacred and mundane, both transcendent and utterly ordinary, as seen in such influential dictums as Chao-chou Ts'ung-shen's (778–897) "Go wash your bowls" as a statement of the highest level of religious practice. They were then acknowledged as teachers themselves to have realized the great freedom of nondualism and to move freely among both the conditioned and the unconditioned. Through this vision and activity Zen monks, nuns, and lay devotees felt they were fulfilling the mission of Mahayana Buddhists to live the lives of a bodhisattva in a world of empty illusion and suffering. The distinctive contribution of the Kitayama Japanese Zen monks was to apply directly to interpretation of the landscape arts these Mahayana ideals of recognizing the illusory character of existence, while acknowledging the value of its provisional existence by undertaking the bodhisattva's mode of nondualistic, free action in the conditioned world. We shall see in the final two chapters how they accomplished this.

Aversion to overly rigid distinctions between the transcendent realm and the ordinary was already part of fourteenth-century Japanese culture both within the Zen sect and outside of it. We find such teaching in other Buddhist schools for whom this ontology was fundamental, such as the Japanese Tantric tradition known as Shingon,[8] in many aspects of the Japanese Tendai school,[9] and in syncretic thought combining Buddhism with Shinto or with Taoism and Confucianism.[10]

In Japanese artistic and literary theory, this Buddhist ontology was already well established in its application to Japanese poetics and prose aesthetics by as early as the Heian period. We find an argument for the absence of difference between enlightenment and the passions in the famous discussion of the truth value of fiction in the early-eleventh-century *Tale of Genji*,[11] and the use of the Tendai Three Truths theory in Fujiwara Shunzei's (also Thshineri; 1114–1204) influential discussion of poetics, the *Korai fūteishō*.[12]

We see the importance of these same teachings early in Japanese Zen history, as in a text attributed to Enni Ben'en, the Kamakura period founder of Tōfuku-ji temple, which would later become one of the most important Five Mountains monasteries. This text, the *Zazenron* or *Seated Meditation Treatise*, combines in typical fashion the teaching of inherent enlightenment with the nondualism of the ultimate and the provisional: "The Buddhas of the three worlds and all sentient beings have this same nature, which is the dharma [or truth] body of the original ground." The text later continues, "[Since] the mind is originally pure, . . . the afflictions are enlightenment."[13] In the later Japanese Zen of fourteenth-century Five Mountains monasteries, interest in the subtle nondualism of enlightenment and illusion seems to have been widespread among Musō Soseki's disciples, and not limited only to his influential dharma heir Gidō Shushin. Shun'oku Myōha, the only disciple of Musō to rival Gidō in influence and importance for the Five Mountains temples, inscribed a *chinzō* self-portrait, "If awakening and sleeping are not one, then how about the real and the provisional?"[14] The presence of this view in Shun'oku's writings certainly does not represent any doctrinal innovation, but only shows the continued importance down into Kitayama Japanese Zen of these general Mahayana Buddhist views in the ontology of perhaps the single most influential Five Mountains monk of the late fourteenth century.

Chūhō En'i shows that he holds a closely comparable view in an explanation he wrote of the name, "At Ease in Centrality," that another monk had given to a young Five Mountains acolyte. Chūhō begins with a discussion of centrality:

> Centrality is the origin of the myriad transformations and the marvelous functionings of One-mind. . . . Our [Zen Buddhist] teachings call it "Middle Way," "Middle View," and "Middle Truth." Ordering and adjusting the myriad dharmas, mixing and combining in the One-mind, its truth is most profound, its tenets are most lofty. When it expands fully, they are still none other than matters proper to daily activities. . . . Oh, how profound is the meaning of centrality! When one examines his throughts and listens and looks with due consideration, and thus is settled in it when practicing, then one will certainly be qualified to enter into the realm of the sages.[15]

Here Chūhō describes the classic Chinese Mahayana Buddhist formulation of the Middle Truth, in which the ultimate and the provisional meet and interact, and its relation to the originally enlightened mind. Yet in typical fashion for a Zen teacher he also asserts its appropriateness to daily activities, including but presumably not limited to religious practice. This linkage of canonical Buddhist philosophy to daily activities characterizes the Kitayama Five Mountains monks in their beliefs that ordinary social affairs are the most appropriate site for the realization and manifestation of the originally enlightened mind underlying Zen Buddhist teachings and practice. We have already seen how central cultural production and interpretation was to the daily lives of the Kitayama Five Mountains monks, and here we see one link of the cultural to the social and ultimately to Buddhist doctrine.

The writings of Taihaku contain perhaps the most representative Kitayama conception of the relation in Mahayana Buddhist ontology of illusion and reality, and one that participates in the tradition of resisting an overemphasis on either the ultimately real or the provisional. In one passage Taihaku developed his conception of the interaction between these two poles in terms of the playful movement back and forth between them, based on the teaching of the "dharma gate of nonduality." In a eulogy read at a cremation ceremony for "The Layman Beyond Delusion" (C. *chen-wai chü-shih*), he described the layman as "beyond delusion disporting his mind, casting his military strategies away and entering the secret room of [the Buddha's] great joy. . . . [He then] awakened to the nondifferentiation of the principle of the Real and the mundane, and knew of the fundamental identity of birth and death."[16] Taihaku alluded to the important Mahayana Buddhist text, the *Vimalakīrti Sutra*, in giving the well-known chapter title, "Dharma Gate of Nonduality." In this chapter Vimalakīrti debates with Mañjuśrī and other bodhisattvas on the meaning of nonduality ends with Vimalakīrti's famous silence.[17]

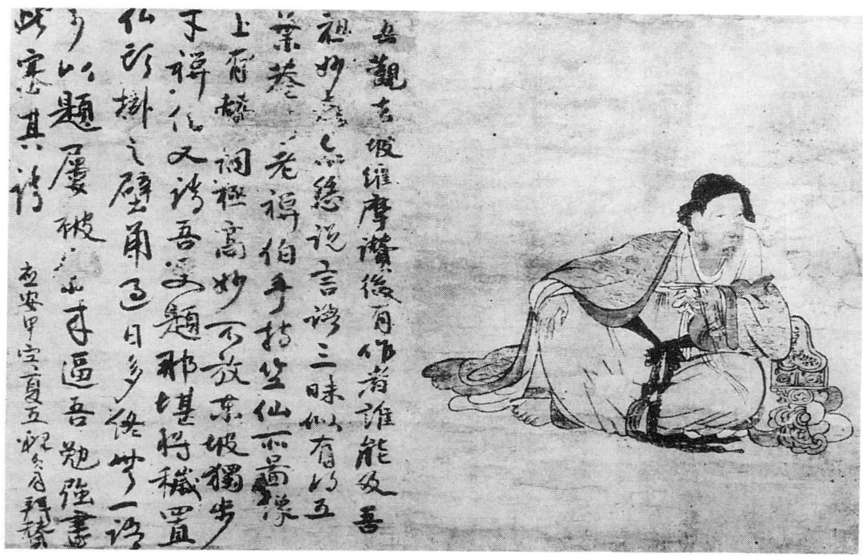

Fig. 3.1. *Vimalakīrti.* Attributed to Chu-hsien Fan-hsien (1292–1348). Inscription by Chūgan Engetsu (1300–75). Handscroll remounted as hanging scroll. Ink and light color on paper. 34.0 x 51.4 cm. 1374. Chōfuku-ji, Kyoto.

In his eulogy Taihaku underlined his reference to the *Vimalakīrti Sutra* by referring in the next sentence to Beyond Delusion's residence in the abbot's quarters as living in "the room of Vaiśālī." While this is a conventional term for the abbot's quarters, it derives from the name of the ancient Indian city known best as the location of Vimalakīrti's debate.

Taihaku's allusions to the sutra would have not gone unnoticed among his contemporaries, since the text was as popular among the Japanese Five Mountains monks as it had been in the earliest centuries of Chinese Zen history and in Sung China. This is attested to by a number of inscriptions in the collected writings of Five Mountains Zen monks and even extant paintings with the lay bodhisattva Vimalakīrti as their subject. For example, we know that the Chinese Zen teacher Chu-hsien Fan-hsien, who was widely influential in the spread of poetry in the Japanese Five Mountains temples after he came to Japan, is reported to have himself painted an image of Vimalakīrti. That image of the popular lay bodhisattva has been preserved, and was inscribed in 1374 by the important Japanese Five Mountains Zen master Chūgan Engetsu (fig. 3.1).[18] Chūgan recalled in this inscription his deep admiration for an inscription on another image of Vimalakīrti by none other than Su Shih, the famous Sung literatus so popular in the Japanese Five

Mountains temples, which he had seen during his travels on the mainland. Just as the sutra had appealed to centuries of their Buddhist predecessors in both China and Japan, the image and teachings of Vimalakīrti were of interest to Chinese and Japanese Five Mountains Zen monks as well as to their literati companions. The image would have been popular in these circles because Vimilakīrti is described in the text as a bodhisattva who lived as the Japanese monks were themselves living in the midst of the samsaric world and working to promote Buddhist insight. The ability to live in the mundane, samsaric world while maintaining correct Buddhist insight would have been of great interest to the Japanese Zen monks in considering their own chosen lifestyles in the metropolitan Five Mountains monasteries. Just as importantly, this model of correct lay Buddhist action in the world would have been important to them in their relations with lay patrons, associates, and disciples who were also powerful figures in the nonordained world.

The sutra itself gives us a good sense of the Mahayana Buddhist thinking that validated them in their lives and challenged those monks who preferred to withdraw into mountain or other rural retreats. In the *Vimalakīrti Sutra* chapter "Dharma Door of Nonduality," we find the various bodhisattvas each in turn giving an interpretation of this teaching before Mañjuśrī and Vimalakīrti finally give their renowned responses. One useful characterization of nondualism for understanding Buddhist nondualism as it applied to the Kitayama monks is that of the bodhisattva Narayana, who gave the following argument:

> To say, "This is mundane" and "That is transcendental" is dualism. This world has the nature of voidness, so there is neither transcendence nor involvement. . . . Thus neither to transcend nor to be involved, . . . this is the entrance into nonduality.[19]

Later on in the chapter, the bodhisattva Ratnamudrāhasta characterized his own insight, "It is dualistic to detest the world and to rejoice in liberation. . . . Liberation can be found where there is bondage, but where there is ultimately no bondage, where is there need for liberation?"[20] These two bodhisattvas explicitly opposed characterizations of ultimate reality as transcendent, or as something that can be separated from the profane world of ordinary experience. It is only in the nondualism of the two, as exemplified of course in Vimalakīrti's own lifestyle, that the Buddhist philosophy of nondualism can be realized.

Placed in the larger context of Buddhist insistence on the nonduality of the ultimate and the ordinary, a conception of the sacred in religious practice as something independent from or transcendent to the profane does not do justice to the Buddhist argument. In this vision of religious practice the Zen practitioner is asked to express enlightened experience through compassionate activity in the sentient world. In this expression, enlightened beings are not active in a realm transcendent to the mundane world, but engage in their bodhisattva practice right in the midst of the profane world of samsaric suffering, desire, and death.

While the Kitayama monks show they were very much a part of mainstream Buddhism generally and in the Zen school in several aspects of their teaching and practice, we touch on only one more in the present study: their conceptions of the mind and its implications for epistemology, soteriology, and ultimately for practice. Of course conceptions of the mind in Zen have changed over the centuries. Practices that dissipate illusions and quiet the mind are generally argued to be the means by which adepts can realize the pure and luminous character of their "original mind," a term grounded in the originally enlightened Buddha-nature in all sentient beings. One important early theory of the mind with which the Kitayama Five Mountains monks differed is seen in important early Zen conceptions of "no-mind" (C. *wu-hsin*; J. *mushin*) or "no-thought" (C. *wu-nien*; J. *munen*). These conceptions are best understood not as a denial of the importance of mind but in the context of practice that leads first to the cessation of the discriminating activities of the mind and then to the end of deluded perception, attachment, and desire.[21] Another important strand of Buddhist theories of the mind is the characterization of original mind as itself "ungraspable," following a well-known phrase in the Perfection of Wisdom text *The Diamond Sutra*: "Past thought is not got at; future thought is not got at; present thought is not got at."[22] In this sense, the original mind cannot itself become an object of dualistic cognition based on a distinction of subject and object.

The Kitayama Japanese Zen monks' approach to the mind is more closely aligned with a conception of the relationship between mind (C. *hsin*; J. *shin*) and object (C. *ching*; J. *kyō*), which is also expressed in terms of subject (C. *wo*) and object (C. *wu*) or of person (C. *jen*) and situation or surroundings (C. *ching*; J. *kei*). The most important aspect in Zen texts of this relationship between subject and object is one of nondualism or even identity, as we find in the discussion of the mind in the T'ang dynasty Chinese Zen master Huang-po Hsi-yun's (d. c. 850) influential *Essentials of the Transmission of the Mind* (C. *Ch'uan-hsin fa-yao*; J. *Denshin hōyō*).[23] As Huang-po stated, "mind and object are one" (C. *hsin-ching i-jo*) or, more commonly, "mind and object are both extinguished" (C. *hsin-ching shuang-wang*).[24] In this advanced state of Buddhist insight, distinctions between subject and object or internal and external ultimately die out and attachments are overcome. The same general view of the mind continued in popularity well after the T'ang, for it is still fundamental to the Zen practice of the important Yüan dynasty Chinese monk Chung-feng Ming-pen, who was so influential in the Japanese Five Mountains temples.[25] The importance of Huang-po's *Essentials* to the Japanese Five Mountains Zen tradition can be seen from its being the first text printed by the Japanese Five Mountains temples. It was widely read during the Kamakura period, only to fall in influence with the rise among the Japanese Five Mountains Zen temples of *kōan* or public case literature, such as the *Blue Cliff Records*, in the late fourteenth and early fifteenth centuries.[26]

A comparative examination of mind in Huang-po's *Ch'uan-hsin fa-yao* with that of the monks of this study can show us how their conception of the mind compares to the conception found in this important Zen text. The Japanese monks applied the relationship of mind and object to their interpretations of the natural world and to landscape painting in ways that reflect this same distinctive Zen Buddhist conception of the mind and of religious practice. Perhaps the fullest discussion of this concept among the Kitayama monks is found in Kiyō Hōshū's explanation of the shogun's sobriquet, "Manifesting the Mountain":

> Therefore, inwardly illumine the mind and outwardly bring the objective world to rest. If you bring the objective world to rest externally, then the mind will be without delusions; if you illumine the mind internally, then the objective world will be without passions. When the mind and its objects are united into one, then luminosity and bringing to rest will be merged.[27]

Kiyō describes the relationship between self and other in terms of the unity of the subject and object, not in terms of extinguishing the two, and in this sense his thinking is closely related but distinguishable from that of Huang-po.

The writings of Taihaku Shingen show that he also used many of the same concepts as Kiyō did. In one of the more important prefaces on an extant landscape painting, Taihaku described the ideal approach to landscape art in his preface to *Small Cottage by a Mountain Stream* (fig. 3.2). In this prose piece Taihaku suggests that the best way of Zen practice is to "attain [the landscape] in the mind and forget external things."[28] Taihaku made the same argument in different terms later in the same preface, bending Chinese syntax to form the following parallel expression: "This then is to be attained in the mind, and not objectified externally."[29] In both passages, Taihaku encouraged the viewers of landscape paintings to avoid objectifying the landscape externally, but to internalize it and appreciate it as part of one's own mind.

While Taihaku did not here argue that both the mind and its object should be extinguished, he was following a line of argument that adheres closely to another aspect of Huang-po's conception of the mind and its place in religious practice. Taihaku was warning his readers to avoid a mistaken view characterized by Huang-po in the following manner: "These days those who study the Way do not find enlightenment in their own minds, and so they become attached to form and are caught up in objectifications. These [practitioners] all turn their backs on the Way."[30] Huang-po indicated that if the practitioner did not concentrate his efforts toward enlightenment or realizing his own innately enlightened mind, then he would fall into the same objectifications and attachments that Taihaku warned his audience away from. In this sense Taihaku's views like Kiyō's accord closely on the topic of mind with those of the T'ang Zen master Huang-po.

The Japanese Five Mountains monks also developed their conceptions of the mind in syncretic terms, emphasizing another major contemporary religious tradition, that of Neo-Confucianism. To see how the Kitayama monks maintained a

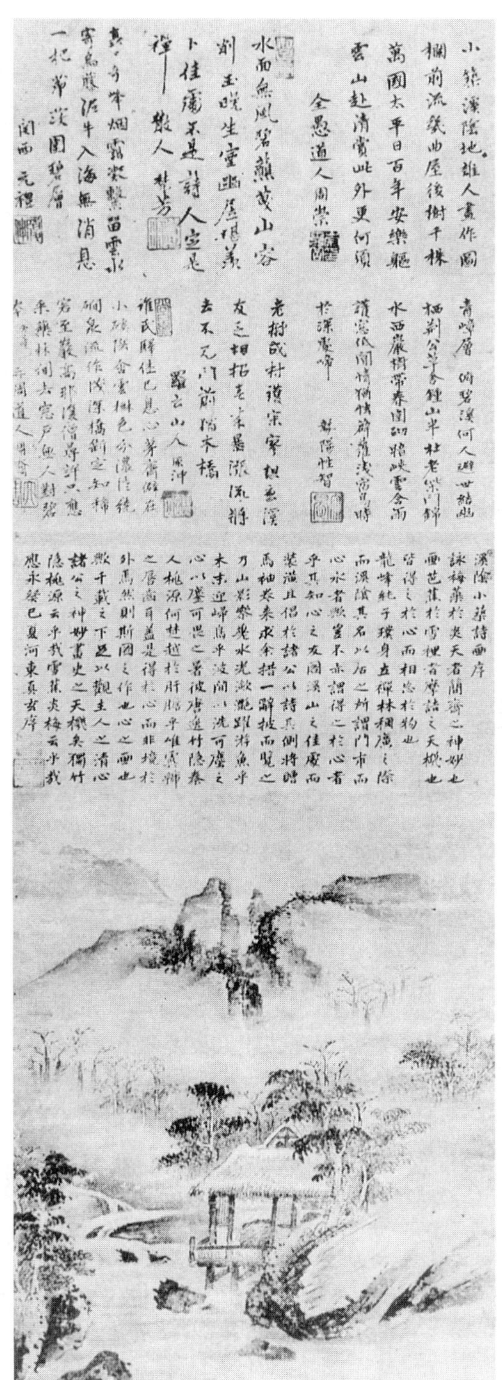

Fig. 3.2. *Small Cottage by a Mountain Stream.* Attributed to Minchō (1351–1431). Inscriptions by Taihaku Shingen (1358–1415) and six others. Hanging Scroll. Ink on paper. 101.5 x 34.5 cm. National Treasure. 1413. Konchi-in, Kyoto.

distinctively Zen style of theory of the mind, we may compare and contrast their views with those of contemporary Neo-Confucians in whose writings the Japanese monks were deeply interested. As did many of their fellow Zen monks beginning in the Sung dynasty on the mainland and throughout the Chinese cultural sphere, numerous Kitayama monks taught a form of Three Teachings syncretism of Buddhism, Taoism, and Confucianism. By the mid-fourteenth century most in Japan who were familiar with mainland developments were well aware of the newly influential Neo-Confucian teachings of Chu Hsi and the thinkers he looked back to earlier in the Sung. Yet again like many other Zen monks, the Kitayama monks argued for the preeminence of Zen teachings in their assimilation of Neo-Confucian and other ideas into their thinking. This syncretic approach to religious theory and practice was certainly very useful to the Five Mountains Japanese monks in developing and maintaining good relations with political elites, who would be most interested in Neo-Confucian theories of government and political authority.

In order to understand better how the Kitayama monks adapted Neo-Confucian ideals to their own Buddhist project, we must introduce the Neo-Confucian theory of the mind. Mind was central to the Confucian tradition, and particularly to conceptions of self-cultivation found among Neo-Confucians of the Sung and Ming. There is an important strain in early Confucian thinking that emphasizes the internal realization of Confucian ideals as a crucial prerequisite for correct action in society. This element was taken up in the Sung dynasty and appeared most prominently in Neo-Confucian thinkers. For many Sung Neo-Confucians the ultimate goal of religious self-cultivation remained the realization of human religious and moral virtue in society, but they shifted the emphasis from practices grounded in the fulfillment of familial and other, larger social relations to the internal, subjectively oriented realization of innate sagehood. For these thinkers, the sacred was more than a realm of perfect morality and government to be realized through following the transcendent Way or will of heaven: it was also an internal state, the innate sagely nature.

The development in the Neo-Confucian tradition of an interest in what we might term the subjective aspects of textual study and self-cultivation must be understood as part of a general reconsideration of religious practice in the Sung dynasty. Many Sung intellectuals ultimately came to emphasize the mind and the internal dimension of the pursuit of the Way. In the Neo-Confucian tradition, full development of the inner attitudes of reverence (C. *ching*) and sincerity (C. *ch'eng*) and the cessation of selfish desires (C. *ssu*) became necessary conditions for correct moral action in society and government. These inner attitudes played a central role in those texts that the Ch'eng-Chu school eventually used for self-cultivation practice in their redefinition of the textual canon, the *Great Learning*, the *Doctrine of the Mean*, and *Mencius*.[31] Neo-Confucians read these and other texts in a manner that emphasized the moral nature of the original mind, a major theme in Sung Neo-Confucian self-cultivation practices, as found in Mencius's notion of the "Four

Beginnings" (C. *ssu-tuan*) and the important phrase in the *Great Learning*, "keeping the inborn luminous virtue unobscured" (C. *ming-ming te*).[32] The Sung Neo-Confucian belief in the internal presence of the sacred is expressed as an ontological identity of man and the transcendent dimension of the cosmos.[33] This is seen most graphically in the straightforward identifications of the human with heaven and earth, as in Chang Tsai's influential "Western Inscription,"[34] and in Ch'eng Hao's use of Mencius 7a4, "All things are already complete in oneself."[35] The importance of the mind in Neo-Confucian self-cultivation derives in part from this confidence that the mind can know the truth of the cosmos because it is in some sense inherently identified with the rest of the cosmos.[36]

While the mind was of course important for the internal aspect of self-cultivation, it also played a central role in Ch'eng-Chu school conceptions of study and interpretation of the objective world. We see the emphasis on the mind in the study of classical texts, perhaps the most important aspect of the "investigation of affairs,"[37] in a widely influential anthology co-compiled by Chu Hsi, the *Chin-ssu lu* or *Reflection on Things at Hand*. In the section on the investigation of affairs, Ch'eng I is quoted as observing that "Only when our minds understand the Way can we distinguish right and wrong. . . . This is what Mencius meant by 'understanding words.'"[38] Chu Hsi's view of the central role played by the mind in textual study gives us a sense both of the reasons why textual interpretation was given such an important place in Neo-Confucian self-cultivation, and why Chu Hsi believed textual study applied to daily affairs:

> Responding to things, handling affairs, and so on, are similar to studying literature. If we drill and polish ourselves in the principles of things and studies, our minds will naturally be penetrating. Take reading, for example. Often, even after a great deal of thought, we cannot see through to the real meaning. But there must be a way to go through. In a case like this there are many difficulties and obstructions, but repeated effort will find a way to go through. To go through means that the mind penetrates.[39]

Through textual study of difficult passages the mind is trained to penetrate obstructions and difficulties and reach principle in a similar way to Chang Tsai's emphasis on the mind's penetration of obstacles to understanding. Chu Hsi points out that the training of the mind in textual study is to be applied to action in the world, the "responding to things" and "handling affairs" of daily life. Through textual study, then, these Neo-Confucian thinkers believed that the study of the Way cultivates the mind to understand the teachings of the ancient sage kings, and so realize the sacred Way of correct moral action in the world of daily experience.

The adaptation by Kitayama Japanese Zen monks of Chu Hsi's influential Neo-Confucian theory of self-cultivation highlighted both important congruences and major differences in Buddhist and Neo-Confucian conceptions of the mind. We can see this in Chūhō En'i's quotation of passages from Chu Hsi's commentary on the *Chung-yung* or *Doctrine of the Mean* in the following discussion of the significance of the name, "At Ease in Centrality," already discussed above:

> Now as for centrality, it is the origin of the myriad transformations but [also] the marvelous functioning of the one mind (*i-hsin*). When it has not yet issued forth, it preserves in perfect condition its flawlessly pure principle with no faults of prejudice or transgression: this is the substance of centrality. When it has already issued forth, the numerous transformations of things and affairs universally follow in reply without arousing any worry of going beyond or not coming up to: this is the functioning of centrality.[40]

While in this passage Chūhō freely used quotes from the first lines of the *Doctrine of the Mean* and its commentary by Chu Shi,[41] Chūhō had significantly changed the meaning of both Chu Hsi's commentary and the *Doctrine of the Mean* itself in integrating these texts into his own Buddhist religious syncretism. To understand his syncretic adaptation and its importance for Five Mountains Zen, we must first examine the idea behind the passage in the *Doctrine of the Mean*.

The *Doctrine of the Mean* makes a distinction in the first chapter that becomes quite important in Chu Shi's enormously influential theory of self-cultivation. This is the distinction between "centrality" (C. *chung*), in which the emotions have "not yet issued forth" (C. *wei-fa*), and "harmony" (C. *ho*), in which the emotions have "already issued forth (C. *i-fa*) and attained due measure" (C. *fa erh chieh chung-chieh*). The former is then characterized in the *Doctrine of the Mean*'s first section as the "great origin of all under heaven," while the latter is designated the "universal path of all under heaven." In Chu Hsi's conception of the ontological and epistemological bases for self-cultivation, centrality together with the state of "not yet issued forth" were associated with the universal principles (C. *t'ien-li*) that, while present in the mind, have not yet been consciously realized or expressed. By contrast, harmony and the issuing forth of the feelings came to be associated with the expression of the nature as present in the mind in response and engagement with the world.[42]

The importance of these analogies is that they define an important bipolarity in Chu Hsi's epistemology and theory of religious practice: the innermost aspect of the mind is closely associated with universal, innate sagely nature; while the engagement of the mind in the world is identified with the feelings, which historically in the Confucian tradition were not generally considered trustworthy, and with the need for constant practice leading to "due measure." In Chu Hsi's model for self-cultivation, this bifurcation becomes the basis for two well-known types of practice: the inner preservation of the innate, virtuous nature (C. *tsun te-hsing*) and the outer-directed study (C. *tao-wen hsueh*) that extends knowledge and investigates things (C. *chih-chih ke-wu*).[43] The ultimate end of self-cultivation in Chu Hsi's model is the merging of the two aspects of the mind, the identification of the human mind (C. *jen-hsin*) and the universal basis of true humanity, the ontological mind (C. *t'ien-hsin*).[44] Only through the union of these two aspects of the mind can innate sagehood be fully realized in engagement in the concrete world of daily affairs, which is of course the ultimate ideal of the Confucian sage and likewise a subject of great importance in Zen Buddhism.

If we return to Chūhō's own reading of centrality, we can now see that it is substantially different from the conception of centrality in the *Doctrine of the Mean* as well as that in Chu Hsi. In the passage quoted above Chūhō associated both of the states of "not yet issued forth" and "already issued forth" with centrality, and did not mention "harmony." Instead, Chūhō distinguished between these two states in terms of the essence or substance (C. *t'i*) and function (C. *yung*) of centrality. Moreover, mind for Chūhō seems to be primarily associated with the latter of the paired conceptions, since he contrasted the "one mind" with the "origin of the myriad transformations," a term often associated with the state of "not yet issued forth."

Chūhō's objective in his placement of both pairs under the rubric of centrality is seen when he turns later in the passage to a brief description of the same ideas in Buddhist terms, in a passage already quoted above:

> Our teachings call it "Middle Way" (*chung-tao*), "Middle View" (*chung-kuan*), and "Middle Truth" (*chung-ti*). Ordering and adjusting the myriad dharmas, mixing and combining in the one mind (C. *i-hsin*), its truth is most profund and its tenets are most lofty. When it expands fully, they are still none other than matters proper to daily activities.[45]

Here Chūhō has taken the notion of centrality from *Doctrine of the Mean* and adapted it to the Buddhist teaching of the "middle truth" or Middle Way. As we saw earlier in this chapter, in Mahayana Buddhist thought the Middle Way generally expresses a medium that transcends the extremes of two views that are each seen to be ultimately opposed from the perspective of the fully accomplished practitioner, views such as empty (C. *k'ung*) and provisional (C. *chia*), being (C. *you*) and nonbeing (C. *wu*), or truth (C. *chen*) and delusion (C. *su*). In Chūhō's Buddhist interpretation of centrality, the Middle Way becomes the ground for a medial position between the contrasting conceptions of the universal truth of innate Buddhahood or sagehood and of the engagement in the mundane world of daily affairs.

As seen in the context of the Buddhist conceptions of the mind I outlined earlier, Chūhō's application of the Buddhist middle way to a theory of self-cultivation did not allow for Chu Hsi's distinction between inner and outer in religious practice. While this distinction is crucial to Chu Hsi's program of study, in ontological terms Chu Hsi's model for religious practice ultimately joins the two aspects of the mind in a manner not unlike that found in Chūhō's reading of the *Doctrine of the Mean.* In this sense we might say that Chūhō here aligns himself with those in the Ma-tsu line of Zen who encouraged the realization of enlightenment in ordinary experience, as seen in his unwillingness to make too fixed a distinction between the internal or even subjective aspect of innate enlightenment and its concrete realization in the objective world. In doing so he assimilates Neo-Confucian conceptions of religious practice into a soteriology and practice better suited to this strand in the Zen tradition. Yet by syncretically integrating Neo-Confucian ideals and concepts into a program of Zen Buddhist study and practice, Chūhō presents a teaching that would have been most useful in his relations with contemporary political elites.

A signficant aspect of Chūhō and other Five Mountains monks' integration of Zen Buddhism with Neo-Confucian self-cultivation theory is the implications they developed for perceiving and cultivating the religious dimension of ordinary, concrete experience. Their Three Teachings syncretism of Buddhism with Taoism and Neo-Confucianism was only one part of the general Five Mountains Kitayama ethos of applying Zen Buddhism to a wide variety of aspects of life in elite society, including the practice and appreciation of landscape arts. In surveying their writings, this application can be found in different venues of their lives ranging from politics to aesthetics. For an example of the broader applications of the Kitayama theory of mind to action in the secular world, I turn to an important area on which I can touch only briefly in this study: the realm of politics.

In the year 1410 Kiyō Hōshū, who would be appointed abbot of the important Five Mountains temple Tōfuku-ji in the following year, was among a group of monks asked by the shogun Yoshimochi to give his interpretation of a sobriquet (C. *hao*; J. *gō*) that Yoshimochi had taken for himself, "Manifesting the Mountain." In his written response to this request Kiyō first noted in his explanation how the land was peaceful and flourishing under his reign, and that Yoshimochi seemed very well disposed to Buddhism and in particular to the Zen sect. Then, in explaining this name, Kiyō writes:

> I respectfully wrote out its meaning, saying, "'Manifesting' is 'luminosity'[46] and 'mountain' is the image of 'bringing to rest.'[47] Now the reason that people cannot conform to this Way is obfuscation[48] and restlessness.[49] Illuminating the obfuscated is called the luminous, and ceasing to be restless is called 'coming to rest.' Coming to rest and luminosity are like the two wheels of a cart or the two wings of a bird.[50] If at first there is not obfuscation, how can there be luminosity? If at first there is not restlessness, how can there be coming to rest? Both coming to rest and luminosity are established only after each movement and each obfuscation, so one who studies this Way should not be separated [from them] for an instant.[51] Therefore, inwardly illumine the mind and outwardly bring the objective world to rest. If you bring the objective world to rest externally, then the mind will be without delusions; if you illumine the mind internally, then the objective world will be without

> passions. When the mind and its objects are united into one, then luminosity and bringing to rest will be merged. Then it becomes apparent that this Way resides in the darkest and obscurest [places] without ever being imperceptible, and is found in the smallest and slightest without ever being diminished. How bright![52] How lofty![53] But mental grasping cannot attain to it. What the Great Teacher Tsao-pai[54] [Cheng-kuan] calls 'Destroying the passions with great wisdom,' this is called 'luminosity'; being without thoughts[55] in pure Zen, this is called 'mountain': we can refer to [your name] in this way."[56]

In his discourse Kiyō skillfully interweaves Neo-Confucian theories of self-cultivation with Zen Buddhist conceptions. He begins with terms that, while common to Buddhist writings on the mind, are clearly derived in this context from the Neo-Confucian canonical collection of the Four Books and Chu Hsi's commentaries on them. The underlying themes, for example, of "luminosity" and "bringing to rest" in the first line, may seem like an odd parallelism, until we recall that together they are important components of the first line to the *Great Learning*: "The way of greater learning lies in keeping one's inborn luminous Virtue unobscured, in renewing the people, and in coming to rest in perfect goodness."[57] After developing this Neo-Confucian theory of practice, Kiyō turns to a Zen Buddhist argument with which we are already familiar. As we saw earlier in this chapter, the pair of terms "mind" and "object(ive world)" is central in Buddhist and particularly Zen Buddhist thinking on the concrete practice centering on meditation that leads to the extinguishing of desires and suffering.

Kiyō then applies these soteriological theories to the specific realities of daily experience in which a layman like Yoshimochi would of course be interested. He does so through a Neo-Confucian reference to the presence of the Way in every moment of experience, finally suggesting in a Zen Buddhist section of the passage that the Way may be found everywhere when an advanced practitioner has mastered the practice of the nondualism of mind and object. Then he closes with allusions to the ideals of political success in the *Mencius* and the *Analects* that, he points out, may only be reached through a combination of Buddhist and Zen practice. In this way Kiyō dovetails classical Confucian and more recent Neo-Confucian allusions and terms into a Zen Buddhist theory of practice applied to the subtleties of daily experience.

As we have seen in this passage, the Five Mountains Zen theory of mind formed the basis for the broader Kitayama Japanese understanding of cultural practice and interpretation, but it also could be directly applied to maintaining a position of power in relations with the political authorities of the day. While Kiyō is distinctive in his interest in the Hua-yan Buddhism of Cheng-kuan, he and the other Kitayama monks were able through such arguments as these to maintain the predominant position of the Zen sect at the shogunal court that was first established by Musō Soseki in the 1330s. In Kiyō's analysis we can see the Kitayama monks actively using their political position at the shogunal court to define even the personal identity of the shogun in terms of this Zen Buddhist theory of the mind. Kiyō was not alone in this among the monks whose views we are presently examining, for the name "Manifesting the Mountain" itself had been given to Yoshimochi by Zekkai Chūshin during a period in which he was at the peak of his influence at the shogunal court.[58] Through their access to the shogun and other high officials, and through their considerable prestige at their court, the Kitayama Five Mountains monks could define the very public and private selves of influential officials through such interpretations of their names as we have just seen.[59] Through such texts and social circumstances the Kitayama monks exercised their wide-ranging influence on Muromachi culture.

The Kitayama monks also followed the Five Mountains tradition of identifying poetic practice with Zen as another important aspect of the Zen role in contemporary society and culture. In this affirmation of the religious importance of poetry, they participated in the general affirmation of the salvific value of language that characterizes much Chinese Mahayana Buddhism and other schools of Chinese religion and philosphy.[60] As we already saw in chapter 1, the affirmation of poetry and other textual study characterized Japanese Zen from at least the Kamakura period. However, the Kitayama monks developed a conception of poetry that centered on the role of the mind, and we now turn to a survey of the place of this theory in Japanese and continental aesthetics.

The central role of the mind in Five Mountains Zen poetics was shared by many aesthetic theories from the earlier centuries of the Japanese court. The earliest poetic theory from the *waka* court poetry tradition opens by finding poetry in the mind, as seen in the famous opening line from both the Chinese and Japanese language prefaces to the *Kokinshū* of the early tenth century, the first imperial anthology of Japanese *waka* poetry. In this line, which reads, "The seeds of Japanese poetry lie in the human heart and grow into leaves of ten thousand words,"[61] the notion of the mind derived, like many of the most important conceptions in Japanese poetics, from the influential preface to the Chinese *Shih Ching* or *Classic of Poetry*, although using natural images that give it a distinctive flavor. Through Heian period poetics the mind only increased in importance, becoming by the time of the enormously influential father and son poets Fujiwara no Shunzei and Fujiwara no Teika (also Sadaie, 1162–1241) the center of the most esteemed element of *ushin* or "intense feeling" (lit., "with mind") crucial to all of the best poetry.[62] Their conception of the highest level of poetic writing was at times clearly influenced by practices that seem to derive from Buddhism, as in Teika's statement that excellent poetry "lies in none other than carefully calming your mind and becoming deeply absorbed [into your object]."[63] By the early fourteenth century we find that this style as it is interpreted by one of the most creative *waka* poets of the age, Kyōgoku Tamekane (1254–1332), has become merged with an attitude of deep contemplation through which the truth (C. *chen*; J. *makoto*) or mind (C. *hsin*; J. *kokoro*) of an object may be discerned.[64] Historians will probably never know whether this shift in significance derives from relations between Tamekane and Zen or other Buddhist monks at the court of Emperor Fushimi, where Tamekane was active.

We find a comparable emphasis on the mind in Five Mountains Zen poetics of the Kitayama period. In chapter 1 we have already seen how important poetry was in Gidō's conception of cultural study.[65] Chūhō En'i also found the religious element to be important to the writing and interpretation of poetry, and argued that this element is found in the degree to which it expressed the poet's and influences the reader's mind internally. In his "Preface to Poems Sent to Head Monk Tokuchū," Chūhō rejected the notion that poetic study was comprised of simply mastering the rules of writing, and developed a conception of poetry in the following manner:

> Poetry is like our teachings which [maintain that] we are all given the great eye. If this eye is correct, then with one look the myriad objects of perception return to their origin, and with each act the numerous delusions leave no traces, and without restraining it the so-called issuing forth of the nature and emotions is correct on its own. . . . Then someone skillful at Zen can also be skillful at poetry.[66]

Chūhō's case for the parallel of Zen and poetry is based on the widely influential analogy of poetry and Zen developed by the important Southern Sung poet and literary theorist, Yen Yü (1180–1235) in his *Ts'ang-lang shih-hua*.[67] Yen Yü used a similar term, "the correct dharma eye" (*chen-fa yan*), as part of his highly laudatory characterization of High T'ang poetry. This passage was then taken as the preface to the *Shih-jen Yü-hsieh*, a widely studied and influential handbook of Chinese poetics in fourteenth- and fifteenth-century Japan.[68]

Here the mind is an important aspect of good art, as evidenced when Chūhō went on in his preface to describe how to tell Zen art from that of heretics and bad poets:

> A student may be Buddhist in his dress and Zen in his teachings, but when you inquire about his speciality, he stupidly does not know anything [about Zen], since his chanting [of poems] obscures his spirit and his propagating [with poems] stains the mind. Not only may our fellow [monks] "attack him openly to the beating of drums," but he is also an offender as a poet.[69]

Chūhō felt that a poet should be judged on the degree to which his writings expressed his inner "spirit" and the innately enlightened character of the mind. While a poet may be technically accomplished, if poetry did not also express this mind of the poet, then Chūhō felt that it was a religious heresy as well as bad poetry. Here we see a conception of poetry as a type of religious practice grounded in Zen beliefs in the importance of the mind in the Ōei period.

We see a similar view of the key role of the mind in literary theory being written by lay writers with whom the Kitayama Five Mountains monks are known to have had contact. We may look briefly at the theories of literature developed by two of these authors and literary theorists, the linked verse poet Nijō Yoshimoto and the dramatist Zeami Motokiyo. During the Kitayama period both Yoshimoto and Zeami were actively creating elite court arts out of cultural forms popular among the lower socioeconomic strata. The authoring of aesthetic treatises arguing for the value of these new cultural forms in terms highly esteemed by members of Yoshimitsu's court was a crucial component in this process, in addition to refinement of literary diction and the composition of literature on themes of interest to court audiences. We can see the importance of Five Mountains Zen monks in these treatises, for both Yoshimoto and Zeami's aesthetics show clear evidence of familiarity both with Zen texts and with Yen Yü's equation of literature with Zen.

Their writings on aesthetics also reveal that both of these literary theoreticians felt that the mind was crucial to the highest forms of their arts, and the mind is defined in terms taken from the Zen tradition. Yoshimoto writes in a treatise from late in his life, *Jūmon Saihisshō*: "Facing the flowers of spring and composing poems beneath the autumn moon, clear your mind, dim your nature [C. *hsing*; J. *shō*], and you will spontaneously attain [Buddhist] enlightenment."[70] In a different way, Zeami emphasizes the mind in the highest level of artistic performance, that is, acting, which he describes with such Zen terms as *mushin* or no-mind and *sokushin* or "the mind itself."[71] In his use of these terms we can see that Zeami is drawing on a different theory of the mind than that practiced by the Kitayama monks we have been studying. However, like Yoshimoto in his writings on linked verse, Zeami is placing a Zen Buddhist conception of the mind at the pinnacle of literary and dramatic practice.

We find comparable conceptions of the role of the mind in artistic practice in the aesthetic theory of the Tendai Buddhist monk Shinkei (1406–75), a student of the Kitayama era *waka* poet Shōtetsu, who lived as an ordained Five Mountains Zen monk from 1414 to sometime early in the 1420s. If we may judge from his writings and what we know of his biography, Shōtetsu was clearly not an active participant in the Five Mountains Zen cultural circles or *yūsha*, yet he still quoted Shunzei in identifying Buddhism with the practice of his literary craft.[72] However, in the case of the monk Shinkei we find he identifies the Way of poetry not with Buddhism generally but with the Way of Zen, and indicates that poetic practice is "the shortest path to sudden enlightenment," thus identifying poetry as a Zen art.[73] While Shōtetsu like Zeami was clearly not being directly influenced by the Kitayama Five Mountains monks we are reading,[74] his interest in the mind functions, on a general level, in the same way as it does in Yoshimoto and Shinkei's aesthetics: to give the writing and appreciation of literature a generally Buddhist or specifically Zen Buddhist orientation.

A more social dimension to the relationship between literature and Zen Buddhism is also developed in the writings of Chūhō En'i. In a cultural permutation on the Three Teachings syncretism of the day, Chūhō employed a similar theory of religious meaning in poetry to establish common ground for overcoming interreligious differences and promoting dialogue between Zen monks and their fellow Confucian thinkers and scholar-officials. His interest in culture as a meeting place for the seemingly disparate realms of religion and politics comes from the key role played, for the Five Mountains monks, by poetry gatherings as their meeting place with non-Buddhist intellectuals, political elites, and potential patrons. In a prose piece, Chūhō memorialized a putative exchange of poems between the Neo-Confucian Chu Hsi and the important Sung dynasty Zen monk and compiler of the widely read *kōan* anthology, *Blue Cliff Records*, Yüan-wu K'e-ch'in. This essay, titled "Preface to a Wilderness," described how a fellow Five Mountains monk was inspired to write a poem and have an illustration done of a poem written by Chu Hsi in response to a poem on plum blossoms written by Yüan-wu. After summarizing Chu Hsi's philosophy and noting his respect for it, Chūhō described Chu's attitude toward Buddhism and the way he reconciled himself to Yüan-wu:

> He denounced heretical doctrines, especially spurning [the teachings of] the Buddha, but when he saw Yüan-wu's "Plum Blossom" poem he wrote poems to him repeatedly and gradually came to have contact with him. Even if [Chu Hsi] does not attain to our [Zen's] deepest teachings, still he seems to know something of the marvelous Way of [our] sages and to be qualified to hold a discussion with us. Thus he proceeded from what appealed to him in approaching [Buddhism].[75]

Chūhō suggests that through the path of poetry Chu Hsi became interested in Yüan-wu, and eventually developed a friendship with him. While this was one consequence of the highly syncretic Unity of the Three Teachings beliefs we have seen were held by the Five Mountains monks, it is important to note that Chūhō here made such an argument not only in terms of doctrine, but primarily in terms of artistic expression and interpretation. It was poetic expression and a common interest in poetry, then, that could reveal for Chūhō a knowledge of the Way, and lay common ground for overcoming philosophical differences and even the polemical attacks that at times divided Buddhists on the continent from followers of the Chu Hsi school of Neo-Confucianism.

This role of poetry would, of course, have been important to the Japanese Five Mountains monks in their own relations with secular officials, who were most interested for their own purposes in Chu Hsi's philosophy. Through emphasizing the similarity between figures as central as these from the two traditions, Chūhō could argue persuasively for an identification between Five Mountains monks and the contemporary leaders of the secular world. I might stress here that this common ground was for Chūhō more than a shared interest in poetry: it was a common understanding of the Buddhist Way and the possibility that poetry could be an effective means of perceiving the level of religious insight of the author. This is a common assumption made in a wide variety of Sung and later mainland Chinese theories of the arts, including Ancient Civilization and literati culture. This foundation of the Kitayama Five Mountains Japanese Zen view of literature allowed monks like Chūhō to argue for the importance of religious understanding to those active outside the Buddhist tradition in a variety of social roles.

Crucially to the present study, the Kitayama monks also applied Zen Buddhist perspectives to the interpretation of the visual arts. While we saw in the last chapter that the act of painting itself was, with one important exception, not of much interest to Five Mountains monks during the Kitayama period, they did not hesitate to describe paintings in profoundly religious terms. We see the central place of the mind in the Kitayama interpretation of art in Taihaku Shingen's conception of the "painting of the mind" (C. *hsin-hua*; J. *shinga*) in an important preface he penned in 1413 to the still extant painting *A Small Cottage by a Mountain Stream* (fig. 3.2). In his preface Taihaku referred again to the theory of Zen practice we have seen alluded to repeatedly, that of "attaining in the mind and not objectifying externally." Taihaku suggests that this practice may allow the Kitayama monks to overcome the separation between the self and the hermit sages of the Chinese past, and then gave a general conception of artistic interpretation:

> Consequently, the creation of this painting is a painting of the mind! So after a thousand years have passed, it will be sufficient to perceive the pure mind of the master [of the hut], the divine marvelousness [C. *shen-miao*] of all of you [who wrote inscriptions], and the natural instinct [C. *t'ien-chi*] of the painter.[76]

By reading the painting as an image of the mind, Taihaku encouraged his readers to view the painting as it applied to the personal significance of the art object and as it applied to the religious cultivation of "attaining in the mind."

The conception of painting and other artistic expression as an image of the mind was certainly not new to Chinese artistic theory, for the *locus classicus* of the conception of art as the "painting of the mind" is found in the writings on calligraphy of Yang Hsiung (53 B.C.E.–18 C.E.). However, the term seems to have become influential in artistic criticism only in the Sung.[77] In the context both of the Five Mountains Zen monasteries and of a wide range of contemporary theories of the place of mind in self-cultivation practices, this conception of painting took on a deeply religious significance.

Gidō Shūshin developed his own view of the relation between poetry and Buddhism in a landscape-painting preface where he responded to a visitor's criticism of his friend Ichū Tsūjo. Ichū had taken the name "White Clouds and Cinnabar Canyons" for his own retreat, from an inscription on the famous residence on Mt. Lu of the Six Dynasties Buddhist, Hui-yüan. In defense of his friend, whose virtue a visitor had attacked for "stealing the name of a recluse," Gidō refers to another important conception in Chinese hermeneutic theory, "spirit communion" (C. *shen-hui*), and associates it with the mind:

> Somebody said, "'Clouds and canyons' are but the traces of Hui-yüan, and not the Way. If with poems and paintings in brush and ink they have traced their traces, then are they not far from the Way?" I [Gidō] replied, "Not so. If one has communed spiritually and attained in the mind, then 'the three realms in an instant' and 'the three thousand worlds in a single hair.' Outside of the Way there are not traces; other than traces there is no Way. Clouds and canyons! Poetry and painting! All are of my Way. Where is there any distance?"[78]

Gidō identified spirit communion with "attaining in the mind" in the sense that they both led beyond conventional distinctions of time and space. Through such a true meeting of spirits between Ichū and Hui-yüan, Gidō argued, deep understanding of Hui-yüan's life on Mt. Lu could be achieved wherever Ichū chose to reside, thus allowing him to surpass conventional conceptions of time and space.

The process of "spiritual communion" has a long history in Chinese philosophy and aesthetics. While it is not necessary here to discuss the history of the term,[79] we might simply point out that it implies a successful "meeting of the minds" of two individuals, a concept that we have seen was important in the textual hermeneutic of the Ancient Civilization, literati, and Neo-Confucian movements in the Sung. In a Buddhist context the term *shen-hui* might be compared to the Buddhist term "the *samadhi* of spirit/marvelous penetration" (*shen-t'ung san-mei*), which is found in a number of important texts including the *Vimalakīrti Sutra*, as well as the "spirit travel" (*shen-yu*) of Taoist philosophy, in the sense of a transcendence of limitations of time and space. However, by the Kitayama period this term ceased to appear very frequently in artistic criticism or in theories of self-cultivation, for the monks chose to emphasize the mind instead of the "spirit" aspect in their interpretation of artistic expression.

The larger implications of this view are indicated in Gidō's conclusion, where he rejected any distinction between religious practice and artistic interpretation. Through spiritual communion and attaining in the mind, Gidō argued, the religious practitioner could find the Buddhist Way in any aspect of the objective world, such as in clouds and canyons, or in any human cultural expression, particularly poetry and painting. Through perception based on the Zen practice the religious practitioner could in Gidō's view reach a deep understanding that realized the important Mahayana Buddhist teachings of "the three realms in an instant." This teaching of this broad claim for religious efficacy of the arts by one of the most influential Five Mountains monks of the early Kitayama period helped provide a foundation for much later Five Mountains Zen writing about the religious value of the arts.

For Chūhō also the art of poetry was very much a part of Zen practice. In a preface to a no longer extant landscape painting that was also inscribed by Ishō Tokugan, Chūhō describes his view of poetry's religious role:

> The ancients said that in literature there are two Ways: one is called that of writing, the other that of metaphor. . . . The techniques for achieving these [qualities] are all most difficult. As for carrying out these two Ways, even though this is not my specialty [as a Zen monk], still they can be of some assistance to the teachings of our school and so we should not discard them lightly.[80]

In this passage Chūhō defines poetry in the subsidiary role of assisting him in his specialty, which would be that of his primary social role as a monk in Zen Buddhism. Chūhō, like Gidō, is able to overcome any significant distinction between art and religion and argue for their close relationship.

Chūhō's use here of the term "Way" (C. *tao*; J. *michi*) of literature may be compared to Gidō's use above of the "Way" of Buddhism. The Five Mountains Zen conception of the Way may be useful in understanding the growth in medieval Japanese culture of the various Ways of artistic practice. While these Ways have been studied by a number of literary historians, they are in disagreement regarding the historical origins and uses of the term.[81] For our purposes we may simply note that the various ways share an emphasis on the maturation and deepening of two different elements: (1) the consciousness of the autonomous social role of a literary writer or actor, as distinct from that of the court official often taken by aristocrats, who undergoes specialized training; (2) the growth of a carefully conceptualized path of progression of literary or dramatic study, culminating with a high level of religious insight at the final stage of study. While one or the other of these two elements is present in the Kamakura period, certainly by the early to mid-fifteenth century we find fully developed conceptions of both the specialized training and deep insight in the writings of such authors as Zeami and the linked-verse poet Shinkei. Their arts of the Nō theater and linked verse are most often associated with the Ways even in twentieth-century popular culture, together with other arts such as calligraphy, painting, and music.

While we may never know with any precision the exact sources of intellectual influence that led to the growth of these Ways, we can see that in the case of both Zeami and Shinkei they developed in an intellectual and cultural environment dominated by views of the Kitayama monks we have been reading and other writers on Zen aesthetics. The Kitayama monks grounded the interpretation of subjective experience in terms of the mind, and so were able to extend their conceptions of religious practice beyond the confines of any particular path, ultimately including such activities as poetry and painting. Their particular interest in art as a mode of expression of Buddhist enlightenment, it should be noted, reveals a fundamentally affirmative conception of Buddhist insight: the ideal expression of

Zen Buddhism was found in the playful poetic, prose, and artistic expression in the very midst of the samsaric world. Now that we have some sense of their views of artistic practice and interpretation, we now turn to their application of this aesthetic to the natural landscape and the landscape arts.

Chapter 4

Zen Buddhist Readings of the Landscape

The Hermit at Court

> Why must one seclude himself in craggy caves, conceal his footsteps in forest and mountain, in order to achieve purity?
>
> —Chao Meng-fu

> A gate like the [busy] marketplace, but a mind like [tranquil] water.
>
> —Taihaku Shingen

In interpreting the landscape arts the Kitayama Zen monks inevitably made them their own, producing meaning out of the concerns and themes at the center of their lives in the large Five Mountains monasteric complexes in Kyoto and Kamakura. By interpreting the natural landscape in terms of their lives in the busy world of the capital, the Five Mountains monks laid claim to its religious value and spiritual authority for themselves at the very center of Japanese culture as they understood it. As we might expect from what we have seen in the previous chapter, they generally accomplished this application of the landscape to their lives through emphasizing the mind, particularly through the process they termed "achieving in the mind." In interpreting landscape imagery in terms that directly applied the natural world to the very centers of Japanese civilization in its twin capitals, the Kitayama monks redefined the relation of "nature" and "culture" as it was understood in their day. While they followed well-established continental Chinese precedents in this interpretation of the landscape arts, they also developed new directions for discovering meaning in city life in a way that remains responsible and attentive to religious, moral, and even political insights derived from a life of reclusion in the natural world.

Before we explore the meaning of landscape in the capital for the Five Mountains Zen monks, I introduce some relevant conventional associations of the natural world, particularly those with the life of the recluse, which the Kitayama monks identified with themselves through the theme of the "hermit at court." In much East Asian elite culture the landscape was traditionally an image of spiritual freedom, religious power, and moral transcendence of the ambitions and avarice of ordinary life in the capital or in various regional centers. Conventionally, the natural imagery of recluse poetry was often associated with a spiritual and moral purity, for example, and contrasted with the "dust" of the busy streets and the dark ambitions of conventional society. Of course, the social value of life outside of these centers rose and fell in different periods of Chinese and Japanese cultural history, but by the fourteenth century life outside of busy metropolitan life was, while often difficult, generally admired.

On the mainland reclusion had been revitalized as a morally virtuous lifestyle during the Southern Sung, although certainly in some earlier periods and in different social sectors it had been given great prestige. Since it was not the exclusive domain of any particular religious, philosophical, or literary school, writing about the landscape was one site for the proliferation of various syncretic integrations of different intellectual traditions. Early philosophical texts such as the *Chuang-tzu*, with its soaring images of freedom and playfulness in pastoral scenes, were widely read in later centuries by intellectuals from a broad range of sectarian traditions and philosophical schools. While life in the natural world may have been the lifestyle of choice for some, it also was the life to which were banished scholar-officials of different intellectual backgrounds who fell into political disfavor, and some of them became known in subsequent generations for their poems of exile.

Yet however popular natural imagery became in their writings or lifestyles, literate elites almost invariably still lived most of their lives in the capital or regional centers. So in the twelfth century and later they developed a variety of ways to apply important natural images and themes to themselves, including those images that they associated with advanced states of religious and moral self-cultivation.[1] The Southern Sung poet Yang Wan-li, who was read and appreciated in the Japanese Five Mountains monasteries, once made just such an association when he wrote, "The flowering plum in the grove is like a recluse/ Full of the spirit of open space, free from the spirit of worldly dust."[2] Through these associations individuals living in busy metropolitan centers could become just like a recluse, Yang and others in the poetic tradition asserted, by planting a plum tree in the garden and enjoying its blossoms as they flourish in the harsh snows of late winter, just as a person of spiritual value thrives even under difficult social and political conditions.

We have already seen in chapter 2 how the virtuous images of plum and other trees and plants were applied to social relations by the Japanese Five Mountains monk Gyokuen Bompō. As on the mainland so also on the Japanese islands: by the fourteenth century the natural landscape had been a site for religious practice and literary self-cultivation for centuries. Whether in Buddhist meditation practices in isolated mountain retreats, in syncretic *shugendō* pilgrimages, in the animistic nature worship of the tradition now known as Shinto, or in the *waka* poetic tradition of the seasonal books of the imperial court poetry anthologies, the natural world was a central part of Japanese culture both in the capital and beyond. In the twentieth century the recluse poet has come to be vaguely associated with Buddhism through the writings of such canonical Kamakura period figures as the Buddhist monk-poet Saigyō and the lay Buddhist poet and essayist Kamo no Chōmei (1153–1216).[3] However, we shall see that the Kitayama Five Mountains monks and many of their ordained and lay contemporaries followed continental precedents in understanding the natural world not strictly in sectarian Buddhist terms but in a syncretic and open fashion.

An interest in the natural landscape and its literary expression was no less true of monks from early in the history of Japanese Zen. The Kamakura Zen teacher Dōgen, who has become so important for twentieth-century Japanese philosophy, did what any enlightened being might be expected to do, and wrote his own sutra on the natural landscape: the *Sansuikyō* chapter to his magnum opus, the *Shōbōgenzō*. Dōgen begins the text by identifying the landscape with the cosmic Buddhas themselves:

> These mountains and rivers of the present are the actualization of the word of the ancient Buddhas. . . . Because the virtues of the mountain are high and broad, the power to ride the clouds is always penetrated from the mountains; and the ability to follow the wind is inevitably liberated from the mountains.[4]

While Dōgen introduces his sutra with a clear Buddhist statement, he turns quickly to the syncretic allusions to Taoist sages who can "ride the clouds" and "follow the wind," the same sort of allusions we will see in the writings of the Five Mountains Zen monks. Yet in the body of the text he develops, in a similar manner as elsewhere in the *Shōbogenzō*, an analysis of his topic through extended discussions of passages selected from the teachings of his Chinese Zen predecessors. The first selections he chose in this text are, as in many of his most eloquent passages, striking images that confound conventional interpretation: "The blue mountains are constantly walking. The stone woman gives birth to a child in the night."[5] While we will return to the function of such seeming paradoxes in the next chapter, here I note only that in his commentary Dōgen plays with the assumption that the landscape is outside of the self:

> One who doubts that the mountains walk does not yet understand their own walking. It is not that they do not walk, but that they do not yet understand, have not made clear, their walking. One who would understand their own walking must also understand the walking of the blue mountains.[6]

In these lines Dōgen presses his reader to reconsider the relation of the landscape to the self, in a maneuver similar in effect although differing in technique to that of the

Kitayama monks' deployment of the conventionally paradoxical "hermit at court" theme to be discussed below.

Yet Dōgen does not draw only on Zen texts, as might a strictly sectarian Buddhist, for he also used the writings of the Sung literati to explore the significance of the natural landscape. The best-known example of this is his use of lines from the important Northern Sung literatus Su Shih's poem to entitle another chapter of the *Shōbogenzō*. These lines compared the sound of streams and the forms of mountains to the tongue and body of the Buddha himself.[7] Such a comparison functions in a similar fashion to the walking mountains, for it leads the reader to reconsider the relation to the landscape to his or her own self, in this case in the literal sense of one's tongue and body. While certainly no Kitayama Five Mountains monks equaled Dōgen in his thoroughgoing application of Zen insight to the physical self, as we shall soon see they did turn to Su Shih and many of the same sources as he did in developing their own distinctive applications of the landscape to Zen insight.

The Kitayama monks applied the landscape to their lives in a variety of ways, but one of the most important in landscape-painting inscriptions was the theme of "the hermit at court" or the "hermit in the marketplace." Through developing this theme in terms meaningful for their lives inside and outside the walls of the Five Mountains monastic complexes, the Kitayama monks were integrating images of nature with those of culture, of the natural world and recluse poets with life at court and textual study. The hermit at court theme favored by the Kitayama Japanese monks is certainly a distinctive development in this tradition of interweaving culture with nature that highlights the relationship of what we might see as two quite distant loci of meaning: the court and the mountains.

An important example of the Kitayama use of the "hermit at court" theme is found in Taihaku Shingen's preface to the extant landscape painting *Small Cottage by a Mountain Stream* (fig. 3.2).[8] Taihaku began by praising the play of illusion in the art of the T'ang painter and poet of reclusion Wang Wei and the Southern Sung poet Ch'en Yü-i, and also alluded to two famous recluses, T'ao Ch'ien and "the bamboo hermit of the T'ang," who may again be Wang Wei. Then he asked rhetorically whether there was any difference between the viewer and these recluses, and rejects that possibility by concluding that they are separated only by the distance between lips and teeth. Taihaku is suggesting that Five Mountains monks might closely approximate the wisdom of these sages of the Chinese cultural tradition, despite the great distances that seem to separate them spatially, temporally, and in terms of their lifestyles.

Taihaku indicated how the apparent distance from the sages of the Chinese past was to be overcome: "This is to be attained in the mind, and not objectified externally."[9] "Attaining in the mind" was also designated by Taihaku elsewhere in the preface as having "attained this in their minds and forgotten [external] things."[10] This is the same epistemological theory that, as we saw in the previous chapter, draws on an important strand in the Chinese theory of Zen religious practice seen in Huang-po and that was influential in the Kitayama period. Elsewhere Taihaku identified, through an allusion to an early Chinese history, the state of mind that this level of practice would lead to: "[This is] the so-called 'A gate [bustling] like the marketplace, but a mind [tranquil] like water.' Is this not also what is called 'attaining in the mind'?"[11] Here Taihaku suggests that, through practice that overcame the habitual objectification of things external to the self and instead internalizes them in the mind, the Zen practitioner could realize the spiritual insight of these individuals at the pinnacle of the Chinese hermit-poet tradition. He draws for this interpretation of the landscape on a Sung and Yüan dynasty tradition, for we see this notion of a "mind [tranquil] as water" in Yüan-wu's Zen letters as well as in painting inscriptions by the literati painter Wu Chen (1280–1354) and others.[12]

The significance of this image for the Kitayama Japanese Zen monks is apparent in the concrete circumstances that led to the creation of this poem-and-painting scroll. As Taihaku tells us in his prose preface, the example of "attaining in the mind" of interest to him is that of a fellow Zen monk in the capital, Junshi Haku. Taihaku tells his readers that he has written the preface to honor Junshi, who named his study [*Small Cottage*] *by a Mountain Stream* even while living in the Japanese capital at the major Five Mountains temple, Nanzen-ji. Through resisting the commonsense impulse to objectify the Chinese mountain recluses outside the mind or the self, Taihaku pointed out, the Japanese Five Mountains monks could themselves join in the spiritual freedom and paradoxical expression of Wang Wei and T'ao Ch'ien while still residing in the capital. Moreover, this would be true not only of their lifestyles but also of their own artistic production, which might through religious and artistic practice become as accomplished as that of Wang Wei's well-known painting of a palm tree, whose leaves still remained despite the late winter scene, or of Ch'en Yü-i's individualistic poem of plum trees blooming out of season under the hot summer sun.

If the painting was understood in terms of "attaining in the mind," Taihaku concluded, "Is it only [the recluses of] the bamboo hermit or peach blossom spring? Only the [paintings of] snowy banana palms or [poems of] fiery plums?"[13] Through his rhetorical questioning Taihaku raised the possibility in the minds of his readers that they could achieve the spiritual freedom of the great Chinese recluses, and their art could be like the marvelous poems and paintings of Wang Wei and Ch'en Yü-i. Taihaku skillfully adapted this ideal of spiritual purity for government officials to the importance of landscape and the landscape arts as they pertained to the lifestyle of a fellow Five Mountains monk, a monk who like himself was serving in a temple system dominated by its close relations to the Japanese shogunate. Taihaku here addressed the spiritual dangers of life in the metropolitan Five Mountains temples, dangers that he suggests could be comparable to those faced by Chinese thinkers and writers when serving a government of less than ideal moral standards. He responded to the problems faced by monks who were active in the metropolitan temples in classically Zen terms, thereby placing them squarely in the mainstream of Zen conceptions of the mind and of religious practice.

The Kitayama Zen use of the theme of "attaining in the mind" drew on centuries of precedent in classical Chinese philosophy and literature. Since the history of interest in the mind in Chinese and Japanese artistic theory is quite long and varied, I will here contain our discussion to this notion alone. "Attaining in the mind" seems to have first been used in artistic criticism in the Sung dynasty.[14] It is commonly paired in its early uses with a related term, "to trust the brush" (*hsin-pi*) or "to trust the hand" (*hsin-shou*), to suggest spontaneity and a loss of distinctions of inner and outer in artistic practice. In this respect, I should note, the term suggests a conception of the mind closely associated with a nondualism of inner and outer that we have already seen was a distinctive characteristic in Chūhō's conception of the mind. An important Sung use of this term can be seen in Su Shih's characterization of his own failure to achieve this nondualistic, subjective state because of insufficient study, in a comment on Wen T'ung's bamboo painting:

> In painting bamboo one must first attain the completed bamboo inside the breast. Then when one grasps the brush and gazes intently, one will see what one wants to paint and rise quickly to follow it . . . like the hare's leaping up when the falcon swoops down. . . . [Wen] Yu-k'o taught me in this way but I could not achieve it, though I understood the way it should be done. Now if one knows the way things should be and cannot do it, inner and outer are not one and mind and hand are not in accord. It is a fault stemming from lack of studying. In other words, the reason why one may see things internally but be awkward in executing them, is that what one sees clearly in everyday life is suddenly lost when it comes to putting it into practice.[15]

I have quoted this passage at length because it is one of the few passages that describes in concrete terms the concept of "grasping in the mind" applied not only to painting in the well-known "completed bamboo inside the breast," but also to self-cultivation in daily life. Attaining something internally for Su Shih was very much the loss of distinction of inner and outer in the mind, and as we have seen the Kitayama conception of attaining in the mind preserved this sense of overcoming the gap between subject (C. *hsin*) and object (C. *ching*).

In this passage Su applied this conception of the mind not only to the actual practice with the brush, however, but also to the process of self-cultivation more broadly. This second sense of "attaining in the mind" is quite close to that of the Japanese Rinzai monks, as we shall see, but it is also reminiscent of the Ou-yang Hsiu's use of "attaining in the mind" that I discussed in chapter 2. Ou-yang and the poet Mei Yao-ch'en conceived of this term as a central part of textual interpretation and in particular of expressing the "inexhaustible meaning outside words" of a poem. This strand of Sung Ancient Civilization and literati aesthetics, combined with an interest very much like that of Su Shih in the role in self-cultivation of artistic practice, was what the Japanese Five Mountains Zen monks emphasized in their own interpretive theory of the landscape arts.

The writings of recluse poets reveal a close relationship between the natural world, traditions of protest, and the values of mainstream Chinese culture. The apparent rejection of human culture that underlay the return to the natural wilderness was accompanied by textual study in the literary tradition of Chinese recluses, a major component of the preservation and transmission of civilization. In one of the most important literary sources for Chinese eremiticism and the Five Mountains Japanese monks, T'ao Ch'ien's narrative poem "Return," we find that after T'ao fled government service he did not reject civilization completely, but "takes pleasure in books and zither."[16] In the Zen tradition, the transcendent playfulness of the recluse Han-shan also incorporates textual study. As is frequently noted in popular writings on Han-shan, he studied the classics of the recluse poetry tradition and such philosophical texts as the *Tao-te ching* and the *Chuang-tzu*. However, his poetry betrays familiarity with many other volumes such as the histories and the *Book of Songs*, as would be expected of the writings of any educated Chinese gentleman. As Han-shan himself remarked, in a statement that runs counter to the popular image of the recluse rejecting all the concerns of civilized society, "And in my house what do I have?/ Only a bed piled high with books."[17] Like T'ao Ch'ien, Han-shan did not turn away completely from civilization in his affirmation of life in the natural world, but continued to participate intellectually in the Chinese cultural tradition.

Indeed, we see the acceptance of the recluse tradition itself into the mainstream elite culture of China during the T'ang dynasty, in which there was a newly pervasive interest among high court officials in reclusion during the first half of the eighth century, most notably in the high esteem given the recluse poetry of Wang Wei. As Stephen Owen has pointed out, exile or reclusion was the only occasion in court poetry in which the violation or rejection of the conventional decorum of style and subject of the court tradition was acceptable. The poetry of reclusion was a poetry of questioning and dissatisfaction with the values of court society and literature, and thus came to serve as the vehicle for expressing of personal, lyrical vision found in the greatest of High T'ang poetry. The High T'ang poets found their model for such poetry in their image of the recluse poet T'ao Ch'ien, Owen indicates, which in its simplicity, seeming lack of technique and artifice, rebellious freedom, and transcendental joy was diametrically opposed to such court poetic values as refined artifice, obsequiousness, and social necessity.[18]

With the establishment in the court poetry tradition of a poetry of protest came the growth of what David Nivison calls "conventions of protest": accepted ways to protest and to transcend convention.[19] Through acceptance into court culture these conventional literary images, techniques, and forms of protest themselves became part of the institution they were protesting, the social institutions of the imperial court and the elite levels of the bureaucracy located in the capital. The values found by the aristocrat Wang Wei and other court poets in the poetry of T'ao Ch'ien served as their model for this movement within the carefully defined hierarchical distinctions of court culture and society. This court poetry was also a poetry of the natural world, however, and through this poetic tradition the image of the mountain landscape as transcendent to the mundane realm of court society became an important part of the court poetic tradition itself.

The mid-T'ang Zen poet Ch'iao-jan voiced sentiments in the same tradition but very closely comparable to those of the Japanese Five Mountains monks. He was following in the court poetic tradition, yet in his Zen training and socialization he surely worked to solve a similar dilemma to that of the Kitayama Japanese. In one poem, he writes:

> Seclude the mind, not the movements,
> Remain living in the world of man.
> Lack a tree? Plant a sapling.
> Without a mountain? Look at a picture.
> Living midst clamor I am not flustered;
> True meaning is found in this.[20]

For Ch'iao-jan peace of mind in the bustle of society was crucial, and through spiritual practice he was able to achieve such a state of mind. He shared with the Japanese Kitayama monks' tradition the view of landscape painting as something that can be a useful representation of the natural world when living far from any mountain retreat. Yet here we see no sign of any interest in the mind, as we find in the later Japanese Zen tradition.

In the Sung dynasty, a growing debate concerning forms of protest occurred fully within the mainstream Confucian tradition itself, a debate that runs counter to conventional descriptions of Confucianism as invariably affirming the Chinese social order. In the Ancient Civilization movement, which protested contemporary moral and cultural values through a return to the Way of the ancients, Ou-yang Hsiu recognized the withdrawal from society as a viable moral alternative.[21] The Confucian classics recognized conditions in which the potential conflict between inner moral values and the integrity of moral government service might lead to the refusal of government service, and there was a limited tradition of such protest within canonical texts.[22] Reclusion as a form of Confucian protest was structurally unlike Taoist and Buddhist reclusion, however, for it was a retreat and disengagement from society that maintained the symbolic order and hierarchical social values of the Confucian orthodoxy, protesting conventional government or morality but remaining within the Confucian social order. While the Confucian mode of protest may take the physical form of retreat or even exile into the natural world, it did not give up its fundamental orientation to religious and ethical life in human society. In contrast, the Taoist designation of the natural world as a model of the sacred for subjective experience established a position that negated fundamentally the moral, cultural, and religious values of structured human society.

In the writings of the Sung literati, we generally find a model of the sacred that does not have structural similarities to the Confucian model, as we might expect from their service in government. Instead, we find a very strong interest in the conceptions of the hermit at court that existed in Six Dynasties Taoist and High T'ang court poetic traditions. The Sung literati were interested in attaining an internal state modeled on the natural world, which was often based on a reading of the *Chuang-tzu* and other such texts, yet they still were most active in society and government. Evidence for this interest argues against any simplistic identification of the literati scholar-officials with Confucian thinking, and is one aspect of syncretic or even eclectic approaches they brought to their understanding of the moral, spiritual, and religious sense of their individual self and of their social roles.

One image of inner spiritual accomplishment modeled on the natural world that received wide acceptance in Sung literati and Kitayama Zen writings was the "hills and valleys" (*ch'iu-huo*) within the practitioner. Huang T'ing-chien, to take an important literatus and close friend of Su Shih, used this phrase and a related phrase "the single hill and valley" (*i-ch'iu i-huo*) to refer to the natural world in which the official enjoyed the pleasures of retirement.[23] In this passage he borrows the terms from the latter Han dynasty (25–220) historian Pan Ku (32–92):

> If one fishes with a line in a valley (*i-huo*),
> the myriad things of the world cannot corrupt this pleasure;
> if one rests for a while on a hill (*i-ch'iu*),
> the affairs of the empire cannot alter this pleasure.[24]

However, Huang employed this theme to describe the internal attitude that characterized expressions of the highest level of spiritual practice. Such views are found primarily in his artistic criticism, as in the following judgment of the artist of a figure painting, "One hill and one valley (*i-ch'iu i-huo*) must be present naturally in the breast."[25] This theme from Huang's writings on art became widely influential in continental artistic interpretation by the twelfth century not only among literati but also in Neo-Confucian and Zen circles and among professional painters, and remained popular at least into the seventeenth century. The Neo-Confucian moral and political philosopher Chu Hsi himself used this conception when he inscribed a painting by a close friend of Huang T'ing-chien and Su Shih, the literati painter and critic Mi Fu. Chu wrote, "These must be the exceptional scenes from the hills and valleys in this old man's breast, spewed forth at the time altogether to embody his true appreciation."[26] The term continues in popularity, as can be seen from its appearance again among Zen lay disciples in mid-twelfth-century inscriptions on the painting to be discussed below, *Dream Journey of the Hsiao and Hsiang*, painted for the Zen monk Yun-ku (d.u.).[27] Finally, the professional painter Yao Yen-ch'ing, whose work may have had some direct impact on the Kitayama Japanese monks, used the phrase, "Hills and Valleys in [my] Breast," to identify himself on two extant paintings other than his illustration of the scroll *Leisure Enough to Spare* inscribed by Yang Wei-chen discussed in chapter 1.[28] From this evidence we may conclude that an impressively wide array of groups in Southern Sung and Yüan China, including literati writers and critics, Neo-Confucian philosophers and moralists, Zen laymen, and professional painters, shared an interest in this phrase suggesting that landscape was best understood by internalizing "the hills and valleys" in one's breast.

The Kitayama monks assimilated this theme into their thinking about how landscape might be applied to their lives in the metropolitan Five Mountains monasteries. In a preface to a painting of a miniature tray landscape, Chūhō En'i indicated that the value of landscape was to be discovered in such artistic renderings as paintings and tray gardens that, despite their small size, "will still be enough to nourish the hills and valleys within."[29] Later in this preface Chūhō suggests why it is that this approach is important: "by nourishing [the hills and valleys] in your breast, you remain composed."[30] We shall see below how this practice of internalizing the landscape was applied by other Kitayama Zen monks to the concrete conditions of life in the Five Mountains monasteries.

More important for understanding Kitayama Japanese Zen Buddhist approach to landscape painting in the social context of their metropolitan temples was the theme of the "recluse at court." The Chinese ideal of the "hermit at court" first became influential in the late third and early fourth centuries, and centered on the reinterpretation of the concept of the recluse in the *Chuang-tzu*. Kuo Hsiang (d. 312), who with Wang Pi (226–49) was one of the important thinkers in the rise of this conception, reversed the praise in the *Chuang-tzu* for the man who left government service, and held up as his ideal individuals who no longer distinguished between the mundane world and the realm of transcendence.[31] Kuo Hsiang commented on a passage in the *Chuang-tzu* about a man who "embraces the ten-thousand things" by describing his own sagely ideal: "Although the sage is in the midst of government, his mind seems to be in the mountain forest. . . . His abode is in the myriad things, but it does not mean that he does not wander freely."[32] The notion of a sage active in government and yet transcending the conditioned world to wander freely about the cosmos was also influential in the writings of Wang K'ang-chu (fl. c. fourth century) and Hsieh K'un (280–322), the former arguing that the ability to combine government service with transcendental freedom was a more profound achievement than that of a life of seclusion.[33] These new developments in conceptions of reclusion took place in turbulent political conditions following the fall of the Han, when, although the Confucian orthodoxy of the Han had crumbled, the risk of leaving government (in a Taoist mode of protest and transcendence of the social order) potentially involved the loss of one's life. These conditions encouraged a rethinking of reclusion, and of the relation of spiritual needs to more tangible circumstances of the day.

In Buddhist terms the tradition of "in the world but not of the world," to use Eric Zürcher's description of this period, is associated with the teachings of the *Vimalakīrti Sutra*. Zürcher contrasted this conception of the relation of social order to Buddhist insight with that of Hui-yüan, who was widely known for his careful distinction between the world of political affairs and the reclusive realm of the Buddhist *saṅgha* or monastic community.[34] In the struggle for the independence of the *saṅgha* from direct political control, Hui-yüan legitimated the Buddhist monastic institution by utilizing the traditional ideal of the retired official and its associated rejection of or independence from the established political order. The symbol of this political neutrality was the Tiger Ravine, which Hui-yüan refused to cross, indicating his separation from the mundane world and his conception of the Buddhist *saṅgha* as beyond the world.[35] This theme in Buddhist history was of considerable interest to the Kitayama Japanese Five Mountains Zen monks, for the Five Mountains temple system had been administered by the Ashikaga shogunate until 1379, when effective control was turned over to Shun'oku Myōha.[36]

However, Hui-yüan came to be known in later centuries and in Muromachi Japan not as the protector of the boundary between the sacred and the mundane, but as the individual capable of deriving great enjoyment from crossing that very boundary. By the Northern Sung the legend of the Three Laughers of Tiger Ravine had gained wide acceptance,[37] but in this legend Hui-yüan with his recluse companions "forgetfully" crosses the bridge of the Tiger Ravine marking the boundary of sacred and profane or, in political terms, the neutral and the politically engaged. In response, however, the legend tells us, the three of them all burst out laughing, and here we see the classical elements of the Buddhist theme of playful nonduality to be discussed in the final chapter.

Crossing the boundary of the sacred and the profane was for these sages very much a laughing matter, something that transformed the all too serious distinctions in the world of religious and political institutions into a matter of the playfulness of nonduality. Hui-yüan here violated conventional Confucian and also Taoist distinctions of sacred and profane, structural differences that were so important to Hui-yüan as the leader of the institution of the Buddhist *saṅgha* in its relations with other institutions of the mundane world. The playful transcendence of dualistic conceptions seen in the Three Laughers legend is much more than "mere play," however, for it derives a seriousness of the highest order from the symbolic and textual traditions of Taoist transcendence and the nondualism of the Buddhist philosophy of emptiness. The lifestyle of the "hermit at court" provided one means by which the transcendent purity of the landscape could be integrated into the highly structured life of medieval Chinese civilization.

This theme played only a minor role in much of medieval Chinese culture, but grew in importance with the fall first of northern China to the Jurchen at the end of the Northern Sung dynasty, and the subsequent conquest of the entire empire by the Mongols. With these developments Han Chinese officials were faced with the new and difficult question of whether or not to serve in the government of a non-Chinese people. One of the most important responses to this dilemma for the purposes of this study, and one that was influential in Kitayama Japan, was the well-known case of Chao Meng-fu. As a member of the Sung imperial family, Chao was naturally expected to refuse to serve in the government of a dynasty that had overthrown that of his own family. After being summoned to the Mongol court, however, he agreed to serve, claiming that if he did not, the survival of Chinese culture would be threatened. Chao received much criticism for his willingness to serve under the Mongols, criticism that was particularly harsh in later dynasties, and Chao seemed to have felt the need to affirm his sense of morality during his own lifetime. His attitude toward this decision is expressed in a eulogy for an unknown friend:

> In order to feel content in your own mind remain unperturbed, without desire for riches and glory, and your neighbors will praise your goodness. This is what "reputation" means. Why must one seclude himself in craggy caves, conceal his footsteps in forest and mountain, in order to achieve purity?[38]

Chao also completed a painting that explained his means of maintaining spiritual purity while serving at the Mongol court, a figure painting, now in the Elliott collection at Princeton University, that depicts in an archaic landscape setting the Six Dynasties recluse Hsieh K'un discussed above.[39] While Chao did not write an inscription on the painting to explain his thinking on this issue, we can gather the significance of the painting for Chao's situation from inscriptions by several friends and literary companions of Chao, as well as by a number of later scholars.

The most important inscription for understanding Yüan interpretations of the "recluse at court" theme is one written by Wang Ch'i (fl. c. 1290–1310), a scholar-poet who may have also been friends with Chao. Like the colophon by Chao's longtime close friend, Yao Shih (d. c. 1318), Wang Ch'i emphasized the parallel between Chao and the high-ranking fourth-century official Hsieh K'un, who is the overt subject of the painting. Hsieh K'un, as I mentioned above, was one of the early pioneers of the "recluse at court" lifestyle in the government of the Eastern Tsin dynasty, and this is the parallel that Wang made in his inscription:

> When Ku [K'ai-chih] [c. 343–406] painted Hsieh [K'un's] portrait, he positioned him among crags and rocks. People asked him the reason, and he replied, "[Hsieh K'un] himself claimed that his 'single hill' (*i-ch'iu*) and 'single valley' (*i-huo*) were superior [to another minister's]; therefore this gentleman should be placed among hills and valleys." When contemplating his excellence in purity and elegance, it deserves to be admired, but he could also remain faithful as a minister. . . . Several hundred years later, it is the old genleman of the Snowy Pine Studio

> [Chao Meng-fu] whose mind understood and whose spirit communed (*hsin-ling shen-hui*) with [Hsieh's].[40]

As Wang noted, Chao's painting followed that of Ku K'ai-chih in depicting Hsieh K'un as seated in the midst of a natural landscape, which Chao has painted in the archaic blue and green style. Wang utilized the theme of internalized hills and valleys to apply the landscape setting directly to the government official, such as Chao Meng-fu, who works to maintain his inner purity under difficult circumstances.

Other colophons on this painting written by his immediate contemporaries, and by the important painter Ni Tsan and other scholars of the mid- and late fourteenth century, show a sympathy and understanding of Chao's response to the call to government office. For them, as for Chao Meng-fu, the spiritual purity associated with the landscape could be preserved even while serving in government office. Unlike scholar-officials of earler centuries who undertook government service in the Confucian mode, conditions under the rule of a foreign people and Chao's own peculiar situation as a member of the Sung imperial family combined to make government service something that had to be justified. It was perhaps these circumstances that led Chao's contemporaries to develop this rationale for Chao's holding public office not based on the traditional Confucian model, but grounded in conceptions of purity associated with the natural landscape. The importance of the natural landscape for spiritual practice even while serving in goverment became an important model for the Kitayama Zen monks.

Ishō Tokugan takes up Chao Meng-fu's willingness to serve as a positive ideal for his contemporaries in a preface on a no longer extant painting attributed to Chao Meng-fu. Ishō justifies Chao Meng-fu's willingness to serve in government through the virtue of his textual and artistic study, which he identified with that of the early sage of recluse poety, T'ao Ch'ien. In this preface, Ishō began by summarizing the value of such study in terms typical of Sung Chinese advocates of the Ancient Civilization movement:

> When the ancients amused themselves in the arts,[41] their long accumulated study was manifested when they encountered a suitable situation. [These practices] were as far apart from unfounded tales[42] and untested skills as the earth from the sky, and [the arts of the ancients] move people deeply, as they should.[43]

In his preface Ishō then identifies the "appropriate circumstances" of his own prose expression, in which a friend of his had taken the name for his study "Splendid Evening" from T'ao Ch'ien's poem "On Drinking Wine," for which he was to inscribe a preface to a scroll that numerous visitors had already praised in poems.

The T'ao Ch'ien poem is most appropriate for understanding the Japanese Five Mountains monks, for it provides an early and very widely admired discussion of the ability to be in reclusion even when surrounded by a busy environment:

> I built my hut in a place where people live,
> and yet there's no clatter of carriage or horse.
> You ask me how that could be?
> With a mind remote, the region too grows distant.
> I pick chrysanthemums by the eastern hedge,
> see the southern mountain, calm and still.
> The mountain is splendid in the evening,
> birds on the wing coming home together.
> In all this there's some principle of truth,
> but try to define it and you forget the words.[44]

Ishō here defined the "Splendid Evening" not just in terms of T'ao Ch'ien's life, particularly his House of the Five Willows residence where T'ao was known to have spent his time reading books, but also as an image appropriate to the Japanese Five Mountains monks: "Thus what is called 'Splendid Evening' is here, and not in the mountains."[45] In this way T'ao Ch'ien's poems were applied by the Japanese Kitayama Zen monks to the life in the Five Mountains monasteries, in a manner similar to the role T'ao's poems took in the recluse poetry of T'ang Chinese court poets such as Wang Wei.[46] The popularity of T'ao Ch'ien among the Kitayama Five Mountains monks can be seen not only in their poetry collections but also in extant paintings, including one inscribed by Ishō (fig. 4.1).

Ishō continues in this preface his application of the T'ao Ch'ien image to life in the Five Mountains temples by turning to discuss Chao Meng-fu, who, though he left retirement and took up high government office, was someone who could live the life of reclusion as depicted in T'ao's poem:

> Even though their going out [to take office] and staying in [retirement] differ, still they could be called members of the "Splendid Evening" circle. They all accumulated [study] for long and after encountering a suitable situation then manifested themselves in poetry or painting, and did not express [themselves] in confusion and empty error. [Even now], many centuries afterwards, people put their trust in them and still discuss them. How admirable they are![47]

It is significant that Ishō's argument for the fundamental identity in values of these two influential Chinese individuals is based on their common interest in study and the expression of the fruits of their study in the arts. Through this study, then, people like Chao Meng-fu were able to express themselves in the arts without falling into error, and so could achieve the high spiritual status of the recluse T'ao Ch'ien even while holding official office. Moreover, this theme is developed in terms of a poem that emphasized the ability of the mind to allow an individual to attain the state of reclusion in a busy, otherwise distracting or troubling environment, the "hermit at court" theme. Finally, as we saw, Ishō explicitly

Fig. 4.1. *T'ao Ch'ien Appreciating Chrysanthemums.* Inscription by Ishō Tokugan (d. 1437). Hanging scroll. Ink and light color on paper. 93.7 x 24.4 cm. Important Cultural Property. 1425. Umezawa Kinenkan, Tokyo.

applied this spiritual ideal to his own life in the Five Mountains monasteries. Like Chinese literati who felt that moral conditions made it difficult to serve in government, many of the Kitayama Japanese Five Mountains monks felt that in living in the capital they were living in the world of deluded sentient beings, thus transforming the capital or regional centers into places of religious practice.

Yet there was certainly not uniform agreement that the ideal of the "hermit at court" was the pinnacle of life in the Japanese Five Mountains monasteries, for on certain social occasions and in certain strands of Five Mountains Zen thought there remained deeply entrenched the longing to leave the busy world of the capital and retreat into the forest. We see such views in the poetic inscriptions on a number of extant poem-and-painting scrolls produced on social occasions of parting, as mentioned in chapter 2. In the inscriptions to such extant paintings as *Distant Thoughts across Rivers and Skies* or *Blue Mountains and White Clouds*, for example, many of the monks longed for the transcendent freedom of life outside the capital. However, even on such social occasions, this view is contradicted by the most prominent monks in the group of inscribers, such as Daigaku Shūsū, who return to the theme of the recluse living contentedly in the city.[48]

Gidō Shūshin referred frequently to the theme "hermit at court" and closely related themes like the "hermit in the marketplace" or the "hermit in the city." For example, Gidō described his own residence at his retreat in the busy headquarters of the Musō lineage, Rinsen-ji, not far west of the imperial palace as "secluded in a corner of the city" (*in ch'eng-wei*).[49] Gidō also developed this theme in a prose preface to a poem scroll compiled at the request in 1380 of the military commander, renowned poet, and later monk Imagawa Ryōshun (also Tokiyo, 1326–1420), who had been a student in *waka* and the linked-verse poetry of Nijō Yoshimoto and was teacher in the early 1400s to the important poet Shōtetsu. After Ryōshun suggested this topic from his distant appointment in the southern island of Kyushu, the shogun Ashikaga Yoshimitsu himself became actively involved in completion of this scroll, which included poems in Chinese by over one hundred Five Mountains monks, whose contributions were coordinated by Shun'oku Myōha, and by a large number of *waka* poems in Japanese by court poets composed at a series of poetry meetings, coordinated by Yoshimitsu and hosted by prominent court poets. In composing the preface to this enormous project, which Gidō had guided to completion, Gidō defined his own role as the "hermit at court" (*shih-yin*) a significant role to take in the political context of this cultural object.[50] The political meaning of Gidō's interpretive reading of this important and grand-scale production can be discerned from the powerful position which Ryōshun had established for himself in 1380, when as *tandai* of the Dazaifu area in northern Kyushu near to the Korean peninsula, he effectively controlled Japan's foreign policy.[51] Yoshimitsu was of course interested in bringing relations with the continent under his direct control, and when Ryōshun's protector, Hosokawa Yoriyuki (1329–92), was toppled in 1379, Ryōshun's independence was weakened. The poem scroll would have been one way for Yoshimitsu in the next year through cultural interaction to improve his relations with the learned Ryōshun. In the midst of these highly charged political conditions, Gidō presents himself in the preface in the tradition of Buddhist monks such as Hui-yüan, whom Gidō admired greatly, as an independent if not neutral player in the cultural politics of the day.[52]

In inscriptions to a no longer extant poetry scroll and landscape painting entitled *White Clouds and Cinnabar Canyons*, Gidō further develops the Zen Buddhist implications of reclusion in the capital. The title of the scroll was given by his friend Ichū Tsūjo (d. 1429)[53] to a study located in the Eigen'an subtemple to the major Five Mountains temple, Kennin-ji. Ichū was borrowing this name for his own residence from the important Sung dynasty Zen monk Ch'i-sung (1007–72), known for his propagation of the Unity of the Three Teachings, who had in admiration inscribed this name on the residence of the influential Six Dynasties Buddhist master Hui-yüan. In this way Ichū alludes to a history of Buddhist teachers known, as were both Ch'i-sung and Hui-yüan, for their willingness to work intellectually and socially with non-Buddhist social elites, and explicitly links his social role with that of the independent-minded Hui-yüan.

Gidō develops his own interpretation of the significance of this tradition, and of Ichū's residence, through exploring the phrase "White Clouds and Cinnabar Canyons" in the following fashion:

> The Higashiyama monk, Master Ichū Tsūjo, named the room where he lives "White Clouds and Cinnabar Canyons." In my view, he chose "clouds" for the going and stopping of no-mind (*wu-hsin*), and "canyons" for their emptiness and consequent skill at response. As for a man of the Way, if inwardly he is of no-mind, and outwardly he responds through emptiness, then he's alright wherever he is.[54]

Gidō uses the classic Zen practice of "no-mind" (*wu-hsin*) here to understand the clouds, and the fundamental Mahayana Buddhist ontology of emptiness to understand the "response" of an echoing canyon. If a practitioner has achieved this difficult level of practice, Gidō asserts, then such a monk may practice in whatever environment he might find himself, whether in the capital or in the mountains, alone or in the midst of complex social relations.

The implications of this hut's significance for understanding Kitayama Five Mountains Zen are explained by Gidō as he concludes the preface with a poem:

> White clouds and cinnabar canyons, abode of the man of the Way;
> Forested mountains are not always far from the world of man.
> Going and stopping like the clouds, originally without ties;
> Body and mind like the canyons, naturally empty.
> Hui-yüan's Lotus Society: an autumn windblown eve;
> Venerable Ta-mei Ch'ang's pine flower: a rainy night's surplus.

If you can only take these ideas and make them one:
In the human world, where could you not make your home?[55]

Gidō demonstrates his literary skill here by weaving simple yet graceful poetic images together with philosophical concepts and allusions to Chinese Buddhist history. He underlines through his choice of allusions the complexities of relations between Buddhist monks and sociopolitical elites. Hui-yüan was known for having formed close relationships with monks and laity, including poets and powerful officials, and his Lotus Society meetings on Mt. Lu were a renowned example of such gatherings.[56] Ta-mei Fa-ch'ang (752–839) was a disciple of the extremely influential Ma-tsu Tao-i who wrote a well-known pine flower poem when he was summoned by a high government official.[57] By integrating these allusions with the Buddhist ideal of emptiness, Gidō reminds his readers of their responsibility to continue their Zen practice even when they find themselves in "the human world." He began and concluded with reminders of the closeness of social centers to mountain retreats, rhetorically suggesting with "Where in human society can we not make our hut?" that there is no place where a Zen monk may not be active in his or her practice. Just as for the Chinese followers of the "hermit at court" lifestyle, the Japanese monks saw the internalized appreciation of the landscape to be central to their preservation of spiritual purity while active in the mundane world of the capital.

We find another argument for the "hermit at court" ideal in a preface by Taihaku Shingen on a no longer extant painting entitled *A Place Surrounded by Screens of Verdure*. In this preface Taihaku described his friend Murō Yūshō's response to being directly criticized by a guest as "stealing the name of a recluse" for living in the capital while identifying his study with such a name as "Screens of Verdure" more appropriate for a mountain retreat. As the critical visitor noted,

> How poor is this dwelling's name. Now the "mountain" is indeed close, but if it is not something you possess, how can you call it "Screens"? Outside your gate there are the jewelled halls of the aristocrats, strollers wandering over the Fifth Ward bridge, and the dust from the carts and the tracks of the horses in confused array. And to the left and right villagers' gates cover the ground while here a pavilion and there a tower, their halcyon [curved eaves like] winged birds soaring high, so numerous they cannot be counted. So you should not take this as the residence of a man of the mountains. Now as I see it, are you not stealing the name of a recluse?[58]

This charge not only questioned Murō's individual morality, it also attacked the fundamental basis of the Kitayama monks' application of the landscape to life in the Five Mountains monasteries. Taihaku tells us in his preface that Murō replied:

> "What you see are only its traces; what I have just named is only its mind. Whether taking a short cut to South Mountain [as did Lu Ts'ang-

yung][59] or coveting a hermit's headband on North Mountain [as did Kung Chi-kuei],[60] these are traces. And both the 'a gate [busy as] the market-place but a mind [pure as] water' of Yeh Sung's [Tsu-yu's] [d.u.] seclusion[61] and the 'living in the city but naming it a mountain' of Shen Tso-pin's [active c. 1200] reclusion[62] are the mind. Why do you neglect my mind and only take up my traces?

"I was born in Shin[ano],[63] grew up in the central country,[64] and then wandered to west of the barrier for study.[65] The wanderings of my blue straw sandals and wisteria staff reached nearly two thousand miles, and the blue peaks and cinnabar canyons, the smoky trees and misty forests now dwell in my eyes, and all are mine to possess. I have attained them in the mind and externalized them as traces; still more tiny Kiyomizu! Where is there any stealing?

"These mica clouds and shining stones, kingfishers[66] and peacocks, marvel upon marvel. [But they are] merely to be used to surround the palatial banquet and to be displayed at an elegant party, and I have nothing to do with such things. Again, where is the coveting? [There is] only what the mind has attained, taking from the creator's inexhaustible treasury without prohibition, just these halcyon screens."[67]

In his response Murō makes a typically Chinese Zen distinction between the mind, assumed to be innately enlightened, and traces, which are the effects of activity not grounded in a fully developed realization of our innate nature. However, he adds to this Zen distinction various allusions to the Chinese classical histories, including two examples of the "hermit at court." But then Murō turns to the concrete personal details of an autobiographical narrative, explaining how in his own life he has achieved the "hermit at court" ideal.

According to Taihaku's preface, Murō then asserts the importance of the mind in this achievement through an important modification in lines from one of the most famous of Chinese poems by Su Shih, the Sung poet so admired by the Kitayama monks, the first Red Cliff Ode. The relevant lines from Su's poem read:

What is there to be envious about? Moreover, everthing in the world has its owner, and if a thing doesn't belong to us, we don't dare take a hair of it. Only the clear breeze over the river, or the bright moon between the hills, which our ears hear as music, our eyes see beauty in—these we may take without prohibition, these we may make free with and they will never be used up. These are the endless treasures of the Creator, here for you and me to enjoy together.[68]

Murō changes Su's emphasis, however, by changing the line where Shih highlights the aural and visual sensory appreciation of the beautiful scenery, to underline that this is what "the mind achieved" (*hsin chih so-te*). It is fairly certain that Murō's changes would have been noticed by many of his educated readers, since Su's ode was included in the late Sung or Yüan literary collection *Ku-wen Chen-pao*, which was widely read and studied in Kitayama society.[69]

In an important passage describing how a state of mind appropriate to Zen is maintained, Taihaku then records Murō's description of exactly how landscape paintings were used by Five Mountains Zen monks in their temples, subtemples, and private studies:

> During free time from the meditation mat, when I sit silently under the eaves, the evening sun lights up half the peaks and the rich halcyon [mountains] are lined up [like] screens, [so that] the mountains of Shin[ano] and the clouds of the barrier [pass] become screen paintings and surround my desk. I do not realize I am near the jewelled halls and the Fifth [Avenue] bridge, and the dust of the carts and horses and the myriad pavilions and towers are all at once annihilated, and do not become afflictions of the eye or ear. If there were something to separate me from [my surroundings], it would be my screens of verdure.[70]

Murō shows his readers why it was that he modified the Su passage here, for he ends with a typically Buddhistic warning against the sensory causes of delusion and suffering. In this idyllic passage we can also see in our mind's eye just how Murō, Taihaku, and their contemporary Five Mountains monks appreciated the landscape paintings. By surrounding his desk with paintings he can enjoy the purity and spiritually uplifting qualities of nature while actually living in the midst of the deluded world right along the largest thoroughfares of the Japanese capital.

In Taihaku's record of this exchange between Murō and his critic, we find the same argument for the life of the Japanese Rinzai monks as a life of the "hermit at court" that Taihaku made in his preface to *Small Cottage by a Mountain Stream.* Here as before Taihaku and his friend Murō interpreted this theme in terms of a theory of the mind.[71] Through this development the Japanese monks took the image of the hermit and rewrote it in a direction different from that which was most common in Sung and Yüan China literati culture, molding it to their own Zen Buddhist ideals and practice. We can see from Taihaku's use of "attaining in the mind" in this preface and also in his preface to the *Small Cottage by a Mountain Stream*, that the mind was the central focus for his conception of landscape. The eclectic Japanese monks used these and other conceptions of the mind in adapting the associations of spiritual purity with the natural landscape to their own lives as Zen Buddhists in the Five Mountains temples.

Chapter 5

Buddhist Illusion and the Landscape Arts

Truths are illusions that we have forgotten are illusions.
—Friedrich Nietzsche

Practice illusion by means of illusion.
—*The Perfect Enlightenment Sutra*

While the Kitayama Zen views of landscape paintings we have surveyed were grounded in the venerable Chinese Mahayana and Zen Buddhist traditions, they also developed their own distinctive vision of the landscape arts. Chinese Zen monks and nuns had modified classical Indian and Chinese Buddhist ontology to emphasize the two premises of the illusory, ultimately empty character of reality and the nondualistic interplay of the realms of samsaric suffering and the enlightened bliss of nirvana.[1] The Kitayama Five Mountains monks applied these premises to artistic creation and interpretation through such canonical Buddhist terms describing meditative states as "the samadhi of [seeing that all is] like an illusion" (C. *ju-huan san-mei*; J. *nyogen zammai*), and "the samadhi of playfulness" (C. *yu-ge san mei*; J. *yuge zammai*). In this and the final chapter we explore the central role played by these two Buddhist themes in the Kitayama religio-aesthetic vision of the landscape arts: Mahayana ontological and heuristic theories of illusion; and a mode of Zen enlightened activity characterized by unimpeded playfulness. It was through syncretic integration of these Buddhist theories of reality and of artistic interpretation with both Chinese painting theory and Taoist and other conceptions of landscape that the Japanese Zen monks developed their reading of landscape art.

The two themes of illusion and playfulness have a similar heuristic function in Buddhist thought. This can be seen in that they, to borrow from Robert Gimello's characterization of another Chinese Mahayana Buddhist school, "are so defined as to actually 'disarm' themselves, as they are being used, of the snares of craving and delusion with which conventional concepts are equipped."[2] Both illusion and playfulness entail an intrinsic sense of movement and transformation that erodes or breaks by means of disjunction and juxtaposition the rigid, clinging grasp of attachment and the rigid bifurcations of deluded, discriminatory thinking. In a similar maneuver both themes also destroy metaphorically the possibility of any settling into a fixed conception of what they themselves mean, since they "offer no sedative dwelling place for the mind," and instead propel the mind onward toward liberation.[3] As we shall see shortly, the notion of "not abiding" is a fundamental one in the Kitayama Zen conception of illusion, one that they borrowed from the important Yüan Zen monk Chung-feng Ming-pen and adapted to landscape painting interpretation. In these ways the Kitayama Japanese monks used two notions that in much of Chinese intellectual history were marginalized and negative, and gave them positive valorization through their theories of cultural interpretation at the center of Kitayama society and politics.

Gidō Shūshin elaborates the significance of the illusory aspect of landscape gardens and paintings in an exchange with three fellow Five Mountains monks sometime around the year 1382. We can see from the nature of their interaction how important some form or another of landscape art is to Gidō's life. Because of the importance of this passage for our discussion, titled simply "Preface to Landscape Poems and Painting," for the coming discussion, I quote it at length:

> I retired to live in the cottage of Great Compassion.[4] In the winter of that year [1382 or 1383], the eleventh month, hoeing by hand the abandoned fields, in a newly built humble dwelling, so to attempt a quiet retirement. I then spent my days enjoying these things. One day I had as a guest the venerable Kōdō. In a samadhi of playfulness (*yuge zammai*) he skillfully built an artificial mountain for me in a tiny space under the eastern eaves, conjuring up the appearance of a thousand precipices and ten thousand canyons.
>
> At that time I noticed two monks coming through the new gate. When I greeted them on the pathway, they were two monks, friends of the Way from the western mountains, Gichū Shō [d.u.] and Kaichū Mo [d.u.]. I led them in to relax in the Pavilion of the Southern [Plum] Branches. After taking our seats, Kaichū brought out a scroll from his sleeve. When he spread it out before me, it was a recent painting of a small scene of mountains and valleys. Above the painting were three inscriptions, and after it were songs (*ke*) by a few more people. All of them were "outstanding people"[5] of the Zen forest known among their contemporaries for their high character and superior writing.
>
> . . . Kaichū had specially set aside a space to the right of the painting, and bid me to write a preface, so I wrote the following: "In general when something is plentiful, then people hold it lightly; when something is scarce, then people treasure it. This is how human sentiment always is. Now I have secluded myself in a corner of the capital and forested canyons are scarce; here I have a temporary dwelling which I value highly: Is this not the same thing? With Kaichū, this is not so. His home

> is in the mountains, and forested springs are plentiful. Now, his eyes are filled by evening vapors freshening the greenery and his ears are satiated by the voices of mountain streams. Furthermore, hundreds of valleys and thousands of caves, and the smokey clouds and grasses and trees appear vague and misty, tempering his vision and hearing: All this is [too plentiful] to describe, yet for Kaichu it is insufficient. Pettily, he had this short scroll painted and these inscriptions written out, taking this as highly valuable. But why?"
>
> At this Kaichū laughed and said, "Have you not read that Master K'ung of Tung-shan [Hsueh-feng Hui-k'ung][6] said, "Truly looking at these valleys and mountains resembles a dream, so on the contrary you should take ink and water and sketch the streams and mountains." I then wrote this preface to thank the two Chus for their good will.[7]

In this passage Gidō characterizes as illusory both the acts of making what seems to have been a small garden and a landscape painting. In the first instance, the small garden is described as having been "conjured up," literally "produced in an illusory manner" (C. *huan-ch'u*; J. *genshutsu*), by his friend Kōdō while in the important Buddhist mental state of the "samādhi of playfulness."[8] We shall see below that this term was applied in the Five Mountains monasteries not only to landscape paintings but also to other subjects, most typically the *chinzō* portrait.

Moreover, Gidō also utilizes a key Mahayana Buddhist term to give the mountains in the garden a status I have here translated as "artificial." The term *saṃvṛti* in Sanskrit is taken from Buddhist ontological theory and often translated as "provisional," "worldly," or "conventional." In a philosophical context it indicates the transitory, causally produced, and ultimately unreal character of the mundane world as conventionally understood, and is generally contrasted with the terms "emptiness" or "ultimate," which designate reality as viewed from the standpoint of the ultimate.[9] Different schools disagree on the relative importance and the ultimate relationship between these two epistemological perspectives, but Gidō and, as we shall soon see, Chūhō seem to adopt a position close to that of the well-known Tendai (C. T'ien-t'ai) triad of emptiness, provisional existence, and the middle way, in which all three visions of reality have equal value and interpenetrate each other.

The propagation by Japanese Five Mountains Zen monks of this strand in Mahayana Buddhist ontology is typical of the mainstream continental Zen schools of the T'ang and later as well as of other Japanese Zen traditions. We find similar ideas in the earliest texts associated with Zen, as well as in the school of Ma-tsu Tao-i, which would come to dominate T'ang and later Chinese Zen.[10]

When applied to the landscape arts, as it was in the circle of Gidō's Five Mountains Zen contemporaries, "artificial" had become a conventional term for hills in an artificial garden, as in the twentieth-century Zen rock garden. Gidō's close friend Tesshū Tokusai, for example, had entitled a poem "Artificial Landscape" describing a miniature rock garden comparable in size perhaps to the twentieth-century *bonsai*. What intrigues Tesshū, as it does Gidō, is the viewer's surprise at finding an expansive scene in such a tiny space: "Who would believe that inside this jar there would be heaven?"[11] The Buddhist significance of this question of scale is found by Gidō and Tesshū in the changeability of even that which might seem the most solid and reliable: the massive, rocky expanse of the natural landscape. Here we encounter the fundamental Buddhist conception of the transitory nature of all reality underlying much early Theravāda as well as later Mahayana and Vajrayāna ontology, epistemology, and psychology.

Yet Gidō saves his most complex discussion of the illusory character of the landscape arts to an exchange with one of the monks who have brought a painting by his retreat. In this exchange we can see the informal nature of much of Five Mountains Zen literature and Gidō's humility in his willingness to record the somewhat peevish response he gives to his friend Kaichū's painting. In his educated reply, Kaichū laughed and reminded Gidō of the verse by Hsüeh-feng Hui-k'ung (fl. after c. 1153), which reads in its entirety:

> All alone, in any place,
> one can achieve simplicity:
> An old man on verdant cliffs
> among layered peaks.
> Truly the view of these streams and mountains
> resembles a dream,
> So on the contrary you should take ink and water
> and sketch the streams and mountains.[12]

In this exchange we also get a sense of the playful quality of Kaichū's remark from his reference to a poem by a monk whose poetry collection Gidō lectured on repeatedly, and whose popularity indicates that their contemporaries seem to have known quite well.[13] Yet Gidō readily acknowledges the serious Buddhist point: rivers and valleys themselves are dreamlike, suggesting that so is the distance between them and Gidō's retreat, about which Gidō had just complained that the forested canyons were so scarce. In such a Buddhist vision of the world, there can be little distinction between the sacred realm of the natural world and that of human civilization, such as we might find in many Taoist texts and in the often Taoist-influenced writings of the Sung and Yüan literati.

Gidō's guest makes a final point through his reference to Hsüeh-feng's poem, suggesting that precisely because the natural landscape is illusory art is the most appropriate medium in which to view it. The view shared by Gidō's guest and the Sung Zen monk Hsüeh-feng of the appropriateness of art for representing illusory reality seems to recur through the broad history of Zen aesthetics. We find, just to take one important Japanese example, comparable views on art other than landscape subjects held by Dōgen, who has been so influential in twentieth-century philosophy and thinking about Zen art. In a chapter from his magnum opus, *Shōbōgenzō*, entitled "Explaining a Dream in a Dream," Dōgen commented on the equivalence in truth value and in ontological weight of dream and awakening, and went on in other chapters to apply this logic to such phrases on the power of art as "Only a painted rice cake can satiate hunger."[14] We might say, then, that Gidō and his guest's views on the religious significance of landscape art participate in a Zen tradition of reading art as ideally suited for the representation of the changeable, illusory aspects of conventional reality.

Another aspect of the Gidō preface with which we began is the topic of miniature landscape gardens, which were a popular topic in Five Mountains literature. The Kitayama Zen monks frequently wrote prose prefaces on this topic even to each other, for we have one such document written by Ishō Tokugan for Taihaku Shingen.[15]

Chūhō En'i held a similar conception of landscape painting, as found in an inscription on a no longer extant painting, "Preface to a Painting Scroll of a Tray Landscape," which likewise combines a miniature landscape garden with the art of painting. Again I translate the full passage:

> The venerable Kengai ko [d.u.],[16] the head monk in the meditation hall of the eastern mountains, brought a painting scroll of a mountain on a tray, showed it [to me], and then asked me to inscribe a few lines. I replied, "You build a mountain before your stairs so you will never tire of viewing its blues and greens. You dig a pond in the front of the garden so you will always be able to wash in its ripples.[17] Even if what you toy with is small, it will still be enough to nourish the hills and valleys within.[18]
>
> "If we compare this to living in the realm of the natural landscape, where you don't know which things should be the most outstanding, it is as far apart as heaven from earth. Now moving the landscape to your garden stairs is already artificial, still more if you give form to a garden on a tray, and still more if you sketch the tray [landscape] in a painting, increasing unendurably its artificiality. However, by nourishing [the hills and valleys] in your breast you remain composed and contemplating this from the perspective of its artificiality, then it is loftier than the Sung and Hua mountains[19] and flows as wide as [all] the rivers and lakes, always making dust fly and streams trickle. Or if you contemplate this from the perspective of its reality, then you can move Mt. Sumeru onto the tip of a tiny autumn hair or place Ch'uang-wang-ch'a[20] on a tray. Its [the painting's] unmoving form and baseless dimensions[21] on its own do not increase or decrease.[22] When self and other (*wu-wo*) have dissolved and the real and artificial (*chen-chia*) have vanished, then I will have already forgotten my words about them."[23]

Kengai clapped his hands and said, "You have argued well, venerable one! Please use this to write a preface."[24]

Chūhō and his friend Kengai here playfully build on a conception of art as illusory to compound the unreality of art threefold, adding layer upon layer of artistic illusion onto the landscape subject until the artificiality and unreality of the subject "becomes unbearable."

Seen from the perspective of reality these art objects are clearly paradoxical in conventional terms, with the largest object in the Buddhist physical universe, Mt. Sumeru, fitting onto the tip of the conventional image of the smallest object in the Chinese literary tradition, the autumn hair. Seen in terms of artificiality, however, the painting also appears to have broken the bonds of common sense, for how can a painting of a small, artificial landscape be larger and wider than the greatest mountains and rivers in the world? Chūhō pointed out that these apparent paradoxes are not simple conundrums, but have a clear pedagogical purport: they are visions of the painting grounded in the ideal Buddhist standpoint, a standpoint which Chūhō defined as "when true and artificial have vanished." In this state of mind, he noted, self and other have dissolved, and questions of scale and movement have on their own ceased to be important.

Chūhō, like Gidō in the passage above, used the Buddhist term that I have again translated as "artificial" to suggest the religious significance of the artistic creation of the various landscape gardens. As discussed above, this term was used in Mahayana ontology to refer to reality viewed from the conventional or mundane perspective: appearing to exist in a net of causal relations and hence only provisionally or temporarily. Chūhō's usage is close to Buddhist conceptions of the world as illusory or evanescent, which understand views that the world exists primarily as deluded and misleading in that they cause attachment and suffering. Here I have translated it with "artificial" in an attempt to suggest Chūhō's double meaning in this passage of human artifice as both produced through human effort and unreal or impermanent.

This notion of "artifice" or "fiction" had a long history in Chinese and Japanese thought, of course, but in much of this history it was given a quite negative valuation. In much Chinese philosophy and artistic theory, for example, fiction and things that appear dreamlike are rejected because they seem to question morality and standards of truth. Even in the early Zen tradition illusions are equated with dust, which may obfuscate the practitioner's innate Buddha Nature and so become an obstacle to correct understanding.[25] This tradition is carried on by the T'ang poet Han-shan, who, in a critique of a Buddhist canonical master, writes:

Fools all shower him with praise,
While wise men clap their hands in mirth,
This hoax! The phantom flowers in the air!
How could he escape from birth and death![26]

A similar strand may be found in early Japanese Zen Buddhist thought, where being "like an illusion" is used in attacking the views of teaching schools.[27] Yet the Kitayama monks were not alone in their positive affirmation of illusion and transformation, for this interpretive tradition also may be found in Zen Buddhist intellectual history; indeed, we have already seen how Dōgen found useful images pointing to the illusory character of reality, such as "a stone woman gives birth to a child."

Chūhō's application of the term "like an illusion" to landscape gardens was itself not new, moreover, for similar conceptions were found in Northern Sung poetry and in Sung-influenced Japanese Five Mountains literature by such influential early Five Mountains Zen monks as Kokan Shiren and Gidō's teacher Musō Soseki. The Japanese Five Mountains monks used these images differently, and these differences are instructive. For example, Kokan's verses on illusory or paradoxical landscapes demonstrate a marked interest in these landscapes as manifestations in the present of Taoist lands of the immortals.[28] In contrast, Musō's interpretation of this type of landscape garden was much closer in conception to Chūhō's notion of unreality. Musō began one poem titled "A Rhyme on an Artificial Landscape," by pointing out the seeming paradox in such an artistic creation as an image of advanced spiritual practice:

> Without arousing a speck of dust, towering mountains soar;
> Never retaining a drop of water, rushing cascades plunge.[29]

Musō agrees with Chūhō in playing on the double significance of the term, suggesting that human artistic creation is a subjective projection into the world of an artificial reality.

The general connotations of these landscape poems and prose pieces include an emphasis on the subjectively derived unreality and illusoriness of art by Gidō together with his teacher Musō and his contemporary Chūhō, as well as other Five Mountains Japanese Zen monks. However, in a maneuver typical of many schools of Buddhism in the Chinese cultural sphere, these monks turned this aspect of artistic creation to positive Buddhist ends. In religious history, teachings like the Buddhist conception of illusion have been understood differently depending on a variety of factors: they have led to a rejection of the mundane world of appearance as deceptive and misleading in the pursuit of truth; or they have become the basis of an affirmation that the changeable world itself is the locus of ultimate religious meaning and value. Even within Mahayana Buddhism both tendencies may be found, for some Mādhyamika schools and in some *Perfection of Wisdom* texts the illusory, changeable world of conventional reality must be transcended, while, in the Yogācāra tradition and much Tathāgatagarbha practice, the same world itself is seen as manifesting ultimate truth. The Kitayama period Zen monks tended to agree more with the latter tendency in their understanding of Buddhist ontology, and associated illusion with the theory of nondualism which is found in both the

Vimalakīrti Sutra and in many Zen schools. In the prose passage quoted above, Chūhō began to develop this positive sense when, after pointing out that the artificial tray landscape shown in the painting is much smaller than the natural landscape, he wrote, "Even if what you toy with is small, it will still be enough to nourish the hills and valleys within." While we have already seen in chapter 4 the Chinese literati values in this characterization, for our present purposes it is a significant statement, given the emphasis we have found in Kitayama Zen on size as a potential marker of artificiality and unreality.

Yet in fully developing the positive implications of this landscape aesthetic, the reader may recall that Chūhō turned in that same prose passage to the "artifice" or "provisional existence" (C. *chia*; J. *ke*) of the world of changeable appearance and of artistic expression and its traditional Mahayana contrast with "ultimate truth" or "ultimate reality" (Ch. *chen*; J. *shin*). As Chūhō's argument draws to a climax, he follows the classic line of argument developed in the Chinese Sanron (C. San-lun) and Tendai (C. T'ien-t'ai) Buddhist schools in contrasting how the painting appears from these two perspectives. There Chūhō pointed out how, when viewed provisionally, the mountain landscape's height and width are undiminished while always "dust fl[ies] and streams trickle," yet when seen from the Buddhist perspective of the Real, dimensions become irrelevant and even great mountains fit like a *bonsai* "on a tray." In the next line Chūhō seemed to take the position of the Real as his own, when he pointed out that "Its unmoving form and baseless dimensions on their own do not increase or decrease." Here Chūhō made a dual reference to subjective and objective in characterizing the painting subject as "baseless," a common term for a tale without basis in fact, characterizing both the perceived artistic object and the subjective, enlightened state of mind in Buddhism. Yet Chūhō quickly turns from this analogy to a line of reasoning centering in the Middle Way of Mahayana nondualism with the assertion, "When self and other have dissolved and the real and provisional have vanished, then I will already have forgotten my words about them." By closing in this fashion, Chūhō made a statement not only about nondualism, but also about the inability of language to fully depict the character of the relation between the art object and the viewer.

It is significant that Chūhō's only direct comment on an art object in his closing discourse on Buddhist epistemology is when he lists the artistic placement of a mountain on a tray as an example of the world seen from "the perspective of the Real." This contradicts any assumptions that art functioned solely for Chūhō and other Kitayama Five Mountains monks as a form of expedient means (S. *upāya*; C. *fang-bien*; J. *hōben*), that they might have used to adapt Zen Buddhist teachings to the interests and levels of understanding of their disciples, lay students, and patrons from elite Japanese society. In Mahayana teachings, expedient means must utilize provisionally real aspects of concrete context or even objects of desire in the eyes of still unenlightened beings in order to reach the understanding level of their intended audience, as in the classic *Lotus Sutra* case of the father who offers his children beautiful carts to ride out of the burning house of deluded sentient existence. The form taken by the formless or the provisional expression of ultimate reality is what would then be of primary interest to Chūhō, its form as found in the ever-changing and unreliable world of samsara itself. In this view the illusory form would itself have been neither true nor false for Chūhō, but simply the play of artifice and truth, of the provisional and the real. Yet in our prose passage Chūhō linked the conventionally unreal or empty (S. *śūnyatā*) with the transformations of scale seen in artistic representations of a landscape painting or miniature garden, not with the provisional reality of the sensory world in which dust flies and streams gurgle. In this sense he is suggesting that such art confronts the viewer with the sudden awareness of ultimate Reality in the Buddhist view, not a gradualist adaptation of conventional reality for Buddhist purposes. In both of these interpretations the artificiality and illusoriness of art were no longer something difficult or troublesome that is to be "endured"; rather, the terms of Chūhō's discussion of the perception of the artistic object have clearly shifted from those of a pejorative description of artistic illusion to those of an affirmation of the soteriological value of art.

Like the use in *kōan* or public case texts of paradox to disrupt the conventional conceptual workings of the mind, Chūhō's rhetoric works to demonstrate that ultimate truth is beyond the conventionally defined spatial and temporal order of existence. From the standpoint of the Zen Buddhist monk, then, ultimate truth is found precisely where it is more than one pole in the opposition of truth and falsity, reality and illusory appearance. In this sense, when the "true and artificial" have vanished, practitioners have reached a point where the true and the artificial are no longer disjunct, but instead are interdependent and are meaningful only in non-dualistic, intimate relation to each other. While there are numerous examples in Buddhist philosophy of this affirmation of the interdependence of illusion and truth, what is distinctive about Chūhō's preface is his application of these conceptions to artistic expression. In doing so, Chūhō affirms the Buddhist value of the art object, and the religious value of the artifice of human creative expression.

In what traditions of religious practice and artistic interpretation might we place the Japanese Five Mountains monks in order to best understand the emphasis on illusion in their religious aesthetics? Conceptions of illusion have long been important in theories of spiritual cultivation, artistic creativity, and cultural interpretation not only in the West, but also in Asia. While the Chinese terms I have been translating as "illusion" are generally used in the Buddhist tradition as a translation of the Sanskrit term *māyā*, Wendy O'Flaherty and others have pointed out that in India the Sanskrit term had historically a wider range of meanings than the modern English term indicates.[30] *Māyā* is produced by a god's expressive power of creation and manifestation,[31] yet this creative power was associated with not only the gods, but also with magicians and artists.[32] The term took on a cluster of meanings closely paralleling that of the English terms "craft" or "play" (*ludens*),[33] and only gradually did it come to be associated primarily with the less positive connotations of marvelous illusion and magical deceit.

Some notion of existence as real in appearance and yet also illusory became important in a number of Indian philosophical traditions, including Buddhist philosophical schools. In some of the earliest Buddhist texts we find comparisons of the world of sensory perception to such images of delusion and transience as dreams, illusions, and the froth on water.[34] With the development of Mahayana texts in the first centuries C.E., these images take on a positive value, however, in which the illusions help the practitioner heuristically.[35] The most common of these images include the rope mistaken for a serpent, the illusory city in the sky, the dream, and the child of a barren woman, although different lists are found in the different textual traditions.[36] These images present a conception of the world as never being what it seems to be and continually changing in unexpected ways, and yet in many cases it is precisely these illusory images and unexpected changes that can lead the practitioner to the perception of the highest truths of the Buddhist tradition.

The arrival of Buddhism in China initiated a period of vigorous intellectual discussion and ferment, leading to new developments beginning in the third century within both the Buddhist tradition and the indigenous religions of Taoism and Confucianism. One important element of this discussion was the interest among the practitioners of Dark Learning (C. *hsuan-hsueh*) in Buddhist conceptions of illusory transformation and its relation with ultimate reality. These Buddhist teachings had a close affinity with such important images in the Taoist philosophical tradition as Chuang-chou's dream that he was a butterfly,[37] and led to similar questions concerning the nature of the relationship of ordinary reality and ultimate reality as well as perception and truth. Zen monks in later centuries both on the mainland and in the Japanese islands were drawn to these texts for similar reasons, and among the Kitayama monks Zekkai explicitly refers to the butterfly dream episode in one of his poems while the theme of dreaming is found scattered throughout the writings of other monks.[38]

The Buddhist significance of illusion is also important in another major benchmark in the development of Chinese Buddhism and the Zen school: the appearance of a number of apocryphal texts claiming to be translations of Sanskrit Indian sutras and commentaries. These texts appeared from around the fifth to the seventh or even eighth centuries, and included the *Awakening of Faith* or *Ta-cheng ch'i-hsin lun*, the *Vajrasamādhi Sutra* or *Chin-kang san-mei ching*, and the *Ta-fo-ting ching* or *Śūraṅgama Sutra*, and most importantly for our purposes, the *Perfect Enlightenment Sutra* (C. *Yüan-chüeh ching*; J. *Engakukyō*). As Peter Gregory has pointed out, these apocryphal texts lent legitimacy to the teachings of the new Zen school, which were taking form during the late seventh and early eighth centuries.

One of these texts provided an important textual basis for the Kitayama understanding of the positive heuristic value of Buddhist illusion, the *Perfect Enlightenment Sutra*, which became important to Japanese Zen Buddhism by the thirteenth and fourteenth centuries.[39] While there seems to have been little significant reaction to the text in the first century or so after its composition, it was raised to a prominent position in Buddhist philosophy when it was given a central role by the influential Hua-yen and Southern School Zen teacher, Tsung-mi. From the mid-eighth century it was used frequently by Buddhists from a number of different sects, most commonly in the Hua-yen, T'ien-t'ai, and Zen sects.

The *Perfect Enlightenment Sutra* was first brought to Japan quite early in its history, as is known from a 736 court record of Buddhist sutras.[40] During the twelfth and thirteenth centuries it was being taught by members of the Daruma sect of Japanese Zen as part of the textual studies offered on Mt. Hiei, and the two monks traditionally designated as the founders of Japanese Zen, Myōan Eisai and Eihei Dōgen, both seem to have known of the text. The Japanese Kitayama monks were also exposed to its teachings, for we know that Gidō and Zekkai both first heard lectures on the *Perfect Enlightenment Sutra* during their studies.[41] It was through Gidō's lectures that many of the monks of the Kitayama era and other lay and ordained students of Zen, including the shogun Yoshimitsu, must have been introduced to its teachings.[42]

When compared to the other apocryphal texts, the *Perfect Enlightenment Sutra* appears to be most closely related to the *Awakening of Faith*, which to a great extent it summarizes, simplifies, and modifies.[43] It follows the *Awakening of Faith* in virtually all of its central tenets, including the important teachings of innate enlightenment and of the original, pure, undefiled mind as the source of both wisdom and ignorance, as well as the importance of the practice of "transcending thoughts" or distancing oneself from thoughts" (C. *li-nien*; J. *rinen*). In these teachings we see the affirmation by Chinese Buddhists of this period of the equivalent value of both wisdom and ignorance or enlightenment and delusion, and a conception of any sharp distinction between enlightenment and delusion as being itself an illusion.

In its relatively strong emphasis on the doctrine of illusion, however, the *Perfect Enlightenment Sutra* differs with the *Awakening of Faith*. While metaphors of illusion are found scattered through the *Awakening of Faith*,[44] the overall emphasis of the text lies more on the immanence of the enlightened mind in all sentient beings, which at times approaches a Yogacārā style realism of the mind. By contrast, the emphasis on illusion in the *Perfect Enlightenment Sutra* is seen most clearly in the central image of the text, the "flower in the sky," a flower mistakenly seen in the sky and so thought to exist because of an eye disease. Such images guard against any perception of the mind as real in any ultimate sense, and yet the conception of illusion in this text is not ultimately a negative one. Like all magical transformations, the image of the empty flower in the sky really does appear to exist, just as reality does to deluded sentient beings, and yet the illusion most obviously does not truly exist, in the same way that any fool knows the magician's tricks are not to be taken as real. This emphasis on illusion and emptiness as found in the

Perfect Enlightenment Sutra is central to Chinese Zen from its earliest period.[45] This affirmation of the value of the illusory world and other themes important in the Zen tradition help explain the appeal the text held for Buddhist monks not only in eighth- and ninth-century China but also in the Japanese Zen tradition.

The Japanese monks' interest in the *Perfect Enlightenment Sutra* can be found in their use of the central image of the sutra, the empty flower in the sky (C. *k'ung-hua*; J. *kūge*), which is found scattered through their writings.[46] To take one important example, Gidō Shushin used this image in the title of his diary, *Kūge nichiyō kufū ryakushū* or "Abbreviated Collection of Daily Practice of the Flower in the Sky." Gidō's life as it is recorded in this diary, it is important to note, does not center on meditation or on *kōan* practice, but on his activities in the most powerful political, social, and cultural circles of his day. This type of activity in the midst of the illusory world of mundane affairs characterizes the daily lives of the vast majority of Japanese Five Mountains monks of the fourteenth and fifteenth centuries, and the monks I am considering in the present study.

The Kitayama Japanese monks were particularly interested in the notion of illusion in the *Perfect Enlightenment Sutra* as found in the phrase, the "samadhi like illusion" (C. *ju-huan san-mei*; J. *nyogen zammai*).[47] This phrase is found only once in the sutra, but it comes at a crucial point at the beginning of the second chapter, when the Buddha summarizes his answer to a question Samantabhadra poses about the practice of the doctrine of illusion with "the samadhi like an illusion." Samantabhadra is responding in his question to the characterization by the Buddha in the first chapter of all reality as illusory, using the image so important in the sutra of the flower seen in the sky by someone with an eye illness. If the body and mind, subject and object are all illusory, how can there be any practice, Samantabhadra asks, and if there is no practice, how is this not annihilation of all things[48] and how can bodhisattvas then save sentient beings? The Buddha responds to Samantabhadra's question by indicating that after practice has progressed to the point where there are no more illusions to avoid, there is no annihilation, and the bodhisattva must "practice illusion by means of illusion" (C. *i-huan hsiu-huan*). From this we can surmise that the "samadhi like illusion" addresses the fundamental issue of how the bodhisattva is to practice his insight and help sentient beings in the samsaric world of illusions.

While we may assume that this practice of the "samadhi like illusion" is a type of seated meditation practice, we find that it instead involves activity in the everyday, mundane world. The phrase is discussed, for example, in the *Mahāprajñāpāramitā Śāstra* (C. *Ta-chih-tu lun*), an important commentary to the *Great Perfection of Wisdom Sutra* (S. *Mahāprajñāpāramitā Sutra*), which is generally attributed to the great Indian Mahayana philosopher Nāgārjuna (c. second century C.E.).[49] The text defines this samadhi in the following way:

> The samadhi like illusion, then, is like residing in the single place of the illusory person and everywhere pervading the world of illusory things

which have been created, such as the so-called four types of soldiers,[50] splendid palaces and walled cities,[51] gluttony and revelry,[52] and death and suffering. The bodhiṣattva is also this way, abiding in this samadhi and working the transformations of the world of the ten directions and everywhere pervading it.[53]

This practice of the "samadhi like illusion" here is interpreted to be not a meditative state, but more appropriate to a bodhisattva's activity in the everyday world of man, the samsaric world of war, wealth, political power, sensual pleasures, death, and continued suffering. Based on the rendering in this important Mahayana text of the heuristic value of illusion, we may conclude that the T'ang Chinese popularity of the *Perfect Enlightenment Sutra*, then, is not simply an interest in illusion in some abstract philosophical way but in affirming ordinary human activity as partaking of ultimate ontological status. It was this dimension of the Mahayana Buddhist heritage and of the Chinese Zen tradition to which Gidō and his visitors returned in their 1382 encounter at Rinsen-ji, and to which they and other Japanese monks turned for understanding their own busy lives in the Five Mountains Zen temples.

Before we turn to other specific examples of Kitayama usage of conceptions of illusion, I would like to introduce an important Chinese Zen interpretation of the doctrine of illusion that was well known among the Kitayama Japanese monks. While the Japanese Five Mountains monks were strongly indebted to a number of Chinese Zen teachers, on the subject of illusion one stands out as particularly important: the influential Yüan dynasty monk Chung-feng Ming-pen. Chung-feng taught a number of Japanese Five Mountains monks during their visits to the mainland, and a total of at least six of these monks received the transmission from him. After they returned to their homeland some Japanese monks who had studied under Chung-feng became known for refusing to serve in the Japanese Five Mountains temple system, instead establishing their own temples in the provinces, the most notable being Jakushitsu Genkō. Chung-feng's reputation also spread quickly in the Five Mountains temples in the first decades of the Nambokuchō or Northern and Southern courts period (1336–92), and this was also when the first Five Mountains Zen printings of his collected sayings and other writings were completed in Japan.[54] His influence is also seen in the writings and activities of a number of the most important Five Mountains monks, including those of the influential Chinese monk Chu-hsien Fan-hsien, the well-known poet Betsugen Enshi, and a painter and close friend of Gidō, Tesshū Tokusai (d. 1366).[55] Perhaps most importantly for the Kitayama monks was the extremely high respect given Chung-feng by the individual monk that historians generally regard as the most important single monk for the establishment of the Japanese Five Mountains system, Musō Soseki. Musō, who was Gidō's teacher in Zen, modeled himself very closely on Chung-feng early in life until he took the abbacy of Nanzen-ji in 1325, through such activities as avoiding calls to head large Five Mountains temples despite requests from his teacher Kōhō Kennichi (1241–1316), the *bakufu* warrior government in Kamakura, and the emperor.[56] We can see the continuing interest in Chung-feng's writings up through the Kitayama period. For example, Gidō gave extensive lectures to his fellow monks and also to the shogun on Chung-feng's writings,[57] while as we have seen Kiyō Hōshū wrote out the text of Chung-feng's collected sayings.

When we examine Chung-feng's own biography, we see that he was known for having refused numerous requests of his contemporaries, including the emperor, to serve as abbot of the most important of the Chinese Five Mountains temples.[58] Instead, Chung-feng spent several years living a mendicant existence literally as part of the floating world while residing on boats. Beginning in 1298 he also resided in small hermitages for periods lasting a few years at a time, until moving on after the number of students who had taken up residence with him became too large. In this way he refused to take up administrative offices or abbacies in the large Zen temples of his day, many of which were located near important political and social centers, thereby implicitly rejecting a mode of activity in the midst of the mundane world.

The importance of the Buddhist teaching of illusion to Chung-feng can be seen in the name he gave to a number of his residences during these years, "Hut of Abiding in Illusion" (C. *huan-chu an*; J. *genjūan*). Some sense of his understanding of illusion and the motivations behind Chung-feng's lifestyle can be gathered from his explanation of the significance of this name as it was recorded by the influential scholar-official, Sung Lien:

> What is revealed by the clear water is the essence of illusion, what is reflected by the bright mirror is the traces of illusion. When illusion is extinguished and awakening reaches emptiness, this is the supreme height of transcendental awareness. We should abide in this samadhi which resembles illusion (*ju-huan san-mei*). Therefore, I will name the temple "Illusory Abode."[59]

Here Chung-feng used the same phrase that we have seen in the *Perfect Enlightenment Sutra*, the "samadhi like illusion," to characterize the way in which those who have awakened should live. Chung-feng felt that the accomplished practitioner should continue to abide in this state even after illusion has been extinguished and through awakening the practitioner has achieved a state of emptiness.

Chung-feng did not disdain all contact with the samsaric, mundane realm that we have seen is associated with this "samadhi like illusion," despite the emphasis in postwar scholarship on his reputation for rejecting the mundane world of political affairs and administrative duties. An examination of Chung-feng's relations with contemporary secular authorities reveals substantial interaction with those active in the secular world. As Yü points out, Chung-feng was following in the tradition of Yang-ch'i (J. Yōgi) line Chinese Zen monks in teaching important public officials.[60]

Chung-feng counted among his disciples at one time or another several of the most powerful secular officials of his day, including the high official and well-known calligrapher and painter Chao Meng-fu,[61] the literatus Feng Tzu-chen, a retired king of Korea, King Bon, and the highest Yüan government official in south China during the second decade of the fourteenth century, Beg Bupa, while the noted Yüan poet Wu Chi wrote a eulogy for Chung-feng.[62] Chung-feng himself was not averse to cultural practice, for he is known to have exchanged poetry with some of the most prominent poets of his day and to have been skilled in the art of calligraphy. While Chung-feng did refuse appointment to be abbot of major Chinese Five Mountains temples, his extensive interaction with these secular scholar-officials suggests that his philosophy of abiding in illusion did not imply in his view that good Buddhists should withdraw from the world of human society.

We can get a sense of Chung-feng's philosophy of "abiding in illusion," which will be useful for understanding Kitayama Japanese Zen views of illusion, from an essay Chung-feng entitled "House Rules for Abiding in Illusion."[63] In this essay Chung-feng began with the self-referential characterization of himself and his lecture as also illusory: "This illusory man [Chung-feng] one day occupied his illusory room and took his illusory seat grasping an illusory whisk. At that time his illusory disciples came and gathered in clouds."[64] This depiction of Buddhist teaching is not unique to the teachings of the Zen sect, for closely comparable ideas may be found in the widely influential *Vimalakīrti Sutra*, the latter reading, "It is as if an illusory person were to teach the Dharma to illusory people,"[65] or in such *Perfect Enlightenment Sutra* passages as, "Practice illusion by means of illusion."[66] Here we see that Chung-feng followed the type of Mahayana teachings found in the *Perfect Enlightenment Sutra* in maintaining the emptiness of emptiness, and the illusoriness of illusoriness.

In his essay Chung-feng then turned to a remarkably clearly argued epistemological discussion of illusion, which I quote at length due to its importance for understanding the Kitayama Japanese views. Chung-feng points out that everything depends on illusion, and our interaction with things occurs only through dependence on illusion:

> One [disciple] asked, "Why is a pine straight, a bramble crooked, a swan white, and a crow dark?" The illusory man stood his whisk up and said to the gathering, "When my illusory whisk stands, it does not stand on its own but relies on illusion to stand. When it lays down, it does not lay down on its own but relies on illusion to lay down. When it is grasped, it is not grasped on its own but relies on illusion in order to be grasped. When released, it is not released on its own, but relies on illusion in order to be released.
>
> "When you clearly observe this illusion, it includes the ten directions [of all space] and fills the three temporal realms [of past, present,

> and future]. When something stands up, it does not stand; when something lays down, it does not lay down; when something is grasped, it is not grasped; when something is released, it is not released. In this way understanding penetrates without obstruction, and you can again see that the pine relies on illusion to be straight, the bramble relies on illusion to be crooked, the swan relies on illusion to be white, and the crow relies on illusion to be dark. Separated from this illusory seeing, pines are fundamentally not straight, brambles are actually not crooked, swans already not white, and crows still not dark. Consequently it is apparent that this illusion blurs your sense of sight and produces illusory seeing. This pervades your consciousness and gives rise to illusory discriminiation, so that you see that straight is not crooked and white is not dark. Everywhere judging the myriad dharmas, you become attached to the nature of the many existences. From the beginningless beginning down to the present, you are bound and tied by birth and death."[67]

By associating the doctrine of illusion with the perception that all discrimination is false, Chung-feng again follows some schools of Mahayana Buddhism, including Yogācāra, and the teachings of such philosophically oriented Zen masters as Tsung-mi.

At this point Chung-feng turned in his essay to what was in essence a reading of the entire Zen tradition in terms of illusion as the basis of teaching, understanding, and practice:

> Even the great practitioner [Shakyamuni] of the snowy mountains suffered from this, so that his eyes were unable to see. Thus when he came from his mother's womb, he then walked seven steps, looked to the four directions, and pointed to heaven and to earth. This sensationalism virtually destroyed[68] the supreme principle [of Buddhism] which has been manifested for a hundred thousand kalpas in the pure aspect of all humans. If we thoroughly realize this most wonderful foundation, from the viewpoint of illusory dharmas it comes to nothing at all.
>
> Venerable Yun-men said, "If at that time I saw [Shakyamuni being born], I would kill him with one blow simply to plan for great peace on earth." Even though he tried to cover gold with yellow, alas he only added another layer of illusion. . . . From that time on, since one man told an idle story, ten thousand have transmitted it as fact. Illusion mutually influences illusion through give and take without end. Then we come to [the founding Zen patriarch Bodhidharma at] Shao-lin [temple] facing an illusory wall, [the second patriarch Hui-k'o] putting to rest his illusory mind, . . . [the sixth patriarch Hui-neng] writing an illusory verse, . . . [Pai-chang's] hanging his illusory whisk, . . . or [Lin-chi's] hitting with his illusory hands. Above all there was one man [Lin-chi] who acted like

> a lunatic, who displayed one illusory shout like angry thunder from a blue sky. Illusory shining and illusory functioning or illusory guest and illusory host were mutually interpenetrated in all directions by giving and taking affirmation and denial with myriad appearances and multiple forms without limit.[69] Even now in all directions old blind monks come forth from this school and succeed to this teaching, receive empty [teachings] and echo them, . . . refine their words and calculate their actions, enhance their character and elevate their appearance, are strict with their commands and increase their temples. But there has absolutely never been anyone who was able to go beyond illusion."[70]

Here we see how in this passage Chung-feng interpreted all Buddhist and Zen Buddhist history based on this single, central teaching of illusion.

For Chung-feng illusion was also the one measure of true understanding, which he described as unobstructed and unstoppable:

> Illusion! Its significance is perfect, its principle is complete, its essence is great, its function is pervasive. Together with the myriad Buddhas and patriarchs, it works at all times through kalpas as [numerous as the grains of] dust and sand without end. [Nevertheless,] there are some that cannot completely understand this great illusion beyond words and images. . . . Above all, they do not know their predecessors' deep and penetrating great illusion. . . . One turn of this wheel is like water going out a break in [in a dike] or like the wind going through an empty sky, rejecting all kinds of treatment and leaving no room for choice, responding to their capabilities and entrusting to their abilities.[71]

True understanding for Chung-feng was to base all perception and action in the realization that all is illusion, and only then can Zen practitioners avoid the poison of discrimination and choice. In this passage Chung-feng capably shows how vital in Yüan Chinese Zen was the classic Mahayana *Perfection of Wisdom* notion of the emptiness of even such key concepts of emptiness, and the illusory character even of the most respected propagators in his own school of the teachings of the truth of illusion.

It is apparent, then, that the teaching of illusion was central to Chung-feng's thinking about Buddhism, and about the teaching and practice of the Zen sect in particular. In his Buddhist vision, illusion is an all-pervasive teaching, and is applied not only to all existences, but to the very acts of teaching and practicing the doctrine of illusion itself. For Chung-feng, abiding in illusion and the "samadhi like illusion" were fundamental images of life in the midst of the natural landscape, the realm of livelihood for his mountain retreats that still encompassed the danger of discriminative views for its Buddhist residents. Chung-feng was careful to keep his world of illusion at what he saw as a healthy distance from the secular world of contemporary politics, and also from the administration of large Five Mountains temples that were closely tied to the secular authorities. In this sense, as we shall see, Chung-feng was less affirmative in practice of the world of ordinary society and mundane experience than were the Japanese Kitayama Zen monks.

One important way in which the Japanese monks applied this conception of illusion to their life in the large metropolitan Five Mountains Zen temples of the capital can be seen in their use of illusion to interpret artistic activity, particularly artistic expression of the theme of the natural landscape. By adapting the Mahayana Buddhist theme of illusion to their lives in the vast Five Mountains monastic complexes in the capital, they were able to maintain a fundamentally Buddhist orientation in their extensive social, cultural, and even political interaction with influential secular figures that their metropolitan lifestyle necessitated.

I shall begin a discussion of the views of the landscape arts in the Kitayama period with a look at Gidō Shūshin's views of the relationship of illusion to the natural world and also to artistic representation of the natural landscape. Gidō discussed his conception of "illusory abode," which we have seen was a theme developed by Chung-feng, in a eulogy[72] written for the well-known painter of ink landscapes, Ūe Gukei.[73] Gidō noted at the beginning of the eulogy that Gukei hung a sign over his door reading, "Illusory Hut" (C. *huan-an*; J. *gen'an*) and recorded a conversation he had with Gukei. Here Gidō alludes to Chung-feng's well-known "Hut of Abiding in Illusion." Gidō then quoted Gukei as saying that in the Hua-yen school "the bodhisattvas' samadhi of abiding in illusion (*huan-chu san-mei*) [is] where they see that all the myriad worlds are like illusion and yet they abide in them."[74] Gidō then remarks that by Gukei's living in his illusory hut, all the realms of the sacred and mundane come to be defined by his Buddhist practice.[75] Gidō elaborates on Gukei's statement in his eulogy:

> Due to the power of [seeing the world] as illusion, the ten thousand forms variously come forth: some are illusory Buddhas and patriarchs, some are illusory demons and spirits; some are illusory grasses and trees, some are illusory mountains and rivers; long ones, short ones; square ones, round ones; flying ones and running ones; ugly ones and beautiful ones. In this way these myriad illusions all through [your] wisdom[76] contemplation, diversely manifest the cosmic and the minute.[77] Even if the worlds were destroyed, your hut would stand solid; even if the empty void were exhausted, your hut would be as before. Therefore now you, a man of the Way, just as an illusion are residing [here].[78]

Gidō agrees with his friend Gukei that by recognizing everything as illusion the bodhisattvas can abide in the samsaric realm without the impermanence of the world affecting them. Here we have a Zen Buddhist philosophy of "abiding in illusion" that is comparable to and based on that found in the writings of Chung-feng Ming-pen.

The Japanese monks further adapt Chung-feng's ideas to apply them to the natural landscape, for in Gidō and Gukei's lifestyles the enlightened bodhisattva sees the samsaric realm of the natural landscape as just as much a manifestation of illusion as all other aspects of experience in the world. Gidō shifts from the Buddhist flavor of his prose eulogy to end with a poem in which he shows how the Five Mountains monks integrated Zen thinking with Sung dynasty literary allusions. In the poem Gidō compared his own act of writing Gukei's eulogy to the famous analogy in a Su Shih poem of the transience and unknowability of human life to the track of a goose in muddy slush. The last two lines of the poem read:

> [I,] Empty flower, write a eulogy:
> Goose tracks in the muddy snow.

This is an allusion to the first lines of the famous Su Shih metaphor for human existence in his poem, "Rhyming with Tzu-yu's 'Remembering Old Times at Mien-ch'i'": "Do you know what the place is like where human life is going?/ It must be like a flying goose's footsteps in the muddy snow:/ By chance it leaves a foot [mark] in the mud,/ But when the goose flies off, how then can you tell if it's gone east or west?"[79] Gidō's use of this conception again echoes Gukei's comments recorded at the beginning of the eulogy, when Gukei instructed Gidō to "grasp your illusory brush and write an illusory eulogy." Here we see that for the Japanese monks, as it was for Chung-feng, the conception of illusory abiding is self-referential: the act of teaching illlusoriness and writings about illusoriness is itself illusory. We have just seen a similair movement at the beginning of Chung-feng's *House Rules for Illusory Abiding*, where he wrote, "This illusory man [Chung-feng] one day occupied his illusory room and took his illusory seat grasping an illusory whisk." This is, of course, an important heuristic point to be remembered by Buddhist monks such as Gidō and his contemporaries, who were more like Vimalakīrti perhaps than Chung-feng in their willingness to enter fully into the realm of samsara, teaching powerful secular authorities not in mountain retreats but in the challenging environment of the metropolitan Five Mountains monasteries. By alluding, however, to Su Shih's concrete yet ultimately expansive image in his poem Gidō makes a point about much more than Zen religious pedagogy narrowly defined: he is also making a statement about the illusory act of literary composition and the significance of the natural landscape as a part of that religious pedagogy and practice. Gidō's allusion to Su Shih's poetry reminds us that he and his Kitayama students were active in circles extending far behond the limits of their narrowly construed roles as religious figures, and their conceptions of Buddhist practice were influential in these arenas of the arts, politics, and society.

We find conceptions of the illusory character of art and of the Zen Buddhist tradition itself in Kitayama thinking about an important artistic practice that had long been central to the Zen tradition: the painting of *chinzō* or *chinsō* portraits.[80] Above these portraits Zen teachers conventionally wrote inscriptions, in which the teacher portrayed commonly referred to the painted image of himself at the end of his inscription as "truth" or, interpolating, "true likeness" (C. *chen*; J. *shin*).[81] However, on occasion monks also refer to their images in these inscriptions as "illusory substance" (*genshitsu*) or "illusory form" (*gensō*),[82] and the Kitayama monks followed this custom.[83] These two terms both play on the dualism implicit in each of the paired opposites, "reality" and "illusion," implied in any statement about the ultimate, true identity of a Zen teacher. This use of the term refers on the one hand to the notion that both body and mind are illusory, a teaching found in many Mahayana texts but that is strongly emphasized in the *Perfect Enlightenment Sutra*. The context of its usage in the *chinzō* inscriptions suggests, however, that the writers of the inscriptions were also referring specifically to the painted image itself. We can see this, for example, in Wu-chun's inscription on the *chinzō* he gave to Enni Ben'en: "They painted my illusory substance and asked me to inscribe [the painting]."[84] The Kitayama monks were effective in propagating this view of the self and of artistic portraiture at the highest level of Muromachi Japanese society. This is seen in the shogun Yoshimochi's inscription on his own father Yoshimitsu's portrait, which was used in Yoshimitsu's memorial services.[85] Here the Buddhist notion that the self is just as illusory as the objective world goes hand in hand with conceptions of artistic representation as based in illusion and not in truthful representation, a view that was influential in the most elite levels of Kitayama culture and society.[86]

Japanese monks in the second half of the fourteenth century often applied this same conception to the act of painting more generally, as is perhaps best seen in their use of such terms to refer not to the painting of figure or devotional paintings with subject matter explicitly linked to Zen Buddhist teaching and practice, but to the painting of landscape subjects. For example, Gidō uses the term "generating illusion" (C. *huan-ch'u*; J. *genshutsu*) to describe the artist in the act of painting. We find his use of this term in an inscription on a no longer extant landscape painting by Ūe Gukei: "The tip of the brush gives off illusions in a ten-thousand form pattern."[87] By choosing not to use more conventional terms, such as "generating a sketch" (*shashutsu*) or "generating a portrayal" (*byōshutsu*), Gidō suggests with this term that artistic activity is the production of illusion. By this he meant that just as all of the myriad illusions derive from the mind, or from the "wisdom contemplation" as he argued above in his "Eulogy for Illusory Hut," art also derives from the human imagination and is illusory.

Kitayama conceptions of art as illusory and fictive were not modeled on Chinese Buddhist concepts alone, but also provide evidence for a syncretic interest in artistic theory based in mainland literati aesthetics. In particular the Kitayama Japanese monks syncretically integrated Buddhist views of illusion with Sung and later Chinese aesthetics that emphasized the importance of rejecting formal likeness in favor of other artistic cum moral and spiritual qualities. As we saw in chapter 1, the Sung literati interest in the spiritual and moral dimension to painting led to a rejection of formal likeness as a criterion of aesthetic judgment. In a famous comment, Su Shih compared the views of those who are interested in verisimilitude in art to the views of a child, and negatively associated representation as an aim of art with the work of professional artists.[88] Such statements as this were part of the growth of the general conception of literati art as contrasted with the art of professionals, begun in the Northern Sung around the time of Su, in which the professional painter's comparatively realistic depiction and reliance on payment was contrasted with the amateurism and deeply meaningful personal expression of literati art.[89] Literati artists and writers of artistic and cultural theory began at this time to emphasize the artist's innermost self at the center of the meaning of a painting. Su's views continued to be influential during the Southern Sung dynasty in the writings of such literati as Ch'en Yü-i (1090–1138), who was never as popular as Su among Kitayama Japanese Five Mountains Zen writings and art. Ch'en Yü-i formulated one classic statement of literati painters in a famous line: "If the meaning is there, don't seek for outward likeness."[90] By the Yüan dynasty these views became very widespread, as seen most clearly in the writings of such theorists as T'ang Hou (fl. c. 1322–29), Wu Chen (1280–1354), and Yang Wei-chen, and this interest in the expression of the artist's inner moral and spiritual state became a definitive characteristic of literati painting generally.

The most important result for our present concern of the new emphasis in literati aesthetics and criticism on personal meaning was the growth of an interest in paintings in which the artist had distorted reality in a manner that expressed his own inner development. The ability of the artist to depict something that could not exist in the phenomenal world was proof to Chinese art theorists of the unreality of art, and it is on this point that there is considerable overlap with Buddhist conceptions of illusion. But in an age when it was precisely inner spiritual significance that defined the highest art, this fabricated character of artistic practice became a highly valued aspect of artistic creativity, rather than a negative defining trait of art as it was in other periods of East Asian cultural and aesthetic theory.

One of the best-known paintings exhibiting this "unreal" character of art depicted a banana palm with its leaves covered in snow, and was titled *Yüan An Lying in the Snow* by the widely loved T'ang poet Wang Wei, who was held up as an ideal of the new literati art during and after the Sung. This painting depicted a conventionally defined impossibility, since the educated literatus knew that the sensitive banana plant lost all its leaves in the harsh winds of the fall and winter. The well-known Northern Sung artistic critic Shen Kua (1031–95), who at one time owned the painting, had the highest praise for Wang Wei's ability as seen in the painting to "penetrate their subtle principles and mysterious creation," concluding that in producing the artwork Wang's creation "partook of the divine, and eminently obtained the ideas of nature."[91] In his passage describing the painting Shen Kua borrows well-known lines from an Ou-yang Hsiu poem making the same point about realistic depiction: "Ancient paintings depict ideas and not forms;/ . . . Few are those who understand abandoning form to realize ideas,/ No less in looking at painting than in poetry."[92] Shen Kua's high opinion of Wang Wei is based on his ability to capture the "ideas" (C. *i*) of the natural world, an aspect of art that was frequently opposed to its "forms" (C. *hsing*). Similar high evaluations of Wang Wei's art can be also found in the writings of Su Shih, who praised Wang for having found the key to his art "beyond appearances."[93] Art that violated expectations and conventional associations was not well tolerated in highly precedent-conscious Chinese elite society, but in the hands of a master like Wang Wei, willingness to take such risks came to be considered the mark of genius. Most importantly for our purposes was the development of a broad-based interest among the Sung literati in what today might be termed "unrealistic" art that violates the norms of court cultural practice.

A comparable interest in inner artistic expression and meaning over and against external appearances is also found in the Kitayama monks' writings on painting, at times with direct reference to Wang Wei's paintings. In one important example of a preface on an extant painting, Taihaku Shingen begins his 1415 preface to the painting *Small Cottage by a Mountain Stream* (fig. 3.2) with high praise for both Ch'en Yü-i's poetry and Wang Wei's image of the banana palm in snow: "Composing a poem on plum blossoms blazing heat was [Ch'en Yü-i's] divine marvelousness; painting a plantain in snow was [Wang Wei's] natural instinct."[94] Ch'en Yü-i, who I noted above followed Su Shih in advocating the primacy of inner meaning over formal representation, associated himself in one of his own poems with this painting by Wang Wei. Taihaku borrowed and built on lines from this poem by Ch'en, which read as follows: "A banana palm beneath the snow: Wang Wei's painting;/ The plum blossoms under fiery skies: Ch'en Yü-i's poem."[95] Ch'en Yü-i was of course comparing the seeming paradox of his own notion of the plum, a tree known conventionally for its blossoms in very early spring, which is blooming in the summer heat to Wang Wei's banana in the winter snow. It should be noted that it is not change per se that captures Ch'en's (and Taihaku's) interest, change being of course a central part of conceptions of the transiency of the world, but the violation of expectation and literary convention with regard to the natural progress of the seasons. Another example of a similar view from the Kitayama period can be found in an inscription by Gyokuen Bompō on one of his bamboo paintings, where he remarks that "The third month is made into autumn, and the eighth month [made into] spring."[96] Here we see the Kitayama monks picking up on what is by the fourteenth century a well-established theme in continental literati culture and developing it for their own purposes. Taihaku in turn took up this tradition, which centered on literary and visual images of bird and flower subjects, and applied it to a Japanese ink landscape painting, which as a scroll combining painting with poetry integrated Ch'en's poetic illusion with Wang's in painting.

While Taihaku followed in the footsteps of these giants of continental culture, he also added a new layer of interpretation by characterizing Wang's painting as

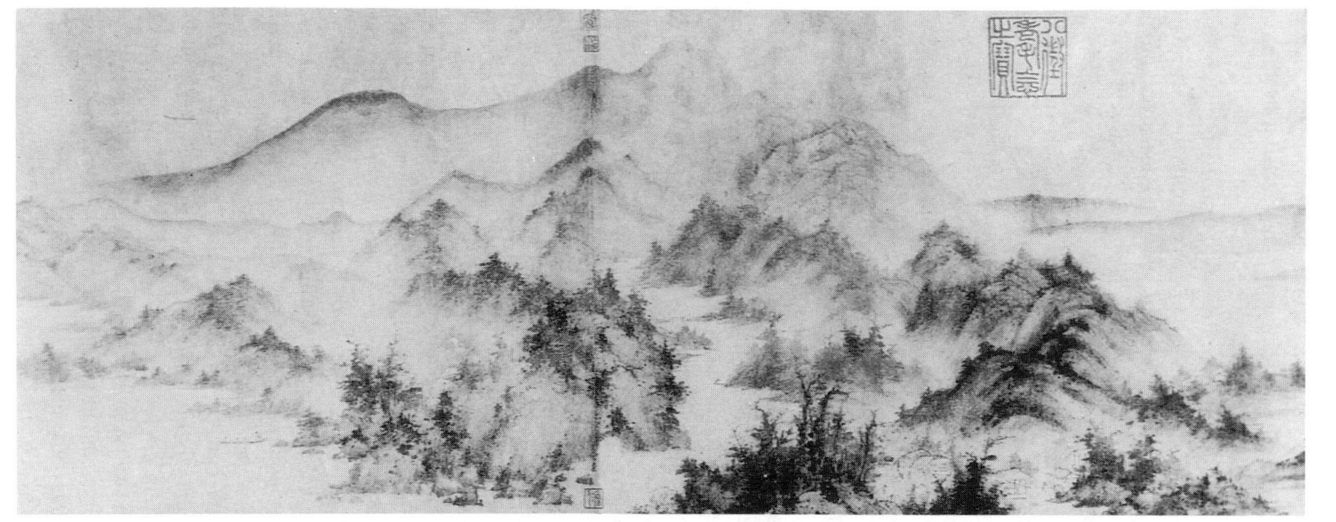

Fig. 5.1. *Dream Journey along the Hsiao and Hsiang Rivers*. By a Mr. Li (d.u.). Inscriptions by Ke Pi (d.u.) and eight others. Handscroll. Ink on paper. 30.3 x 403.6 cm. National Treasure. 1170. Tokyo National Museum. Detail.

"natural instinct" and Ch'en's poem as "divine marvelousness." These are terms of high praise taken from literati painting theory[97] that Taihaku used to praise images that are possible only in a world defined by the magical illusions of human creativity, comparable illusions to those that Mahayana Buddhists believed were the source of all phenomenal appearances. It was through the affirmation of these illusions that Gidō, Taihaku, Bompō, and their predecessors on the continent developed conceptions of art that found deep philosophical and religious meaning in the productions of the human imagination.

Literati views of art as fabricated and illusory were widespread in influence, extending well beyond the limits of Chinese literati and court circles to become influential among Buddhist monks and their secular patrons and companions in Sung and Yüan China. The Chinese Zen monk Hsüeh-feng's views on the appropriateness of mountains for art due to its illusory character, as quoted earlier in this chapter by Gidō's visitor, focus on what seems to have been a common subject of interest in Southern Sung continental culture. We can judge this from similar comments made in inscriptions on a painting done for the otherwise unknown Buddhist monk Yun-ku (fl. c. 1140–70), a contemporary of Hsüeh-feng.[98] The inscriptions on the painting *Dream Journey along the Hsiao and Hsiang Rivers* (fig. 5.1) were completed in 1170 and 1171, and inscribed for Yun-ku by some ten of his lay disciples so that he could enjoy wandering among the mountains now that he was too old to leave his hut.[99] In the inscriptions we see a good deal of discussion of the issue of illusion and art, including the following comment: "The great earth and the mountains and rivers are illusion, and painting is an illusion of an illusion, while this explanation of illusion is yet another illusion."[100] This reading of a landscape painting as an illusion posing as yet another illusion is quite close to Hsüeh-feng's conception of painting cited by Kaichū and Gidō above. It also shares with Chung-feng and others' views the insistence that illusion is self-reflexive, an important pedagogical point when we remember that these literati and also the Japanese Zen monks functioned in society as advisors and instructors. Moreover, this passage characterizes painting in terms of its illusory nature, but instead of contrasting this with the world of appearances, this illusory quality to art is thought to make it the perfect medium for representing the seeming reality of the illusory world as understood in Buddhism. The teachings of Hsüeh-feng and the beliefs of Yun-ku's lay disciples together suggest that this tradition of interpreting landscape and landscape painting as images of Buddhist illusion had become influential in the social circles shared by continental Zen monks and literati by the mid-twelfth century, only some half century after Su Shih's death and the spread of literati interest in artistic illusion.

Inscriptions on the same painting show interest in the related theme of the relationship between illusion and truth or conventional reality and ultimate reality that Chūhō applied to the complex layering of painting and miniature garden above. In an 1171 inscription by Chang Ch'uan-pu (d.u.), after noting that several of the other inscriptions discuss the issue of truth (*chen*) and illusion (*huan*), Chang, like Chūhō, argued for the nondualism of illusion and reality.[101] Chang suggested that it was not necessary to judge according to these two criteria, for they were intimately related: "Illusion is born in opposition to truth, and truth operates relying on illusion."[102] To describe a more appropriate attitude for understanding painting, he cited a line from Su Shih's comments on the famous painter of bamboo Wen T'ung's method of painting, "When the hare leaps up as the falcon swoops down, if there is the slightest hesitation then all will be lost."[103] The state of mind of the hare in such a situation may be compared to Chūhō's "vanishing of the self and other," and certainly represented a very high state of religious practice that goes beyond the distinction between truth and illusion, reality and appearance. This resistance to an overemphasis on either illusion or truth, two poles of Buddhist ontology, and a preference for some middle path, are characteristics of both much of Zen soteriology and a Tendai Buddhist–style Three Truths theory in which these two are combined with the principle of the Middle. The same refusal to discriminate between the two falls within the affirmative Mahayana Buddhist tradition of refusing to designate any ultimate difference between form and emptiness, right and wrong, or between samsara and nirvana.

The Japanese Kitayama monks were probably not as familiar with the views of Yun-ku and his lay disciples as they were with those of Hsüeh-feng, so we cannot assume any direct historical influence. Yet they shared a common interest with both of these Chinese predecessors in developing a conception of landscape themes in artistic practice that addressed the fundamental values of both the worldview of their lay colleagues and their own religious vision. The continued interest in this issue of truth and illusion in subsequent artistic theory can be seen in a line from a poem written by the important Yüan literati painter Ni Tsan to the monk-painter Fang Yai (fl. fourteenth century), with whom he seems to have had a close spiritual relationship:

I ask my master Fang I,
What is illusion, what is real?
From the ink well I take some ink drops,
To lodge in my painting a boundless feeling of spring.[104]

In this poem Ni Tsan answers his own question with the "boundless feeling of spring" that, we might surmise, somehow bridges the contradictory impulses of illusion and the real. As in Chūhō's preface, Ni Tsan and Chang's considerations of illusion in art make the rubric "illusory" central to an understanding of the meaning of art while moving in the direction of the characteristically nondualist logic of the affirmative strain in Mahayana Buddhist ontology.

An example of this application of nondualist ontology to aesthetics with direct historical connections to the Japanese Five Mountains Zen tradition is found in a painting inscription by the late Yüan and early Ming Chinese Zen master, Chien-hsin Lai-fu (1319–91). This inscription is found not on a landscape painting but on an image of Mañjuśrī, the Buddhist bodhisattva of wisdom, wearing a hemp robe.[105] Chien-hsin began his inscription by telling the viewer how the image was to be perceived: "The body is not short or long . . . and the form is not ultimately [real] or conventionally [real]."[106] The teachings of Chien-hsin were important to the Kitayama monks, for they were transmitted to Japan in the late 1360s and mid-1370s when interest in recent developments in continental Zen continued unabated but relatively few monks were returning to the Japanese islands from the continent. More importantly for the early landscape poem-and-painting scrolls, Chien-hsin's teachings were brought back to Japan by one of Gidō's disciples, the Japanese monk Ikō Tokuken,[107] who as we saw in chapter 2 was the most important monk in the circle active under Gidō's leadership in the early years of the Japanese *shigajiku* in Kamakura. Ikō's importance to the Kamakura monks surrounding Gidō, and perhaps to Gidō himself, would have been strengthened by his extended, direct contact with the mainland Zen tradition. While the Japanese Zen interpretation of the teaching of the nonduality of truth and illusion is not necessarily derived directly from Chien-hsin, his application of the teaching to the interpretation of painting is important for understanding the aesthetics theories applied to early landscape poem-and-painting scrolls by the Kitayama monks in the 1370s.

We see how Gidō himself applied his thinking on the nonduality of illusion and truth in a discourse he wrote on the name "Dream Mountain" (C. *meng-shan*).[108] In this essay Gidō set up a somewhat forced analogy of dream with the play of the demonic spirit of man and of mountain with the unmoving. He then pointed out that neither one of these had any meaning without its polar opposite, and concluded, "Dream and mountain are merely the single awakening from sleep, and not two. It is unknown which dreams and which awakens. Mountains or dreams? Right or wrong? We cannot judge [which is which]."[109] Here Gidō applied the principle of nonduality to the illusory quality of landscape, and refused to discriminate between the dualism of dreaming and awakening or of truth and reality. This argument is consistent with his views in the dialogue described previously between Gidō and Kaichū about the similarity of mountains and dreams. Yet here Gidō applies it not just to an art object but to the very naming of the identity of a close companion of his, the artist Gukei, now known primarily for his landscapes. As Chūhō and Shunoku did in their arguments for the nondualism of ultimate and conventional reality in painting, Gidō applied this same principle to the natural landscape while bringing the full weight of the Buddhist tradition to bear on this mode of artistic interpretation. These passages are significant in their suggestion of a Five Mountains Zen tradition of interpreting dreams in a non-Freudian and yet nonrationalistic manner, comparable perhaps to the contemporary popularity of dreaming in local branches of the Sōtō school of Zen and in other aspects of contemporary Japanese elite culture.[110]

In this act we can see that Gidō and his contemporaries understood the landscape not only as a realm to be explored in free moments from their administrative duties in the capital, but also as something crucial to their own identities in a fundamental way. This use of the landscape to understand their own sense of self is comparable to the application of landscape to their self-images we have already seen in the discussion of "achieving in the mind" and the hermit at court. The distinctive and I would suggest fundamentally Buddhist aspect of this conception of the world and of the self is the Kitayama Zen emphasis on the theme of illusion in understanding the significance of the "reality" of the landscape. Through applying Buddhist conceptions of illusion to the natural world in these and other passages, Gidō, Chūhō, and their fellow Five Mountains Zen monks developed a fundamentally Buddhist mode of interpreting their own lives in metropolitan monasteries together with landscape paintings, small gardens, and other of the landscape arts. By seeing the landscape as illusory in this distinctive sense, they freed themselves of any attachments to what might be seen as a traditional sense of worship of the idyllic mountains and pastoral fields that characterizes some nature-based religious movements. Instead, illusion became for these Kitayama monks a basis for the unimpeded, free-roaming practice of enlightenment in the midst of ordinary life of elite Japanese society. They accomplished this difficult intellectual and personal task through the Buddhist ideal of the playfulness of enlightened nondualistic activity in a world that is at once both real and illusory, and it is to this ideal of playfulness that we now turn.

Chapter 6

Buddhist Playfulness and the Landscape Arts

> Penetrating heaven and earth, we cannot know its expansiveness;
> encompassing past and present, we cannot know its duration.
> Buddhas and sentient beings both have this Way,
> differing only in being joyful or not.
>
> —Kiyō Hōshū

> Art is the highest form of play and the genuinely creative realm of the imagination.
>
> —Paul Tillich

In this final chapter we encounter the Buddhist theme of playfulness, a theme closely associated in popular culture with Zen Buddhism but that has been the subject of considerable disinterest among Buddhologists and religious historians.[1] As indicated in the previous chapter, playfulness like illusion is potentially a powerful heuristic tool for Buddhist purposes, since through its imaginative, wandering, and transformative aspects play disrupts the settled attachments of deluded perception. Japanese Zen monks of the Five Mountains insitutions took playfulness quite seriously, for it was intimately connected in their minds with Buddhist illusion and with the artistic practices of Chinese literati poets and artists.

Certainly their pursuit of playfulness also had important social effects in which they would not have been uninterested, for play often offers an alternative reality to that defined by conventional symbols and social or religious institutions.[2] The seemingly unconventional or even antinomian implications of playfulness underlie perhaps much of the popular association of this theme with the eccentric and wild behavior of Zen masters at the center of its twentieth-century image.

In contrast to such associations of playfulness with unconventionality, East Asia images of playfulness such as those we find in the *Vimalakīrti Sutra* and *Chuang-tzu* are complex symbol systems that have been fully integrated into the cultural traditions of Asia. In Zen Buddhism playful elements have been perpetuated through such institutional and doctrinal means as an extensive textual tradition, religious rituals of meditation and *kōan* practice, elaborate conventions of expression and interpretation, and a vast, wealthy, and powerful religious institution. The turn of the fifteenth century in Japan found Five Mountains Zen monks in just such an institution very much drawn to playfulness in their writings, and as we have already seen they ultimately applied it to interpretations of the landscape arts. It is through concepts such as playfulness that they seem to understand their own activity in social and cultural circles outside the monastery walls. In some sense the notion of play represented their own rendering of much of what has come to be seen in the nineteenth and twentieth centuries as the more controversial aspects of Zen activity.

One basis for much of the Five Mountains emphasis on playfulness may be found in the theories of illusion we have just examined. If we ask how the Kitayama monks described the specific relationship between illusion and play, we find in one view that it is the illusory objects of the senses themselves that are at play. Chūhō once described this relationship in the following manner:

> The four great form bodies manifest
> as Vairocana's true form,
> The six senses' deluded objects play about
> in the Tuṣita Heaven.[3]

Play in this sense is the appearance of the illusory world as seen from the standpoint of enlightenment. Moreover, Chūhō suggested with his parallel construction that this playful appearance is equal in value for Buddhist practice with the true form of the Buddha Vairocana, a deity of central importance in Japanese Tantric Buddhism as the origin of the entire cosmos. Illusion for Chūhō was not something to be avoided or despised, it was something that the adept could enjoy by contemplating its playful transformations in the samsaric world. Chūhō seems to assert here that, while grounded in the Buddhist philosophy of illusion we discussed in the last chapter, the vision of enlightenment ultimately goes beyond illusion to a perspective that engages the play of illusion and truth.

The most articulate Kitayama Japanese spokesperson for the Buddhist vision of the playfulness of the illusory world was the monk Kiyō Hōshū. Kiyō described his understanding of playfulness in a 1408 exposition on the shogun Yoshimochi's *gō* (C. *hao*) or pen name, "Enjoying the Way" (*etsudō*). Significantly for our understanding of the sociopolitical circumstances of Five Mountains cultural production, Kiyō wrote out his interpretation at the request of a powerful daimyo, Hosokawa Mitsumoto (d.u.). Kiyō tells us in his explanation that Hosokawa had an important relationship with Yoshimochi's wife, Hino Yasuko (also Kitayama-in; 1368–1419), and had received a copy of this *gō* in Yoshimochi's own hand. The precise term for "enjoying the way" chosen as a form of his own identity by Yoshimochi ultimately derives from the Chinese classics, and is not peculiar to the Zen Buddhist tradition.[4]

Yet Kiyō interprets this summation of Yoshimochi's character in terms of his Zen heritage, which includes the theme of "Enjoying the Way" (C. *le-tao*), a popular subject of Zen verses also known as "Songs of Enjoying the Way" (*le-tao ke*), which are found beginning in the T'ang and are especially common in writings by Sung and Yüan Zen monks.[5] Verses on this subject are particularly frequent in the T'ang Zen poetry of Ming-ts'an (also Lan-tsan; active c. 742–62), Tao-wu Yüan-chih (769–835), and Han-shan, whose poetry became associated not long after his death with life in the mountains in which he "enjoyed the Way."[6] It was to explain the association of the shogun's worldly activity with this theme from the Zen tradition that Kiyō wrote out his explanation.

As we might expect from a monk known by his chosen name of "Nondualism," Kiyō began his discussion of Yoshimochi's "enjoying the Way" with a discourse on "the Way of nondualism":

> Now our sages have the Way of nondualism of the real and the provisional. The real is not the provisional, yet it cannot endure; the provisional is not the real, yet it cannot be eliminated. Perpetuated or diminished: when they have been fused with each other, then we call this the realm of unfathomable liberation.[7] Penetrating heaven and earth, we cannot know its expansiveness; encompassing past and present, we cannot know its duration. Buddhas and sentient beings both have this Way, differing only in being joyful or not.
>
> If we have a root of faith in our hearts,[8] and truly put it into practice and really carry it out, progressing more and more without rest, suddenly doubts will melt away. Then self-affirmation and self-contentment will be achieved. However, we are unable to talk of this with others, because we are in the midst of the utmost in happiness and joy which gushes forth, and even the joys of tasting a feast or of hearing stringed and wind instruments will still be insufficient to describe it. Those who treat the real and the provisional as strictly opposed, definitely cannot speak of this with us.[9]
>
> Then extending and fulfilling this [Way] brings all under heaven and later generations to enjoy this Way. Then while roaming at ease in a world of peaceful reign and roving at leisure in a realm of benevolent longevity, self and other have exactly the same essence. Real and conventional! Happiness and joy! These are what is called "The marvelousness of making oneself happy and making other men happy."[10] The reason the shogun wrote [these characters] out and gave them to you is found in this.[11]

Kiyō grounds his definition of the joy of the Zen path firmly in the classical Chinese Buddhist theory of innate enlightenment and the Mahayana nondual ontology of the conventional and real. While pointing out that all beings have this character, in his interpretation enjoyment and the release from suffering occur only through sustained, intensive practice and are not based on any fundamental or ultimate difference between the enlightened Buddha and ordinary individuals.

In his closing Kiyō applies this soteriology directly to the important political examples of the shogun Yoshimochi and also Hosokawa Mitsumoto in terms that political elites would understand clearly. In his use of the phrase, "extending and fulfilling," for example, Kiyō borrows from a Mencius passage on the "four beginnings" popular in Cheng-Chu school of Neo-Confucianism. The passage from Mencius reads:

> If a man is able to develop all these four germs that he possesses, it will be like a fire starting up or a spring coming through. When these are fully developed, he can take under his protection the whole realm within the Four Seas, but if he fails to develop them, then he will not be able even to serve his parents.[12]

By referring to the moral and political model of the Confucian sage king and his ministers who "bring all under heaven" under their sway, Kiyō flatters his audience while at the same time pushing them in the direction of a Buddhist rendering of how this may be achieved. In suggesting that Buddhist practice leads to "roving at leisure in a realm of benevolent longevity," Kiyō makes a similar maneuver through an allusion to the Confucian *Analects*, where "The Master said, 'The wise find joy in water; the benevolent find joy in mountains. The wise are active; the benevolent are still. The wise are joyful; the benevolent are long-lived.'"[13] This passage was a favorite of Kiyō that as we saw in chapter 3 he also quoted in his discourse on Yoshimochi's pen name, "Manifesting the Mountain," pehaps due to its association of wisdom with the long life that is customarily wished by subjects to their kings. Through his choices of Confucian and Neo-Confucian references, Kiyō syncretically integrates these traditions of political thought into a Buddhist framework.

Yet Kiyō's stress on playfulness through such phrases as "roaming at leisure," "the realm of unfathomable liberation," and "happiness and joy" make his interpretation distinctively representative of Kitayama renderings of Zen Buddhist philosophy and soteriology. This rendering is aligned with the Mahayana notion of unfettered, free movement through cosmic space and time, for in this state, "Penetrating heaven and earth, we cannot know the expansiveness [of this realm]; encompassing past and present, we cannot know its duration." Kiyō's thinking on nondualism in this passage was close to the teachings of the famous bodhisattva Vimalakīrti, as interpreted in the major Zen text that Kiyō wrote an important commentary on, *The Blue Cliff Record*. The climax of the "Dharma Door of Nonduality" chapter from the *Vimalakīrti Sutra* is itself made the subject of a *kōan* in *The Blue Cliff Record* case 84, which begins with a discussion of the freedom realized on leaving behind the dualistic views of "is" (*shih*) and "is not" (*fei*):

"When 'is' and 'is not' are left behind, and gain and loss are forgotten, then you are clean and naked, free and at ease."[14] In the same chapter we find that the various views of the bodhisattvas are characterized in the very same terms Kiyō used, the "nonduality of real and provisional."

To fully understand the Kitayama adoption of these views, we must introduce the East and South Asian Buddhist and other religious context of playfulness. When we consider the notion of playfulness in Indian philosophy and religion, we can see the positive dimension to the theories of illusion as it was understood in its early Indian senses. The Indian notion of play (S. *līlā*), often associated with Kṛṣṇa, is thought of as divine in that the gods continue to act even though they do so neither to respond to any particular cause nor to fulfill any desire.[15] In this sense their activity is unconditioned, purposeless, completely free, and intrinsically satisfying, and as a result becomes at times spontaneous, unpredictible, and disruptive. In its Indian Buddhist context, playfulness was most appropriate to the bodhisattva's unconditioned activity, which was free of the bonds of desire and occurred in the mundane, samsaric world. As I noted in the last chapter, the cluster of meanings associated with early conceptons of *māyā* were comparable though not coextensive with the range of meanings of the English derivitives of the Latin term *ludo*. What may be "illusory" and leading to "delusion" may also lead to "elusive" new meanings of words and new layers of significance through poetic "allusion," in a process of seeing through the literal or conventional meaning to new perceptions of reality and new facets of what was thought to be already completely understood. From this perspective we might risk oversimplifying to read the Buddhist teachings of playfulness, in a sense that is positive and deeply religious, as the willingness to remain open to the transformations of illusory appearances.

Playfulness is found in a number of different guises throughout Buddhist philosophical history both in India and in China. In some strands of Yogācāra thought play is an extremely important state defined in terms of nondichotomous absorption, a state of mind that was also important in Sung Chinese literati cultural production.[16] The concept is also found throughout the *Vimalakīrti Sutra*, a text important in early Zen history and that we have already seen is important to the Kitayama Japanese monks. We find the term "playfulness" (S. *vikrīdita*; C. *yu-hsi*; J. *yuge*) in the second chapter on expedient means, where it is an attribute of Vimalakīrti, "liberated through the transcendence of wisdom."[17] This skill of Vimalakīrti is manifested in the sutra through his power to move freely among the various Buddhalands of the Buddhist cosmos, a power seen in different beings throughout the Mahayana Buddhist tradition, and also in the ability to transform the various lands in size and location at will. These two types of playfulness are suggestive of two different aspects of this power: "unobstruction" (*wu-ai*) by physical and conceptual boundaries or limits; and "transformation" (*hua*) of the world. An example of this latter power is seen in one of the best-known passages in the sutra, a passage that has become representative of the entire sutra: Vimalakīrti's transformation of his house "into emptiness"[18] so that Mañjuśrī and his thousands of attendants and companions could be enthroned inside his "ten-foot-square room" without crowding and without the city, the land of India, or the world changing in appearance.[19] It is in this power of Vimalakīrti that we find another Buddhist context for Kiyō's interest in the artistic play of illusory appearance of size: the transcendence of limitations of time and space.

Such playful transformations of size and spatial dimension are possible only when conventional conceptions of the world have been relativized through the recognition of the emptiness of illusory appearances. While we may be tempted to demythologize these "flights of fancy" as allegories with little literal significance, we should also consider what they may have meant in the context of the Buddhist philosophy of emptiness and illusion. In Vimalakīrti's magically expansive "house of emptiness" and in Kiyō's "penetrating heaven and earth" and "encompassing past and present" we find that the Buddhist philosophies of illusion and of playfulness join. The magical transmutations in this view of reality are not illusions in the negative sense of deception, nor are they the products of mistaken sensory perception, mere subjective hallucinations of "flowers in the sky." Instead, they are the products of the play of enlightened beings, reveling in the perception of the many realities behind surface appearances and conventional, discriminatory conceptions. This perception is part of a continuing, playful process of *prajñā* or wisdom vision of the myriad possibilities of a world defined by illusion.

While Indian Buddhists may have been comparatively more interested in transcending the cosmic necessity of the samsaric world of karmic cause and effect, this playful quality has not always been at the forefront of the Buddhist philosophical tradition. In early Chinese Buddhist history the emptiness philosophy led not to theories of playfulness but to a scholastic identification of samsara and nirvana, and this also holds for many other periods and schools in Buddhist history. Religious historians locate the beginning in Chinese Buddhism of this element of joy and playfulness as grounded in this vision of both samsara and nirvana as an illusory, dreamlike state. Yanagida Seizan has argued that this vision first becomes prominent in Chinese Buddhist history through the apocryphal texts so important to the early Chinese Zen teachers and also lectured on at the Muromachi shogunal court by Gidō and Zekkai. These texts, such as the *Śūraṅgama Sutra*, and in particular the *Perfect Enlightenment Sutra*, became known for several teachings, but in the present context were especially important for their philosphy of "the samadhi like illusion." It may also be that this new playful element in Buddhist philosophy and practice arose with the growing interest in living out nondualism in the samsaric world that accompanied the eighth-century flourishing of the Zen school in China.[20]

We do find an interest in playfulness as a serious philosophical concept in the early texts of the Chinese Zen Buddhist tradition. The phrase "the samadhi of playfulness," which as we have already seen was used by the Kitayama Japanese monks in their writings on art, appears in the writings of such early Ma-tsu line masters as Nan-ch'uan P'u-ÿan (748–835) and in the formative early Zen text, the *Platform Sutra* of the late eighth century. The latter used this term to explain the state attained after "seeing into one's own nature," one of the central conceptions of the text.[21] There playfulness is described in the following manner:

> Those who have seen their nature, realize [buddhahood] whether they establish [things] or not, come and go freely, are unbound and unobstructed, respond immediately when acted on and answer immediately when spoken to, everywhere manifesting their transformation body without [ever] being separated from their own nature, thus realizing the autonomous divine power of the samadhi of playfulness: this is called "seeing one's Nature."[22]

This playful state is described here as a characteristic of the highest enlightened state, in which the practitioner *qua* bodhisattva roams about the cosmos freely and without obstacles, independent of the conditioned limitations of the phenomenal world. While this conception is also found in early Chinese Pure Land teachings and is not peculiar to the Zen school, we can see from its importance in this central Zen text that the Zen tradition found such a teaching to its liking.[23]

While the *Platform Sutra* was not well known in Kitayama Japan, playfulness retained much of the same significance in Sung dynasty Zen thought, and it was through this avenue that the ideal of playfulness seems to have become central to the Kitayama formation of the concept. In Sung Zen we see, for example, the term used in the commentary by Wu-men Hui-k'ai (1183–1260) to the important *kōan* anthology, *Wu-men kuan* (J. *Mumonkan*) or *Gateless Gate*, compiled circa 1228. This text was first brought to Japan by a Japanese disciple of Wu-men, Shinchi Kakushin (1207–98) in 1254, and must have been fairly widely read, judging from its having been repeatedly printed in the Five Mountains temples.[24] We find an interpretation of playfulness in Wu-men's comments to the first *kōan*,

> After long practice inner and outer will of their own accord be fused into one. . . . [S]uddenly fusing, you astonish heaven and move the earth, as if you had grasped the great sword of General Barrier. [Then] if you meet the Buddha, you kill the Buddha; if you meet a patriarch, you kill the patriarch. On the brink of life and death you attain great autonomy, enjoying the samadhi of playfulness (C. *yu-hsi san-mei*) in the six realms[25] and the four births.[26]

As in the *Platform Sutra*, playfulness in the *Gateless Gate* is characteristic of religious activity of the highest order, in which the practitioner moves independently, freely, and without discrimination through the samsaric realm.

While playful transformation did not always take a prominent place in East Asian Buddhism, it was a prominent topic in the Taoist tradition. Taoist alchemy and thaumaturgy are transformational arts *par excellence*, though the playful character of Taoism is perhaps best seen in the widely influential *Chuang-tzu*, which might be described as a playful study in the understanding of transformation. The Japanese Five Mountains Zen monks were quite interested in the teachings of Taoism, even more so than in those of the other Chinese classics.[27] A comparision of the conception of play in the *Chuang-tzu* will help us understand more fully the context for the Kitayama Japanese interest in playful transformation, an interest that was central to their interpretation of landscape art to be discussed shortly.

The *Chuang-tzu* begins with one of the most effective images in world literature of unrestricted cosmic wandering: the giant fish K'un that transforms itself into the marvelous bird P'eng. In this chapter and in such sections as the "Discussion on Making All Things Equal" and the teachings of the god of the North Sea in "Autumn Floods," we find spirited discussions of the effects of perspective on understanding and the impossibility of correct perception when bound to any single viewpoint. The attitude of the man who dreamt he was a butterfly, as Michael Crandell has pointed out, and indeed the overall tone of the *Chuang-tzu*, is one of quiet pleasure in a life at sea in a flood of change.[28] Throughout the *Chuang-tzu* we find the players in the text reveling in the transformations of the small into the large, the useless into the essential, and numerous other examples used to indicate the importance of avoiding attachment to any particular viewpoint and to other conceptual distinctions. This imagery came to the Japanese Kitayama monks not only through their study of the *Chuang-tzu* directly, but also indirectly through their reading in literary texts such as the poetry of the popular Yang Wan-li (1124–1206), who favored Taoist images of playfulness and transformation.

The *Chuang-tzu* play of nondual perception may be compared to and may have been used for many of the same intellectual and institutional purposes as that found in Buddhist contexts. The sophisticated arguments in the "Discussion on Making All Things Equal"[29] against distinguishing between "is" (*shih*) and "is not" (*fei*) are just as effective in countering conceptual discriminations as those of Buddhist arguments couched in terms of the nondualism of the real and the conventional. On the level of concrete imagery, we find images like "Mt. Sumeru on the tip of an autumn hair," which Chūhō used in his miniature garden preface, in such *Chuang-tzu* passages as, "There is nothing in the world bigger than the tip of an autumn hair, and Mount T'ai is tiny. No one has lived longer than a dead child, and P'eng-tsu died young."[30] Following the thread of such arguments takes a certain nimbleness of wit and flexibility of mind, but the ability to "make sense" of such "nonsense" was as highly prized in the Taoist intellectual tradition broadly understood as it was in the Zen temples of China and Japan.

Although the aimless, playfully wandering characters of the *Chuang-tzu* and the individuals it influenced are able to transcend obstacles in space and time as well as the conceptual barriers of the mind, they are to be found most often in narratives of the mountainous wilds. The typical Taoist sage is like the man on Ku-she mountain, described by a man whose words "never come near human affairs," who "climbs up on the clouds and mist, rides a flying dragon, and wanders beyond the four seas."[31] The sacred state of cosmic playfulness and wandering in Taoist-influenced Chinese and Japanese culture, then, was generally associated with a particular spatial realm, the sacred realm of the natural world.

Yet when considering the religious significance of this East Asian mode of interest in the natural landscape, it is necessary to keep in mind the internal component of such mountain wanderings. Many of the terms we have been considering are used to refer to an advanced internal state in addition to unobstructed action in the external world. As a case in point central to the present discussion, we might consider the Chinese term *yu*, which we have been translating variously as "playfulness," to refer to the subjective state and "wandering" to refer to physical movement. We see this double reference in the *Chuang-tzu* when the character is used as in the important term for wandering in the world, "free and easy wandering" *hsiao-yao-yu*, and in such passages of internal significance as, "Just go along with things and let your mind wander freely."[32] The reference of this and other terms to both a subjective state of mind and a mode of activity in the objective world is important when considering the significance of objective natural imagery for internal spiritual development.

We see the same doubled use in the Chinese and Japanese Zen traditions, where "playing in the mountains" or "wandering in the mountains" is a central component of religious practice. On the one hand this term denotes the physical wandering of monks from one teacher to another, many of whom were known by the name of the mountain where they resided. These roving monks often spent years searching for a master who could help them with their "great ball of doubt" and perhaps provoke an enlightenment experience. On the other hand, the internal dimension of the Zen practice of "wandering in the mountains" is suggested in passages we find in T'ang and Sung texts. For example, the well-known T'ang master Yun-men Wen-yen (864–949) responded to the question, "What is the self of the student?" with "Wandering in the mountains, playing in the waters."[33] In a similar vein Tung-shan Liang-chieh (807–69) had the following discussion with one of his disciples:

Master: Where have you been?
Yun-chu: Walking in the mountains.
Master: Which mountain was suitable for residing on?
Yun-chu: None was suitable for residing on.
Master: In that case, have you been on all the country's mountains?
Yun-chu: No, that isn't so.
Master: Then you must have found a path of entry.
Yun-chu: There is no path.
Master: If there is no path, I wonder how you were able to see this old monk.

Yun-chu: If there were a path, then a mountain would stand between us, Teacher.

Master: Henceforth, a thousand or ten thousand people will not hold fast to Yun-chu.[34]

Tung-shan's discussion of his disciple's wandering on the mountains turns on many of the most important issues we have been discussing, including "abiding," the Way, and conceptual grasping or attachment. Through his questions Tung-shan probes to see if his student objectifies outside of himself both a place of resting or attachment and the path or Way, and when the monk shows he does not Tung-shan praises him as impossible to tie down and restrict in his wanderings through the internal and external landscapes. In this passage then the natural landscape is also an internal state in which the self playfully engages with the world without falling into the intellectual abiding and grasping that characterizes the dualism of conceptual discrimination.

We find a passage from Sung dynasty Chinese Zen similarly suggestive of the internal aspects of traveling in the mountains in Yüan-wu's writings in *Blue Cliff Record* 25, which would have been familiar to several of the Kitayama Japanese monks. In this passage we find a discussion of the hermit of Lotus Flower Peak (d.u.) in which Yüan-wu playfully moves back and forth between the physical landscape and the inner implications of the images:

> Thus the hermit of Lotus Flower Peak said, "It's because they didn't gain strength on the road." To get it you simply must go into the myriad peaks [as the hermit said in answering, "In the end, how is it?"]. But say, what is being called "the myriad peaks"? [In his verse commentary] Hsueh T'ou is just like him saying, "With my staff across my shoulder, I pay no heed to people—I go straight into the myriad peaks." . . . But tell me, where does he go? Is there anyone who knows where he goes?[35]

By questioning his readers in this way (and not providing any answers), Yüan-wu directed them to discover the inner significance for themselves of the hermit's entering the mountains. By resisting the literal interpretation of the mountains as a place outside the self or a physical location through which the monk literally travels, Yüan-wu, Tung-shan, and Yun-men all pushed their followers to transcend the boundaries of inner and outer, self and other, and to consider the subjective significance of the landscape as sacred space in which these dualities do not hold. They also shared the same image of this sacred internal state as undirected wandering and unobstructed play, a play that allowed their fellow monks to roam far and wide in their own inner landscape just as they did in the mountain wilderness.

As we might expect, the Kitayama Five Mountains monks develop interpretations of landscape exploring both the external and internal facets of mountain wandering and playful transformation. Taihaku Shingen gives us an example of the

Japanese Zen use of "wandering in the mountains" as an act in the objective world in his record of a visit he paid to Gyuin-ji temple near Arima, a popular hot springs. Taihaku tells his readers how he went to the hot springs at Settsu to cure a case of beriberi and, after his condition improved, hiked over the mountains to the west of Kamakura Gorge. Taihaku began what sounds like a simple record of a journey in his 1392 preface, entitled "Preface for Wandering to Gyūin-ji in Kamakura Gorge," by alluding to famous Chinese Buddhist monks who made the mountains where they resided famous. On reaching the valley where the temple was, however, the tone and literary style of the tale changed. Taihaku began a lyrical description in four character phrases of an area so beautiful, "it was just as if we had wandered into the picturesque realm of the immortals."[36] Instead of finding Taoist immortals, however, he and his companions encountered "Several country monks sit[ting] bolt upright on meditation cushions in Dead Tree Hall."[37] After talking over the history of the temple with the monks, Taihaku composed on the spot a verse in which he further developed the association of the temple grounds with the land of the immortals:

> Expansive spring feelings,
> the urge to roam aroused.
> Chanting staffs break the green
> of the crude bridge's moss.
> Peach blossoms crowd the bank,
> searching for a hermit's retreat.
> Greens and leaves follow the flow,
> drawing the guest they come.
> Water encircles the stilled gate,
> twining an azure belt.
> Mountains surround a humble hut,
> opening verdant screens.
> Among the pines I sit on a stone,
> meeting these monks we talk.
> In the evening sun staying on and on,
> entranced I do not return.[38]

Taihaku likened his journey to that of the Chin dynasty fisherman in T'ao Ch'ien's famous prose piece, "Preface to the Poem on the Peach Blossom Spring,"[39] who by chance visits a land of immortals there but cannot find it again. He also suggests that the monks of Gyūin-ji are like the members of the utopian community the Chin fisherman found in a mountain cave.[40] The sacred character of this mountain retreat is seen in its timelessness, as Taihaku suggested in the absorption in the conversation that led him to forget to return.[41] Taihaku then closes the poem with an allusion to the last lines of the famous poem by the T'ang poet Wang Wei, "Chung-nan Country Home": "By chance I meet an old man of the forest;/ talking and laughing we forget to return."[42] In his wanderings in the mountains, then, Taihaku's poetic subject first transcended the formidable barriers of time and space that separated a Kitayama Japanese monk from the utopian community of Chin dynasty China, and then lost sense of time completely in his fascination with the marvelous manifestations of the mountains as sacred space. Through allusions to well-known poems by T'ao Ch'ien, Wang Wei, and others, Taihaku suggested that he was able to achieve the freedom of the Chinese sages and roam freely about through the world in a manner structurally similar to that of Taoist wanderers through sacred space and time.

The poetic theme of T'ao Ch'ien's Peach Blossom Spring existing not in a distant land but in the present was a popular theme in Sung Chinese poetry and painting. We find an example of this theme in the poetry of Su Shih, a favorite poet of Taihaku and other Kitayama monks. Su responded to the popular T'ang poet Li Po's characterization of Peach Blossom Spring as "another world, not that of men" with "The peach flowers, the stream are in the world of men!/ Wu-ling is not for immortals only."[43] A Japanese Five Mountains example of a similar theme of the discovery of the lands of the Taoist immortals in the present can be found in the poetry of Kokan Shiren, where he wrote in a poem on an artificial landscape, "Right now before your eyes is P'eng[-Lai] and Ying[-chou]."[44] Taihaku and other Five Mountains monks took their place in this tradition of seeing these sacred realms as available to those with a playful attitude free to move beyond the limitations of ordinary time and space.

In Su and Taihaku's poems the playful wandering of the sage transforms the world of man into the world of the immortals, and the mundane world becomes potentially a locus of the sacred. With this transformation, however, the distinction between the realm of the sacred as natural landscape and that of profane, everyday reality also begins to break down. The power of the Taoist adept and his Chinese literati followers to transcend all spatial and temporal limitations is also a power to move freely between the sacred and the mundane, between the paradises of the immortals and the realm of mundane bureaucratic reality for the Chinese literati or of metropolitan temple administration for the Kitayama Japanese monks. In their relations with the sociopolitical elites the Zen Buddhist monks of Kitayama Japan utilized religious symbols and practices grounded in the Buddhist, Taoist, and literary traditions to bring about a similar transformation of the mundane into the sacred.

Another important tradition of playfulness in Chinese culture that served as an important model for the aesthetics of the Kitayama Japanese monks was that of "ink play" (C. *mo-hsi*). The art historian Susan Bush has traced the history of this term back to the frequent use of "playfully" (*hsi*) in the titles of Tu Fu's poems, but finds the beginnings of its general application to all the arts of the brush in Su Shih's circle.[45] While Bush suggests that this term has "a deprecatory tone," when we consider the term in its context in Buddhist- or Taoist-influenced theories of self-cultivation we might also find a strongly positive sense to this artistic playfulness.

We can see that "playfulness" in art is associated with the difference between amateur and professional painting in a poem by Huang T'ing-chien, "A Prose Poem on the Retired Scholar [Su] Tung-p'o's Ink Play":

> The retired scholar [Su] Tung-p'o played with Master Brush and Master Paper, making a dried out stump, an ancient tree, a clump of dwarf bamboo, and cut-off hills. . . . Perhaps what is easy for a man of the Way and difficult for an artisan is like impressions in seal paste: frosty branches and wind-blown trees were first formed in his breast.[46]

Here we see that Huang's characterization of Su's art as playful removes it from the context of conventional criteria of judgment, and also from the social context of the professional painter. By associating playful artistic practice with the art of an amateur, Huang T'ing-chien was also valuing the moral and spiritual significance of the artistic accomplishment of the man of the Way over the artistic practice of the artisan painter.

The playful quality of the amateur art of the literati was what distinguished it from the work of the artisan, who was entangled in the web of social, political, and economic ties of patronage in court society. Playfulness served a dual function here, extricating literati art from judgment according to conventional social values, while at the same time placing it above professional art in spiritual value. Amateur art was given this high seriousness through its association with the eclectic mix of moral and spiritual values that Su Shih and his companions in ink play, Huang T'ing-chien, Mi Fu, and his son Mi Yu-jen, brought to the aesthetic evaluation of art.

Many of the most important terms in discussions of the spiritual significance of artistic activity in Su's circle, however, were drawn from the *Chuang-tzu*. Su and his circle borrowed conceptions from it that suggest that the elevated states of spiritual freedom so central to the text were achieved through artistic expression. Su and other members of his circle used such terms from the *Chuang-tzu* as "creative transformation" (*tsao-hua*) and "the creator" (*tsao-wu-che*) and used the tales of master craftsmen like the ferryman, Cook Ting, and Wheelwright Pien.[47] By mastering the secrets of artistic practice, the literati argued, artists could come to embody the transformative powers of the cosmos and attain sagehood. We see this conception of art in a colophon by Su Shih written on a bamboo painting by Wen T'ung:

> When [Wen] Yu-k'o painted bamboo,
> He saw bamboo, not himself.
> But did he merely not see people?
> Trance-like, he left his body.
> [Then] his body transformed with the bamboo,
> giving forth inexhaustible purity and freshness.
> Chuang-[tzu] is no longer of this world,
> So who can understand such concentration?[48]

Su believed that through artistic practice, Wen could attain such a high level of insight into the cosmic process of transformations that only the great sage Chuang-tzu could comprehend his subtlety.

Su and his friends' interest in the playfulness of true perception in artistic practice became widely influential by the Chin and Yüan dynasties. The Chin scholar Yuan Hao-wen (1190–1257) wrote: "When an accomplished man's skill is advanced, it is not called skill;/ In play one can also penetrate to true essence."[49] Here too we can see that artistic play has the same dual function we found in Northern Sung writings: it so differs from conventional categories of judgment, that it is "not called skill" but rather linked with a spiritually advanced state, an internal state in which the artist is capable of deep understanding. We see such a usage by the Kitayama Japanese Zen monks in an inscription by Gidō Shūshin on an extant painting now at the Art Museum of Princeton University by his close friend Tesshū Tokusai (fig. 6.1). The image is of an intimate landscape scene of *Orchids and Bamboos*, known by art historians as a flower and bird subject, and in his inscription Tesshū praises the brushwork of the playful (*yuge*) old Zen master as "divine" or "demonic" (*shen*).

Kitayama Japanese monks also associated ink play with Mi Yu-jen, a member of Su's circle who frequently used the term in his painting inscriptions.[50] In the earliest recorded Japanese poem-and-painting scroll inscription, which was written by Gidō on a painting in the style of Mi Yu-jen, Mi's brushwork is characterized as "playful" (C. *hsi-pi*).[51] An extant figure painting may give us some sense of the style that the early Muromachi *gozan* monks thought of as playful, the extant painting of *Ling-yun [Chih-ch'in] Viewing Peach Blossoms*.[52] The inscription by the Five Mountains Zen monk Sokuan Reichi (d. 1419) ends with a seal that reads, "Ink play in free time from Zen" (*Ch'an-yu mo-hsi*).[53] Here the playfulness is turned against the Zen institution itself, so that the serious value structure of institutionalized religious practice are inapplicable to the act of painting.

The application of conceptions of playfulness and leisure to individual Kitayama religious practice is seen most clearly in the names the monks chose for themselves, a surprisingly large number of which contain characters that mean "playful," "lazy," or "at leisure." Chūhō En'i gave the name "Drafts from the Room of Laziness" (*lan-man shih-kao*) to his literary collection,[54] while he also took the name of "Child of the Lazy Clouds" (*lan-yun tzu*) for himself. A similar trend is found in a number of names during the Yüan dynasty, including one important individual for the Kitayama Japanese monks, the influential monk, poet, painter, and later high government official Yao Kuang-hsiao (Tao Yen). Yao took as his *hao* or pen name "Old Fellow of the Tower of Laziness" (*lan-ke weng*). As we saw briefly in chapter 1, Yao's taste in such matters was influential in Kitayama Japan not only because of his fame on the continent, having been a close friend of the important poet Kao Ch'i, but also because he had written prefaces for Zekkai's poetry collection and Shun'oku Myo-ha's collected sayings. These conceptions of

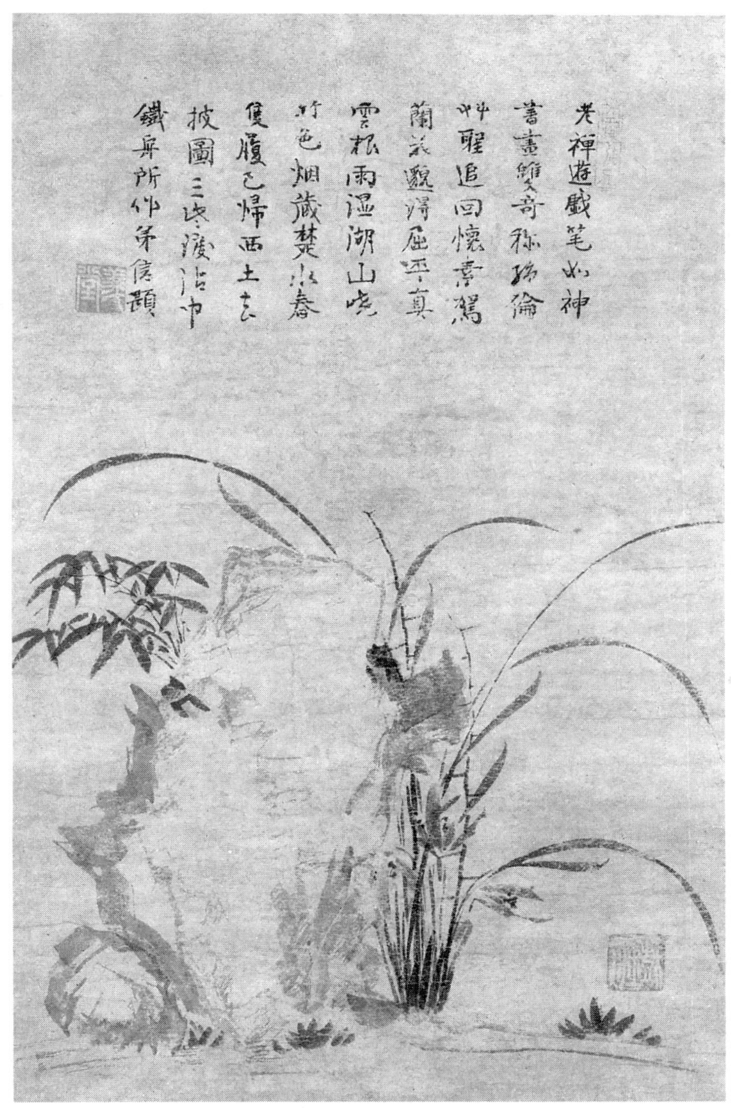

Fig. 6.1. *Orchids and Bamboo*. By Tesshū Tokusai (fl. 1342–66). Inscription by Gidō Shūshin. Hanging scroll. Ink on paper. 51.3 x 32.6 cm. C. 1381. The Art Museum, Princeton University. Anonymous loan.

laziness, like those of the "amateurish" character of the literati *mo-hsi* or ink play, served both on the mainland and in Japan to move the artistic activities out of the realm of conventional value judgments and conceptual distinctions and open them up to interpretations based in newly developing aesthetic and religious conceptions.

Play and leisure were associated in Zen texts, but became important for the Kitayama monks primarily in their application to artistic practice and interpretation. We find that this is not a new development in the Zen tradition, however, but is also found in the writings of T'ang Zen teachers and lay devotees, such as the early T'ang Northern School monk Ming-ts'an, who took as his sobriquet "Lazy Ts'an" (C. Lan-ts'an), and the late T'ang poet Han-shan. Han-shan, who was highly popular in the Zen temples of Sung and Yüan China, explicitly linked these states of mind to the highest ideals of the Zen tradition:

> A thousand clouds and ten thousand streams,
> In their midst lives an idle man,
> In the daytime wandering over green mountains,
> At night returning to sleep by the cliff.
> Swiftly springs and autumns pass,
> At peace and free from ties to the dusty world.
> How pleasant with nothing to rely on,
> Still as the waters of autumn rivers.[55]

A life of leisure and mountain wandering was for Han-shan how a man lives when free of attachments and dependencies, whose mind is still as autumn waters. In this highly advanced state of mind adepts express their release from the bonds of the conventional world through idleness and wandering in the sacred landscape, yet at the same time they achieve another state valued by many people in both metropolitan and rural settings, but perhaps especially important in the lives of Zen monks: peace of mind.

Playful transformation plays a major role in Zen practice, and can be said to lie at the heart of literary genres traditionally associated with Zen, such as the exchanges found in *kōan* texts and in encounter dialogues or *mondō*. One dramatic image of transformation, already familiar from its appearance in the *Chuang-tzu* and in Chūhō's miniature landscape preface, is that of the miraculous appearance of the very large in the very small and vice versa. We find examples of this type of imagery in classical Chinese Zen texts, such as the *Transmission of the Lamp*, as in the following passage by the important ninth-century Zen teacher Mu-chou Tao-ming (also Tao-tsung) (780–877), who was a teacher for both the enourmously influential Lin-chi and the powerful Zen spokesman Yun-men. Mu-chou once asked: "When one understands, a drop of water on the tip of a hair contains the great sea, and the great earth is contained in a speck of dust. What do you have to say about this?"[56] Such seemingly gratuitous paradox can also be understood as the play of Mu-chou with the illusory appearances of the mundane world, play that however asks that the abbot rise to the occasion and join in with the playful manifestation of his own nondual insight into the emptiness of the objective world. As we saw in the Chūho passage, the Kitayama monks often used such natural images as mountains and the fine autumn hair of animals to build these images. The common occurrence of such natural imagery of cosmic transformation in size indicates that they had become conventionalized representations of the play of perception in the changeable, illusory world. We find the Japanese Five Mountains monks took pleasure in these conventions and utilized them often in their writings on the landscape arts.

Another common Buddhist image in Kitayama Zen landscape painting inscriptions of cosmic transformation is that of the free movement of the enlightened person through time and space. In his inscription on the landscape painting of Sekidō Mountain already discussed, Kiyō Hōshū described his own vision of the power of the adept to transcend conventional conceptions of space and time.[57] Kiyō first described the beauty of the landscape in the painting, and noted the association of the mountain with the Nara period poet Chitoku (d.u.). Then Kiyō pointed out that he himself did not live in the mountains but "in aristocrat sponsored temples," and that "the capital is separated by 500 miles of land from Nōtō and Etchū, and I live more than 700 years after the virtuous [Chitoku]."[58] Kiyō used this to introduce what must have been a common problem for the Japanese Five Mountains monks: their separation in time and space from many of the sages that they were studying and emulating in their life and literature. As Kiyō commented, "Whether speaking of the region or of the person, I have never set foot there or set eyes on him. If you were to have me speak well of this [mountain], how can I write a preface without straying into speculation and fiction?"[59] In developing this point, the reader may recall that Kiyō turned to a visitor for its solution who, instead of resolving the practical dilemma of writing, turned to the larger question of spiritual practice and introduced Buddhist Hua-yen metaphysics. While making the common point about the need to transcend conventional conceptions of time and space, Kiyō's visitor also associated this with the Buddhist theme of the playful interrelation of the subject and object. By composing his preface in this manner, Kiyō is able to introduce a significant Buddhist dimension to his discussion of the obstacles to inscribing landscape paintings.

A more obvious aspect of the Kitayama Zen interest in playfulness is in the Five Mountains monks' use of the term "samadhi of playfulness." In a preface we have already touched on in chapter 2, Chūhū En'i used this notion "samadhi of playfulness" to characterize the production process of a landscape poem-and-painting scroll by his friend Kengan Genchū. Specifically Chūhō indicated that because Kengan wrote his poetry in this state of playfulness, Chūhō considers his literature to be comparable to that of the three great Zen poets of T'ang China, Chiao-jan, Kuan-hsiu, and Ch'i-chi. These would be terms of the highest praise in the Japanese Zen literary tradition.

In another preface we discussed in the last chapter, Gidō Shūshin told of a garden built for him by a friend at his new retreat where Gidō enjoys his attempted retirement by hoeing the surrounding, abandoned fields. The reader may recall that when his venerable guest Kōdō drops by, Gidō records that his guest attains "the samadhi of playfulness" as he completes his artistic production of Gidō's garden, and so Gidō established the playful quality of the appropriate Buddhist attitude toward such artistic activity. In this advanced state of mind, Gidō tells his readers that his visitor playfully produced the unreal qualities of the landscape garden: "In a samadhi of playfulness he skillfully built an artificial mountain in a tiny space under the eastern eaves, where he illusorily conjured up the appearance of a thousand precipices and ten thousand canyons."[60] It is in the state of playfulness that Gidō's friend was able to create his own illusory transformations, transformations that conform to the conventions of the natural landscape seen in terms of its empty, changeable character.

The application by Kiyō's visitor, Gidō, and Chūhō of the subjective state of playfulness to artistic perception and interpretation was for these monks only one aspect of the larger issue of the proper mode of activity in the world of ordinary society outside of their monastery walls. We can see in some passages how seriously the Kitayama monks took playfulness in their application of such notions to their politically charged social relations. In one example terms of playfulness are used at a funeral memorial service of none other than the shogun himself to describe advanced religious activity in the mundane world in a lecture delivered by Chūhō En'i in 1412.[61] In this lecture, Chūhō referred to the shogun as a praiseworthy student of the Buddhist teachings who had "played (*yuge*) among the deep meaning of the Buddhas and patriarchs"[62] while he characterized the life of the shogun as "the playfulness (*yuge*) of the samadhi of the king of the inexhaustible treasury."[63] His use of the conception of playfulness at an occasion which clearly called socially and conventionally for deep seriousness and lavish praise suggest that "playfulness" was for Chūhō a category of religious practice of the highest order. More importantly, this playfulness is the mode of activity that Chūhō chose to emphasize in his relationship with the most powerful figures in the world of ordinary social relations.

However, for the Kitayama Zen monks one of the more important images of this activity was the image of the eccentric Zen character Hotei (C. Pu-tai). Hotei had long been a popular Zen personage on the mainland, together with other semilegendary eccentrics, such as Han-shan, his companion Shih-te, and Pu-hua.[64] It was to this tradition, which had been particularly strong in the Chinese Zen monasteries of the Yüan and early Ming dynasties where the Japanese monks studied, that the Kitayama monks turned in their application of the theme of playfulness to their social interaction with secular elites.

We also learn from an inscription by Kiyō Hōshū on a now lost Hotei painting by none other than the shogun Ashikaga Yoshimochi[65] that for the Kitayama monks

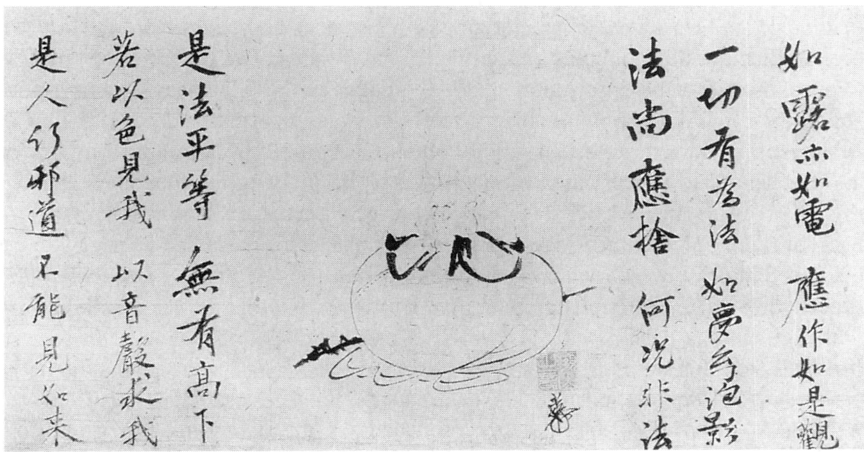

Fig. 6.2. *Hotei*. By Ashikaga Yoshimochi (1386–1428). Inscription by Ashikaga Yoshimochi. Hanging scroll. Ink on paper. 31.2 x 56.1 cm. Important Cultural Property. Fukuoka Art Museum, Fukuoka Prefecture.

Hotei was more than just another member of the Zen pantheon. Hotei was known to the Ōei monks as an image of the highest level of spiritual practice, in which the practitioner returns from seclusion in the mountains to the world of man, just as Vimalakīrti was active in the samsaric world. In his inscription Kiyō characterized Hotei at this high stage of spiritual practice in the following manner: "When at the crossroads, his thinking abides in playfulness."[66] The playfulness of Hotei is what allowed him to transcend such obstructions as the distinction of the transcendent realm of practice and the mundane world of the marketplace at the busy crossroads of the world, enabling him to reenter the world of samsara and again participate freely in everyday social and political relations. Yoshimochi also completed paintings of the eccentric and poet Han-shan,[67] and we may surmise that Kiyō or other influential Kitayama monks may have been instrumental in provoking the shogun's interest in these playful characters while also directing his understanding of them in a direction fully supportive of Zen Buddhist readings of literature, religious practice, and the Zen institutional basis.

Another possible example of the importance of Hotei in Kiyō's relationship with Yoshimochi that gives us important information about the Buddhist context for their relationship is found in an extant painting of Hotei in Yoshimochi's hand. In this painting, now in the Matsunaga collection (fig. 6.2), the inscriptions surrounding the lightly inked image are taken from an assorted collection of several passages from the *Diamond Sutra* (S. *Vajracchedikā Sutra*; J. *Kongōkyō*), a popular text in the *Perfection of Wisdom* tradition.[68] Included in this list are several images of illusion and transience characterizing all existences and taken from the sutra: a dream, illusion, dew, bubbles on the water, and the like. The character of both the lines chosen for the inscription and the image in the Matsunaga painting are suggestive. The lines are taken from one of the most important and popular texts in Mahayana Buddhism, one that might commonly be used by a monk from Zen or another school to instruct an advanced lay student in Buddhist fundamentals, and this is precisely the relationship that Yoshimochi seems to have had with Kiyō. Moreover, the Hotei image is associated with the *Ten Oxherding Pictures*, to be discussed shortly, which were (and still are) often used to instruct students in the progression of Zen religious practice. We know that Kiyō had a close relationship with the shogun Yoshimochi, for we have seen evidence of that in a number of passages from his writings. We also know from Kiyō's extant writings that he had a particularly close relationship to Yoshimochi's predecessor, Yoshimitsu, for he wrote two inscriptions on portraits produced on the occasion of Yoshimitsu's death.[69] It is not unlikely that Kiyō continued to have close relations with Yoshimochi after Yoshimitsu's death, since Yoshimochi may well have been involved in the selection of Kiyō to compose and inscribe these two important inscriptions on images of his father. Since we know that Kiyō worked closely with Yoshimochi on another Hotei painting, we may conclude that this painting could well have been the result of instruction by Kiyō of Yoshimochi in the fundamentals of Buddhist philosophy and Zen practice. Whether or not this is the case, the existence of this inscription shows clearly that Yoshimochi saw these Buddhist images of illusion as an important enough statement of Buddhist philosphy to select them from the *Diamond Sutra* in connection with his own artistic practice, and that he associated this fundamental Buddhist teaching with the playful image of Hotei. This documentation of Yoshimochi's views of popular Zen images of playful engagement in social relations shows how successful the Kitayama monks were in encouraging interest among political elites at the highest level in the Zen Buddhist culture of playfulness. More centrally for the argument of the present chapter, this image also shows how closely linked were themes of playfulness with Buddhist images of illusion in the minds not only of the Five Mountains Zen monks but also of Kitayama political elites.

I conclude this final chapter by examining a group of paintings and inscriptions with which Japanese monks and nuns may have begun their religious practice of Zen in the Kitayama temples: the "Ten Oxherding Pictures." The playful image of Hotei was known to the Kitayama monks for his role in this popular series of drawings and explanatory inscriptions. The series was used pedagogically in the Zen tradition, as it had been from the Sung dynasty in China, Central Asia, and elsewhere, to illustrate the stages of spiritual progress of the Zen mendicant, becoming very popular by the end of the thirteenth century.[70] We also know that it was used for these purposes in the Kitayama period, for records indicate that Zekkai lectured on the series to the shogun Ashikaga Yoshimitsu.[71] The series

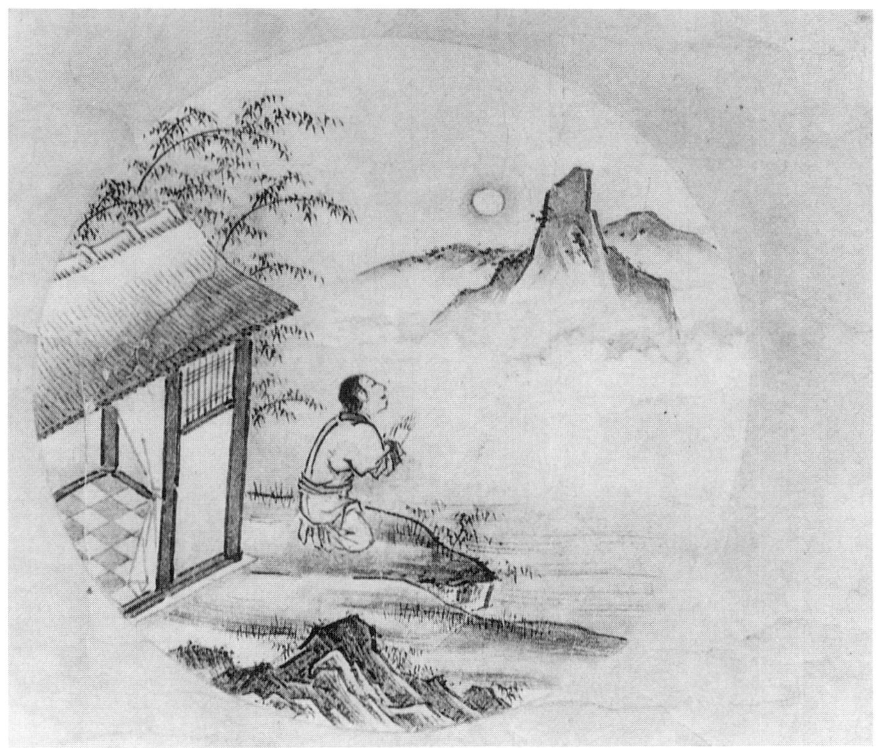

Fig. 6.3. Ten Ox Herding Pictures (#7—*Forgetting the Ox, the Person Remains*). Muromachi Period. Jōtenkaku Museum, Shōkoku-ji, Kyoto.

begins with six scenes depicting the journey of an oxherd taming an ox as a metaphor for deepening Buddhist understanding of attachments and the innately enlightened character of the mind. Once this journey has been completed, the seventh scene generally shows a person living the leisurely life of the recluse in a mountain retreat, illustrating the state of forgetting the ox and living one's life as one pleases (fig. 6.3). However, the tenth and final image is no longer of this transcendent realm of freedom outside of society, but one of a laughing Hotei entering the marketplace (fig. 6.4).

This sequence of the Ox Herding Pictures show clearly that at least in this period of Zen history in China and Japan the practitioner was expected to go well past the stage of retreat from society into the mountains in order to return to the realm of ordinary social relations. Zekkai Chūshin's own explanatory inscriptions to one of the earliest extant Japanese examples of a complete group of the Ox

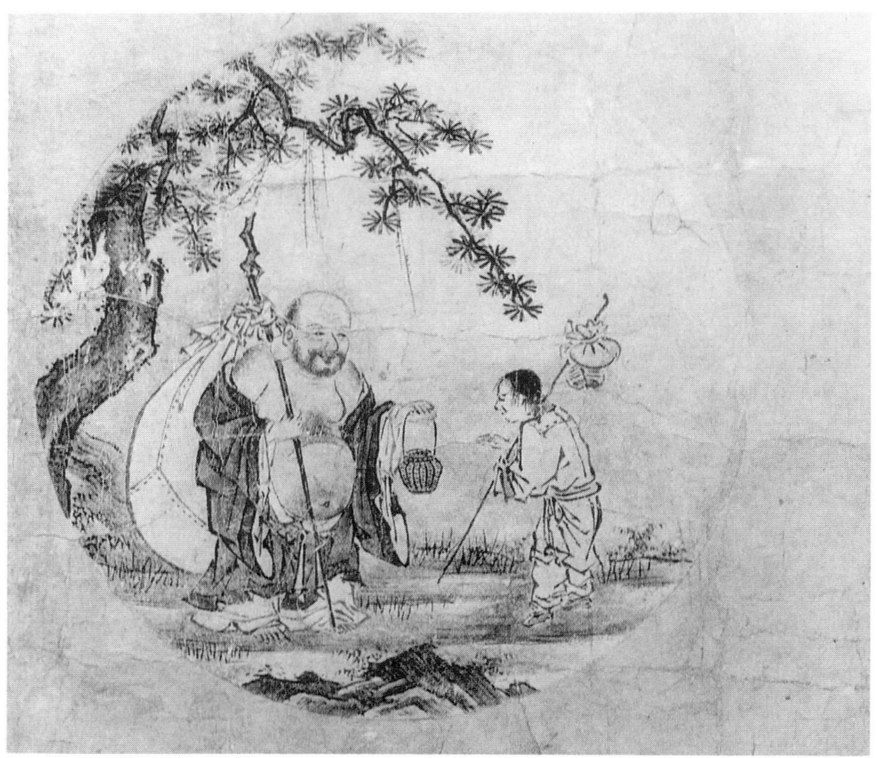

Fig. 6.4. Ten Ox Herding Pictures (#10—*Entering the Market with Basket in Hand*). Muromachi Period. Jōtenkaku Museum, Shōkoku-ji, Kyoto.

Herding series have been preserved, though the original paintings are now lost.[72] Zekkai describes the seventh stage with the traditional images of the monk still dreaming away while residing in a grass hut in the mountains.
The seventh poem reads,

> Riding the ox, [the oxherd] has finally returned to his mountain home;
> The ox has vanished into emptiness, and the person is tranquil.
> With the red sun high in the sky, he is still dreaming;
> A whip and rope discarded emptily, under the thatched hut (fig. 6.5).[73]

His explanation of the final stage in the series also follows the traditional text in depicting Hotei as an enlightened sage who, after passing through the various stages of religious progress, enters the bustling marketplace, dressed in ragged clothes and laughing wholeheartedly.

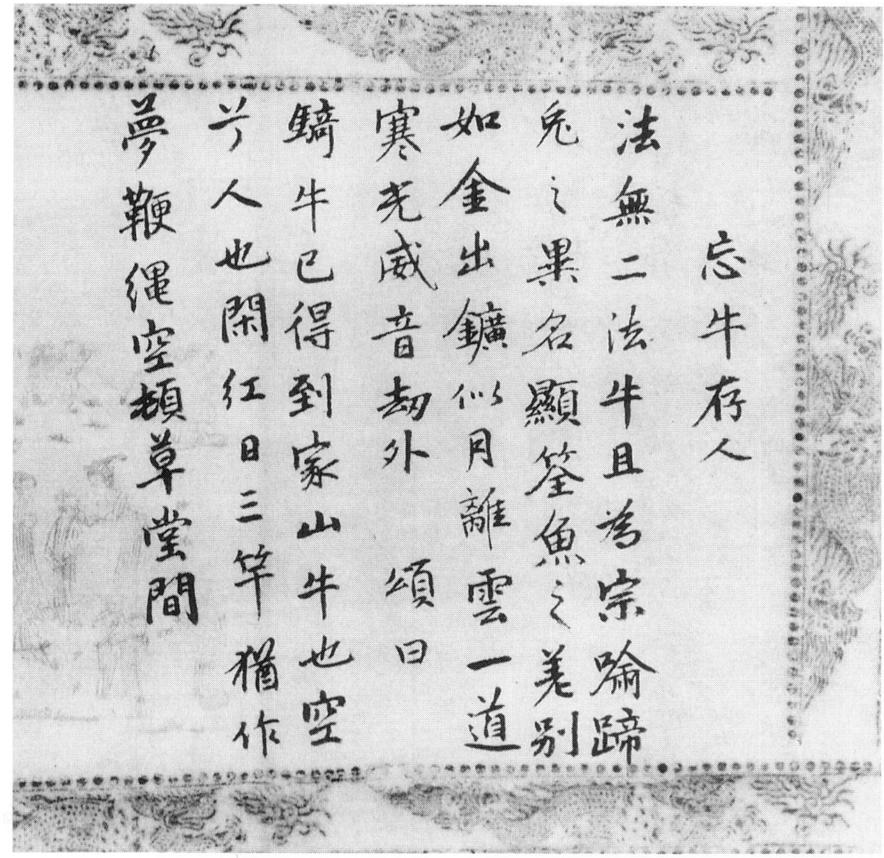

Fig. 6.5. Ten Ox Herding Verses (#7). By Zekkai Chūshin (1336–1405). Ink on paper. 33.4 x 33.4 cm. C. 1395. Jōtenkaku Museum, Shōkoku-ji, Kyoto.

Zekkai inscribed the final verse:

> Barechested and barefooted he enters the market place;
> Smeared with mud and ashes, he smiles broadly.
> No need for the gods and sages' divine powers;
> Directly leading dried branches, fragrant flowers blossom (fig. 6.6).[74]

In closing with this playful image, Zekkai underlines the importance of continued enlightened activity in the midst of the social world only after experiencing the freedom and leisure of the seventh stage's reclusive lifestyle in a mountain retreat.

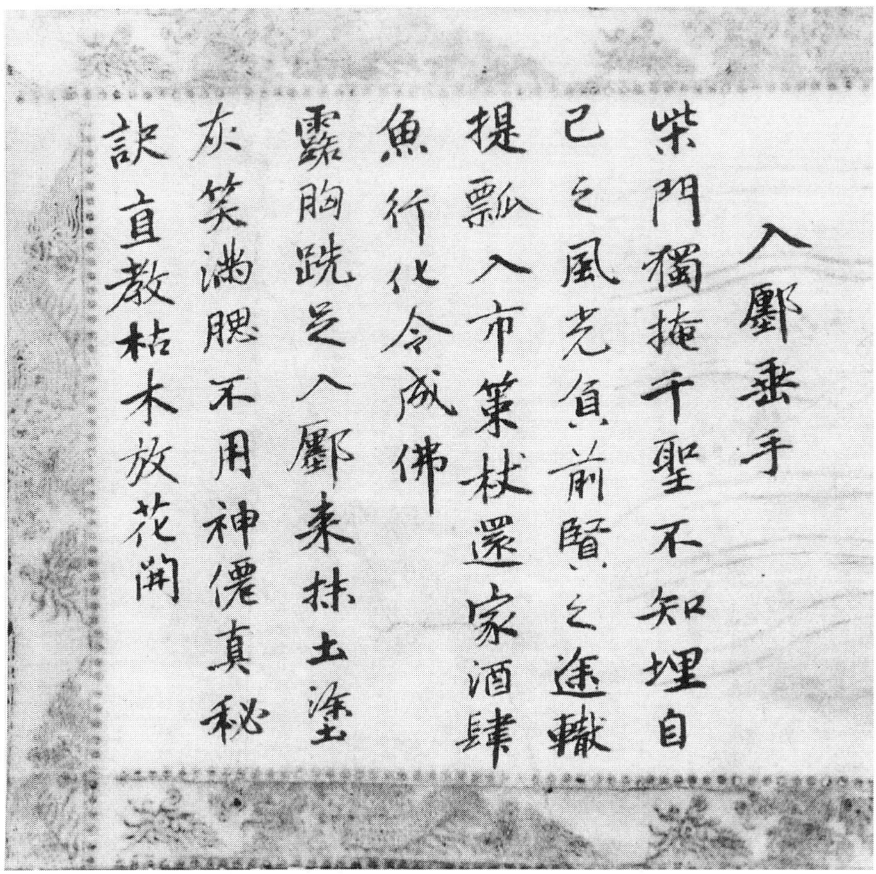

Fig. 6.6. Ten Ox Herding Verses (#10). Zekkai Chūshin (1336–1405). Ink on paper. 33.4 x 33.4 cm. C. 1395. Jōtenkaku Museum, Shōkoku-ji, Kyoto.

The relationship between landscape imagery and the playful wandering of enlightened beings in ordinary society seen in these images very much accords with interpretations of the landscape arts found in the other Kitayama documents we have surveyed. For the Japanese Five Mountains Zen monks the natural landscape took a central role in their lives, yet their lives in the capital were highly social and cultural in character. The Kitayama monks applied their visions of the landscape to their lives undertaken in the midst of the play of illusion and suffering in the mundane realm of ordinary social relations.

Conclusion

Through the Buddhist themes of playfulness and illusion the Kitayama Japanese Five Mountains monks developed a distinctive vision of the landscape arts. As a site for roaming free of the obstructions in Buddhist enlightenment, they read the landscape as a joyful and deeply religious state of mind present to all yet perceived only by those who have realized Zen insight. As a world of changing seasons and trickling streams, the natural world well represented to them the ever-transforming, unreliable, and even paradoxical or dreamlike nature of sentient existence in the Buddhist view, which made an ideal subject in their view for the heuristic functions of Buddhist art. While the two themes were certainly not without precedent, this Kitayama Zen vision of the natural landscape is perhaps their distinctive contribution to East Asian religious and cultural history.

The Five Mountains monks introduced this Buddhist vision of the landscape into early Muromachi period culture through their application of the "hermit at court" to their lives in the urban monasteries. In their explorations of this theme in elite culture, they were able to draw on the already well-established Chinese and Japanese tradition of a subtle moral critique implicit in the reclusion theme of craving for political influence and material affluence in court society. While this gave them an independent symbolic system of valorization of popular landscape themes in the heritage of Hui Yüan and predecessors in the Zen tradition, it simultaneously placed them in the delicate position of negotiating the difficult moral and spiritual terrain of life in court society, replete as it was with its own possibilities for corruption, avarice, and greed. However successful the Kitayama monks may have been individually in negotiating this terrain, we can tell clearly from their writings that they were quite consciously aware of these moral and religious tensions, and discussed them openly in attempting to inspire and model positive behaviors and in chastising their contemporaries and carefully monitoring their own monastic community. Moreover, in integrating seclusion in the natural world into their urban lives, these Japanese monks and their Chinese teachers may provoke considerations for those of us today who struggle with comparable moral, spiritual, and material issues of the problematic relation of nature to culture and civilization as it is defined in the twentieth century.

As we saw in earlier chapters, the Japanese Five Mountains monks drew on classical ideas and practices prominent in Zen and other schools of Chinese Mahayana Buddhism for this distinctive Buddhist vision of the landscape arts. Through the traditional emphasis on the innately enlightened mind, they developed and cultivated a realization of the nondualism of mind and object at the level of perception and of enlightenment and suffering at the experiential level. These same conceptions also provided them with a Buddhist philosophical basis for their participation through cultural study and interpretive appreciation of Buddhist and non-Buddhist texts and art objects in the long-established tradition of "literary Zen."

Like their Sung and Yüan Chinese predecessors, the teachings by Kitayama Zen monks of traditional Zen Buddhist ideals and practices were interwoven with elements borrowed syncretically from Chinese literati, Ancient Civilization, Confucian, and Neo-Confucian thinkers, writers, and artists. This Buddhist syncretism proved most effective in the propagation of Zen teachings and the strengthening of the Zen institutional base among male and female elite social and political strata. Ultimately the success of the Kitayama monks affected not only privileged members of the court cultural and political circles but also local elites in the domains of influential *shugo* daimyo and, through the flourishing Five Mountains temple system, some members of nonelite social strata both in the capital and in peripheral regions where there were found *shosan* and *jissatsu* temples. In the end, however, their close affiliation with the Ashikaga shoguns and the most powerful daimyo of the Muromachi *bakufu* also spelled the decline of the Five Mountains temple system in the late fifteenth century, as the Ashikaga authorities grew increasingly unable to effectively retain centralized power and gradually lost their access to symbolic and revenue resources.

Yet the literary, artistic, and aesthetic production of the Five Mountains Zen monks had an enduring impact on subsequent centuries of Japanese cultural history well outside the limits of Japanese literature in Chinese. These monks saw culture as a crucial means for the preservation of enduring spiritual value, and history found that to be the case. The works of the Kitayama and other Five Mountains monks were important to the cultural practices, aesthetic interpretations, and religious dimensions to the increasingly popular *michi* or Ways of linked verse and *waka* poetry, the Nō theater, ink painting, the garden arts, and the tea ceremony, as well as the *haikai* or haiku poetry and other arts of the Edo period. Through this influence the Five Mountains monks diffused into Japanese culture the ideals and interpretive conventions of the Chinese Zen literary and cultural tradition, as well as those of the Sung, Yüan, and early Ming proponents of literati learning and art, the Ancient Civilization movement, and Neo-Confucianism. This highly cosmopolitan dimension to Muromachi culture and indeed to premodern Japanese civilization argues quite forcefully against essentialist and monolithic characterizations of the uniqueness of Japanese culture. Further study is still much needed of the importance of continental aesthetic, social, political, and institutional forms for those aspects of premodern Japanese culture that have been privileged in the construction of twentieth-century Japanese cultural nationalism.

The Kitayama practice of a cultural form of Zen was highly social in nature, with its institutional basis in the friends societies and *tatchū* subtemples of the Five Mountains temple complexes but also extending into literary and social circles outside of the monastic walls. This cultural and social dimension to Zen religious practice had its origins in T'ang and Sung dynasty Zen Buddhism together with the affirmation of culture as a site for the discovery and production of enduring human value seen in the Ancient Civilization and literati tradition of Su Shih and others. While Su Shih may have lost the debate to the Ch'eng-Chu school Neo-Confucians in the Sung and Yüan on the proper locus of universal truths, particularly with Neo-Confucian successes in determining the Yüan and Ming state orthodoxy, this tradition continued to flourish in the Zen temples of the Sung and later dynasties as well as in some literati cultural production. By using *shigajiku* poem-and-painting scroll inscriptions as my central documentary source, documents which so clearly demonstrate the links of this mainland Zen cultural tradition to the Japanese islands, I have emphasized the cultural aspects of early Muromachi Zen Buddhist history. The Kitayama period when these scrolls became popular was the peak of Japanese Five Mountains culture, and the Kitayama monks were highly conscious of their participation in the literary and other artistic practices established by Chinese Zen monks of the T'ang and later dynasties. This historically important instance of a highly social and fundamentally cultural form of Zen reminds us that their Sung, Yüan, and Ming predecessors in this "literary Zen" tradition await future study.

Finally, the Muromachi Five Mountains monks certainly provide us with still more evidence useful in rethinking characterizations of Zen as radically antitextual, individualistic, anti-institutional, paradoxical or mystical, and iconoclastic. For these Japanese monks, Zen Buddhist religious insight is inseparable from textual study, written expression in prose or poetry, cultural appreciation, and the mainstream social and institutional context for these behaviors. Whether or not we may agree with them, in their day the Kitayama Japanese monks embodied the most respected form of Zen Buddhism in the eyes of their contemporaries. Their Zen Buddhism affirmed the importance of the landscape arts to understanding the Mahayana Buddhist vision of human experience in the bustling Japanese capital. They may still have much to teach us about the relation of religion with human culture, society, and politics.

Epilogue

Every methodology has its blind spots, while every set of assumptions has its limitations. As I have revised this manuscript, it has become more and more obvious how my own chosen approach led me to ignore aspects of the subject matter that might have otherwise been important or even central to my analysis. It has also become all too apparent how these limitations were produced through my own claims, which might broadly be characterized as humanist, objectivist, and in some fundamental ways Orientalist. These claims are, most fundamentally, that the privileged males I have written about were somehow representative of the Muromachi period, and that I have somehow come to authoritatively know and interpret a culture that is somehow "other" than my own. If the reader accepts these claims, then the present study may be seen to have a certain value for understanding the Japanese past even as it participates in the construction of a certain network of present, transnational relations.

During the decade since I first conceived of this study, the fields of Japanese studies and Buddhist studies have been changed irrevocably through the increasing penetration of a surprising wealth of new methods for the study of culture(s). As the array of methodologies increases, those like myself who were trained in area studies and the humanities as if there were only one way to research and write are now confronted with important choices. For this volume I have chosen to complete the project as I began it: as a study based on unselfconscious translation and "objective" or "factual" historical information. In doing so I defined myself as a member of what is probably the last generation of Asian studies scholars who will be able to make claims to knowledge of "their" subject without at least having to assert their veracity and authority more explicitly than I have done here.

Here I do not wish to defend the method I have used. I simply note that the approach used in this study led me to what seem now to have been important oversights. For example, I completed this decade of work completely unaware until just a few years ago that there flourished during the Kitayama period an entire Five Mountains system of Zen nunneries; hence I wrote with virtually no explicit reference to gender. On discovering this lacuna in what I felt was thorough research in a traditional sense, and believing that I had somehow just missed references to these nuns and temples in the Japanese scholarship that I had taken as my benchmark, I searched high and low for information on the Five Mountains nuns and nunneries in that scholarship. I was naively surprised to discover that there was no explicit discussion of nuns in the secondary works by the male religious and literary historians on whose work I had relied so heavily, unless I already knew what names to look for in primary documents. So in the present study we are missing analysis of women in Five Mountains culture, as well as any discussion of the consequences of the relations of monasteries to nunneries in Japanese history.

Nor did it ever occur to me to examine the implications of my location in North America, having been trained and then writing "here" about the "over there" that is Japan and Asia. I wrote without asking what significance my positionality had as a white, male subject in the context of U.S. assumptions about and relations with Japan, and how that positionality may have shaped or privileged my perceptions of Japanese cultural history. Moreover, my own positionality is of course dependent on an inversely positioned "object" of study, most significantly for this study being of course the vague yet persistent association of Japan with nature, and the implicit positioning of Japan in "the East" that this association inevitably implies. I have attempted to question some aspects of the distinctiveness or essential character of Japan deriving from Japanese cultural nationalism and *nihonjinron* theory, primarily through emphasizing the close relationship of the culture of the Japanese islands to that of the mainland. Yet I did not take the further step of asking why the landscape is associated with the "east" more broadly understood, and not just with the particular constructions of "Zen culture" that so persistently confront us. While writing about representations of the landscape arts and the natural world in East Asia, then, I did not ask about the origins of the association in the scholarship and in my own mind of Japan and of Asia with images of landscape, images that were certainly formative in my early selection of research topics, not only as an historical legacy of Orientalist scholarship in the "West" but also as a continuing reproduction of neocolonial relations in the late twentieth century. So in this study these associations remain fundamentally unquestioned, as does the related positioning of Japan as my "object" of study in the feminine and subordinated "east" and of myself as the "subject" of the study in the masculine and privileged "west."

Finally, throughout this study it seemed to make no sense that some authors felt that Zen literature expressed the highest religious insight while other authors argued that Zen literature represented a period of spiritual ennervation and corruption. So I explored the contradiction between two approaches: a rigid separation of religion from culture in scholarly and sectarian literature on Zen and Zen culture on the one hand; and on the other an enthusiastic identification of religion with culture in popular literature and scholarship on Zen culture. Ultimately I developed a critique of both bodies of work in this book, one that attempts to redefine the relation between the religious and the cultural or between the religious and the sociopolitical. Yet in examining questions raised of the corruption in the monasteries that many scholars assert in order to maintain their critique of "secularized" Zen, I faithfully followed my training and looked only at those documents studied in the humanities. For example, while my examination of religious, cultural, aesthetic, and intellectual history together is in a limited sense interdisciplinary, I never once even considered topics or documents taken from the realms of history and the social sciences, such as looking closely at the socioeconomic role of the monasteries or at the political and economic consequences and bases of Five Mountains Zen culture. This oversight may have already seemed apparent to many, since the Five Mountains monks were so directly involved in domestic and overseas politics and trade, yet their cultural production certainly also had broad-ranging effects in the production of centralized authority and discursive formations. Yet it is precisely such divisions of labor and of areas of study as those between the disciplines broadly conceived that preserve the past as the realm of study for the humanities and the present as the realm of study for the social sciences and their linkages with foreign policy, development policy, and other instruments of the nation-state and of transnational corporations. Examining such divisions would have raised questions of how interpretations of the past support present sociopolitical formations, and how culture works to produce certain unequal political, social, and economic relations.

These are some of the blindnesses with which I afflicted myself as well as the reader through my methodological choices. I do not lay out these lacunae here in order to deplore the weaknesses of the study the reader has just completed. Given the parameters and assumptions of this book, I do believe that it makes an important contribution to a large and relatively unexplored area of Japanese culture and of Zen Buddhist history in the particular tradition of scholarship to which it belongs. Rather, I merely wish to state explicitly that this study is limited in its vision of Japanese cultural and religious history, and that this limitation is not simply because there were certain documents that remain unexplored or untranslated. The reader surely knows that the ways culture is studied are changing quite dramatically in North America, Japan, and elsewhere, and I only wish to leave a clear reminder that this book is very much a part of that changing situation. Indeed, I have begun to explore some new methods for understanding and problematizing "culture" in my more recent work. Who knows what role Muromachi Japanese cultural history as here presented plays in producing the present, and how it may come to be understood in the future?

Notes

ABBREVIATIONS

GBS	*Gozan bungaku shinshū*
GBZ	*Gozan bungaku zenshū*
GSS	*Gozan shisō*
SBT	*Suiboku bijutsu taikei*
SPPY	*Ssu-pu pei-yao*
SPTK	*Ssu-pu ts'ung-k'an*
T	*Taishō shinshū daizōkyō*
Z	*Zokuzōkyō*
ZGS	*Zenrin gasan*

INTRODUCTION

1. Recent Japanese historians have emphasized the place of Japan in its East Asian context linguistically, culturally, and historically, as I do in this study. See the six-volume series, *Ajia no naka no Nihonshi*, ed. Arano Hironori, Ishii Masatoshi, and Murai Shōsuke (Tokyo Daigaku Shuppankai, 1992), and for the medieval period see especially Murai Shōsuke, *Ajia no naka no chūsei Nihon* (Azekura Shobō, 1988) and also his *Higashi Ajia ōkan: kanshi to gaikō* (Asahi Shinbunsha, 1995). For important articles applying this approach to Muromachi Japanese landscape paintings, see Shimao Arata, "Jūgoseiki ni okeru Chūgoku kaiga shumi," *Museum*, 463 (Oct. 1989): 22–34; Ebine Toshio, "Kan no sekai no seiritsu to tenkai," in *Suibokuga to chūsei emaki*, Nihon bijutsu zenshū, vol. 12, Kōdansha, 1993, 146–53; and Suzuki Hiroyuki, "Ōkansuru kaiga—Jūgo seiki kanji bunkaken no naka no 'karae' no igi," *Bijutsu kenkyū* 361 (1995): 1–23. I am grateful to Shimao Arata for bringing this last reference to my attention.

2. See in particular the discussion of religious and philosophical value of culture in Peter K. Bol, *"This Culture of Ours": Intellectual Transition in T'ang*

and Sung China (Stanford, CA: Stanford University Press, 1992) and Robert M. Gimello, "Mārga and Culture: Learning, Letters, and Liberation in Northern Sung China," in *Paths to Liberation: The Mārga and Its Transformation in Buddhist Thought,* ed. Robert E. Buswell Jr. and Robert M. Gimello (Honolulu: University of Hawaii Press, 1992), 371–437. I draw for this term "home tradition" on the important work of Judith A. Berling, in her *The Syncretic Religion of Lin Chao-en* (New York: Columbia University Press, 1980), 1–13 and passim. See also below.

3. A useful introduction to this temple system may be found in Martin Collcutt's *Five Mountains: The Rinzai Zen Monastic Institution in Medieval Japan,* Harvard East Asian Monographs, 85 (Cambridge, MA: Council on East Asian Studies, Harvard University, 1981) and his "Zen and the Gozan," in *Cambridge History of Japan,* vol. 3, Medieval Japan, ed. Kozo Yamamura (Cambridge: Cambridge University Press, 1990), 583–651.

4. A useful Western language introduction to the economic and political aspects of Japanese Zen temples during this period may be found in Collcutt's *Five Mountains.* For a somewhat dated but still useful introduction to the history of the period, see also the essays in John Whitney Hall and Toyoda Takeshi, eds., *Japan in the Muromachi Age* (Berkeley: University of California Press, 1977) and the more recent Kozo Yamamura, ed., *The Cambridge History of Japan,* vol. 3, Medieval Japan.

5. John McRae, *The Northern School and the Formation of Early Ch'an Buddhism,* Kuroda Institute Studies in East Asian Buddhism, vol. 3 (Honolulu: University of Hawaii Press, 1986), 51–54, 61–70, 239–43.

6. Tsung-mi's relations with literati elite members of the T'ang imperial court are documented by Peter Gregory, *Tsung-mi and the Sinification of Buddhism* (Princeton, NJ: Princeton University Press, 1991), 73–88.

7. Also known as the Council of Tibet and the Council of bSam yas'. See the important early study by Paul Demiévielle, *Le Concile de Lhasa: Une controverse sur le quiétisme entre bouddhistes de l'Inde et de la China au VIIIe siècle de l'ére chrétienne,* vol. 7 (Paris: Bibliothèque de l'Institut des Hautes Études Chinoises, 1952); and Y. Imaeda, "Documents tibétains de Touen-houang concernant le concile du Tibet," *Journal Asiatique,* 1975: 125–46.

8. Ko Ik-chin, "Introduction of Ch'an (K. Son) in the Later Silla," in *Assimilation of Buddhism in Korea: Religious Maturity and Innovation in the Silla Dynasty,* ed. Lewis R. Lancaster and C. S. Yu (Berkeley, CA: Asian Humanities Press, 1991), 169–229; and Cuong Nguyen, "The Teachings of Trần Thái Tōng: A Model of Syncretic Chan in Thirteenth Century Vietnam," forthcoming in *Creating the World of Zen: The Transmission of Sung Dynasty Ch'an Buddhism in East Asia,* ed. John McRae and Albert Welter, Fo Kuang Shan Buddhist Studies Series.

9. These contacts are well discussed in Miriam Levering, "Ch'an Enlightenment for Laymen: Ta-hui and the New Religious Culture of the Sung" (Ph.D. dissertation, Harvard University, 1978). For analysis of Ta-hui's importance in Zen history and the relationship between Zen style and his secular relations, see Robert

E. Buswell, "The 'Short-Cut' Approach of *K'an-hua* Meditation: The Evolution of a Practical Subitism in Chinese Ch'an Buddhism," in *Sudden and Gradual: Approaches to Enlightenment in Chinese Thought*, ed. Peter N. Gregory (Honolulu: University of Hawaii Press, 1987), 321–77. On Chung-feng, see Chün-fang Yü, "Chung-feng Ming-pen and Ch'an Buddhims in the Yüan," in *Yüan Thought: Chinese Thought and Religion under the Mongols*, ed. Hok-lam Chan and Wm. Theodore de Bary (New York: Columbia University Press, 1982), 419–78; and on Chung-feng's relations with lay disciples, see Fujishima Tateki, "Genchō bukkyō no ichiyōsō: Chūhō Myōhon o meguru kojitachi," *Ōtani Gakuhō* 57.3 (Dec. 1976): 147–63.

10. T. Griffith Foulk has argued convincingly against the existence of a Chinese Five Mountains Zen temple system, in his "The Japanese Views of Zen Institutions in Sung China," forthcoming in McRae and Welter, *Creating the World of Chan*. For a recent Japanese historian who has been examining evidence for such a Chinese temple system, see Nishio Kenryū, "Nitchū no gozan no ue o megutte," *Nihon rekishi* 447 (1985).

11. In English see Collcutt's *Five Mountains* for an introduction to the Kamakura and Muromachi period history of this topic. In Japanese, see, e.g. Imatani Akira, "Gozan Zen'in no Kokuōkan," *Shin Nihon koten bungaku taikei geppō* 18 (July 1990): 5–7. I have begun to explore linkages between the medieval and twentieth-century cultural politics of Five Mountains Zen culture in "Contested Orthodoxies in Five Mountains Zen Buddhism," in *Religions of Japan in Practice*, ed. George Tanabe, Jr. (Princeton, NJ: Princeton University Press, 1998), and in "Writing Cultural Struggle Past and Present: Orthodoxy and Literary Practice in the Transmission of Sung Chinese Ch'an Buddhism to Japan," forthcoming in *Creating the World of Zen: The Transmission of Sung Dynasty Ch'an Buddhism in East Asia*, ed. John McRae and Albert Welter, the Fo Kuang Shan Buddhist Studies Series.

12. Please see epilogue.

13. Collcutt, *Five Mountains*, 100. Collcutt here draws similar conclusions to those of the widely influential Japanese historian, Tamamura Takeji, as do the Japanese religious historian Akamatsu Toshihide and the American Zen scholar, Philip Yampolsky, in their important early article, "Muromachi Zen and the Gozan System," in Hall and Toyoda, eds., *Japan*, 313–30. See, e.g., Tamamura, *Gozan bungaku*, rev. ed. (Subundō, 1966), 198–200. This conception is surprisingly widespread in scholarship by other postwar Japanese religious historians. For an important review and critique of Tamamura's influence in art historical scholarship, see Shimao Arata, "Shoki shigajiku no yōsō—*Kūgeshū* ni mieru *Unjuzu* shigajiku o chūshin to shite," *Bijutsushi* 114 (1983): 98–99.

14. Berling, *Syncretic*, 1–13. For a survey of Chinese syncretism, see Kubota Ryōen, *Chūgoku Judōbutsu sankyō shiron* (Kokusho kankōkai, 1931). Japanese syncretism awaits a useful survey; for important studies see, e.g., Alicia Matsunaga, *The Buddhist Philosophy of Assimilation* (Tokyo: Sophia University Press, 1969),

and Allan G. Grapard, *The Protocol of the Gods: A Study of the Kasuga Cult in Japanese History* (Berkeley: University of California Press, 1992). Three Teachings syncretism as practiced in the Japanese Five Mountains monasteries is surveyed in Haga Kōshirō, *Chūsei Zenrin oyobi bungaku ni kansuru kenkyū* (Kyoto: Shibunkaku, 1981), 221–46, and its application to Five Mountains Zen painting is described in John M. Rosenfield, "The Unity of the Three Creeds: A Theme in Japanese Ink Painting of the Fifteenth Century," in Hall and Toyoda, *Japan*, 205–25.

15. In the Confucian and Neo-Confucian case, see the important work of Tu Wei-ming, e.g., his essays in *Humanity and Self-cultivation: Essays in Confucian Thought* (Berkeley, CA: Asian Humanities Press, 1979). For literati culture, see particularly Peter Bol, "*This Culture*," and also see the writings of Beata Grant, *Mount Lu Revisited: Buddhism in the Life and Writings of Su Shih* (Honolulu: University of Hawaii Press, 1994) and others.

16. Different scholars have suggested reasons for the popularity of this ideal according to whether they see culture as determined more by intellectual tradition or by geographic region. Bernard Faure, in his *The Rhetoric of Immediacy: A Culture Critique of Chan/Zen Buddhism* (Princeton, NJ: Princeton University Press, 1991) suggests (p. 56) the popularity comes from Mahayana Buddhism, while Robert Buswell associates it with religions deriving from the Chinese (and not Indian) geographic region in his "Short-Cut," 323.

17. For a useful survey of these developments as they apply to early Chinese Buddhism, see Robert M. Gimello, "Apophatic and Kataphatic Discourse in Mahāyāna: A Chinese View," *Philosophy East and West* 26.2 (1976): 117–36.

18. For a useful discussion of the relation of these ideas to Chinese Zen, see Peter Gregory, *Tsung-mi*, 12, 160, and 219–36.

19. Buswell, "Short-Cut," 356, quoting Araki Kengo, *Daiesho*, Zen no goroku 17 (Tsukuma Shobō, 1969), 80, and Christopher Cleary, trans., *Swampland Flowers: The Letters and Lectures of Zen Master Ta hui* (Grove Press, 1977), 41–42.

20. For an influential argument that such behavior is evidence of spiritual decline, see Tamamura Takeji, *Gozan bungaku*, passim, and Bernard Faure's critique of the "excesses" following from the identification of the passions with Buddhist awakening, potentially being used "to legitimate a kind of apology for the phenomenal world that verges on secularism and monism" (*Rhetoric*, 56) and coming at times "at the expence of transcendental values, and [leading] to legitimation of the profane enjoyment of the world of passions" (*Rhetoric*, 76). This may be contrasted with the approach of Robert Buswell, who finds this identity to positively characterize all of Chinese area religions, and Ta-hui in particular ("Short-Cut," 325).

21. See the range of historical and twentieth-century views of Zen Buddhism in James W. Heisig and John C. Maraldo, *Rude Awakenings: Zen, the Kyoto School, & the Question of Nationalism* (Honolulu: University of Hawaii Press, 1994). For the impact on objectivist Zen historical scholarship, see, for example, a special

issue of *Cahiers d'Extrême-Asie* 7 (1993–94) for interviews and personal reflections on how Japanese militarism affected the Zen scholarship of two of the most important twentieth-century Zen philologists and historians, Yanagida Seizan and Iriya Yoshitaka.

22. Collcutt, *Five Mountains*, provides a useful survey of monasteries for men during this period. Study of Kamakura and Muromachi Zen nunneries has only developed recently: see, e.g., Ushiyama Yoshiyuki, "Chūsei no amadera to ama," *Shiriizu josei to Bukkyō*, vol. 1: *Ama to Amadera*, ed. K. Osumi and J. Nishiguchi (Beibonsha, 1989), and Ōishi Masaaki, "Bikuni goshō to Muromachi bakufu: Amagozan Tsūgenji o chūshin ni shite," *Nihonshi kenkyū* 33.7 (1990): 1–28. While there did exist a Five Mountains system of Zen nunneries during the early fourteenth century, the unavailability of documents on the thought of Zen nuns while I was researching this project made it impossible to include them as a topic in the present study. For recent research on individual Zen nuns, see Barbara Ruch, "The Other Side of Culture," in *The Cambridge History of Japan*, vol. 3, ed. Kozo Yamamura (Cambridge: Cambridge University Press, 1990), 503–11; Joseph Parker, "Historicizing Gender Representations: Zen Buddhist Nuns from 13th Century Japan," unpublished manuscript; and the work of Anne Lazrove and others in various issues of the newsletter for Columbia University's Institute for Medieval Japanese Studies.

23. By the late fourteenth century the largest of these temples actually numbered eleven, for Nanzen-ji had been elevated to a status of "above the Five Mountains."

24. Collcutt, *Five Mountains*, 122. Murai, *Chūsei*, 259–81 and 295–311, discusses the importance of Five Mountains monks in political relations with the continent.

25. Like many of the teachers of the early Five Mountains monasteries, Dōgen and Daitō attempted to gain patronage at the Japanese court in Kyoto but both ultimately failed in different ways in the medieval period for different reasons. The Zen teachings of Dōgen became popular in Japan only in the twentieth century through the influence of the Kyoto school philosophers. Despite some significant early successes in securing patronage, the importance in Japan of Daitō's Zen in recent centuries has derived largely from Edo period developments in Zen history and textual study, and today virtually all of the Zen temples of the Rinzai school in Japan are led by abbots of Daitō's lineage.

26. Following the pioneering work of Kamimura (also Uemura) Kankō just after the turn of the century, Japanese-language Five Mountains Zen scholarship flourished in the 1930s and early 1940s, then revived again in the late 1950s only to increase substantially in the late 1970s and early 1980s. The more recent Japanese scholarly study of Five Mountains Zen has grown very rapidly, and will be referred to below. The Western language literature has consisted, with the exception of the art historical literature, largely of translations: Marian Ury, trans. and intro., *Poems*

of the Five Mountains, rev. ed., Michigan Monograph Series in Japanese Studies, vol. 10 (Ann Arbor, MI: Center for Japanese Studies, University of Michigan, 1992 [1977]); Thomas Cleary, trans. and ed., *The Original Face: An Anthology of Rinzai Zen* (New York: Grove Press, 1978); David Pollack, trans. and intro., *Zen Poems of the Five Mountains* (Decatur, GA: Scholars Press, 1985); Musō Soseki, *Dream Conversations: On Buddhism and Zen*, trans. Thomas Cleary (Boston: Shambala, 1996); and W. S. Merwin and Sōiku Shigematsu, trans. and intro., *Musō Soseki: Poems and Sermons* (San Francisco, CA: North Point Press, 1989). However, see also Collcutt, *Five Mountains*, and David Pollack, *The Fracture of Meaning: Japan's Synthesis of China from the Eighth through the Eighteenth Centuries* (Princeton, NJ: Princeton University Press, 1986), 111–57.

27. See, e.g., Carl Bielefeldt, "Filling the Zen Shū: Notes on the *Jisshū Yōdō ki*," *Cahiers d'Extrême Asie* 7 (1993–94): esp. 225; T. Griffith Foulk, in a volume forthcoming from Stanford University Press, questions conceptions of a "pure" Zen and other aspects of the Sung model of Zen; and Bernard Faure, *Rhetoric*, who develops a historically based critique of such preconceptions of Zen as being iconoclastic, antiritual, rationalistic, or nonsuperstitious. For reevaluations of Zen history without using the lens of the Sung Chinese histories, see Peter Gregory, who in his *Tsung-mi* has reconstructed the Zen landscape of the T'ang pre-Sung documents; and Robert Buswell, in "Short-Cut," who has concluded that the Sung (and not the T'ang, as in Sung views) represented the culmination of Chinese Zen in a reconsideration of the historical development of practice and pedagogy. For important recent critiques of the relation of Zen to Japanese nationalism, see *Rude Awakenings* and Robert H. Sharf, "The Zen of Japanese Nationalism," *History of Religions* 33.1 (Aug. 1993): 1–43.

28. Peter Gregory, *Tsung-mi*, 15–16, points out that while these phrases may be found scattered in early texts, as a group they have been retrospectively attributed to Zen's legendary founder Bodhidharma even though they occur together only in an early-twelfth-century text. For a convincing critique of the stereotypes of Zen based on these four phrases, see Robert E. Buswell Jr., *Zen Monastic Experience: Buddhist Practice in Contemporary Korea* (Princeton, NJ: Princeton University Press, 1992), 217–23.

29. T'ang Zen poets active during the eighth century are described in Stephen Owen, *The Great Age of Chinese Poetry* (New Haven, CT: Yale University Press, 1981); Thomas P. Nielson, *The T'ang Poet-Monk Ch'iao-jan*, Occasional Paper No. 3, Center for Asian Studies (Tempe: Arizona State University, 1972); and Ishihara Kōkichi, "Chūtō shoki ni okeru Kōsa no shisō ni tsuite," *Tōhō gakuhō* (Kyoto) 28 (Mar. 1958): 219–48. These poets were well known in Five Mountains Japanese Zen, as we will see below, and predate the Zen monk-poets and monk-artists of the ninth century who have become better known in twentieth-century popular culture, such as Kuan-hsiu (832–912) and Han-shan (active late eighth to early ninth centuries).

30. In this description of the function of these phrases and the changing objectives and contexts of Zen teaching during the T'ang and Sung, I follow Robert E. Buswell, "Short-Cut," 321–22 and passim. A comparable analysis may also be found in Peter Gregory, "What Happened to the 'Perfect Teaching'? Another Look at Hua-yen Buddhist Hermeneutics," in *Buddhist Hermeneutics*, Kuroda Institute Studies in East Asian Buddhism, vol. 6, ed. Donald S. Lopez Jr. (Honolulu: University of Hawaii Press, 1988), 207–8.

31. See esp. David W. Chappel, "Hermeneutical Phases in Chinese Buddhism," in *Buddhist Hermeneutics*, ed. Lopez, 175–206, and Gregory's summary of Tsung-mi's description of early Zen schools in *Tsung-mi*, passim. For an opposing view, see Faure, *Rhetoric*, 66–67, where he argues that early Zen thinkers disavowed the ontology of Buddhist scholasticism.

32. A groundbreaking English-language article discussing relations of Sung Zen monks with writers and artists is by Robert M. Gimello, "Mārga and Culture," 371–437. Discussions of the Sung debate on the appropriate role of textual and literary study are available in Buswell, "Short-Cut"; Evelyn Hsieh Ding-hwa, "Yuan-wu K'o-ch'in's (1063–1135) Teaching of Ch'an *Kung-an* Practice: A Transition from the Literary Study of Ch'an *Kung-an* to the Practical *K'an-hua* Ch'an," *Journal of the International Association of Buddhists* 17.1 (1994); and Ōno Shūsaku, "Ekō *Sekimon monjizen* no bungaku sekai," *Zengaku kenkyū* 67 (1989): 1–27. A history of relations between Chinese Zen monks and lay elites is also available in Abe Jōichi, *Chūgoku Zenshūshi no kenkyū* (Seishin shobō, 1963). See below regarding the debate in Japan.

33. For an English language introduction to this tradition in Chinese thought, see Conrad Holzman, "The Conversational Tradition in Chinese Philosophy," *Philosophy East and West* 6.3 (1956): 223–30.

34. These relations are discussed in the present author's "The Religious Meaning of Poetic Practice in Nijō Yoshimoto's Poetics," unpublished manuscript.

35. See Kōsai Tsutomu, *Zeami shinkō* (1962): 40–68, and Kasai Kiyoshi, "Manbō Kiichi—Funi Ōshō to Zeami," *Zen bunka* 61 (1971).

36. See epilogue.

37. Jan Fontein and Money Hickman, *Zen Painting and Calligraphy* (Boston: Museum of Fine Arts, 1970), xxxii.

38. The one exception to this problem has been the twentieth-century interest in the Daitoku-ji monk Ikkyū Sōjun, although the extent of his relations with contemporary artists, poets, and tea masters is still uncertain. For a carefully documented discussion of his relations with the Nō playwright and aesthetic theoretician, Zenchiku (1405–68?), see Arthur H. Thornhill III, *Six Circles, One Dewdrop: The Religio-Aesthetic World of Komparu Zenchiku* (Princeton, NJ: Princeton University Press, 1991). Studies and translations of his writings may be found in, among others, James H. Sanford, *Zen-Man Ikkyū*, Studies in World Religions, vol. 2 (Chico, CA: Scholars Press, 1981); Sonja Arntzen, trans. and intro., *Ikkyū and the*

Crazy Cloud Anthology: A Zen Poet of Medieval Japan (Tokyo: University of Tokyo Press, 1986); and Yanagida Seizan, *Ikkyū: "Kyounshu" no sekai* (Kyoto: Jinbun Shoin, 1980).

39. *The Nō Plays of Japan* (Grove Press, 1957), 59.

40. *Japan: A Short Cultural History*, rev. ed. (1943), 391.

41. See, e.g., William R. LaFleur, *The Karma of Words: Buddhism and the Literary Arts in Medieval Japan* (Berkeley: University of California Press, 1983), 23, and Faure, *Rhetoric*, 72–73. For a conception of literary or artistic spontaneity much closer in assumptions and intellectual heritage to the Five Mountains Zen monks, see Michael Fuller, "Pursuing the Complete Bamboo in the Breast: Reflections on a Classical Chinese Image for Immediacy," *Harvard Journal of Asiatic Studies* 53.1 (1993): esp. 18–19.

42. One important exception to this tendency in Western language scholarship is the work of Pollack, e.g., *Fracture*, 121–33. The recent surge of publications of Zen philological materials and Japanese Five Mountains literature with extensive and very reliable annotated modern translations has now made these texts more accessible to readers trained in classical Chinese. See such advances in references for reading in colloquial Zen materials as the *Zengo jiten*, edited by Iriya Yoshitaka with Koga Hidehiko (Kyoto: Tanaka Shūji, 1991), and other reference materials discussed in Urs App, "Reference Works for Chan Research: A Selected Annotated Survey," *Cahiers d'Extrême-Asie* 7 (1993–94): 357–409. See also the CD-ROM, *ZenBase CD 1*, ed. Urs App (Kyoto: International Research Institute for Zen Buddhism, 1985). For very reliable annotated modern translations in addition to those listed above, see *Kunchū kūge nichiyō kufū ryakushū—chūsei Zensō no seikatsu to bungaku*, Gidō Shūshin, Kageki Hideo, trans. (Kyoto: Shibunkaku, 1982); *Zenrin gasan: Chūsei suibokuga o yomu*, ed. Shimada Shūjirō and Iriya Yoshitaka (Mainichi Shinbunsha, 1987) (hereafter ZGS); and Iriya Yoshitaka, trans., *Gozan bungakushū*, Shin Nihon koten bungaku taikei, vol. 48 (Iwanami Shoten, 1990).

43. For an early trenchant critique of the association of Japanese religion and culture with nature, see John M. Steadman, *The Myth of Asia* (New York: Simon and Schuster, 1969), esp. 215–42; similar conclusions from a very different perspective are reached by Royall Tyler in his article, "A Critique of 'Absolute Phenomenalism,'" *Japanese Journal of Religious Studies* 9.4 (1982): 261–83. The general reasons for this phenomenon have been explored in Edward Said, *Orientalism* (New York: Vintage Books, 1979) and a substantial body of subsequent literature. Some of Said's conclusions are developed in application to Zen Buddhism by Bernard Faure in his *Chan Insights and Oversights: An Epistemological Critique of the Chan Tradition* (Princeton, NJ: Princeton University Press, 1993), 15–88. The historical development of these associations and the production of an internalized Orientalism in Asia are presented in Stephen Hay, *Asian Views of East and West: Tagore and His Critics in Japan, China, and India* (Cambridge,

MA: Harvard University Press, 1970); Stefan Tanaka, *Japan's Orient: Rendering Pasts into History* (Berkeley: University of California Press, 1993); and other works.

44. Perceptive discussions of the sociocultural and political implications of Chinese landscape poetry may be found in Owen, *The Great Age*, esp. 27–51, and of early Japanese landscape poetry in Gary L. Ebersole, *Ritual Poetry and the Politics of Death in Early Japan* (Princeton, NJ: Princeton University Press, 1989), e.g., 23–45.

45. I am indebted here to Peter Bol's discussion of Confucian cultural theory in Chin dynasty China in his "Chao Ping-wen (1159–1232): Foundations for Literati Learning," in *China under Jurchen Rule: Essays on Chin Intellectual and Cultural History*, ed. Hoyt Tillman and Stephen West (Albany: State University of New York Press, 1995), esp. 115–44.

46. See, e.g., Peter Bishop, *The Myth of Shangri-La: Travel Writing and the Western Creation of Sacred Landscape* (Berkeley: University of California Press, 1989); Alexander Wilson, *The Culture of Nature: North American Landscape from Disney to the Exxon Valdez* (Cambridge, MA: Blackwell, 1992); Paul Carter, *The Road to Botany Bay: An Exploration of Landscape and History* (Chicago: University of Chicago Press, 1987); Sally Price, *Primitive Art in Civilized Places* (Chicago: University of Chicago Press, 1989); Andrew Ross, *The Chicago Gangster Theory of Life: Nature's Debt to Society* (New York: Verso, 1994); and Marilyn Strathern, "No Nature No Culture: The Hagen Case," in *Nature, Culture and Gender*, ed. Carol P. MacCormack and Marilyn Strathern (Cambridge: Cambridge University Press, 1980). (I am grateful to Emily Chao for this last reference.) For an important contribution on this topic in Japanese studies, see Thomas Keirstead, *The Geography of Power in Medieval Japan* (Princeton, NJ: Princeton University Press, 1992), esp. 46–72.

47. See, e.g., Konishi's article, "Yoshimoto to Sōdai shiron," *Gobun* 14 (Mar. 1955): 1–9; Timothy Wixted's important study, "The *Kokinshū* Prefaces: Another Perspective," *Harvard Journal of Asiatic Studies* 43.1 (1983): 47–70; David Pollack, *Fracture*; and Arthur H. Thornhill III, *Six Circles*.

48. Gimello, "Apophatic," 133.

1. THE CHINESE RELIGIOUS AND CULTURAL CONTEXT

1. Chappell, "Hermeneutic Phases," 193–94, but see also John McRae, *The Northern School*, 134–35 and 342n322, on the problematic identification of some early Zen schools with specific sutras.

2. This possibility is suggested by Peter Gregory, "Perfect Teaching," 207–8.

3. Gregory, *Tsung-mi*, 79, 173–204.

4. Tsung-mi's relations with mid-T'ang literati are described in Gregory, *Tsung-mi*, 73–88.

5. See Introduction, note 19.

6. For a translation of an important Hui-yüan prose essay on landscape and discussion of his literary circle, see Susan Bush, "Tsung Ping's Essay on Painting Landscape and the 'Landscape Buddhism' of Mount Lu," in *Theories of the Arts in China*, ed. Susan Bush and Christian Murck (Princeton, NJ: Princeton University Press, 1983), 132–64; see also Richard Mather, "The Landscape Buddhism of the Fifth-Century Poet Hsieh Ling-yün," *Journal of Asian Studies* 18 (1958): 67–79; and Obi Kōichi, *Chūgoku bungaku ni arawareta shizen to shizenkan—chūsei bungaku o chūshin to shite* (1963).

7. Exceptions to this trend in modern scholarship are found in Yanagida Seizan, *Zen no jidai: Yōsai, Musō, Daitō, Hakuin* (Tsukuma Shobō, 1987), 191; and Iriya Yoshitaka, "Chinese Poetry and Zen," *Eastern Buddhist* 6.1 (May 1973): 54–67, and his essays, "Zen to bungaku," 3–10, and "Chūgoku no Zen to shi," 74–92, in his *Kyūdō to etsuraku: Chūgoku no Zen to shi* (Iwanami Shoten, 1983). Iriya has consistently argued that the highest level of Zen practice is precisely that which involves the linguistic or poetic expression of religious insight.

8. Tamamura Takeji, an influential historian of Five Mountains Zen in art historical and historical scholarship, frequently uses a distinction based on whether Zen monks have become "aristocratized," "degenerate," or "secularized," depending on whether they have begun to use the eclectic teachings and literary forms commonly used among the elite levels of Chinese society. See his *Gozan bungaku*, passim, and *Musō Kokushi—Chūsei Zenrin shuryū no keifu*, Sara Sōsho 10 (Kyoto: Heiraku-ji Shoten, 1958), 160–61, which is in part the basis for Akamatsu Toshihide and Philip Yampolsky, "Muromachi Zen," 313–30. Ogisu Jundō, in his "Mujun Shiban to Kidō Chigu," *Zenbunka* 56 (Mar. 1970): 31–35, distinguishes the "pure Zen" of "transmission outside the teachings" or "patriarchal Zen," in which he includes Three Teachings syncretism, from syncretic Zen, which he characterizes in terms of opposition to a combination of *nembutsu* practice and Zen. Imaeda Aishin characterizes the eclectic (J. *kenshū Zen*) forms as "merely Zen as something mixed with the teaching schools" in his "Chusei Bukkyō no tenkai (sono ni)," in *Nihon Bukkyōshi II, Chūseihen*, ed. Akamatsu Toshihide (Kyoto, Hōzōkan, 1967), 161. However, he also distinguishes between two different types of "pure" Zen. The first is reclusive and refuses the possibility of court patronage, which Imaeda associates with Dōgen and several disciples of Wu-chun Shih-fan, although Imaeda elsewhere notes that Dōgen attempted to gain patronage at the court in Kyoto but failed. Imaeda associates his second type with Zen beliefs of the Sung court, which he argues does not become "aristocratized," however, and which maintains an emphasis on rigorous meditation practice ("Chūsei Bukkyō," 160–62). While Imaeda's first type closely corresponds to Tamamura's, the second introduces the possibility of discussing Zen beliefs of the court without Tamamura's pejorative sense. The criteria for these various critical evaluations of Zen have a quite lengthy history, and are discussed in the context of fourteenth-century apologetics in the present author's "Contested Orthodoxies."

9. Buswell, "Short-Cut," 322, 328, 359–60n8, and passim. "Ch'an Education in the Sung: Ideals and Procedures," in *Neo-Confucian Education: The Formative Stage*, ed. William Theodore deBary and John W. Chaffee (Berkeley, CA: University of California Press, 1989), 99, and see also 79–88. On the Zen study of Confucian texts, see Eirk Zurcher, "Buddhism and Education in T'ang Times," in deBary and Chaffee, *Neo-Confucian Education*, 19–56.

10. The scholarship on this period in Zen history is not well developed. An English introduction is found in Ding-hwa Evelyn Hsieh's "Yüan-wu K'o-ch'in's (1063–1135) Teaching of Ch'an *kung-an* Practice: A Transition from the Literary Study of Ch'an *Kung-an* to the Practical *K'an-hua* Ch'an," *Journal of the International Association of Buddhist Studies* 17.1 (1994): 66–81, while the textual developments leading up to Northern Sung Zen poetry are surveyed in Yanagida Seizan, "The 'Recorded Sayings' Texts of Chinese Ch'an Buddhism," trans. John McRae, in *Early Ch'an in China and Tibet*, ed. Whalen Lai and Lewis R. Lancaster (Berkeley, CA: Berkeley Buddhist Studies Series, 1983), 185–206. Also see Robert Gimello, "Poetry and the *Kung-an* in Ch'an Practice," *Ten Directions* 7.1 (Spring–Summer 1986).

11. Discussed in Buswell, "Short-Cut," 345ff.

12. Yüan-wu and Ta-hui were not the first to use this term, but their employment of it became widely influential. Robert Buswell gives a useful summary of their approach in his "Ch'an Hermeneutics: A Korean View," in *Buddhist Hermeneutics*, ed. Gregory, 231–56.

13. For the importance of the Three Teachings and the conciliatory attitude taken by Ta-hui and his followers toward Confucian and Taoist teachings as well as officials, see Miriam Levering's article "Ta-hui and Lay Buddhists' Ch'an Sermons on Death," in *Buddhist and Taoist Practice in Medieval Chinese Society*, ed. David W. Chappell (Honolulu: Hawaii University Press, 1987), 181–206.

14. For discussion of the literary Zen of the earliest Chinese monks in Japan, see the present author's "'Scribbling without End': Chinese Zen Monks' Views of Textual and Artistic Study in Kamakura Japan," unpublished manuscript, and see also below.

15. I use the term "teacher" throughout to refer not to the master under whom a monk formally accepted the transmission of the Buddhist teachings, but to a teacher understood in the broader sense of a Zen master under whom a monk studied for a significant period of time. My information on teacher-student relationships is taken in this section from a wide variety of sources, the most useful being "Zenshū denrai kankei shiryō," in *Zen to bijutsu: kenkyū happyō to zadankai*, Bukkyō bijutsu kenkyū Ueno kinen zaidan josei kenkyukai hōkokusho 10 (Mar. 1983): 21–48, and the chart in a Tamamura article, "Nihon Zensō no tokai sangaku kankei o hyōjisuru shūhazu," in his *Nihon Zenshushi ronshu*, 3:151ff., both of which show study relationships in addition to formal transmission lines.

16. Collcutt, *Five Mountains*, 41–48.

17. Imaeda discusses the importance of the *Tsung-ching lu* in early Japanese Zen and Enni's use of the text in his *Chūsei Zenshūshi no kenkyū* (Tokyo Daigaku Shuppankai, 1970), 73–75.

18. Ogisu Jundō, "Nihon Chūsei Zenshisō no tenkai," in Ogisu Jundō ed., *Zen to Nihon bunka no shomondai* (Kyoto: Heiraku-ji Shoten, 1969), 21–25.

19. Ogisu Jundō, "Mujun Shiban to Kidō Chigu," 31–35.

20. Haga, *Chūsei Zenrin*, 57–61, 105–6, and 124.

21. Haga, *Chūsei Zenrin*, 105.

22. Tamamura describes the relationship between court society and Wu-chun as well as his disciples in his "Nihonsō no gunsanshita Sōmatsu Gensho Chūgoku Zenrin no shoeka," *Nihon Zenshūshi Ronshū*, vol. 2 (Shibunkaku, 1976), 781–82.

23. This "pure" Zen is also associated with the Zen teachings of his disciple, Shūhō Myōcho, the temple Shūhō founded, Daitoku-ji, Shūhō's disciple, Kanzan Egen (1277–1360), and the temple he in turn founded, Myōshin-ji. One reason these temples and their founders have played a prominent role in modern scholarship is because they are the source of modern Japanese Rinzai Zen, and the description of spiritual purity of their founders of course reflects their own claims to spiritual vitality.

24. See, e.g., Iriya Yoshitaka, "Kidō no geju o yomu tame ni," *Daitoku-ji bokuseki zenshū*, ed. Maruoka Muneo (Mainichi Shinbunsha, 1984), 1:249–51 and passim.

25. Hsü-t'ang's Zen is described by Ogisu, in "Mujun," 35–40. The importance of Hsu"-t'ang's literary activities for the Japanese Zen tradition is discussed in Tamamura's "Nihonsō no gunsanshita," 782–85.

26. Wu-hsüeh is quoted in Kageki Hideo, *Gozan shishi no kenkyū* (Kasama Shoin, 1979), 37. Ta-hui P'u-chüeh Ch'an-shih yü-lu, *Taishō Shinshū Daizōkyō*, ed. Takakusu Junjirō, et al. (Society for the Publication of the Taishō Edition of the Tripitaka, 1924–32) (hereafter cited as T.), vol. 47, kan 18.

27. These poems in their original scroll format have been lost, but the texts have been preserved in an Edo period edition. See Tamamura, "Nihonsō no gunsanshita," 783.

28. I am grateful to Ebine Toshio for bringing this type of literary meeting to my attention.

29. "Nihonsō no gunsanshita," 784–85.

30. *Lan-ch'i Yü-lü*, cited in Haga, *Chūsei Zenrin*, 245. The Musō admonition has been widely translated and discussed; see, e.g., Pollack, *Fracture*, 129.

31. Discussed by Kageki Hideo, *Gozan shishi*, 38ff.

32. See Tamamura, *Gozan bungaku*, 60–106; Kageki, *Gozan shishi*, 25–88; Ōmura Toyotaka, "Sōgendai raichōsō to Kamakura Zen—Gozan bungaku no engen o megutte," *Tōhoku Fukushi Daigaku ronsō* 10 (1971): 119–30.

33. Haga Koshirō, "Zensō no bungakukan no hensen," *Nihon koten bungaku taikei geppō* 2.23 (Feb. 1965): 6.

34. *T'ung-shu* 28, in *Chou-tzu ch'uan-chu*, 10.180. Trans. in James J. Y. Liu, *Chinese Theories of Literature* (Chicago: University of Chicago Press, 1975), 114. Chu Hsi's response to this passage is translated in Richard John Lynn's "Chu Hsi as Literary Theorist and Critic," in *Chu Hsi and Neo-Confucianism*, ed. Wing-tsit Chan (Honolulu: University of Hawaii Press, 1986), p. 337.

35. *Yu-chang Huang hsien-sheng wen-chi, Ssu-pu ts'ung-k'an*, comp. Chang Yüan-chi, et al. (Shanghai: Han-fen-lou, 1919–33) (hereafter *SPTK*), 7:26.9b. My translation adapted from Susan Bush, *The Chinese Literati on Painting: Su Shih (1037–1101) to Tung Ch'i-ch'ang (1555–1636)*, Harvard-Yenching Institute Studies, 27 (Cambridge, MA: Harvard University Press, 1971), p. 44; text no. 74, p. 191.

36. Here I follow in part Hoyt Cleveland Tillman's suggestions for developing a new classification system for Sung intellectual history, in his "A New Direction in Confucian Scholarship: Approaches to Examining the Differences between Neo-Confucianism and *Tao-hsüeh*," *Philosophy East and West* 42.3 (July 1992): 455–74, esp. 469–70.

37. Important exceptions to this problem have been the work of Ronald Egan on the Ou-yang Hsiu and the *ku-wen* movement, and the substantial body of scholarship on Su Shih, particularly, for the present purposes, that of Peter Bol. See Ronald E. Egan, *The Literary Works of Ou-yang Hsiu (1007–72)* (Cambridge: Cambridge University Press, 1984), and Bol, "*This Culture*." Important Sung and later texts on this topic by literati scholar-officials have been translated with very useful annotations by Stephen Owen in his *Readings in Chinese Literary Thought*, Harvard Yenching Institute Monograph Series, 30 (Cambridge, MA: Council on East Asian Studies, Harvard University, 1992), 391ff. This volume, which is perhaps the best single source in a Western language for understanding Chinese literary theory, was unfortunately not available to me when preparing the present study.

38. "*This Culture*," 22–27, and "Chao Ping-wen (1159–1232): Foundations for Literati Learning," in *China under Jurchen Rule: Essays on Chin Intellectual and Cultural History*, ed. Hoyt Tillman and Stephen West (Albany: State University of New York Press, 1995), 115–44.

39. In this section I rely on Peter Bol, "*This Culture of Ours*" and Ronald Egan, *Ou-yang Hsiu*. On the topic of the religious meaning of textual study, see also Egan, "Ou-yang Hsiu and Su Shih on Calligraphy," *Harvard Journal of Asiatic Studies* 49.2 (Dec. 1989): 416, and Fuller, "Bamboo," esp. p. 14.

40. Kuo Shao-yu, *Chung-kuo wen-hsueh p'i-p'ing shih* (Shanghai: Wen-i Ch'u-panshe, 1956), 141, cited in Egan, *Ou-yang Hsiu*, 16. Egan notes that Kuo Shao-yu believed this anticipated much of Sung Ancient Civilization and Neo-Confucian literary theory.

41. *Ou-yang Hsiu ch'üan-chi* (Taipei: Shih-chieh Shu-chü, 1961), 1:499; translation from Bol, "Culture and the Way," 72; s.a. "*This Culture of Ours*," 184.

42. *Ou-yang Wen-chung-kung chi, SPTK*, 63.6b–7a; trans. Egan, *Ou-yang Hsiu*, 23–24.

43. "Liu-i shih-hua," *Ou-yang wen-chung-kung chi, SPTK*, 128.5a–b; my translation is adapted from Jonathan Chaves, *Mei Yao-ch'en and the Development of Early Sung Poetry* (New York: Columbia University Press, 1976), 110–11.

44. The differing Sung theories of the place of poetry in self-cultivation are surveyed in Peter Bol, "Culture and the Way in Eleventh Century China" (Ph.D. dissertation, Princeton University, 1982), 35–37, 129–38, and 263–74. See also Bol's "*This Culture of Ours*," 148–342.

45. Egan, *Ou-yang Hsiu*, 80ff.

46. Here and in the next paragraph I rely on Egan, *Ou-yang*, 29ff. As Egan notes, Ou-yang is the individual who establishes this lyrical and personal element in these prose genres as an important aspect of literati prose.

47. Yoshikawa Kōjirō, *An Introduction to Sung Poetry*, trans. Burton Watson (Cambridge, MA: Harvard University Press, 1967), 24–28. See also Egan, *Ou-yang Hsiu*, 81–96.

48. See Egan, *Ou-yang Hsiu*, 98.

49. Discussed by Egan in *Ou-yang Hsiu*, 93–95.

50. Discussed and translated by Egan, *Ou-yang Hsiu*, 87–91, 95, 215–17. This record was included in a number of collections, including the late Sung or early Yüan *Ku-wen chen-pao*, which was studied in Japan by Chuho En'i and his contemporaries. See *Kobun shinpō*, ed. Hoshikawa Kiyotaka, Shinshaku kanbun taikei 16 (Meiji Shoin, 1963), 163–68.

51. In his "Record of Transcendence Pavilion," Ogawa Tamaki and Yamamoto Kazuyoshi, *So Toba shishū* (Tsukuma Shobō, 1986), 3:615–19.

52. Egan, *Ou-yang*, 95.

53. Bol, "Chao Ping-wen," 140–44.

54. A study of these poems and their differences with earlier poems on paintings can be found in Ronald C. Egan, "Poems on Paintings: Su Shih and Huang T'ing-chien," *Harvard Journal of Asiatic Studies* 43.2 (1983.12): 413–51; also see Aoki Masaru, "Daiga bungaku no hatten," *Aoki Masaru Zenshū* (Shunchōsha, 1970), 2:491–504, and Stuart Sargent, "Colophons in Countermotion: Poems by Su Shih and Huang T'ing-chien on Paintings," *Harvard Journal of Asiatic Studies* 52.1 (1992): 263–302.

55. The development of this rise in the status of painting has been outlined by Susan Bush in *Chinese Literati*, esp. 22–51. A discussion of the formative development of the Sung relationship between poetry and painting through the popular theme "Eight Views of the Hsiao and Hsiang" can be found in Alfreda Murck, "Eight Views of the Hsiao and Hsiang Rivers by Wang Hung," in Wen C. Fong et al., *Images of the Mind* (Princeton, NJ: The Art Museum, Princeton University, 1984), 214–35. For general treatments of the relationship in East Asia of poetry with painting, see Jonathan Chaves, "Some Relationships Between Poetry and Painting

in China," *Renditions* (1976): 88–97, James Cahill, *The Lyric Journey: Poetic Painting in China and Japan* (Cambridge, MA: Harvard University Press, 1996), and Robert E. Harrist, Jr., *Painting and Private Life in Eleventh-Century China:* Mountain Villa *by Li Gonglin* (Princeton, NJ: Princeton University Press, 1998).

56. Bush, *Chinese Literati*, 30–31.

57. This discussion is based largely on Bush, *Chinese Literati*, 29ff.

58. *Chi-chu fen-lei Tung-p'o hsien-shen shih, SPTK*, 10:24.39a. My translation modifies Bush, *Chinese Literati*, 30.

59. I have modified Bush's translation, *Chinese Literati*, 25.

60. Bush, *Chinese Literati*, 25. The translations are mine.

61. Descriptions of this painterly tradition may be found in Marsha Weidner, "Ho Ch'eng and Early Yüan Dynasty Painting in Northern China," *Archives of Asian Art* 39 (1986): 6–22, and Susan E. Nelson, "On Through to the Beyond: The Peach Blossom Spring as Paradise," *Archives of Asian Art* 39 (1986): 23–47. Julia Murray has authored an important full-length study of the Southern Sung political and social context for such artworks in her *Ma Hezhi and the Illustration of the Book of Odes* (New York: Cambridge University Press, 1993).

62. Egan, "Poems on Paintings," 421–26.

63. *Tung-p'o Ch'uan-chi, Ssu-pu pei-yao*, comp. Kao Yeh-hou et al. (Shanghai: Chung-hua Shu-chu, 1927–31), *hsu-chi*, 2.5b (hereafter referred to as *SPPY*). Translated and discussed by Egan, "Poems on Paintings," 422.

64. "Poems on Paintings," 419. This approach to landscape painting in particular has been termed by James Cahill the "mind landscape," meaning a painting on which a cultural interpretive framework is overlaid over the actual landscape image. See his introductory essay in *Artists and Patrons: Some Social and Economic Aspects of Chinese Painting*, ed. Chu-tsing Li (Seattle: University of Washington, 1989), 9–10.

65. *Chi-chu fen-lei Tung-p'o hsien-sheng shih, SPTK*, 10: 60.10a; my translation adapts Bush, *Chinese Literati*, 31.

66. Egan, "Calligraphy," 403.

67. Ibid., 408–9.

68. For an introduction to the role of Buddhism in Su's life and writings, see Beata Grant, *Mount Lu Revisited.*

69. Translated in Egan, "Calligraphy," 409.

70. Ibid., 409.

71. Mi Fu, *Hai-yueh t'i-pa*, in *Chin-tai pi-shu*, comp. Mao Chin (Shanghai: Po-ku-chai, 1922), 2b. Discussed and translated in Bush, *Chinese Literati*, 70.

72. *T'u-hua chien-wen chih*, 1.12a, in Alexander Soper's *Kuo Jo-hsu's "Experiences in Painting"* (Washington, DC: American Council of Learned Societies, 1951), p. 15. I here follow James Cahill's translation, "Wu Chen: A Chinese Landscapist and Bamboo Painter of the Fourteenth Century" (Ph.D. dissertation, University of Michigan, 1958), 19.

73. Sung attitudes toward formal representation are a continuing theme in Bush's *Chinese Literati*. See esp. 13–22, and 32–34 on Su Shih. Bush argues that there was a continuing concern with representation in the Sung, followed by a more completely expressive theory of art in the Yüan. For a comparable view, see also Wen C. Fong, *Beyond Representation: Chinese Painting and Calligraphy, 8th–14th Century* (New York: Metropolitan Museum of Art, 1992). By contrast, James Cahill, in his thesis "Wu Chen" (pp. 27–39), argues for a more expressive theory of painting and interpretation in the Sung dynasty. In my own understanding of these texts I find that artistic interpretation in the Sung and later generally emphasizes a broader range of aspects of the artist's character than that of feeling most commonly associated with Neo-Romantic notions of art as expression.

74. Egan, "Poems on Paintings," 419.

75. *Chi-chu fen-lei Tung-p'o hsien-sheng shih*, *SPTK*, 5:11.29a. Translation adapted from Bush, *Chinese Literati*, 26. Also translated in Egan, "Poems on Paintings," 426.

76. *Chung-kuo li-tai shih-hua chuan*, ed. Tai Hsiao-jo (Chang-sha: Yueh-lu Shu- sha, 1985), 1:377.

77. Maggie Bickford, *Ink Plum: The Making of a Scholar-Painting Genre* (Cambridge: Cambridge University Press, 1996), 115ff.

78. James Cahill has argued that the Sung interest in intention or idea (*i*) is a representational theory of art, as opposed to the expressive interests of Yüan literati painters. See *Hills beyond a River: Chinese Painting of the Yüan Dynasty, 1279–1368* (Weatherhill, 1976), 165. Here I am emphasizing the continuity between the writings of Su on *i* and those of later Yüan literati, and ultimately with Kitayama Japanese views.

79. *Chi-chu fen-lei Tung-p'o hsien-sheng shih*, *SPTK*, 9:54.9a–b; translation adapted from Bush, *Chinese Literati*, 42.

80. Stephen Owen argues that such an assumption is found throughout the Chinese poetic tradition. See, e.g., his *Traditional Chinese Poetry and Poetics: Omen of the World* (Madison: University of Wisconsin Press, 1985), 251ff.

81. This argument is found in Tu Wei-ming's "'Inner Experience': The Basis of Creativity in Neo-Confucian Thinking," in *Humanity and Self-Cultivation: Essays in Confucian Thought* (Berkeley, CA: Asian Humanities Press, 1979), 106–7.

82. *Chu Tzu Yü-lei* comp. Li Ching-te, 1880 ed., 33.8b; trans. by W. T. Chan in *Reflections on Things at Hand: The Neo-Confucian Anthology Compiled by Chu Hsi and Lü Tsu-ch'ien* (New York: Columbia University Press, 1967), 96.

83. The implications of this group for understanding Zen culture is ably discussed in Robert M. Gimello, "Mārga and Culture," 371–437. The importance of Buddhism for this circle of scholar-officials is demonstrated in Harrist, *Painting and Private Life*.

84. Bush, *Chinese Literati*, 8–9. Bush also describes (pp. 9–10) a meeting of six members of Su's circle where Su and Li together completed a painting, *Resting*

in Contemplation, based on a line from a Tu Fu poem. Also see Gimello, "Mārga," passim.

85. Bush, *Chinese Literati*, 105–7.

86. The hesitant response of the educated elite to the call to government service during the period of unrest is described in some detail in Frederick W. Mote, *The Poet Kao Ch'i (1336–1374)* (Princeton, NJ: Princeton University Press, 1962). Discussions of the philosophical arguments behind these developments during the Yüan can be found in Mote's "Confucian Heremitism in the Yüan," in *Confucianism and Chinese Civilization*, ed. Arthur F. Wright (Stanford, CA: Stanford University Press, 1975), 252–90; and Tu Wei-ming, "Towards an Understanding of Liu Yin's Confucian Eremitism," in *Yüan Thought: Chinese Thought and Religion Under the Mongols*, ed. Hok-lam Chan and Wm. Theodore de Bary (New York: Columbia University Press, 1982), 233–78.

87. Yoshikawa Kōjirō finds Yang Wei-chen to be the first example of a literati who felt no need to serve in government. Yoshikawa also notes that although there had been some tendency in this direction during the Southern Sung among the Chiang-hu school poets, none of those poets were important and this trend had not continued after their time (*Genminshi gaisetsu*, Chugoku Shijin senshū nishū, 2 [Iwanami Shoten, 1963], 104). While Yoshikawa focuses his discussion more on Yang Wei-chen, both of these individuals are described by Susan Bush as early examples of the "Confucian recluse." See *Chinese Literati*, 118.

88. Zekkai Chūshin may have had contact with Kao Ch'i during his travels on the mainland (Kageki Hideo, personal communication, Dec. 1985), and Kao Ch'i's poetic style definitely influenced the Japanese Kitayama monks. (Discussed by Kageki in his *Gozan shishi*, 305–6.) Yang Wei-chen is known to have written a farewell poem for the Japanese painter-monk Chōun Reihō (d.u.) as Chōun prepared to return to his homeland, although it is unclear when or if he ever returned to Japan. (See *Japanese Ink Paintings from American Collections: The Muromachi Period, An Exhibition in Honor of Shūjirō Shimada*, ed. Yoshiaki Shimizu and Ann Yonemura [Princeton, NJ: The Art Museum, Princeton University, 1976], 241 and 243n8.) See also below for less direct ways in which Yang's writings played an important, formative role in the Japanese *shigajiku* inscriptions.

89. Evidence of contact between a Japanese monk active in the Kitayama period and Wang Meng is discussed in an article by Ebine Toshio, "Ō Mō ni atta Nihonjin," *Bunjinga suihen, Chūgokuhen*, Monthly Report 3 (Dec. 1985): 1–2. This contact is evidence for interest among the Japanese monks of the late fourteenth century in the art and aesthetics of Wang Meng.

90. For an extended study of eremitism and the reclusive scholar's study in early Yüan dynasty landscape painting, see Shou-chien Shih, "Eremitism in Landscape Paintings by Ch'ien Hsüan, c. 1235–1307" (Ph.D. dissertation, Princeton University, 1984), esp. 122–38. The scholar's study continued to be important for a number of late Yüan and early Ming painters, including Ch'en Ju-yen (active

c. 1341–68) and Hsü Pen (active c. 1372–97). See Claudia G. Brown, "Ch'en Ju-yen and Late Yüan Painting in Suchou" (Ph.D. dissertation, University of Kansas, 1985).

91. Several examples of the scholar's study image from earlier painting that were important for Yüan painters are listed by Ōnishi Hiroshi in *ZGS*, 222.

92. Brown, "Late Yüan Patronage," 104.

93. One example of Wang Meng's image of the scholar's study is developed in heavily Buddhist terms in a painting inscription from his literary collection, modern Japanese translation and commentary by Iriya Yoshitaka, *Chūgoku bunjin shisen* (Chūō Kōronsha, 1982), 69–73. See the collection of Wang Meng's painting inscriptions in Chuang Shen, comp., *Huang-ho Shan-ch'iao Shih-chao*, in *Yuan-li Ssu-hua-chia Shih-chiao-chi.*

94. Ōnishi, ZGS, 222.

95. See his collected writings, *Liao-an Ch'ing-yü Ch'an-shih Yü-lü*, in *Dai Nihon Zokuzōkyō* (hereafter cited as *Z*) (Kyoto: Kyoto Zōkyō Shoin, 1905–12), 2, 6, 4 (vol. 614): 291a–396a.

96. Published in Tayama Hōnan, *Zenrin bokuseki shūi* (1977), pl. 87. Ch'u-shih's collected sayings have been translated by J. C. Cleary, *A Tune beyond the Clouds: Zen Teachings from Old China* (Berkeley, CA: Asian Humanities Press, 1990).

97. Liscomb, "Wang Fu," 42, and Ōnishi Hiroshi, in *ZGS*, 222.

98. Brown, "Late Yüan Patronage," 102.

99. Liscomb, "Wang Fu," 42.

100. Published in Sherman E. Lee and Wai-kam Ho, *Chinese Art under the Mongols: The Yüan Dynasty (1279–1368)* (Cleveland: The Cleveland Museum of Art, 1968), pl. 260; and Wai-kam Ho et al., *Eight Dynasties of Chinese Painting* (Cleveland: The Cleveland Museum of Art, 1980), pl. 112; and inscription texts transcribed with painting in Ishikawa Jun et al., eds., *Kō Kōbō, Gei San, Ō Mō, Go Chin*, Bunjinga suihen (Chūō Kōronsha, 1985), 3:178–79. Publication record of the painting can be found in *Eight Dynasties*, 138. Descriptions of extant paintings and a biography of Yao T'ing-mei may be found in Richard Barnhart, "Yao Yen-ch'ing, T'ing-mei, of Wu-hsing," *Artibus Asiae* 39 (1977): 105–23.

101. Shimada Shūjirō, "Muromachi jidai no shigajiku ni tsuite," *ZGS*, 13 and 17.

102. Kageki, *Gozan shishi*, 365–6.

103. Yoshikawa, *Genminshi*, 103–4; Western-language discussions of Yang's literary activities in the circle surrounding Kao Ch'i can be found in Mote, *Kao Ch'i*, 195–96 and 245, and in the circle surrounding Ku Te-hui (1310–69) in David A. Sensabaugh's "Life at Jade Mountain: Notes on the Life of the Man of Letters in Fourteenth-Century Wu Society," *Suzuki Kei sensei kanreki kinen Chōgoku kaigashi ronshū*, ed. Suzuki Kei sensei kanreki kinenkai (Yoshikawa Kobunkan, 1981), 50–55.

104. Wai-kam Ho, *Eight Dynasties*, 138.

105. Further discussed in the next chapter.

106. Wai-kam Ho, *Eight Dynasties*, 137–38.

107. Two of the inscriptions comment on the problem of the *chün-tzu* who lives in reclusion, that of nos. 10 and 15; see Ishikawa Jun et al., ed., *Kō Kōbō, Gei San, Ō Mō, Go Chin*, 178–79.

108. Translated by Susan Bush and Hsio-yen Shih, comps. and eds., *Early Chinese Texts on Painting* (Cambridge, MA: Harvard University Press, 1985), 248. Also translated in part by James Cahill, *Hills*, 165. Note that important characters in the last phrase differ in two extant texts of this preface: the text in Yang's literary collection has *hsin-ch'uan shen-ling*, while the text in the preface to Hsia's history has *hsin-ch'uan i-ling*. See Yang's *Tung-wei-tzu chi, SPTK* ed., 11.9a, and Hsia's *T'u-hui pao-chien*, in *Hua-shih Ts'ung-shu*, comp. Yu Hai-yen (Shanghai, 1963), 3:1.

109. For a discussion of Yang's artistic theory, see Maeno Naoaki, "Min Shichishi no senshō—Yō itei no bungakukan ni tsuite," *Chūgoku bungakuhō* 5: 41–69.

2. JAPANESE FIVE MOUNTAINS ZEN AND THE POEM-AND-PAINTING SCROLLS

1. *Gozan bungaku zenshū*, ed. Kamimura (also Uemura) Kankō (Shōkabō shoten, 1906), 3:2511–12 (hereafter referred to as *GBZ*).

2. We learn of the importance of Yüan-wu's poem for Kengan's scroll later in the preface. Two lines from this poem are preserved in the *Shih-jen Yü-hsieh* comp. Wei Ch'ing-chih (13th c.) (Shanghai: Ku-chi Ch'u-pan-she, 1978), 452, which was widely read in the Kitayama monasteries.

3. The identity of Sekiho is unknown, but his high social role is suggested by Chūhō's ending to the preface, in which he encourages Sekiho to strive to equal the Chinese sage-emperor Shun.

4. Kageki, *Gozan shishi*, 35–37.

5. Ibid. Further discussion of early attitudes toward literary and other textual study may be found in the present author's "Scribbling without End."

6. See Kawaguchi Hisao, "Zenrin sankyoshi no tenkai ni tsuite—Dōgen sankyo jūgoshu to Zekkai sankyo jūgoshu," *Kokugakuin zasshi* 72 (1971.11): 206–18, who also provides a comparative discussion of Dōgen's poems on landscape hermitages with those of the influential Kitayama monk Zekkai Chūshin.

7. The general topic of literary and cultural activities of Chinese Zen monks is a neglected topic in twentieth-century Western-language research, with the exception of recent work by Robert Gimello. Secondary literature on the Japanese monks and their cultural production has increased substantially in the last two decades. Japanese Zen literature is surveyed in Tamamura, *Gozan bungaku*; Kageki, *Gozan shishi*; Asakura Hisashi, *Zenrin no bungaku* (Seibundō Shuppansha, 1985); and Kageki, *Chūsei Zenrin shishi* (Chikuma shoin, 1994). The last volume was unfor-

tunately unavailable to me during the writing of the present manuscript. Western-language translations of Japanese Five Mountains poetry can be found in Marian Ury, *Five Mountains*; David Pollack, *Zen Poems*; and Alain Colas, "Gozan no shisō," *Furansu no bungaku (Rikkyō Daigaku)* 13 (1983), 15 (1985), 17 (1987), 18 (1988), and 19 (1989). A survey of the travels of Japanese monks in this generation on the continent may be found in Shimizu Yoshiaki, "Problems of Moku'an Rei'en (?–1323–1345)" (Ph.D. dissertation, Princeton University, 1974). The early intellectual history of Japanese Five Mountains literature is surveyed in Chisaka Takashi, "Gozan bungaku e no michi—Joron," *Seiwa* 14 (1977.3): 25–42, and "Gozan bungaku e no michi—juyon seiki no gozan ni okeru shisōteki tokuchō o megutte," *Seiwa* 15 (1978.3): 23–57.

8. Cultural activities other than literature of these monks are documented in Haga, *Chūsei Zenrin*, while the best discussion of their interests in Neo-Confucianism may still be found in Ashikaga Enju, *Kamakura Muromachi jidai no Jukyō* (rpt. Ariake Shobo, 1970).

9. In this paragraph I rely on Tamamura Takeji's "Gozan sōrin no tatchu ni tsuite," *Nihon Zenshūshi ronshū* 1:197–243. See also Colcutt, *Five Mountains*, 181, 215, and 224.

10. Personal communication, T. Griffith Foulk, 1995.

11. Ōnishi Hiroshi in his "Sesshū shiryō o yomu," *Nihon bijutsu kōgei* 452 (May 1976): part 5, pp. 85–86.

12. See, for example, Ōnishi's discussion of paintings by Sung and Yüan dynasty artists on the same poem of parting by Li Po that would be the basis for the extant Kitayama era painting *Blue Mountains and White Clouds* (*ZGS* 193).

13. See David Pollack, "Literature as Game in the T'ang," in *Legend, Lore, and Religion in China*, ed. Sarah Allan and Alvin P. Cohen (San Francisco: Chinese Materials Center, 1979), 205–24, and Cahill, *Lyric Journey*.

14. Japanese literary gatherings are recorded as early as the eighth century; see Paula Doe, *A Warbler's Song in the Dusk: The Life and Work of Ōtomo Yakamochi (718–785)* (Berkeley: University of California Press, 1982), 30ff. For information on illustrations of poems in the tradition of the Thirty-Six Sages of Poetry (Sanjurokkasen), including a 1347 image of the important Japanese Shingon monk Kukai in a landscape setting, see among others Umezu Jirō, "Shakyōkasen giri ni tsuite—Kōbō Daishizō ni yosete," *Yamato bunka*, 5 (1952.1): 56–58. I am grateful for suggestions on this topic from Joshua Mostow.

15. David Pollack discusses the participation in linked-verse meetings of two important *gozan* Zen monks, Kōhō Kennichi (1241–1316) and his enormously influential student Musō Soseki (1275–1351), in *Fracture* 124–25. Pollack also discusses the alternating of Japanese and Chinese verses, *wakan renku*, with particular attention to Gidō Shūshin's verse and literary theory in *Fracture*, 140–70. See also Haga, *Chūsei Zenrin*, 393–421, for further information about these meetings in the Five Mountains temples.

16. There has been comparatively little study of poetry meetings in the Five Mountains temples during the fourteenth century. My discussion here is based on examples I have collected from Five Mountains documents of descriptions of various paintings from the first three decades of the fifteenth century (discussed further below) combined with information on late-fifteenth-century poetry meetings from Asakura Hisashi, "Zenrin ni okeru shikai no yōsō—Shōkoku-ji," *Chūsei bungei*, Sōsho bekkan 3, p. 235–57 and 50 (May 1972): 19–40. I am grateful to Professor Asakura for sending me a copy of this and his other articles on Five Mountains poetry meetings. See also Pollack, *Fracture*, 140–170.

17. Tamamura, *Gozan bungaku*, 201, and "Gunsanshita," 784 (2022).

18. This fourteenth- and fifteenth-century history awaits future study, with much evidence for these groups scattered through the literary works of the various monks. Some sense of the nature of these groups can be gathered from a later source, the fifteenth-century *Inryoken nichiroku*, which provided the basis for the useful two-part study of friends societies in the late fifteenth century by Asakura, "Shikai no yōsō." See also Nanami Hiroakira, "Musō Soseki no geju to shisō—'yūsha' no genkei o chūshin to shite," *Nihon bungaku* (*Nihon bungaky kyōkaikan*) 28.7 (1979.7): 53–63.

19. Tamamura, *Gozan bungaku*, 198–200.

20. *ZGS*, 223ff. See below for further discussion of the painting.

21. Both *po* and *yi* are gambling games, which in the *Analects* are compared favorably to being idle; *po* is beleived to be a board game in which moves were decided by a throw of the dice, while *yi* is now better known by the Japanese name *go*.

22. Each of these three characteristics are the representative traits of the "three beneficial friends" discussed below, following the *Analects* 16.4, trans. D. C. Lau (Penguin Books, 1979), 139.

23. *ZGS*, 223–29.

24. Their early development as a theme in Chinese culture is discussed by Wai-kam Ho in "Chinese Art under the Mongols," in Lee and Ho, *Chinese Art under the Mongols*, 97–98.

25. Ibid.

26. Tamamura Takeji, "Daikyū Shōnen bokuseki 'Ishihashi gejikujo' ni tsuite," in idem, *Nihon Zenshūshi ronshū* (Kyoto: Shibunkaku, 1976), 1:1121–35.

27. Tamamura, "Nihonsō no gunsanshita," ibid., 2:779–85. A survey of poem scrolls by Tamamura Takeji may be found in his "Shijiku shūsek kaidai," *Gozan bungaku shinshū*, ed. idem (Tōdai shuppansha, 1972), 1177–1235.

28. Tamamura, "Gunsanshita," 784.

29. Tamamura, *Gozan bungaku*, 147.

30. For a postface by Mugai Ninkō (d. 1359) written for a poem scroll compiled on the occasion of parting, which also included poems by several of his friends, see Akazawa Eiji, "Ōei shigajiku kenkyū," *Tokyo Gakugei Daigaku kenkyū hōkoku* 11 (1960): 18.

31. Tamamura, *Gozan bungaku*, 147.

32. *Kamakura no shigajiku—Muromachi suibokuga to gozan Zensō no shūhen* (Kamakura: Kamakura Kokuhōkan, n.d.), 38.

33. See, e.g., Kanazawa Hiroshi, *Japanese Ink Painting: Early Zen Masterpieces*, trans. Barbard Ford (Kōdansha International and Shibundō, 1979), 29–31. Akazawa Eiji surveys documentary sources in his "Ōei shigajiku kenkyū," *Tokyo Gakugei Daigaku kenkyū Hōkoku* 11:20.

34. Kanazawa, *Early Zen Masterpieces*, 90.

35. Akazawa, "Ōei," 19. Akazawa also lists a number of examples of such poem scrolls from the 1350s, 1360s, and 1370s.

36. "Byōbu uta," *Waka bungaku jiten*, ed. Ariyoshi Tamotsu (Ōfūsha, 1982), 544–45; see also Kuranaka Shinobu, "Daigashi no hassei," *Kokugo to kokubungaku* 65.12 (1987): 17–36.

37. *Waka bungaku jiten*, 555; Phillip Tudor Harries, "Shikashū," *Monumenta Nipponica* 35.3 (Autumn 1980): 312; and Joshua Mostow, "Painted Poems, Forgotten Words: Poem-Pictures and Classical Japanese Literature," *Monumenta Nipponica* 47.2 (1992): 323–46. For a discussion of this type of poem in the first imperial *waka* anthology, the Kokinshū, see Helen Craig McCullough, *Brocade by Night: "Kokin Wakashu" and the Court Style in Japanese Classical Poetry* (Stanford, CA: Stanford University Press, 1985), 235–40 and 251ff.

38. Kanazawa Hiroshi, *Muromachi kaiga*, Nihon no bijutsu 207 (Shibundō, 1983), 27.

39. Shimada Shūjirō, "Shūbunkei sansuiga ni kansuru ni, san no mondai," in *Zaigai Nihon no shihō*, ed. Shimada (Gakushū Kenkyūsha, 1968), 92–93; the article is also published in Shimada's *Nihon Kaigashi kenkyū* (Chūō Kōronsha, 1987), 124–30. The text of the inscriptions may be found in Tamamura Takeji, "'Shokoku-ji Zenjūseki' fusai no gasan shiryō," *Gasetsu* 59 (1941): 868.

40. Akazawa, "Ōei," 20, lists a sampling of landscapes recorded in literary collections. It is likely but not certain that all of these recorded poems were actually inscribed on paintings.

41. It may be significant that of these four early landscape painters, three of them had some substantial contact with Gidō, who was also at the center of the earliest *shigajiku* poem-and-painting scrolls. Tesshū's relationship with Gidō is discussed in Kanazawa, *Japanese Ink Painting*, 224–29, and below. For an example of Sōen's relationship with Gidō, see Shimao, "Shoki shigajiku," 103. The documents and extant works of these painters are surveyed by Shimada Shūjirō in "Shūbunkei," 92–93. For information on Tesshū Tokusai, see, e.g., entries by Shimizu and Wheelwright in *Japanese Ink Painting*; and Nakamura Tanio, "Tesshū Tokusai no gaji," *Museum* 98 (1959): 20–22. Yoshiaki Shimizu has written a useful study of Mokuan as an unpublished Princeton University Ph.D. dissertation, "Problems of Moku'an." An article on Sōen Ōsei by Ebine Toshio, "Sōen Ōseihitsu Byakue Kannonzu," *Kobijutsu* 53 (July 1977): 89–96, contains some information on his

landscape paintings. Gukei's landscape paintings can best be studied through an article by Shimada, "Ūe Gukei no sakuhin nishū," *Kokka* 707 (1951) (also published in Shimada, *Nihon kaigashi*, 112–123), and Richard Edwards's article, "Ūe Gukei—Fourteenth-Century Ink Painter," *Ars Orientalis* 7 (1968): 169–78; see also below.

42. See Akazawa, "Ōei," 30–31.

43. Source materials for the study of Gidō are rich and varied, and I do not list here all of them. Perhaps the most important document historically is Gidō's diary, the *Kūge nichiyō kufū ryakushū*, ed. Tsuji Zennosuke (Taiyōsha, 1939). An important modern translation with annotation of Gido's diary is by Kageki, *Kūge*; while Kageki has also studied his poetry in *Gozan shishi*, 240–74. Modern annotated translations of some of the poetry from Gido's poetry collection, the *Kūgeshū*, in Tamamura Takeji, *Gozan shisho*, 76–105 and 167–281; other reliable translations are available in Iriya Yoshitaka, *Gozan bungakushū*, 196–235. See also Terada Tōru's monograph, *Gidō Shūshin Zekkai Chūshin*, Nihon shijinsen 24 (Tsukuma Shobō, 1977). English translations are available in Ury, *Five Mountains*, 67–76; Pollack, *Five Mountains*, passim; and Bruce E. Carpenter, "Poetry and Prose of Gidō Shūshin," *Teizukayama Daigaku kiyō* 24 (1987): 18–76.

44. Unless otherwise noted I rely for the biography on the "Gidō Shūshin" entry in Tamamura Takeji, *Gozan Zensō denki shūsei* (Kōdansha, 1983), 85–96.

45. Sasaki Tomoko, "Kamakura zaiju no Gidō Shūshin," *Nihon bungaku*, 29.11 (1980): 18–19. For a thoughtful analysis of how literature was useful in the expansion of the Musō school in Kamakura, see Sugihara Takuya, "Gidō Shūshin no Dōjakukenki ni tsuite," *Kamakura* 55 (1987): 39–57.

46. Shimao, "Shoki shigajiku," passim.

47. Gidō's views on Neo-Confucianism have been studied in Kusumoto Fumio, *Nihon Chūsei Zenrin no Jugaku* (Sankibō Busshorin, 1992), 135–59.

48. Discussed in Pollack, *Fracture*, 142–46.

49. Both Zekkai's collected sayings and a poetry collection are extant in modern, annotated editions. See Kageki Hideo's reliable translation and notes to Zekkai's poetry collection, *Shokenkō*, published as *Shokenkō: Zenchū* (pub. Kageki Hideo, 1977); this study was published privately, however, and is not widely available. (I am indebted to Professor Kageki for a copy of his translation.) Iriya Yoshitaka has also translated a large number of Zekkai's poems in *Gozan bungaku shū*, 3–194. A biography of Zekkai can be found in Tamamura's *Gozan shisō*, 105–26, with translations of a number of his poems, 285–300. Poetry criticism is available in Terada Tōru's volume together with Kageki's *Gozan shishi*, 274–94. See also the flawed but useful translation of both Zekkai's collected sayings and his poetry collection by Kajitani Sonin *Zekkai goroku*, 3 vols. (Kyoto: Shibunkaku, 1976). English translations may be found in Ury, *Five Mountains*, 83–88 and Pollack, *Zen Poems*, passim.

50. On Zekkai's Zen studies in Ming China, see Makita Tairyō, "Zekkai Chūshin to Minsō to no kōshō—bungaku e no imashime," *Zengaku kenkyū* 57

(Feb. 1969). For importance of his stay on the mainland for Muromachi international relations, see Nishio Kenryū, "Muromachi bakufu gaikō ni okeru gozansō—Zekkai Chūshin o chūshin ni," *Nihon Rekishi* 537 (1993): 35–54.

51. This preface, which would have been read widely by his younger contemporaries, is a discourse on the ways in which poetry is important for Zen monks and describes the way in which it should be written and read. See Kageki, *Shokenkō*, 4–7.

52. A survey of Zekkai's role in relations with Ming China while in this office is found in Nishio, "Muromachi bakufu gaikō," 48–51.

53. Kusumoto, *Nihon Chūsei*, 159–75.

54. Shimao Arata, *Hyōnenzu-Hyōtan namazu no ikonorojii*, E wa kataru 5 (Heibonsha, 1995), 13. For an important article discussing the general significance of such names in establishing social prestige and authority, see Satō Dōshin, "Kaiga to gengo, 2: Gagō to risō no sekaikan," *Bijutsu kenkyū* 353 (1992.3): 17–33.

55. For example, temple records show that Chūhō was appointed as the eighty-first abbot of Kennin-ji in the third month of 1409, while Taihaku becames the ninetieth abbot of Kennin-ji in the eighth month of 1411. Note that in the fifteen months between their tenures there were eight abbots, for an average term of less than two months each.

56. On Yoshimochi's interest in Zen, see Tamamura Takeji, "Ashikaga Yoshimochi no Zenshū shinkō ni tsuite," *Zengaku kenkyū* 42 (Mar. 1951): 20–43.

57. Taihaku Shingen, *Taihaku oshō goroku* (undated National Diet Library manuscript), 40a–41a; Chūhō En'i, *Chūhō oshō goroku* (1885 handwritten copy of Tenryū-ji text, Tokyo Daigaku shiryō hensanjo), 31b–33b.

58. Ashikaga, *Kamakura Muromachi*, 384.

59. Tamamura, *Denshū*, 462.

60. Kitamura, *Gozan bungaku shikō* (Fuzanbō, 1941), 482.

61. *Gaun nikkenroku*, entry for second month, seventeenth day of 1453; cited in Shimao, "Hyōnenzu," 36n9. The text of this entry with the poem topics and lines from some of the poems composed are discussed in Kitamura Sawakichi, *Gozan bungaku*, 492.

62. For this biography I rely on Yoshiaki and Wheelwright, *Japanese Ink Paintings*, 244–47, and Hoshiyama Yukinari, "Gyokuen Bompō ni tsuite," *Geijutsugaku kenkyū* 2 (1976): 33–57.

63. Text in Tamamura, "*Shokoku-ji Zenjūseki* fusai no gasan shiryō," *Gasetsu* 59 (1941): 876–77.

64. I rely for this biography on Taihaku's extant writings, Gidō's diary, and Tamamura, *Denki shūsei*, 400.

65. Cited in Kitamura, *Gozan bungaku*, 478.

66. Shimao, "Shoki shigajiku," 101.

67. Kageki discusses his relationship with Ishō, *Gozan shishi*, 333–34.

68. Kageki, *Gozan shishi*, 335.

69. The literary collection, also known simply as the *Ashūshu*, is published in *GBZ*, 3:2217–66, while the collected sayings are available only in a manuscript edition in the National Diet Library.

70. See, e.g., Kageki, *Gozan shishi*, 296–97, for a discussion of the general characteristics of *gozan* Zen during the first decades of the fifteenth century.

71. Shimada Shūjirō, personal communication, February 1986.

72. "Hyōnenzu no kenkyū—Daigaku Shūsū no jo ni mirareru 'shin'yō' o chūshin to shite," *Bijutsu kenkyū* 335 (Mar. 1986): 28. See *GBZ*, 3:2237, where Taihaku discusses Su Shih's theory of art as an expression of the "creative change" (*tsao-hua*) in a Buddhist context. See also Chūhō's use of this same conception of art, *GBZ*, 3:2527.

73. Kageki, *Shishi*, 337. Kageki believes that this poetic theory is distinctive among those found in Japanese Five Mountains Zen literature.

74. In this biography I rely on Chūhō's extant writings and Tamamura, *Denki shūsei*, 461–62.

75. Shimao, *Hyōnenzu*, 30 and 31n27.

76. Shimada Shūjirō, "Motsugai no bokubai," *Kokka* 770 (May 1956): 148–56; see also *ZGS*, 401–6. For a useful discussion of the painting criticism in the inscriptions on this painting, see Ōta Takahiko, "Muromachi jidai no okeru kaiga hihyō ni tsuite—Masaki Bijutsukanzō bokubaizu no daishi o chūshin to shite," *Geijutsu no riron to rekishi*, ed. Kyoto Daigaku Bigaku Bijutsushigaku kenkyūkai (Kyoto: Shibunkaku, 1989), 76–85.

77. Akazawa, "Ōei," 31; the text can be found in *GBZ*, 3:2526–27.

78. I have examined the two *kan* handwritten texts of this *goroku* based on an edition preserved at Tenryu-ji and now kept at the Tokyo University Documents Department; there is another *kan* kept at Ryosoku-in that I have not seen.

79. I have not seen this text.

80. Only *kan* five to seven are extant; they are published in *GBZ*, 3: 2501–2630. A no longer extant literary collection was titled *Ranshitsushū*.

81. Discussed by Kageki, *Gozan shishi*, 296–97. See Chūhō's discussion of study, *GBZ*, 3:2529–30.

82. *Kamakura Muromachi*, 387–88. See, e.g., Chūhō's explanation of the study name, "Examining the Mind" (J. *shūshin*) in *GBZ*, 3:2535–36.

83. A survey of his Neo-Confucian views may be found in Kusumoto, *Chūsei Zenrin*, 178–81, and Ichikawa Hontarō, *Nihon Jukyōshi*, vol. 3, Chūsei (Tōa gakujutsu kenkyūkai, 1992), 354–58.

84. Ashikaga, *Kamakura Muromachi*, 384–88.

85. For text, see *GBZ*, 3:2518–19; Kamimura Kankō's "Sekikarōzusan kaidai," *Kokka* 319 (1916): 196–204; and Fujita Tsuneo, "Muromachi jidai gasanshū," in *Kōkan bijutsu shiryō zokuhen*, comp. idem (Kamakura: Kōkan bijutsu shiryō kankōkai, 1985), 2:169–71.

86. The Su Shih passage is translated and discussed by Susan Bush, *The Chinese Literati*, 35.

87. For this biography I rely on Kiyō's extant writings and Tamamura, *Denki shūsei*, 70–71, unless otherwise indicated.

88. Mugan had become known for his knowledge of Chinese learning in the capital after lectures he gave in 1369 on *Mencius* that reflected the growing contemporary interest in recent continental developments in Neo-Confucian thinking. Mugan also seems to have played an important role in education of many of the Five Mountains monks who were to be most active in the inscription of paintings during the 1420s and 1430s.

89. Ashikaga, *Kamakura Muromachi*, 360.

90. Kageki, *Nihon shishi*, 323.

91. Ibid., 325.

92. Ibid., 324.

93. *GBZ*, 3:2877–3027.

94. In *Dainihon Bukkyō zensho*, vol. 111, ed. Busshō Kankokai (Busshō Kankōkai, 1912).

95. *GBZ*, 3:2911, 2912.

96. *GBZ*, 3:2903–4.

97. An early edition dated 1425 is extant, as are others from the 1650s. See Sueki Fumiakira, "*Hekiganroku* no Chūshakusho ni tsuite," *Matsugaoka Bunko Kenkyū hōkoku* 7 (1993): 26–28.

98. Two handwritten transcriptions of this text are extant: one with Kiyō's preface dating from 1420 at Tōfuku-ji; the second from the mid-Muromachi period at the Daitōkyū Kinen Bunko.

99. Ashikaga (*Kamakura Muromachi*, pp. 362–63) has pointed out that although Kiyō was known among Edo period Japanese Neo-Confucians as the first to lecture in Japan on these commentaries, at least two other monks had given lectures at court on them, including Gidō Shushin. For evidence that these commentaries were known in the first half of the fourteenth century, see Andrew Goble, "Social Change, Knowledge, and History: Hanazono's Admonition to the Crown Prince," *Harvard Journal of Asiatic Studies* 55.1 (1995): 61–128. Full discussion of Kiyō's Neo-Confucianism may be found in Kusumoto, *Nihon Chūsei*, 182–90, and Ichikawa, *Nihon Jūkyoshi*, 342–48.

100. See, e.g., *GBZ*, 3:2892.

101. Ashikaga, *Kamakura Muromachi*, 365–66.

102. Ibid., 364, 367.

103. See chapter 3. For his views on nondualism that will not be treated in the following chapters, see his "Explanation of the Name 'Kaishuku'" (J. *Kaishuku jisetsu*, *GBZ*, 3:2998) and "Explanation of the Name 'Etsuin'" (J. *Etsuin jisetsu*, *GBZ*, 3:3000).

104. See, e.g., Tsung-mi's critique of the interest in illusion and dream in his critique of Ox Head lineage Chinese Zen, in Gregory, *Tsung-mi*, 234–36.

105. Unless otherwise noted, I rely in this biography on Ishō's extant writings and Tamamura, *Denki shūsei*, 20–22.

106. See his "Preface after Poems on the Pavilion of Evening Splendor," *GBZ*, 3:2518–19; also transcribed in Kamimura, "Sekikarōzu," 200, and Fujita, "Gosanshū," 2:171. Textual problems remain with these different documents.

107. Of course, extant *shigajiku* scrolls may be found with subjects other than landscape, as discussed below, but here I concentrate my discussion on the landscape *shigajiku* scrolls.

108. Shimada Shūjiro (in "Shūbunkei," 95) distinguishes between paintings of "poetic intent" and of the scholar's study. See also his "Gozan bungaku to Muromachi kaiga," in *Gozan no gakugei*, ed. Okazaki Hisashi (Daitokyū kinen bunko, 1985), 80–82.

109. Secondary scholarship on this painting is considerable. For an important reconsideration and survey of relevant scholarship, see Shimao Arata, "Hyōnenzu no kenkyū," 24–38.

110. There has been much discussion of whether the painting was completed for Yoshimitsu or Yoshimochi; most scholars now agree that it was probably completed for Yoshimochi. The date of the painting is also unknown; Shimao Arata has suggested that the most likely date is perhaps closer to 1410 than to 1415, judging from the biographies of the inscribers and the seal used by Gyokuen Bompō ("Hyōnenzu no kenkyū," 26–27, and *Hyōnenzu*, 27ff.).

111. Ōnishi Hiroshi, "Hyōnenzu to hyōtan no jujutsusei," in *Uri to Ryōda*, Ima wa Mukashi, Mukashi wa ima (Ippuku Onkan Shoten, 1989), cited in Shimao, *Hyōnenzu*, 15.

112. This general point was made in early articles on the *shigajiku* by Kumagai Nobuo, "Ōei nenkan no shigajiku—toku ni sono sansuiga no hatten ni okeru ichi ni tsuite," *Bijutsu kenkyū* 4 (1932); Matsushita Takaaki, "Shigajiku ni tsuite," *Nihon suibokuga ronshū* (Chūō Kōron Bijutsu Shuppan, 1983), 84–92 (orig. pub. 1940); and Shimada Shūjirō, "Shigajiku no shozaizu ni tsuite," *Nihon shogaku shinkō iinkai kenkyū hōkoku* 4 (1943), also published in Shimada, *Nihon kaigashi*, 124–29. The precise history of the development may be found in Shimao, "Shoki shigajiku."

113. Hou-mei Sung Ishida, "Early Ming Painters in Nanking and the Formation of the Wu School," *Ars Orientalis* 17 (1987): 83.

114. Sensabaugh, "Jade Mountain," 96.

115. Robert Treat Paine and Alexander Soper, *The Art and Architecture of Japan* (Baltimore, MD: Penguin Books, 1955), 412–13; I am also grateful to Bruce Coats for information on these architectural developments.

116. See his *Hua-chi pu-i*, in *Hua-chi, Hua-chi pu-i* (Peking: Jen-min Mei-shu Ch'ü-pan-she, 1963), 1:21. I am grateful to Valérie Malenfer for this reference.

117. *GBZ*, 2:1713.

118. "Preface to [a Painting of] a Place Surrounded by Screens of Verdure," *GBZ*, 3:2233; see also his "Preface to Traveling to Gyūin-ji in Kamakura Gorge," *GBZ*, 3:2232. The term used by Taihaku's friend in "Screens of Verdure," however, may indicate that the desk was surrounded by screen paintings rather than scrolls hung on walls.

119. "Hyōnenzu," 27–28.

120. Akazawa, "Ōei," part 2, p. 24. See also the discussion below of the painting *Returning Home Out of Filial Piety*.

121. "Ōei," part 1, p. 19.

122. See Akazawa, "Ōei," part 2, p. 24. Shimada discusses several ways in which the Japanese monks associated the virtues of individuals from Chinese culture with their own lifestyle in his "Gozan bungaku," 84, and in "Shigajiku no shosaizu," 142. These articles and subsequent discussions with Professor Shimada were important for my thinking about the significance of the study for the Japanese Five Mountains monks.

123. Shimada, "Shosaizu," 142–44.

124. Max Loehr suggests that the datable paintings of scholars' studies by Ni Tsan cover the years 1339 to 1372, and those by Wang Meng cover the period between 1343 and c. 1370, in his *The Great Painters of China* (New York: Harper & Row, 1980), 248, 249.

125. *GBZ*, 3:2089–2170.

126. For a survey of Muromachi ink paintings of Su Shih, see Kunigō Hideaki, "Nihon ni okeru So Shoku zō—Tokyo Kokuritsu Hakubutsukan hokan no mohon o chūshin to suru shiryō shōka—," *Museum* 494 (May 1992): 4–22.

127. For Gidō and his fellow monks, the prose category was not the public prose that we have seen was so important for writers in the mainland Ancient Civilization movement, but informal genres of prose, the preface *hsü* (J. *jo*) and postface.

128. Shimao discusses Gidō's conception of the religious value of these arts in "Shoki shigajiku," 102–3.

129. Ibid., 103-4.

130. Ibid., 100.

131. I rely in my discussion of Ikō on the short biography in Kageki Hideo, *Kūge nichiyō*, 440n109, together with the comments in Shimao, "Shoki shigajiku," 100. I am grateful to Ide Seinosuke for a chronology of Ikō's life; see also Ide's "Manzai-ji no Ikō Tokukenzō," *Bukkyō Geijutsu* 166 (1986.5): 50–63.

132. Gidō, *Kūgeshu*, in *GBZ*, 2:1340. See also Shimao, "Shoki shigajiku," passim.

133. Shimao, "Shoki shigajiku," 101.

134. See, for example, *Wang Hsi-chih Writing on a Fan* in the Kyoto National Museum and *Noble Scholar Admiring Plum Blossoms*, *ZGS*, 152ff. and 177ff.

135. If we consider only paintings inscribed by more than one person, important examples of such paintings would include: several plum paintings by Motsugai; paintings by unknown artists of a lotus and plums flanking a Kannon painting that is often attributed to Isshi; and a chrysanthemum painting attributed to Shūbun. For discussions of these paintings, see Shimada Shūjirō, "Motsugai," 148–56, and *ZGS*, 401ff. and 417ff.

136. See *ZGS*, 406ff.

137. This will be further discussed in chapter 3.

138. This role and its importance in understanding the social position of painters in the *gozan* monasteries is described by Ōnishi, ZGS, 223.

139. Barnhart, "Yao Yen-ch'ing," 123.

140. See, for example, Bompō's preface to the *Study of the Three Friends*, where he refers to the painter as "ordering a skilled [person] to make a painting [of the study]" (*ZGS*, 223–24). The economic role of the craftsmen and other workers in the "eastern ranks" of the Five Mountains temples is surveyed in Fujioka Daisetsu, "Zen'in uchi ni okeru tōhanshū ni tsuite: toku ni muromachi bakufu no zaisei to kanrenshite," *Nihon rekishi*, 145: 19–28.

141. For his extant paintings, see Shimada Shūjirō, "Ūe Gukei," also published in *Nihon Kaigashi*, 112–23, and Richard Edwards, "Ūe Gukei," 169–78.

142. These ties are discussed in Shimao, "Shoki shigajiku," 104; general information on this painter may be found in Ebine Toshio, "Sōen Ōsei," 89–96.

143. Published in *Nihon no suibokuga* (Tokyo National Museum, 1987), pl. 97.

144. The significance of this term has been carefully studied by Shimao, "Hyōnenzu," passim.

145. Discussion of this revival may be found in the work of several scholars, for example, Kathlyn Maureen Liscomb, *Learning from Mount Hua: A Chinese Physician's Illustrated Travel Record and Painting Theory* (New York: Cambridge University Press, 1993), 96–110, as well as in Hou-mei Sung Ishida, "Early Ming Painters," 73–115.

146. Art historians have primarily pursued the former possibility by examining paintings in the shogunal and other collections. See Yoshiaki Shimizu, "A Chinese Album Leaf from the Former Ashikaga Collection in the Freer Gallery of Art," *Archives of Asian Art* 37 (1984): 96–107; Richard Stanley-Baker, "Some Proposals Concerning the Transmission to Muromachi Japan of Styles Associated with Painters from Chekiang of the Late Yuan and Early Ming: With Particular Reference to the Styles Favored in the Hung-chih Academy," in *Suzuki Kei Sensei Kanreki Kinen: Chūgoku Kaigashi Ronkō* (1981): 71–96; and Stanley-Baker, "The Ashikaga Shogunal Collection and Its Setting: A Matrix for Fifteenth-Century Chinese Landscape Painting," in *Influence in Oriental Art: International Symposium on Art Historical Studies*, no. 7, Landscape Painting, 1990. An important recent article by Suzuki Hiroyuki explores these same paintings not stylistically but as

they contribute to understanding the circulation of cultural artifacts in the Chinese cultural sphere. See his "Ōkansuru kaiga," 1–23.

147. Hou-mei Sung Ishida has suggested that this distinction, which has been quite widely applied, derives ultimately from the writings of the influential critic Tung Ch'i-ch'ang, in "Nanking," 81.

148. Kathlyn Liscomb, "Shen Zhou's Collection of Early Ming Paintings and the Origins of the Wu School's Eclectic Revivalism," *Artibus Asiae* 52 (1992): 239; see also her "Wang Fu's Contribution to the Formation of a New Painting Style in the Ming Dynasty," *Artibus Asiae* 48 (1987): 39–78. An important discussion of the complex relations in the early Ming between painting styles and the social roles of scholar-painters and court professionals may be found in Sung Ishida, "Early Ming Painters in Nanking," 73–115.

149. In the discussion below I recognize questions of authenticity and the practice of unacknowledged copying of paintings, but I here follow the general custom of Japanese art historians in assuming that copies still have value as documentary sources.

150. All but a few of the less well-known paintings have been widely published, and the secondary literature on the paintings is substantial. A recent bibliography of relevant art historical materials can be found in *ZGS*, 26–32, including other works that publish paintings not included in *ZGS* (p. 33), while the *ZGS* entry on each of the paintings lists all previous publications of the painting. The most useful source for understanding the paintings is now the entries in *ZGS*, but other reliable sources include the English language catalog, *Japan: The Shaping of Daimyo Culture, 1185–1868*, ed. Yoshiaki Shimizu (Washington, DC: National Gallery of Art, 1988). Other citations are also given below.

151. *ZGS*, pl. 66, p. 182ff.

152. Tu Fu was one of the two or three most popular poets among the Five Mountains literary circles; for a discussion of his place in Zen poetry, see Asakura Hisashi, *Zenrin no bungaku*, 225–33, 286–376.

153. Shimada groups this painting under the rubric of "parting" (J. *sōbetsu*) or "visiting friends" (J. *hōyū*) in *ZGS*, 182.

154. The approximate dating of the painting is discussed by Yokota Tadashi in *ZGS*, 199.

155. For further discussion of these inscriptions, see the present author's "Attaining Landscapes in the Mind: Nature Poetry and Painting in Japanese Gozan Zen of the Early Fifteenth Century," *Monumenta Nipponica*, 52.2 (Summer, 1997): 235–56.

156. Not all questions have been answered regarding the dating and authenticity of this painting, although even if problematic in this regard it would retain significant iconographic and documentary value.

157. Ōnishi Hiroshi discusses the implications of paintings depicting parting scenes that appear little different from an ordinary landscape painting in *ZGS*, 193.

158. Based on the paintings included in *ZGS*, we can see this decline quite clearly. The two earliest extant *shigajiku*, *New Moon over a Brushwood Gate* and *Plantain in Evening Rain*, each has fifteen or more inscriptions. Those inscribed between 1410 and 1420 average around ten each, but after a gap in extant paintings in 1420–25, the average number of inscriptions drops to between five and seven, and then around 1440 the number drops again to only one to four inscriptions. I am grateful to Ebine Toshio for bringing this trend to my attention. This change also seems to indicate a weakening of the social networks of the Five Mountains monks, at least in their relation to painting scrolls.

159. The identity of the monk, who is referred to in the inscriptions only as Ikka, is discussed by Watanabe Akiyoshi in *ZGS*, 290.

160. "Ōei," part 2, p. 23.

161. Watanabe has also noted that differences in the seasonal allusions in the poems may indicate that they were composed at different times of the year (*ZGS*, 289). It is always difficult, however, to determine whether differing seasonal allusions in literature are based on the seasonal context of the biographical act of composition or on different imaginative poetic interests among the inscribers.

162. A modern Japanese edition and translation of his diary is available in Murai Shōsuke's *Chūsei Wajinden* (Iwanami Shoten, 1993). Murai discusses medieval cultural relations between Japan and Korea in his "Chūsei Nicchō kōshō no naka no kanshi," in his *Higashi Ajia*, 182–223.

163. Yamana's office is mentioned by Yoshiaki Shimizu in *Japan: The Shaping of Daimyo Culture*, ed. Yoshiaki Shimizu (Washington: National Gallery of Art, 1988), 143–44. See also the discussion of "Mountain Villa" below for the importance of the *shugo daimyō* to the Ōei landscape poem-and-painting scrolls.

164. Watanabe, *ZGS*, 290.

165. See Parker, "Attaining Landscapes," passim.

166. Shūbun's early style is generally distinguished from the later or classic style of such paintings as *Reading in a Bamboo Study* of 1447 in the Tokyo National Museum and the 1445 painting *Watery Forms and Mountainous Brilliance* in a private collection. Of the six paintings that are generally cited as representative examples of the early style, five of them are products of around the years 1415–25 and the sixth is a painting (not discussed here) in a private collection from c. 1437 titled *Hermit of the Rivers and Mountains* (also known as *Setting Sun on Rivers and Mountains*) (Shimada, "Shūbunkei," 98).

167. The exact date of the painting is problematic, but the last possible date of completion is before the death of Genchū in 1428. See *ZGS*, 304.

168. For a discussion of the religious significance of the image of the scholar's study in the earliest extant poem-and-painting scrolls, see the present author's "The Hermit at Court: Reclusion in Early Fifteenth Century Japanese Zen Buddhism," *Journal of Japanese Studies* 21.1 (1995): 103–20.

169. Ōnishi, *ZGS*, 222–23.

170. The painting is published in *Bulletin of the Cleveland Museum* 73.1 (Jan. 1986), where it is identified only as attributed to a "Korean painter living in Kyoto" in the fifteenth century. The introduction of this little known, new painting to the otherwise already well-established corpus of Ōei *shigajiku* is an event of great importance, and one looks forward to hearing the reaction of art historians to this painting. I am grateful to Elizabeth Lillehoj for calling this painting to my attention.

171. Both the "Record" and Su Shih's poem are included in the *Ku-wen chen-pao*, a mainland prose collection that was well known in the Ōei period and lectured on by Chūhō En'i. See *Kobun shinpō*, Shinshaku kanbun taikei 16, ed. Hoshikawa Kiyotaka (Meiji Shoin, 1963), 160ff and 194ff., respectively.

172. See Shimizu, *Daimyo*, 144–46. A Japanese language publication on this artwork is found in Ōta Takahiko, "Masaki Bijutsukan zō "Sansōzu" ni tsuite," *Museum* 450 (Sept. 1988): 4–11.

173. *ZGS*, 222.

174. Other members of this literary circle are listed by Ota Takahiko in *ZGS*, 296.

175. See Yoshiaki Shimizu's description in *Daimyo Culture*, 146, of the events leading up to Morimi's welcoming into the capital during the first decade of the fifteenth century.

176. Another extant painting with an inscription by Ishō Tokugan directly related to Morimi's activity is *Listening to the Pines Hut*, discussed in *ZGS*, pl. 77, p. 234ff. and *Daimyo Culture*, pl. 86, pp. 146–48.

177. The inscriptions on this painting are further discussed in Parker, "Attaining Landscapes," passim.

178. This painting is also known by the title, *Waiting for Spring Hut*.

179. See, e.g., Kanazawa's entries in *Josetsu, Shūbun, San'ami*, Suiboku Bijutsu Taikei, vol. 6, ed. Matsushita Takaaki (Kōdansha, 1978), entries no. 34 and 35, p. 152.

3. THE EAST ASIAN RELIGIOUS CONTEXT FOR CULTURAL PRACTICE

1. *GBZ*, 3:2899–30. This passage is further discussed in the final chapter.

2. A useful survey of the range of Mahayana bodhisattva ideals and practices may be found in Luis O. Gómez, "From the Extraordinary to the Ordinary: Images of the Bodhisattva in East Asia," in *The Christ and the Bodhisattva*, ed. Donald S. Lopez Jr. and Steven C. Rockefeller (Albany: State University of New York Press, 1987), 141–91.

3. Translated by Edward Conze, *Buddhist Wisdom Books: The Diamond Sutra, The Heart Sutra* (New York: Harper & Row, 1972), 81.

4. Imaizumi Yoshio develops this point with reference to the Japanese Five Mountains tradition in his *Tōgo Seiwa: Muromachi bunka sunbyō* (Yoshikawa Kōbunkan, 1994), 176–83.

5. Translated Thomas Cleary and J. C. Cleary (Boulder, CO: Shambala, 1977), 1:3; *T*, 48:140b14–19.

6. Eliade, *The Sacred and the Profane* (Harper Torchbook, 1961), 99–100.

7. *Baso no goroku*, trans. Iriya Yoshitaka (Kyoto: Zenbunka kenkyujo, 1984), 32. Discussed by Iriya, pp. 34–35.

8. See, for example, Robert Morrell, "Shingon's Kakukai on the Immanence of the Pure Land," *Japanese Journal of Religous Studies* 11.2–3 (1984): 195–220.

9. The extensive literature on the impact of *hongaku* thought in Japan has focused on the Tendai school, largely through the work of the Japanese scholars Nakamura Hajime and Tamura Yoshirō. In English, see, for example, the discussion of the relationship of the Buddhist theory of innate enlightenment to conceptions of nonduality in Tamura Yoshirō, "Critique of Original Awakening Thought in Shōshin and Dōgen," *Journal of Japanese Religious Studies* 11.2–3 (June–Sept., 1984): esp. 243–47. For a review of this literature and a critique, see Royall Tyler, "A Critique of 'Absolute Phenomenalism,'" *Japanese Journal of Religious Studies* 9.4 (Dec. 1982): 261–83.

10. Scholarship on this tradition in Japan is not well developed at this time. For discussion of Chinese examples from the Sung and later, see Judith Berling on Three Schools syncretism in which the Buddhist Pure Land is found to be immanent in the mind and other teachings, in *Syncretic Religion*, 35 and 58–60 and passim. Three Teachings syncretism as practiced in the Five Mountains monasteries is surveyed in Haga, *Chūsei Zenrin*, 221–46.

11. *Genji Monogatari*, Nihon Koten Bungaku Taikei, 15:433; English translation by Arthur Waley, *The Tale of Genji* (New York: The Modern Library, 1960), 502. This passage has been neglected in most discussions of Murasaki's "Defense of the Art of Fiction."

12. Hayashiya Tatsusaburō, *Kodai chūsei geijutsuron*, Nihon shisō taikei (Iwanami Shoten, 1973), 23:263; English translation and discussion in William LaFleur, *The Karma of Words*, 91.

13. Translated by Carl Bielefeldt, "No-Mind and Sudden Awakening: Thoughts on the Soteriology of a Kamakura Zen Text," in Buswell and Gimello, *Mārga*, 485.

14. Tanaka Ichimatsu, ed., *Kaō, Mokuan, Minchō*, Suiboku bijutsu taikei 5 (Kōdansha, 1978), 83, inscription transcribed p. 170.

15. *GBZ*, 3:2540.

16. *Taihaku oshō goroku*, 39b–40a.

17. *The Holy Teaching of Vimalakīrti*, trans. Robert A. F. Thurman (University Park, PA: The Pennsylvania State University Press, 1976), 73–83; *Taishō Shinshū Daizōkyō*, ed. Takakusu Junjirō, et al. (Society for the Publication of the Taishō Edition of the Tripitaka, 1924–32) (hereafter *T*), 14:550b.

18. The portrait of Vimalakīrti is now in Chōfuku-ji (reproduced in *ZGS*, pl. 41 and Kanazawa, *Japanese Ink Painting*, pl. 39); Chūgan's inscription is tran-

scribed and discussed in Motonaka Kunihiko, ed., *Nambokuchō Muromachi Momoyama*, Shōdō Zenshū (Heibonsha, 1966), 8:157–58 and in *ZGS*, 115ff. Despite the attribution to Chu-hsien in Chūgan's inscription, some art historians have not accepted it without other documentation.

19. *Vimalakīrti*, 74.

20. *Vimalakīrti*, 76.

21. Quieting the mind as preparation for correct insight into reality is a teaching found in virtually every aspect of the Buddhist tradition. For a discussion of this teaching in Chinese Yogācāra and its importance in Buddhism generally, see Alan Sponberg, "Meditation in Fa-hsiang Buddhism," in *Traditions of Meditation in Chinese Buddhism*, ed. Peter N. Gregory, Kuroda Institute Studies in East Asian Buddhism, 4 (Honolulu: University of Hawaii Press, 1986), 30ff. and 38–39. For its importance in early Chinese Zen, see, e.g., McRae, *Northern School*, 223.

22. Edward Conze, trans., *Buddhist Wisdom Books*, 60.

23. I have used the text translated and edited by Iriya Yoshitaka, *Denshin hōyō, Enryōroku*, Zen no goroku 8 (Tsukuma Shobō, 1969).

24. *Denshin hōyō*, 38 and 30.

25. See, e.g., his collected sayings in *T'ien-mu Ming-pen chien-tz'u ts'a-lu*, in *Zokuzōkyo*, Zengakubu 17, p. 373b.

26. Yanagida Seizan introduction to Iriya, *Denshin*, 182–83. Kawase Kazuma dates this printing to 1283, in *Gozanban no kenkyū* (The Antiquarian Booksellers Association of Japan, 1970), 421. While Yanagida does not specify when the *Blue Cliff Records* and other such texts became popular in Japan, the first commentaries to this text were written primarily by Kiyō Hōshū's contemporaries. Kawase notes that the text is reprinted in the Nambokuchō and early Muromachi period (*Gozanban*, 421).

27. *GBZ*, 3:2994–5.

28. *ZGS*, 216ff. This argument in its application to landscape will be discussed more extensively in the next chapter.

29. Ibid.

30. *Denshin hōyō*, 13.

31. A survey of the history of interest in these texts that lead to the Sung Neo-Confucian adoption of them as part of the new canon can be found in Daniel K. Gardner, *Chu Hsi and the Ta-hsueh: Neo Confucian Reflection on the Confucian Canon* (Cambridge, MA: Council on East Asian Studies, Harvard University, 1986).

32. This is the definition of "Great Learning" found in the first line of the text. I here follow Gardner in his translation of *ming-ming te*; Gardner discusses the translation of this term in his *The Ta-hsueh*, 89n53. See also his discussion of the significance of this passage and Chu Hsi's interpretation of it, p. 51ff.

33. A useful discussion of the link between these inner attitudes and Neo-Confucian ontology may be found in Tu Wei-ming, "'Inner Experience': The Basis of Creativity in Neo-Confucian Thinking," in *Humanity and Self-Cultivation:*

Essays in Confucian Thought (Berkeley, CA: Asian Humanities Press, 1979), 102–20.

34. Translated by Chan, *A Source Book in Chinese Philosophy* (Princeton, NJ: Princeton University Press, 1963), 97–98.

35. Ch'eng Hao passage translated by Chan, *Source Book*, 523; Mencius translated by Chan, *Source Book*, 97–98.

36. The degree to which the mind can be identified with the inherent universal principle (C. *i-li*) or heavenly nature (C. *t'ien-hsing*) was a topic of intense debate in the Neo-Confucian tradition. I here follow Ch'ien Mu and Tu Weiming's view that the principal disagreement between the Ch'eng-Chu and more liberal strands of Sung Neo-Confucianism centers on different conceptions of the degree of identification of the mind with innate heavenly principle, and not on the importance of mind as compared to the importance of principle. See Tu Wei-ming's discussion of Ch'ien Mu's views in "Reconstituting the Confucian Tradition," *Humanity*, 126–30 and Tu's "Neo-Confucian Concept of Man," *Humanity*, 77–78. The ontological continuity of humans and the cosmos is also apparent in Ch'eng-Chu school Neo-Confucianism, however, which argues against simple identification of the mind with principle. Instead, Ch'eng I and Chu Hsi emphasized the difficulty of the process of self-cultivation due to the dual presence in the mind of both universal principle, identified with the nature, and the *ch'i* that is turbid and obstructs the correct understanding of principle.

37. See, for example, Ch'eng Yi's comments on the importance of study of the classics for entering the Way and for studying moral principles in the *I-ch'uan wen-chi*, supplement, p. 3a; also in Chu Hsi and Lu Tsu-ch'ien, comps., *Chin-ssu lu*, 2:15; translated by Wing-tsit Chan, *Reflection on Things at Hand: The Neo-Confucian Anthology Compiled by Chu Hsi and Lu Tsu-ch'ien* (New York: Columbia University Press, 1967), 47–48.

38. Quoted as the first passage in the section on the "investigation of affairs" in the *Chin-ssu lu*; see also *Wen-chi*, 5:7b. I here use Wing-tsit Chan's translation, *Source Book*, 88. The Mencius quote is *Mencius* 2a2.17, trans. D. C. Lau (Baltimore, MD: Penguin Books, 1970), 78. Chu Hsi glosses the Mencius passage as "I understand the principles of things as expressed in words." See Chan translation of *Chin-ssu lu*, 88n2.

39. Written as a comment on Chang Tsai's view of textual study in the *Chin–ssu lu*; trans. W. T. Chan, *Source Book*, 96.

40. *GBZ*, 3:2540.

41. The phrase "not yet issued forth" is from *Chung Yung*, 1.4: "Before the feelings of pleasure, anger, sorrow and joy are aroused it is called equilibrium. When these feelings are aroused and each and all attain due measure and degree, it is called harmony. Equilibrium is the great foundation of the world, and harmony its universal path" (tr. W. T. Chan, *Source Book*, 98). The term "faults of discrimination" in Chūhō's passage quotes Chu Hsi's commentary on *Chung Yung* 1.4, while

"(faults of) transgression" is from Chu Hsi on *Chung Yung* 1.3. See *Shisho shūchū*, vol. 2, *Shushi Taikei* 8, ed. Suzuki Yoshijirō (Meitoku Shuppansha, 1943), 451a.

42. Here and below I follow Tang Chun-i's interpretation of Chu Hsi's philosophy in his "The Development of the Concept of Moral Mind from Wang Yang-ming to Wang Chi," in Wm. Theodore de Bary, *Self and Society in Ming Thought* (New York: Columbia University Press, 1970), 94. See also David Gaedalacia, "Wu Cheng's Approach to Internal Self-cultivation and External Knowledge-seeking," in *Yuan Thought*, 184–91, and Tu Wei-ming, "Reconstituting," 126–27.

43. These two practices and their relationship to the *i-fa* and *wei-fa* distinction are discussed in some detail in Gaedalacia, "Wu Ch'eng," 284ff.

44. Tu Wei-ming, "Reconstituting," 126–27.

45. The last phrase is taken from *Doctrine of the Mean* 1.2: "The Path may not be left for an instant. If it could be left, it would not be the path" (trans. James Legge, *Confucius: Confucian Analects, The Great Learning, and the Doctrine of the Mean* [New York: Dover Publications, 1971 (1893)], 384). Chu Hsi used the term "daily" (*jih-yung*) in his explanation of the meaning of this phrase.

46. See the *Great Learning* 1.1: "The way of greater learning lies in keeping one's inborn luminous Virtue unobscured, in renewing the people, and in coming to rest in perfect goodness" (translated by Gardner, *Chu Hsi*, 88–90).

47. While Kiyō's association may initially seem groundless, that of "mountain" (C. *shan*) and "bringing to rest" (C. *chih*) is plausible based on the similarity of the graphs when written quickly.

48. This use of "obfuscation" derives from Chu Hsi's commentary on *Great Learning* 1.1: "[Inborn luminous Virtue] . . . may be concealed by human desire, so at times it will become obscured. Never, however, does its original luminosity cease. Therefore, the student should look to the light that emanates from it and seek to keep it unobscured, thereby restoring its original condition." (Translated Gardner, *Chu Hsi*, 89n53.)

49. *Great Learning* 1.2 defines *chih* in terms of tranquility (C. *ching*): "Only after knowing what to abide in (*chih*) can one be calm (*ting*). Only after having been calm can one be tranquil (*ching*). Only after having achieved tranquility can one have peaceful repose (*an*)." (Translation by Chan, *Source Book*, p. 86.) Kiyō here follows Chu Hsi's commentary on this definition of *chih*, when Chu reads "The mind not moving recklessly is called tranquility." (Translated Gardner, *Chu Hsi*, 89.)

50. For the implications of both of these metaphors, cf. the discussion of "cannot be separated for a moment" from the *Doctrine of the Mean* quoted below.

51. Kiyō quotes the *Doctrine of the Mean* 1.3; translated by Chan, *Source Book*, 104: "The Way cannot be separated from us for a moment."

52. Kiyō here associates Yoshimitsu's government with that of a sage. See *Mencius*, 7.b.20: "Mencius said, 'A good and wise man helps others to understand clearly by his own clear understanding. Nowadays, men try to help others understand by their own benighted ignorance." Translated by D. C. Lau, *Mencius*, 198.

53. Now Kiyo associates Yoshimitsu with the sage emperors Yao and Shun. See *Analects*, 8.19: "Great indeed was Yao as a ruler! How lofty!" (Translated by D. C. Lau, 94–95.)

54. This is Cheng-kuan, the important early Hua-yen and Zen teacher, also referred to in Kiyō's "Inscription on Sekidō Mountain."

55. "Without thoughts" (C. *wu-nien*) is a very important term in Zen Buddhism. For its importance in Zen thought, see *Platform Sutra of the Sixth Patriarch* 17, trans. Philip B. Yampolsky (Columbia University Press, 1967), 137–38, see esp. note 69.

56. *GBZ*, 3:2994–45.

57. See Gardner, *Chu Hsi*, 88–90.

58. Tamamura, *Denki*, 380.

59. In a groundbreaking article, Satō Michinobu discusses the political and social significance of the act of taking a formal name and the sobriquets so popular in Muromachi society. See his "Kaiga to gengo," 243–55.

60. Gimello, "Apophatic," 119. On the Zen Buddhist conception of language, see chapter 1 above.

61. Translated in Wixted, "*Kokinshū*," 67; the same line from the Chinese preface is translated on p. 53.

62. This style has received considerable attention both historically and in twentieth-century scholarship. English discussion of the style may be found in Robert H. Brower and Earl Miner, *Japanese Court Poetry* (Stanford, CA: Stanford University Press, 1961), 258–59. A useful Japanese-language survey of the permutations of this term may be found in Konishi Jin'ichi, "Ushintei shiken," *Nihon gakushiin kiyō* 9.2 (1951): 115–42.

63. *Meigetsushō*, cited in Konishi Jin'ichi, "Shunzei no yūgentei to shikan," *Bungaku* 202 (1952): 110. An early English-language general discussion of the relation between religion and Japanese poetic writing may be found in Herbert Eugen Plutschow, "Is Poetry a Sin?—Honjisuijaku and Buddhism versus Poetry," *Oriens Extremus* 25.2 (1978): 206–18.

64. See, e.g., the passage from *Lord Tamekane's Notes on Poetry*, trans. Robert N. Huey and Susan Matisoff, *Monumenta Nipponica* 40.2 (1985): 135. See also Brower and Miner, *Poetry*, 361.

65. For studies of Gidō's conception of poetry, see Sasaki," Kamakura"; Nanami Hiroaki, "Gidō Shūshin shironkō—geju to bungeishi to no kanten kara," *(Kokubungaku) Gengo to bungei* 77 (1973): 103–21; and Toyoda Setsuko, "Gidō Shūshin no shiteki taido ni tsuite," *Kanazawa Daigaku kokugo kokubun* 4 (1971): 1–9.

66. *GBZ*, 3:2509–10.

67. *Sōrō shiwa*, trans. Arai Ken, *Bungaku ronshū*, Chūgoku bunmei sen 13 (Asahi Shinbunsha, 1972). This analogy has been the subject of considerable discussion for centuries; for recent Western scholarship on the analogy, see Richard

John Lynn, "The Sudden and Gradual in Chinese Poetry Criticism: An Examination of the Ch'an-Poetry Analogy," in *Sudden and Gradual: Approaches to Enlightenment in Chinese Thought*, ed. Peter N. Gregory (Honolulu: University of Hawaii Press, 1987), 381–427, and also his "Orthodoxy and Enlightenment: Wang Shih-chen's Theory of Poetry and Its Antecedents," in *The Unfolding of Neo-Confucianism*, ed. Wm. Theodore de Bary (New York: Columbia University Press, 1975), 217–70. A very reliable translation and annotation with Chinese text may be found in Stephen Owen, *Chinese Literary Thought*, 391–420.

68. *Shih-jen Yu-hsieh*, 1:3. The importance of *Shih-jen Yu-hsieh* for fourteenth-century Japanese poetics is discussed by Ōta Seikyu, *Nihon kagaku to chugoku shigaku* (Kiyomizu Kobundo shobo, 1978), 161 and Konishi Jin'ichi, "Yoshmoto" and "Gyokuyōshū jidai to sōshi," *Chūsei bungaku no sekai*, ed. Joko Kan'ichi et al. (Iwanami Shoten, 1969), 151–81, passim.

69. *GBZ*, 3:2509–10.

70. *Rengaronshū Haikaironshū*, Nihon kokubungaku taikei, vol. 66, ed. Kidō Saizō and Imoto Nōichi (Iwanami shoten, 1961), 110. Yoshimoto's use of Zen terms is discussed further in Parker, "NijōYoshimoto," unpublished manuscript.

71. *Nōgakuronshū*, ed. Nishio Minoru, Nihon koten bungaku taikei, 65 (Iwanami shoten, 1961), 458–59. In English, see Richard Pilgrim, "Some Aspects of *Kokoro* in Zeami," *Monumenta Nipponica* 24.4 (1969): 393–401, and for a general discussion of Zeami's use of Zen in his Nō theory, see Pollack, *Fracture*, 167–71.

72. *Conversations with Shōtetsu*, trans. Robert H. Brower and intro. Steven D. Carter (Ann Arbor: Center for Japanese Studies, University of Michigan, 1992), 89.

73. Shinkei, *Sasamegoto*, in *Rengaronshū Haironshū*, Nihon Koten Bungaku Taikei, vol. 66, ed. Kidō Saizō aand Imoto Nōichi (Iwanami Shoten, 1961), 94 and 182; cited and translated by David Pollack, *Fracture*, 159.

74. Although Morisue Akira argues that Zeami's Zen beliefs come from Kiyō Hōshū ("Tōgen Zuisen no *Shikishō* ni miru Zeami," in *Yōkyoku, Kyōgen*, ed. Nihon Bungaku Kenkyū Shiryō Kankōkai [Yūseidō, 1981], 44ff.), Zeami's conception of mind gives credence to Yasuraoka Kōsaku, who has argued that Zeami is primarily influenced by the Zen teachings of Getsuan Sōkō (1326–89) of the non-Five Mountains temple Daitoku-ji. See his *Chūseiteki bungaku no tankyū* (Yūseidō, 1971), 220–30, cited in Pollack, *Fracture*, 167.

75. *GBZ* 3:2511–12. Chūhō here sounds as if he believed that Chu Hsi and Yuan-wu actually became acquainted, an historical impossibility, since Chu was born only five years before Yüan-wu's death in 1135. The source for this misunderstanding appears to be the record of this event in the *Shih-jen Yu-hsieh* (2:452), which records two lines from Yüan-wu's poem and indicates that the two "exchanged poems."

76. *SBT*, 5:168–69; *ZGS* 216–23.

77. See Wen Fong, *Images of the Mind*, 76, for a discussion of the influence of this dictum in calligraphic practice that derives from Kuo Jo-hsü's revival of the

term. Bush translates Kuo Jo-hsü's influential use of the term (fl. C. 1075) in her and Hsio-yen Shih's *Early Chinese Texts on Painting* (Cambridge, MA: Harvard University Press, 1985), 96.

78. *GBZ*, 2:1713.

79. Tu Wei-ming has discussed the philosophical importance of this term for artistic theory in his "The Idea of the Human in Mencian Thought: An Approach to Chinese Aesthetics," *Humanity*, esp. p. 69. Bush, *Chinese Literati*, discusses the term in the aesthetic theory of Huang T'ing-chien, pp. 44, 49–50, where she equates it with the related term which she translates as "entering the spirit" (*ju-shen*), and suggests that the term has close relations to Zen practice. Adele Austin Rickett discusses the same term *ju-shen* in the critical theory of Yen Yü, Huang T'ing-chien, and Ch'en Shih-tao, in her "Method and Intuition: The Poetic Theories of Huang T'ing-chien," in *Chinese Approaches to Literature from Confucius to Liang Ch'i-ch'ao*, ed. Richett (Princeton, NJ: Princeton University Press, 1978), 108 and 117–18.

80. *GBZ*, 3:2519. I have not yet identified who "the ancients" are that Chūhō refers to in this preface.

81. See, e.g., Konishi Jin'ichi, *Michi: chūsei no rinen* (Kōdansha, 1975), largely summarized in an English article, "Michi and Medieval Writing," trans. Aileen Gatten, in *Principles of Classical Japanese Literature*, ed. Earl Miner (Princeton, NJ: Princeton University Press, 1985), 181–208, and Ogisu Jundō, "Chūsei bungaku michi no shinka to kotei—Shōtetsu Shinkei kara Sōgi e," *Kokugo to Kokubungaku* (1947): 20–30.

4. ZEN BUDDHIST READINGS OF THE LANDSCAPE

1. Bush, *Literati*, describes this evolution as it applies to painting, 103ff. A survey of Chinese conceptions of reclusion may be found in Chi Li, "The Changing Concept of the Recluse in Chinese Literature," *Harvard Journal of Asiatic Studies* 24 (1962): 234–47.

2. Translated by Herbert Frankl, "The Plum Tree in Chinese Poetry," *Asiatische Studien* 6 (1952): 104.

3. The literature on these writers is quite considerable. For a treatment of Saigyō in generic Buddhist terms, see William La Fleur, "Saigyō and the Buddhist Valorization of Nature, Parts I and II," *History of Religions* 13.2 (1973): 93–128 and 13.3 (1974): 227–48, but see also an argument for his affiliation with particular Esoteric Buddhist practices by Manabu Watanabe, "Religious Symbolism in Saigyō's Verses: A Contribution to Discussions of His Views on Nature and Religion," *History of Religions* 26.4 (1987): 382–400. On Kamo no Chōmei, see, e.g., Marian Ury, trans., "Recluses and Eccentric Monks: Tales from the Hosshinshū by Kamo no Chōmei," *Monumenta Nipponica* 27 (1972), and Thomas Blenman Hare, "Reading Kamo no Chōmei," *Harvard Journal of Asiatic Studies* 49.1 (June 1989): 173–228. An overview of reclusion imagery in Japanese literature and painting may

be found in Kendall H. Brown, *The Politics of Reclusion: Painting and Power in Momoyama Japan* (Honolulu, HI: University of Hawai'i Press, 1997), 19–52.

4. "Treasury of the True Dharma Eye: Book XXIX, The Mountains and Rivers Sutra," trans. Carl Bielefeldt, in *The Mountain Spirit*, ed. Michael Charles Tobias and Harold Drasdo (Woodstock, NY: Overlook Press, 1979), 41.

5. Ibid. Bielefeldt discusses the function of disjunctive images in Dōgen's writings in his *Dōgen's Manuals of Zen Meditation* (Berkeley: University of California Press, 1988), 156–57.

6. Bielefeldt, "Treasury," 41–42.

7. For an extended discussion of the chapter of the Shōbōgenzō that takes these lines as its title, see Bernard Faure, *La vision immédiate: Nature, Eéveil, et selon le Shōgōgenzō* (Paris: Le Mail, 1987), 121–42. For a comparative analysis of Dōgen's landscape poetry with that of Zekkai Chūshin, see Kawaguchi, "Zen no sankyoshi," 206–18.

8. The text of this preface is not preserved in Taihaku's extant writings. For my text I used *SBT*, 5:168–69; also translated into modern Japanese and discussed by Ōnishi Hiroshi in *ZGS*, 216–23.

9. *SBT*, 5:169; *ZGS*, 217.

10. *SBT*, 5:168–69; *ZGS*, 217.

11. *SBT*, 5:168–69; *ZGS*, 217. The quoted phrase was used unsuccessfully by Yeh Sung (d.u.), a minister of the Former or Western Han (206 B.C.E. – 7 C.E.), to defend his behavior as a responsible minister against trumped up charges brought against him by court rivals; he was then executed by the last emperor of the dynasty, Emperor Ai-tsung.

12. Yüan-wu K'o-ch'in, *Zen Letters: Teachings of Yuan-wu*, trans. J. C. Cleary and Thomas Cleary (Boston, MA: Shambala, 1994), 66, and *Mei-tao-jen i-mo*, in *Mei-shu Ts'ung-shu*, comp. Huan Pin-huan and Teng Shih (Shanghai: Shen-chou kuo-kuang-she, 1947), 3.4:45.

13. *SBT*, 5:168–69; *ZGS*, 217.

14. James Cahill does not find any pre-Sung examples, "Wu Chen," 63. See also, Bush, *Chinese Literati*, 35–36.

15. *Ching-chin Tung-p'o wen-chi shih-lueh, SPTK*, 9.49:1a–2a; my translation modifies Bush, *Chinese Literati*, p. 37, Chinese text no. 60, p. 190.

16. Translated by James Robert Hightower, *The Poetry of T'ao Ch'ien* (Oxford: Clarendon Press, 1970), 269. The importance of this poem in later poetry, painting, and intellectual history is described by Shou-chien Shih in "The Mind Landscape of Hsieh Yu-yü by Chao Meng-fu," in Wen C. Fong, et al., *Images of the Mind* (Princeton, NJ: The Art Museum, Princeton University, 1984), 247.

17. Trans. Iriya Yoshitaka, *Kanzan*, Chūgoku shijinsenshū 5 (Iwanami Shoten, 1958), 26–27; Burton Watson, trans., *Cold Mountain: 100 Poems by the T'ang Poet Han-shan* (Columbia University Press, 1970 [1962]), 20.

18. Stephen Owen, *The Great Age*, 27.

19. "Protest against Convention and Conventions of Protest," in *Confucianism and Chinese Civilization*, ed. Arthur F. Wright (Stanford, CA: Stanford University Press, 1975), 227–52.

20. Translated Nielson, *Ch'iao-jan*, 32.

21. Discussed in terms of "voluntary eremitism" by Frederick Mote, "Confucian Eremitism," 259–70, and Bol, "Culture and the Way," 192–96. I here follow Bol, who disagrees with Mote on Ou-yang's position; see also Bol's discussion of the implications of Ou-yang's position for the thinking of Su Shih, p. 196ff.

22. Mote, "Confucian Eremitism," 256–59, discusses the positions in Confucius, Mencius, and Hsun-tzu, as well as their implications for later thinkers.

23. Bush, *Chinese Literati*, 45. Discussion of a related theme in painting theory, internalization of bamboo in the breast, may be found in Fuller, "Bamboo," 5–23.

24. Pan Ku, in *Han-shu* (Shanghai: K'ai-ming Shu-tien, 1935), 100:632d, cited in Bush, *Chinese Literati*, 45n49.

25. *Yu-chang Huang hsien-shen wen-chi, SPTK*, 8:27.5a–b. My translation modifies Bush, *Chinese Literati*, p. 46; Chinese text no. 81, p. 191.

26. Bush, *Chinese Literati*, 47.

27. Ishikawa Jun, ed., *Tō Gen, Kyo Nen*, Bunjinga suihen (Chūō Kōronsha, 1985), 2:148.

28. Barnhardt, "Yao Yen-ching," 105, 107.

29. *GBZ*, 3:2514.

30. Ibid.

31. Feng Yu-lan, *A History of Chinese Philosophy*, trans. Derk Bodde (Princeton, NJ: Princeton University Press, 1953), 2:234–36.

32. Wing Tsit-chan's translation cited in Tu Wei-ming, "Profound Learning, Personal Knowledge, and Poetic Vision," in *The Vitality of the Lyric Voice: Shih Poetry from the Late Han to the T'ang*, ed. Shuen-fu Lin and Stephen Owen (Princeton, NJ: Princeton University Press, 1986), 8–10.

33. Shou-chien Shih, "The Mind Landscape," 239–40.

34. *The Buddhist Conquest of China; the Spread and Adaptation of Buddhism in Early Medieval China* (Leiden: Brill, 1959), 216–17.

35. Zurcher, *Conquest*, 211.

36. Collcutt discusses the political circumstances, particularly Shun'oku's role with the powerful daimyo Shiba Yoshimasa in struggles between different Zen factions, that led to these changes (*Five Mountains*, 119–22).

37. John Rosenfield has discussed the history of this legend in his "The Unity of the Three Creeds," 210–11. Analysis of the Five Mountains interest in the *Three Laughers of the Tiger Ravine* may be found in Asakura, *Zenrin no bungaku*, 59–100.

38. Manuscript from the Taipei National Palace Museum; translated by Shih, "The Mind Landscape," 238–39.

39. Published with English translations of several of the colophons by Shou-chien Shih, "The Mind Landscape," 238–54 and cat. no. 6, pp. 280–83.

40. Inscription transcribed in Ishikawa et al., eds., *Kō Kōbo*, 176; my translation modifies Shih's in "The Mind Landscape," 242.

41. Quoting the Confucian *Analects* 7.6, trans. D. C. Lau, p. 86: "The Master said, 'I set my heart on the Way, base myself on virtue, lean upon benevolence for support and take my recreation in the arts.'" While the arts in the *Analects* passage included ceremony, music, archery, charioteering, writing, and arithmetic, Ishō makes clear in this preface that he has in mind just the arts of poetry and painting.

42. This is a common characterization of fiction in contemporary China and Japan that is countered, for example, in the important "Defense of the Art of Fiction" in the *Tale of Genji* and other aesthetic theories.

43. *Gozan bungaku shinshū*, comp. Tamamura Takeji (Tokyo Daigaku Shuppankai, 1967–72), 2:779–80 (hereafter cited as *GBS*). The preface was originally on a painting attributed in the fifteenth century to Chao, though Ishō questions the attribution in his preface; the painting is now lost and only the inscriptions remain. The inscriptions are published and briefly discussed by Uemura Kankō in "Sekikarōzu," but the text differs significantly from that found in *GBS*.

44. I modify Burton Watson's translation, *The Columbia Book of Chinese Poetry: From Early Times to the Thirteenth Century* (New York: Columbia University Press, 1984), 135.

45. *GBS*, 2:779.

46. Owen, *Great Age*, 6–7, 48–50.

47. Ibid.

48. Discussed in the present author's "Attaining Landscapes in the Mind: Nature Poetry and Painting in Japanese Gozan Zen of the Early Fifteenth Century," *Monumenta Nipponica*, 52.2 (Spring, 1997): 235–56.

49. *GBZ*, 2:1710.

50. "Preface to Collected Poems and Songs on the Eight Views of Great Compassion [Temple]," *GBZ*, 2:1710.

51. The political and military events leading to this role are described in Kawazoe Shōji, "Foreign Relations: Early Muromachi," *Cambridge History of Japan*, vol. 3: *Muromachi*, 423–29.

52. Discussed in Horikawa Kishi, "'Daiji Hakkeishi' ni tsuite," *Kokugo to Kokubungaku* 67.6 (1990): 30–43.

53. Ichū was a student of Gidō and the important Kennin-ji monk Mugai Ninkō (1294–1359), who had spent twenty-eight years on the mainland, and went on to become abbot of the important Five Mountains temples of Kennin-ji, Tenryū-ji, and Nanzen-ji. He was also one of the two most prolific inscribers of poems on paintings during the Kitayama period.

54. I use as my main text that found in *GBZ*, 2:1610, but I also rely on the annotation in Tamamura Takeji's modern Japanese translation in *Gozan shisō* Nihon

no Zen goroku 8 (Kōdansha, 1978) (hereafter *GSS*), pp. 214–16. The full context for the composition of this poem can be found in Gido's "Preface to Poems and a Painting on White Clouds and Cinnabar Canyons," *GBZ* 2:1713, discussed above.

55. Ibid.

56. While this group gathered for Buddhist devotional practices, Japanese Zen monks looked up to Hui-yu"an not primarily for the Amida devotional practices carried out by the group but as a venerated precedent for gatherings of monks together with influential lay followers to practice Buddhism together.

57. Gidō alludes to the second line of Ta-mei's poem: "In a solitary pond lotus leaves: clothing without end./ On numerous trees pine flowers: Food enough for a surplus." (Cited in Tamamura, *GSS*, 216.)

58. *GBZ*, 3:2233.

59. Lu Ts'ang-yung (active c. 701–5) retired to Chung-nan shan (South Mountain) when he was not given an office after passing the *chin-shih* examination, only to practice the arts of immortality and then be given official office. When Ssu-ma Ch'eng-chen visited the mountain, Lu indicated a number of places with beautiful scenery, but when Su-ma commented that the mountain had been a short-cut to official service, Lu became ashamed.

60. Kung Chi-kuei, active during the Southern Ch'i dynasty, was scolded by the god of the mountain for pretending to be a recluse. This headcloth is illustrated in Morohashi Tetsuji, *Daikanwa jiten*, reduced size imprint (Daishūkan Shoten, 1960), 4:8995c.

61. *Han-shu*, 77; quoted in Morohashi, *Daikanwa jiten*, 11:39647.184.

62. I have been unable to locate the source of this phrase.

63. Most likely Shinshū, modern Nagano Prefecture.

64. Literally, "central flower," this may refer either to the central area of the country, i.e., the capital region around Kyoto, or it may refer to the area west of the Kinki region, centering on modern Hyogo Prefecture.

65. "West of the barrier" can refer either to the Kansai area around modern Osaka, or to west of the Kantō barrier near modern Tokyo, which seems less likely. The phrase "west of the barrier" is also used in Five Mountains literature to refer to Kyūshū, where travelers arrived from the mainland and where there were several important Zen temples. I am indebted to Takahashi Noriko for this information.

66. Here Taihaku plays on the name of the essay, which I have translated as "verdure."

67. *GBZ*, 3:2233.

68. Translated by Burton Watson, *Su Tung-p'o: Selections from a Sung Dynasty Poet* (Columbia University Press, 1965), 90. Chinese text in *Kobun Shinpō*, 53.

69. Haga, *Chūsei Zenrin*, 141–43. For an in-depth study of the importance of the popular Su Shih in Five Mountains Zen literature, see Asakura, *Zenrin no bungaku*, 377–530.

70. *GBZ*, 3:2233.

71. For a closely comparable argument by Chūhō En'i that self-cultivation centering on the mind is at the base of learning how to "make one's recluse hut anywhere," see his "Explanation of Reflecting on the Mind Hut," *GBZ*, 3:2535–36.

5. BUDDHIST ILLUSION AND THE LANDSCAPE ARTS

1. Faure, *Rhetoric*, 66–67. While Faure suggests in this section that Zen disavowed Buddhist canonical ontology, I here follow David Chappell's argument for continuity between early Zen texts and the Buddhist canonical heritage in "Hermeneutical Phases in Chinese Buddhism," *Buddhist Hermeneutics*, ed. Donald S. Lopez Jr. Kuroda Institute Studies in East Asian Buddhism, 6 (Honolulu: University of Hawaii Press, 1988), 193–94.

2. Gimello, "Apophatic," 133.

3. Ibid.

4. Gidō's cottage was located at the time along the banks of the Katsura river in the Sankai-in subtemple of Rinsen-ji temple; the temple was the headquarters of the Musō school that dominated the Five Mountains Zen system.

5. This term is found in the *Mencius*, where it refers to the most talented individuals in the kingdom who are pupils of the true sagely gentleman, or *chun-tzu*.

6. Hsüeh-feng Hui-k'ung (fl. c. 1153) was the author of the *Tung-shan Wai-chi* or *Tung-shan K'ung Ho-sheng Wai-chi*, which was widely read among the Japanese Five Mountains monks. This monk and Gidō's knowledge of him are discussed further below.

7. *GBZ*, 2:1725.

8. While we will return to this important theme of playfulness in our next and final chapter, here we might merely note the close relationship Gidō suggests between such a state of mind and the artistic production of illusion.

9. Analysis of this term in Indian Buddhist philosophy may be found in Nagao Gadjin, "An Interpretation of the Term 'Saṃvṛti' (Convention) in Buddhism," in *Silver Jubilee Volume of the Zinbun-Kagaku Kenkyusyo* (Kyoto: Institute for Humanistic Studies, 1954), while Junjirō Takakusu gives an English introduction emphasizing the various philosophical interpretations of the term in Chinese and Japanese Buddhism in his *The Essentials of Buddhist Philosophy* (Delhi: Motilal Banarsidass, 1975 [1947]), 103ff., 134–42.

10. For an example in an early text, see *Daruma no goroku*, 2, Zen no goroku, vol. 1, ed. and trans. by Yanagida Seizan (Tsukuma Shobō, 1969), 31. For this concept in the Ma-tsu line of Chinese Zen, see "Verse on not falling into distinction between sagely and common" by Tung-shan Liang-chieh, trans. by William Powell, *The Record of Tung-shan*, Kuroda Institute Classics in East Asian Buddhism (Honolulu: University of Hawaii Press, 1986), 66.

11. *GBZ*, 2:1282.

12. This poem is preserved in Gidō's important collection of Sung and Yüan Zen verse, *Jōwashū*, found in *Jūkan Jōwa ruijū soen renpōshū Shinsen Jōwashū, Dainihon Bukkyō Zensho*, ed. Bussho Kankōkai (Bussho Kankōkai, 1912), 229, 432.

13. Gidō himself wrote out a text of this collection, which is no longer extant, and gave three series of lectures on the collection in 1371, 1380, and 1385. See Gidō's *Kūge*, 69, 102, 106, 212, 215, 217, and 340. Kawase concludes from the large number of Japanese Five Mountains printings that Hsüeh-feng's poetry collection underwent, totaling more than six in the Nambokuchō period alone, that it was one of the most popular literary collections among the Japanese Five Mountains monks. See his *Gozanban*, 401–3.

14. T.82, 2582: 161–63. Discussed and translated in Faure, *Rhetoric*, 218–19.

15. Modern Japanese translation in Imaizumi, *Tōgo Seiwa*, 229–31. Useful studies for understanding miniature gardens in their Chinese intellectual, religious, and aesthetic context may be found in John Hay, *Kernels of Energy, Bones of Earth: The Rock in Chinese Art* (Chinese Institute of America, 1985); and Rolf A. Stein, "Miniature Gardens in the Far East," in idem, *The World in Miniature: Container Gardens and Dwellings in Far Eastern Religious Thought*, trans. Phyllis Brooks (Stanford, CA: Stanford University Press, 1990 [1943]), 1–119.

16. Biography unknown.

17. Mencius, 4.a.8.2–3:

There was a boy who sang,

"If the blue water is clear
It is fit to wash my chin-strap.
If the blue water is muddy
It is only fit to wash my feet."

Translated D. C. Lau, *Mencius*, p. 121.

18. See Bush, *Literati*, 44–47, on this theme in Sung literati theory. Ashikaga (*Kamakura, Muromachi*) discusses the related term, "to nourish the mind" (C. *yang-hsin*), in the writings of Kiyō Hōshū, pp. 365–66. See also chapter 6 below.

19. Mt. Sung and Mt. Hua were two of the largest mountains in China, and taken together were a common epithet for immense size.

20. I have been unable to identify this object, and must assume that it is a Chinese transliteration of the Sanskrit name of a very large object, perhaps associated with Mt. Sumeru.

21. This phrase has two meanings: objectively, it indicates measurements of the size of the painting (and its miniature garden), with no basis in reality (since they are smaller than a real landscape); conceptually, it indicates the Buddhist conception of thought or judgment that is not based on sensory perception.

22. *Mencius*, 7.a.21.3 (trans. D. C. Lau, pp. 185–86): "That which a gentleman follows as his nature is not added to when he holds sway over the Empire nor is it detracted from when he is reduced to straitened circumstances. . . . That which

a gentleman follows as his nature, that is to say, benevolence, rightness, the rites and wisdom, is rooted in his heart."

23. Chūhō is here suggesting by poetic allusion that he goes beyond even the poetic sage T'ao Ch'ien in transcending T'ao's well-known distinction between truth and falsehood, from T'ao Ch'ien's fifth verse on "Drinking Wine." The verse ends with the words, "In all this there's some principle of truth,/ but try to define it and you forget the words" (translation by Burton Watson, *The Columbia Book of Chinese Poetry: From Early Times to the Thirteenth Century* [Columbia University Press, 1984], 135).

24. Ibid.

25. McRae, *Northern School*, 147.

26. Translated by Burton Watson, *Han-shan*, 102.

27. Bielefeldt, "*Jisshū*," 232.

28. See, e.g., his poem on "An Artificial Landscape," *GBZ*, 1:86.

29. Yanagida seizan, trans., *Musō Kokushi goroku* Gendai goyaku Zen no koten 4 (Kōronsha, 1983), 145.

30. *Dreams Illusion and Other Realities* (Chicago: University of Chicago Press, 1984), 117–19. For an important critique of the notion of dream and *māyā* in Indian civilization, see also Ronald Inden, *Imagining India* (Oxford: Basil Blackwell, 1990), 40, 55–56, 108.

31. Jan Gonda, *Change and Continuity in Indian Religion*, Disputationes Rheno-Trajectionae, 9 (The Hague, 1965), 166.

32. A discussion of the importance of *māyā* in Indian conceptions of art can be found in O'Flaherty, *Dreams*, esp. chapter 6, "The Art of Illusion."

33. O'Flaherty, *Dreams*, 118 and 322n79, cites Arthur A. Macdonell's description of the parallel between what he calls the "moral ambiguity" of *māyā* and the connotations of the English word "craft": old signification of occult power and magic, as in "witchcraft"; more recently skillfulness and art, as in "arts and crafts" or "handicrafts"; and also deceitful skill and wile, as in "crafty character." O'Flaherty also draws on Johan Huizinga's *Homo Ludens* (Boston: Beacon Press, 1955) to mention the "cluster of meanings" of the English derivatives of the Latin word for play, "*ludo*," such as "de-lusion," "il-lusion," "e-lusive," to which for the present purposes we might add "(poetic) al-lusion" and "word play."

34. See, e.g., *Buddha's Teachings: Being the Sutta-Nipāta or Discourse-Collection*, trans. Lord Chalmers, Harvard Oriental Series 37 (Cambridge, MA: Harvard University Press, 1932), 195, 203.

35. For important Mahayana examples, see the discussion of dreams by Dharmodgata in chapter 31 of the *The Perfection of Wisdom in Eight Thousand Lines*, trans. Edward Conze (Bolinas, CA: Four Seasons Foundation, 1973), 291–92, and the "Parable of the Conjured City" in *The Scripture of the Lotus Blossom of the Fine Dharma*, trans. Leon Hurvitz (New York: Columbia University Press, 1976), 130ff. Images of illusion are especially central to the *Laṅkāvatāra*

Sutra, a text central to some schools of early Chinese Zen, discussed in D. T. Suzuki, Studies in the *Laṅkāvatāra Sutra* (Boulder, CO: Prajñā Press, 1981; orig. pub. Routledge & Kegan Paul, 1930), e.g., 114–121 and 392. English-language discussion of the Gandharva city in the sky as found in the *Lankāvatāra* is available in O'Flaherty, *Dreams*, 262, 271–75.

36. See Edward Conze, *Buddhist Thought in India* (Ann Arbor: University of Michigan Press, 1967), 222. Other images of illusion widely influential in East Asian Buddhism are those found in the "Expedient Means" chapter of the *The Holy Teaching of Vimalakīrti*, 22. For a survey of Buddhist dream images, see Masaaki Hattori, "Yume no hiyu ni tsuite," *Indogaku Bukkyōgaku kenkyū* 3.1 (1954). For an extensive bibliography of materials on dreams in Chinese and Japanese culture, see Faure, *Rhetoric*, 212nn6–7 and 214n13; for Faure's critical discussion of stereotypes of Zen rationalism based on historical examples of dreaming in Zen as a source of shamanic revelatory insight, see pp. 209–30.

37. *The Complete Works of Chuang-tzu*, trans. Burton Watson (Columbia University Press, 1968), 49.

38. Modern Japanese translation by Kageki in Zekkai, *Shōkenkō*, 70–71.

39. Scholars now agree that the text was probably composed in Chinese by some unknown author or group of authors sometime at the end of the seventh or early in the eighth century. Full discussion of the early translation legends surrounding the text and different dates of the purported translation (ranging from 693 to 718) can be found in Yanagida Seizan, *Chūgoku senjutsu kyōten, ichi: Engakukyō*, Bukkyō kyōtensen 13 (Tsukuma Shobō, 1987), 268–72, and Mochizuki Shinkō, *Jōdokyō no kigen to hattatsu* (Tokyo, 1930), 244–45. English-language descriptions of the text may be found in Gregory, *Tsung-mi*, 54–58 and 167–70, and in Whalen Lai, "Illusionism (*Māyāvāda*) in Late T'ang Buddhism: A Hypothesis on the Philosophical Roots of the Round Enlightenment Sutra (*Yüan- chüeh-ching*)," *Philosophy East and West* 28.1 (Jan. 1978). An English translation is available in Charles Luk (Lu K'uan Yü), "The Sūtra of Complete Enlightenment," in *Ch'an and Zen Teaching: Third Series* (rpt. Berkeley: Shambala Publications, 1973 [1962]), 149–278.

40. In this brief summary I depend on Yanagida's discussion of the text's early use in Japan, *Engakukyō*, 263–68.

41. Gidō first heard lectures on the fifth day of the eleventh month, 1367 (*Kufūshū*), while Zekkai first heard lectures in 1350 at the age of fifteen. (See his chronology appended to his poetry collection, *Shōkenkō*, ed. and Japanese translation by Kageki Hideo, p. 185.)

42. There are numerous references to the text and to his lectures on the text throughout Gidō's diary, *Kufūshū*. See, e.g., his lecture with other monks to Yoshimitsu on a number of sutras, including the *Perfect Enlightenment Sutra* starting on the eighteenth day of the sixth month of 1382, at the temple that later was to become the important Five Mountains administrative temple Rokuon'in.

43. Yanagida, *Engakukyō*, 264–65.

44. See, e.g., the discussion of the relationship between enlightenment and nonenlightenment, where *The Awakening of Faith* says, "The various magic-like manifestations (*huan*) of both enlightenment and nonenlightenment are aspects of the same essence, Suchness." Yoshito S. Hakeda, trans., *The Awakening of Faith Attributed to Asvaghosha* (New York: Columbia University Press, 1967), 46.

45. John McRae, *The Northern School*, 212–13 and 342n322.

46. While this image is very prominent in the *Perfect Enlightenment Sutra*, it is, of course, not limited in use to the text, but is a common image of illusion, and is also found on the two standard lists of ten images of illusion mentioned above.

47. Of course, this phrase is found in Buddhist texts other than the *Perfect Enlightenment Sutra*, such as the *Laṅkāvatāra Sutra*. Evidence that the Kitayama Japanese interest in the term is not an original development but more likely reflects Southern Sung or Yüan dynasty Chinese Zen can be found in the use of the term by a Zen monk from outside the Five Mountains system, the important early Japanese Sōtō master, Keizan Jokin (1268–1325), in his *Denkōroku*, 2 (T82.360b).

48. Nagarjuna's tetralemma and the problem of annihilationism have been discussed in a wide variety of sources; see, e.g., Conze, *Buddhist Thought in India*, 219 and 225.

49. *T* 25.416c. My translation is based on Yanagida's modern Japanese rendering in *Engakukyō*, 37.

50. The four types of soldiers in ancient India: those who ride elephants, horses, and chariots, and foot soldiers.

51. Splendid palaces refers to the capital, while walled cities can refer to any large city; these examples may also refer to the illusory cities in the sky, a common metaphor for illusion in Indian literature.

52. Literally, eating and drinking, singing and dancing. To classically trained Chinese and Japanese readers, the first of these compounds, "eating and drinking," would be recognized as common pejorative terms in the Chinese classics, where it is used for people who desire only to eat and drink. The second compound, "singing and dancing" is the object of one of the eight Buddhist precepts, which prohibits these two activities.

53. Yanagida, *Engakukyō*, 37.

54. Kawase Kazuma, *Gozanban* 1:420–21, points out that the alleged late Kamakura date of the earliest edition of Chung-feng's *Kōroku* is doubtful, considering that the original edition was not completed in China until 1335, and that a date in the early Nambokuchō is more likely.

55. Chu-hsien was abbot of Kenchō-ji and Engaku-ji, among others, and his influence was extremely wide as a representative of continental Zen in Japan during a period when relatively few other Chinese masters were coming to Japan. Betsugen held the Five Mountains temple abbacy of Kennin-ji, while Tesshū was abbot of Manjū-ji in Kyoto.

56. Yanagida Seizan, *Zen no jidai: Eisai, Musō, Daitō, Hakuin* (Tsukuma Shobō, 1987), 126–28. Cf. Especially Musō's verse composed on the occasion of Chung-feng's death, translated by Yanagida, 127–28.

57. Imaeda Aishin, *Chūsei Zenshūshi*, 458 and 461n13.

58. I rely in this biographical sketch on Chün-fang Yü's biography in "Chung-feng Ming-pen," 419–30.

59. "Wu-men ch'ung-chien Huan-chu ch'an chi," in *Sung wen-hsien kung ch'uan-chi, SPPY* ed., 29:5a; trans. by Yü, "Chung-feng," 466–67n28.

60. Yü, "Chung-feng," 423.

61. Yü, "Chung-feng," 433–44 and 269n52, points out that Chao and Chung-feng refer to each other as master and disciple in letters they wrote to each other. For discussion of the circle of literati, poets, and artists in which Chao participated in the Hangchou area near some of Chung-feng's residences, see Marilyn Wong Fu, "The Impact of the Re-unification: Northern Elements in the Life and Art of Hsien-yü Shu (1257?–1302) and Their Relation to Early Yüan Literati Culture," in *China under Mongol Rule*, ed. John D. Langlois Jr. (Princeton, NJ: Princeton University Press, 1981), 371–433.

62. Discussion of these and other of Chung-feng's lay followers can be found in Fujishima Tateki, "Genchō Bukkyō," 14–26, and also in Nishio Kenryu's "Genchō ni okeru Chūhō Minhon to sono dōzoku," *Zengaku kenkyū* 64 (Nov. 1985): 31–56.

63. *T'ien-mu Chung-feng Ho-sheng Kuang-lu*, *Dainihon Zokuzōkyō* (also *Manji Zokuzōkyō*), ed. Nakano Tatsue (Kyoto: Zōkyō shoin, 1905–12) (hereafter cited as Z.), 31.6–7. I rely for my translation on notes found in a woodblock print edition with commentary and a preface of 1387 in the Hanazono University Library, *chuan* 16, p. 1ff., and on minor character corrections suggested to me by Professor Iriya Yoshitaka.

64. *Chung-feng Kuang-lu,* Z., 31.6–7.

65. Trans. Robert Thurman, *The Holy Teaching of Vimalakirti: A Mahayana Scripture* (University Park: Pennsylvania State University Press, 1976), 25.

66. Yanagida, *Engakukyō*, 35.

67. *Chung-feng Kuang-lu,* Z., 31.6–7.

68. Here Chung-feng used a slang expression for sensationalist or alarmist behavior, as when, for example, somebody thinks they see a ghost and is scared out of their wits and causes a big disturbance.

69. This and the previous sentence allude to important incidents and concepts in Lin-chi's *Recorded Sayings*.

70. *Chung-feng Kuang-lu,* Z., 31.6–7.

71. *Chung-feng Kuang-lu,* Z., 31.6–7.

72. *GBZ*, 2:1888–89.

73. English-language introductions to Gukei's art may be found in Richard Edwards, "Gukei," 169–78, and Ann Yonemura's entry in Shimizu and Yonemura,

Japanese Ink Paintings, 192–93; a definitive Japanese-language study is by Shimada Shujiro, "Gukei Ūe no sakuhin nishū," *Kokka* 707 (1951): 83–90; also published in idem, *Nihon Kaigashi*, 112–23.

74. *GBZ*, 2:1888–89.

75. Literally come to be "communal property of the monastery" (*jojumotsu*).

76. Gidō here played on the character "*e*" or "wisdom" in Ūe Gukei's name.

77. "Great thousand" (*ta-chien*) is an abbreviation for *san-chien ta-chien shih-chieh*, a Buddhist term for the myriad worlds making up the cosmos; the term "hair tip" (*hao-tuan*) is a common epithet for the tiniest of things.

78. *GBZ*, 2:1888–89. Also translated in Edwards, "Ūe Gukei," 177–78.

79. Su Shih text with modern Japanese translation in Ogawa Tamaki, trans., *So Shoku*, Chugoku shijinsen, vol. 6, rev. ed. (Iwanami Shoten, 1983), 5–7.

80. An important revisionist discussion of the significance and usage of these portaits in Zen Buddhism may be found in T. Griffith Foulk and Robert Sharf, "On the Ritual Use of Ch'an Portraiture in Medieval China," *Cahiers d'Extrême Asie* 7 (1993–94): 149–219.

81. Ibid., 160ff.

82. Examples of Chinese uses important to the Japanese Five Mountains monks of this term can be found on the *chinzō* inscribed by Wu-chun Shih-fan for Enni Ben'en, discussed below (text reproduced in *Zensō to bokuseki—Shōichi Kokushi o megutte* [Nara National Museum, 1986], pl. 1 and p. 17) and a *chinzō* of Wu-an Pu-ning (text reproduced in *Suiboku bijutsu taikei*, vol. 5, no. 27). I am grateful to Ebine Toshio, who first pointed this usage out to me.

83. See for example Kiyō's use of the term *gensō* on a *chinzō* recorded in *GBZ*, 3:2926.

84. *Zensō to bokuseki*, pl. 1, p. 1; text transcribed p. 17.

85. Discussed by Shimao in *Hyōnenzu*, p. 29; see also fig. 20.

86. Foulk and Sharf, "Ritual Use," 202–6, mention this general Zen-style notion in passing, but do not develop this point in any detail.

87. *Kūgeshū, GBZ*, 2:1414. Cited in Akazawa, "Ōei," 1.26. I am again grateful to Ebine Toshio for pointing out Gidō's use of this type of term to me in an April 1986 personal communication, and also to the discussion by Ōta Takahiko's in 1987 lectures at Kyoto University on the significance of this term in fourteenth- and fifteenth-century Japanese conceptions of painting.

88. Bush, *Literati*, 26, 32.

89. Bush, (ibid., 3) points out that literati painting and aesthetics was first defined in terms of social class and amateur status, and only later developed something approaching a unified style.

90. Trans. Bush, *Literati*, 110.

91. *Meng-ch'i pi-t'an, Chin-tai pi-shu*, Comp. Mao Chin (Shanghai: Po-ku-chai, 1922), 15:17.2a–b (composed c. 1090); my translation modifies Bush, *Texts*, 100.

92. *Ou-yang Wen-chung-kung wen-chi, SPTK*, 2:6.7b; trans. Bush, *Texts*, 203 and *Literati*, 23–24.

93. Chinese text in Bush, *Literati*, 29 (text no. 39, p. 188).

94. I based my translation on the text in Tanaka Ichimatsu, ed., *SBT* 5: *Kaō, Mokuan, Minchō*, 198–99. A modern Japanese translation and discussion of Taihaku's preface by Ōnishi Hiroshi is also found in *ZGS*, 216ff. The importance of this preface was first indicated to me by Shūjirō Shimada in a personal communication, November 1985. See also his article, "Shosaizu," passim.

95. These are the last two lines of the third of three poems written with the title, "Three Poems Inscribed on Chao Shao-in's [Chao Tzu-yen, fl. c. 1129–62] Blue and White Hall," *Ch'en Yü-i chi*, ed. Wu Shu-in and Chin Te-hou (Beijing: Chung-hua shu-chu, 1982), 423.

96. *SBT* 5, pl. 77; text transcribed p. 170.

97. "Divine marvelousness" (C. *shen-miao*) is a term used in Chinese art criticism and in Buddhist texts to describe an accomplishment beyond the range of normal human capability. The term "natural instinct" (C. *tien-chi*) was used in Sung literati theory for unselfconscious artistic activity, and was also close in meaning to "spiritual communion" (C. *shen-hui*). (See Bush, *Chinese Literati*, 60–62.)

98. Valerie Malenfer describes the sociocultural context of Buddhist and literati relations underlying the production of this painting in her 1990 Harvard University dissertation, "'Dream Journey over the Xiao and Xiang': Scholar-Amateur Landscape Painting in Southern Sung China (1127–1279)."

99. Stylistic issues and the identity of the painter of this painting are discussed by Suzuki Kei in a two-part article, "Shōshō unyū zukan ni tsuite," *Tōyō bunka kenkyūjo kiyō*, 61 (Mar. 1943): 1–63, and 79 (Mar. 1979): 1–84; see also Malenfer, "Dream Journey." I have used as my text for the translations the transcriptions found in Ishikawa Jun, et al., eds., *Tō Gen, Kyo Nen, Bunjinga suihen*, vol. 2 (Chūō Kōronsha, 1985), 147–48. I am grateful to Valerie Malenfer for discussing with me the inscriptions and the translations.

100. Found in the inscription by Chang Kuei-mou (d.u.), *Tō Gen, Kyo Nen*, 148.

101. The sixth inscription, *Tō Gen, Kyo Nen*, Bunjinga suihen 2, p. 148.

102. Ibid.

103. Translation modifies Susan Bush, *Literati*, p. 37, text 60.

104. Translated in Wen Fong, *Images of the Mind*, 120. A discussion of the early history in artistic criticism of the term "truth" (*chen*) and its relation to the terms "conventionality" or "artificiality" (*chia*) and "fake" (*wei*) through developments in the Kung-an school of Ming criticism can be found in Jonathan Chaves, "The Panoply of Images: A Reconsideration of the Literary Theory of the Kung-an School," in *Theories of the Arts in China*, ed. Susan Bush and Christian Murck (Princeton, NJ: Princeton University Press, 1983), 347ff.

105. Attributed to Hsieh Chien, published and inscription transcribed in *Gendai dōshaku jinbutsuga* (Tokyo National Museum, 1977), pl. 37.

106. Ibid.

107. Tamamura notes (*Denshū*, 19) that Ikō returned from the mainland in 1368 after a stay of two or three decades, where he was active at Kenchō-ji in 1368 and headed the meditation hall at Engaku-ji and lived again at Kenchō-ji around 1374. Ikō's literary collection and his collected sayings are unfortunately not extant. More biographical information is available in Ide Shosuke, "Ikō," passim.

108. *GBZ*, 3:1809.

109. Ibid.

110. See Bernard Faure, *Rhetoric*, 214ff., for description of these aspects. While he suggests that dreams are underdeveloped in Zen, the Kitayama monks provide an example of just such a interpretive tradition.

6. BUDDHIST PLAYFULNESS AND THE LANDSCAPE ARTS

1. See, for example, the comparative study by Conrad Hyers, *Zen and the Comic Spirit* (Philadelphia: Westminster Press, 1974). For work on this topic by Buddhologists, see below. Discussion of the theme of playfulness in other Japanese Buddhist schools may be found in Yokoi Kiyoshi, "Yuge to Jōdo—*Ryōjin Hisshō* o sozai to shite," *Zen bunka* 63 (1972): 44–50; and on its importance among marginal social groups with Buddhist affiliations, see Emiko Ohnuki-Tierney, *The Monkey as Mirror: Symbolic Transformations in Japanese History and Ritual* (Princeton, NJ: Princeton University Press, 1987).

2. The religious and social value of play has been the subject of a considerable academic literature. For my own early thinking on the topic, the following were formative: Roger Caillois, *Man, Play, and Games*, trans. Meyer Barash (Schocken Books, 1979); and Johan Huizinga, *Homo Ludens*.

3. *Chūhō oshō goroku*, 2.4a.

4. See, e.g., *Mencius*, 7a.8, trans. D. C. Lau (p. 183): "Mencius said, 'Wise kings in antiquity devoted themselves to goodness, forgetting their own exalted position. How should wise gentlemen in antiquity be any different? They delighted in the Way, forgetting the exalted position of others."

5. I am grateful to Iriya Yoshitaka for introducing me to this subject in Zen verse.

6. Information on Ming-ts'an, who was important for the spread of the Northern School of Zen to the south, is available in English in McRae, *Northern School*, 68–70. For a discussion of the "Enjoying the Way" theme in Han-shan's poetry, and of a poem by Kuan Hsiu on the contemporary image of Han-shan, see Iriya Yoshitaka, *Kyūdō to etsuraku*, 13–15.

7. The realm of unfathomable liberation is a favorite expression of Kiyō and a common expression in Zen and other Buddhist texts for the world as seen from the state of all-pervasive wisdom.

8. Here Kiyō seems to mean faith in one's own innate enlightenment. On the importance of this faith in Zen from its earliest period, see McRae, *Northern School*, 112.

9. This is a conventional expression for people whose way of thinking is completely different from one's own.

10. This seems to be a proverb, but I have been unable to locate any source.

11. *GBZ*, 3:2995–96.

12. 1.b.6–7; Translated by D. C. Lau, p. 83.

13. 6.23; translated by D. C. Lau, *Analects*, 84.

14. T. 48.209a and c; *The Blue Cliff Record*, Cleary trans., 3:541, 542.

15. David R. Kinsley, *The Sword and the Flute: Kali and Krsna, Dark Visions of the Terrible and the Sublime in Hindu Mythology* (Berkeley: University of California Press, 1975), 73–74.

16. Discussed in, e.g., Masatoshi Nagatomi, "*Mānasa-Pratyaksa*: A conundrum in the Buddhist Pramāna System," in *Sanskrit and Indian Studies: Essays in Honor of Daniel H. H. Ingalls*, ed. idem (Boston: D. Reidel, 1983), 243–60. For the history of this conception in Sung literati aesthetic theory, see Egan, "Calligraphy," 409.

17. *Vimalakīrti*, trans. Thurman, p. 20; *T*, 4:539a.

18. *Vimalakīrti*, 43.

19. *Vimalakīrti*, 51–52.

20. Yanagida, *Engakukyō*, 72–73.

21. The literature on the *Platform Sutra* is extensive; see, e.g., Philip Yampolsky, *The Platform Sutra*, 90–91, 99–104. Information on the transmission of the sutra to Japan can be found in Yampolsky; it does not seem to have been widely read or available until the Edo period.

22. This passage is not to be found in the Tun-huang edition, but is found in the Kōshō-ji and Ming editions. My translation here is based on Yanagida Seizan's Japanese rendering of the Ming tripitaka text in *Zenke goroku I*, Sekai koten bungaku zenshu, 36A, ed. Yanagida Seizan and Nishitani Keiji (Tsukuma Shobo, 1972), 144.

23. Yanagida, *Zenke goroku I*, 146, notes that this conception derives from T'an-luan's (476–542) *Ching-tu lun-chu*, where it is characterized as the highest of his five stages of "entering" and "leaving," in which the practitioner manifests his transformation body, as in the *Platform Sutra*, and moves about among the realms of suffering, desire, and birth and death.

24. Kawase, *Gozanban*, 243 and 453, lists printings first in 1291, then during the latter half of the Nambokuchō period, and again during the Kitayama epoch in 1405.

25. The six paths of existence in Buddhist cosmology.

26. *T*, 48:293a. English translation available in Thomas Cleary, *No Barrier: Unlocking the Zen Koan* (New York: Bantam Books, 1993), 2.

27. Haga Kōshirō has documented Gidō's interest in the *Chuang-tzu* in his *Chūsei Zenrin*, 201. Ishō Tokugan's study of the *Chuang-tzu* while he was at Nanzen-ji is recorded in his inscription on a portrait of his teacher (Haga, *Chūsei Zenrin*, 203).

28. "On Walking without Touching the Ground: 'Play' in the *Inner Chapters* of the *Chuang-tzu*," in *Experimental Essays on Chuang-tzu*, ed. Victor H. Mair (Honolulu: University of Hawaii Press, 1983), 108.

29. *Sōshi*, Chūgoku kotensen 8, trans. Fukunaga Mitsuji (Mainichi Shinbunsha, 1966), 1:46–57; *The Complete Works of Chuang Tzu*, trans. Burton Watson (New York: Columbia University Press, 1968), tr. pp. 39–41; *Chuang-tzu, the Seven Inner Chapters: And Other Writings from the Book "Chuang-tzu,"* trans. A. C. Graham (London: Allen & Unwin, 1981), 52–53.

30. Fukunaga, 1:71–72; Watson, 43; Graham, 56.

31. Fukunaga, 1:19; Watson, 33; Graham, 46.

32. Fukunaga, 1:165; Watson, 61; Graham, 71; also discussed by Crandell, "On Walking," 119.

33. *Unmon goroku*, in *Shika goroku, goke goroku*, ed. Yanagida Seizan (Kyoto: Chubun shuppan, 1983), 11a (p. 162). I might note that Yun-men playfully breaks up the Chinese compound for "landscape" into its two components, "mountain" and "water," in order to establish that the mendicant "wanders" in both of them.

34. *Tung-shan lu*, in *Shika goroku, goke goroku*, 10b (p. 128); my translation modifies William Powell's in his *The Record of Tung-shan* (Honolulu: University of Hawaii Press, 1986), 39.

35. *The Blue Cliff Record*, 170.

36. *GBZ*, 3:2232–33.

37. Ibid.

38. Ibid.

39. English translation by Burton Watson, *The Columbia Book*, 142–43.

40. Taihaku explicitly makes the same association of Five Mountains monks to the immortals of Peach Blossom Spring in a preface to a poem scroll on T'ao Ch'ien, *GBZ*, 3:2235.

41. Taihaku alluded with this forgetfulness most specifically to a poem by Li She (fl. c. 810–830) in the *San-t'i shih*, Japanese translation Murakami Tetsumi, *Santaishi*, Chugoku kotensen 16 (Asahi Shinbunsha, 1966), 1:171.

42. This poem is found in the *San-t'i shih* (2:398–99), which was the most likely source for the Japanese Five Mountains monks. English translation may be found in Watson, *Columbia Book*, 202, and Pauline Yu, *Wang Wei: New Translations and Commentary* (Bloomington, IN: Indiana University Press, 1980), 171.

43. Ogawa, *So Toba shishū*, 1:203–10; I use Burton Watson's translation in *Su Tung-p'o*, 111.

44. *GBZ*, 1:103. P'eng-lai and Ying-chou are two of the best known of the legendary islands of the immortals that were thought to be off the coast of China.

45. *Literati*, 70–72.

46. *Yu-chang Huang hsien-sheng wen-chi, SPTK* ed., 1:1.8a. My translation modifies Bush, *Chinese Literati*, 70–71.

47. See Bush, *Chinese Literati*, 36, 39, 47–48.

48. *Collected Poems*, 5:11.28b; my translation modifies Bush, *Chinese Literati*, 41; Chinese text no. 66, p. 191. For an extended discussion of the importance of Sung images of bamboo in aesthetics, see Fuller, "Bamboo," passim.

49. *Yuan I-shan shih chien-chu, SPPY* ed., 2:5.8b. My translation modifies Bush, *Chinese Literati*, 109; Chinese text no. 168, p. 197.

50. On Mi's use of the term, see Bush, *Chinese Literati*, 71–72.

51. *GBZ*, 2:1340–41; Gidō's inscription is discussed in Shimao, "Shoki shigajiku," passim.

52. Now in the Powers collection; reproduced in *Muromachi*, Nihon kaigakan 5, ed. Matsushita Takaaki (Kodansha, 1971), pl. 31.

53. Seal published in *Muromachi*, p. 31. Not all questions have been answered regarding the authenticity of this seal.

54. The name of this literary collection may also have been given to it by its anonymous editor, but either way it is most likely based on his own sobriquet, mentioned below.

55. *Han-shan*, 79–80. My translation modifies Watson, *Cold Mountain*, 79.

56. Translated in Chang, *Original Teachings*, 108–9.

57. *GBZ*, 3:2899–90.

58. Ibid.

59. Ibid.

60. *GBZ*, 2:1725.

61. Chūhō's collected sayings record two of these lectures given while offering incense, and I here refer to the contents of both of them. See *Goroku*, 2, 31b–33b. It possible to date this lecture from the date of a lecture at the same ceremony given by Taihaku in 1412. See Taihaku's *goroku*, 40a–41a.

62. *Goroku*, 2, 32a.

63. *Goroku*, 2, 33a.

64. See Faure, *Rhetoric*, 96–131, for a discussion of these figures in the Chinese context of the thaumaturgical and trickster traditions.

65. Kiyō's description of Hotei relied heavily on the influential hagiography by Meng T'ang, *Dai Nihon zokuzōkyō* (Kyoto: Zōkyō Shoin, 1905–12), II.B.15.5 (vol. 146, p. 471b ff.).

66. *GBZ*, 3:2903–4.

67. The painting, in a private collection, is published in *SBT*, 6:28.

68. See Ikeda Hisako, "Ashkaga Yoshimochi hitsu, 'Hoteizu,'" *De Arute* 8 (1992).

69. *GBZ*, 3:2911, 2912.

70. Sung dynasty versions of this series and other pictures on this topic are described by Scarlett Ju-yu Jang, "Ox-Herding Painting in the Sung Dynasty," *Artibus Asia* 52.1/2 (1992): 54–93. See also Yanagida Seizan and Ueda Shizutera, *Jūgyūzu: Jiko no genshōgaku* (Tsukuma Shobō, 1982).

71. Tamamura, *Denki*, 380.

72. The oldest extant Japanese version of the "Ten Oxherding Pictures" is dated to 1278 on the basis of an inscription. Three panels and the inscription have been published by Shinbo Tōru in "Shinshutsu no Kōanbon jūgyūzu kan," *Bukkyō geijutsu* 96 (May 1974): 77–79. The Zekkai inscriptions are preserved in the Jōtenkaku Museum collection at Shōkoku-ji, where they are now paired with a series of illustration attributed to Shūbun.

73. Motonaka, *Nambokuchō, Muromachi, Momoyama*, 163.

74. Ibid.

Glossary

This selective glossary includes names of individuals from the premodern period; terms in Chinese and Japanese; and a small number of selected temple names and documents. Filled-in squares represent unknown characters for individual names.

an 安
Ashikaga Motouji 足利基氏
Ashikaga Takauji 足利尊氏
Ashikaga Yoshimitsu 足利義滿
Ashikaga Yoshimochi 足利義持
Ashūshū 鴉臭集
batsu 跋
Beb Bupa 別不花
Betsugen Enshi 別源圓旨
Bon Wang 藩王
bunjin 文人
byōbu uta 屏風歌
byōshutsu 描出
Ch'an 禪
Chang Ch'uan-pu 張泉甫
Chang Kuei-mou 張貴謨
Ch'an-yu mo-hsi 禪余墨戲
Ch'an-yüan chu-chüan-chi tu-hsü 禪源諸詮集都序
Chao-chou Ts'ung-shen 趙州從諗
Chao Meng-fu 趙孟頫
chen 真
chen-chia 真假
Ch'en Ching-yüan 陳景元
cheng-fa yan 正法眼
ch'eng 誠
Ch'eng-kuan 澄観
Ch'en-wai Chü-shih 塵外居士
Ch'en Yu-i 陳與義
chi 記
ch'i 氣
chia 假
Chiang-hu 江湖
Chiao-jan 皎然
chiao-wai pieh-ch'uan 教外別傳
Ch'i-chi 齊己
Chien-hsin Lai-fu 見心來復
chih 止
chih-chih ke-wu 致知格物
Chin-kang san-mei ching 金剛三昧經
Chin-ssu lu 近思錄
ching 景
ching 敬
ching 靜
ching 境

Ching-cho Cheng-ch'eng 清拙正澄
Ching-sou (Pei-chien) Chü-chien 敬叟(北磵)居簡
ch'ing-t'an 清淡
Ch'ing-t'ang Chüeh-yüan 鏡堂覺圓
chinzō (chinsō) 頂相
Ch'i-sung 契嵩
Chitoku 智德
ch'iu-huo 丘壑
ch'i-yun 氣韻
chōka 長歌
Chōkei Oshō goroku 長慶和尚語錄
Chōun Reihō 頂雲靈峰
Chou Tun-i 周敦頤
Chuang Su 莊肅
Chuang-tzu 莊子
Ch'uan-hsin fa-yao 傳心法要
Chuan-shih Tsung-le 全室宗泐
Chüeh-fan Hui-hung 覺範慧洪
Chūgan Engetsu 中巖圓月
Chūhō En'i 仲方圓伊
Chūhō Oshō goroku 仲方和尚語錄
Chu Hsi 朱熹
Chu Hsiang-hsien 朱象先
Chu-hsien Fan-hsien 竺仙梵僊
chung 中
Chung-feng Ming-pen 中峰明本
Chung-jen 仲仁
chung-kuan 中観
Chung-nan shan 終南山
chung-tao 中道
chung-ti 中諦
Chung-yung 中庸
chun-tzu 君子
Chu Shan-jen 朱山人
Ch'u-shih Fan-ch'i 楚石梵琦
chu-yü san-mei 句語三昧
Daibutchōkyō 大仏頂經
Daidō Ichii 大道一以
Daidō-ken 大同軒
Daigaku Shusū 大岳周崇
daigashi 題畫詩
Daigo-ji 醍醐寺
Daigu Shōchi 大愚性智
Dainichi Nōnin 大日能忍
Daitō Kokushi 大燈國師
Denkōroku 伝光錄
Denshin hōyō 伝心法要
dōbōshū 同朋衆
Dōfuku-ji 道福寺
dōgō 道號
e 慧
Eihei Dōgen 永平道元
Ekyō Chūwa 慧嶠中和
emakimono 絵巻物
Engakukyō 圓覚經
Enni Ben'en 圓爾弁円
etsudō 悦道
fa erh chieh chung-chieh 發而皆中節
Fa Hsiu 法秀
fang-pien 方便
Fang Yai 方崖
Fan Kuan 范寬
fei 非
Fen-yang Shan-chao 汾陽善昭
Feng Tsu-chen 汾子振
Fujiwara no Shunzei 藤原俊成
Fujiwara no Teika 藤原定家
fu-ku 復古
Fumon-ji 普門寺
Funi Ikō 不二遺稿
Funi-ken 不二軒
Gabi Ashūshū 峨眉鵶臭集
gakō 画工
Gakuin Ekatsu 鄂隠恵奯
Gaun nikkenroku 臥雲日件録
gen'an 幻菴
Genchū Shūgaku 厳中周噩
genjūan 幻住庵
Genkō shakusho 元亨釈書
genshitsu 幻質
genshutsu 幻出
gensō 幻相
Gichū Shō 義中■勝

Gidō Shūshin 義堂周信
gō 号
Go Daigo Tennō 後醍醐天皇
goroku 語録
Gottan Funei 兀庵普寧
gozan (gosan) 五山
Guchū Shūkyū 愚中周及
Gukei Yūe 愚溪右慧
Gyokuen Bompō 玉畹梵芳
haikai 俳諧
Han-shan 寒山
Han Yü 韓愈
hao 號
hao-tuan 毫端
Hekiganroku 碧巖録
Hiei 比叡
Hino Yasuko 日野康子
ho 和
hōben 方便
Hogyū Kōrin 放牛光林
Hōjō Tokiyori 北條時頼
hōki 法諱
hongaku 本覚
Hōrin-ji 宝林寺
Hosokawa Yoriyuki 細川頼之
Hosokawa Mitsumoto 細川滿元
Hotei 布袋
Hōun-ji 宝雲寺
hōyū 訪友
hsi 戲(戯)
Hsia Kuei 夏圭
hsiao-yao yu 逍遙遊
Hsia Wen-yen 夏文彥
Hsieh Chien 雪澗
Hsieh K'un 謝鯤
Hsieh Ling-yün 謝靈運
Hsi-k'un 西崑
hsin 心
hsin chih so-te 心之所得
hsin-ching i-jo 心境一如
hsin-ching shuang-wang 心境雙忘
hsin-ch'uan 心傳
hsin-ch'uan i-ling 心傳意領
hsin-ch'uan shen-ling 心傳神領
hsing 形
hsing 性
hsin-hua 心畫
hsin-ling shen-hui 心領神會
hsin-pi 信筆
hsin-shou 信手
hsi-pi 戲筆
hsü 序
hsuan-hsueh 玄學
Hsüeh-feng Hui-k'ung 雪峰惠空
Hsüeh-tou Ch'ung-hsien 雪竇重顯
Hsü-t'ang Chih-yu 虛堂智愚
hua 化
Hua-chi pu-i 畫繼補遺
hua-kung 畫工
huan-an 幻菴
huan-chu an 幻住庵
huan-chu san-mei 幻住三昧
huan-ch'u 幻出
Huan Hsuan 桓玄
Huang-po Hsi-yun 黃檗希運
Huang T'ing-chien 黃庭堅
hua-t'ou 話頭
hui 會
Hui-yüan 惠遠
Hung-chih Cheng-chüeh 宏智正覺
huo-chu 活句
i 意
Ichijō Kaneyoshi (Kanera) 一条兼良
i-ch'iu i-huo 一丘一壑
Ichū Tsūjo 惟忠通恕
i-fa 已發
i-hsin 一心
i-huan hsiu-huan 以幻修幻
Ikka Kenbu 一華建悳
Ikkyū Sojun 一休宗純
Ikō Tokuken 以亨得兼
i-li 一理
i-ling 意領
Imagawa Ryōshun (Tokiyo) 今川了俊

in ch'eng-wei 隱城隈
Inryōken nichiroku 蔭涼軒日録
I-shan I-ning 一山一寧
Ishō Tokugan 惟肖得巖
Isshi 一之
Jakushitsu Genkō 寂室元光
jen 人
jen-hsin 人心
jih-yung 日用
jissatsu 十刹
jo 序
jojumotsu 常住物
Josetsu (Nyosetsu) 如拙
Joshin Chūjo 如心中恕
Jōwashū 貞和集
ju-huan san-mei 如幻三昧
Jūmon Saihisshō 十問最秘抄
Junshi Haku 純子■璞
ju-shen 入神
Kaichū Mo 楷中■莫
kaiyūzu 懐友図
Kakinomoto no Hitomaro 柿本人麻呂
Kamo no Chōmei 鴨長明
Kan'ami 観阿弥
Kanchū Chūtai 観中中諦
k'an-hua 看話
kanrei 管領
Kanzan Egen 関山恵玄
Kao Ch'i 高啓
ke 假
kei 景
Keijō Shūrin 景徐周麟
Keizan Jokin 瑩山紹瑾
Kempō Shidon 乾峰士曇
Kengan Keieki 謙巖景易
Ke Pi 葛邲
Kitayama 北山
Kiyō Hōshū 岐陽方秀
kōan 公案
Kobun shinpō 古文真宝
Kōhō Kennichi 高峰顕日
Kōkakau-ji 広覚寺
Kokan Shiren 虎関師錬
Koken Myōkai 古剣妙快
Kokinshū 古今集
kokoro 心
Kongōkyō 金剛經
Korai Futeishō 古来風体抄
Kōsei Ryūha 江西龍派
Kotohira 琴平
koyō 古様
Kuan-hsiu 貫休
kūge 空華
Kūge nichiyō kufū ryakushū 空華日用工夫略集
Kujō Michiie 九条道家
Ku K'ai-chih 顧愷之
Ku-lin Sei-mo 古林清茂
k'ung 空
kung-an 公案
Kung Chi-kuei 孔稚珪
k'ung-hua 空華
Kuo Hsi 郭熙
Kuo Hsiang 郭象
Kuo Jo-hsü 郭若虛
ku-wen 古文
Ku-wen chen-pao 古文真寶
kyō 境
Kyōgoku Tamekane 京極為兼
Lan-ch'i (Lan-hsi) Tao-lung 蘭溪道隆
lan-ke weng 嬾閣翁
lan-man shih-kao 懶漫室稿
lan-ts'an 懶瓚
lan-yun tzu 懶雲子
le-tao 樂道
le-tao ke 樂道歌
li 理
Liao-an Ch'ing-yü (Nan-t'ang) 了庵清欲(南堂)
Liao-an ho-shang yü-lu 了庵和尚語錄
Li Ch'eng 李成
Li Kung-lin 李公麟
Ling-ch'e 靈徹

Ling-yi 靈一
li-nien 離念
Li Po (Pai) 李白
Li She 李涉
Li-tsung 理宗
Liu K'ai 柳開
Liu Tsung-yüan 柳宗元
Liu Yü-hsi 劉禹錫
Lu Ts'ang-yung 盧藏用
Lu Tsu-ch'ien 呂祖謙
makoto 真
Manzai Jugō 滿済准后
Matsuo Bashō 松尾芭蕉
Ma-tsu Tao-i 馬祖道一
Ma Yüan 馬遠
Mei-tao-jen i-mo 梅道人遺墨
Mei Yao-ch'en 梅堯臣
meng-shan 夢山
Meng T'ang 夢堂
michi 道
Mi Fu 米芾
Minchō 明兆
Ming-chi Ch'u-chün 明極楚俊
ming-ming te 明明德
Ming Tai-tsu 明太祖
Ming-ts'an (Lan-ts'an) 明瓚(懶瓚)
Mi Yu-jen 米友仁
mo-hsi 墨戲
Mokuan Reien 默庵靈淵
mondō 門答
monji Zen 文字禅
Motsugai 物外
Mu Ch'i 牧谿
Mu-chou Tao-ming (Tao-tsung) 睦州道明(蹤)
Mugai Ninkō 無涯仁浩
Mugaku Sogen 無学祖元
Mugan Soō 夢巖祖応
Muga Shōgo 無我省吾
Mumonkan 無門関
munen 無念
Murata Jūkō 村田珠光
Mu-shan 慕山
Mu-shan Lao-jen 慕山老人
mushin 無心
Musō Soseki 夢窓疎石
Muzō Jōshō 無象靜照
Myōan Eisai (Yōsai) 明庵栄西
Nampo Jōmyō (Jōmin) 南浦紹明
Nan-ch'uan P'u-yüan 南泉普願
Nankei Shū 南溪■周
Nanrei Shietsu 南嶺子越
Nihon sōhōden 日本僧宝伝
Nijō Yoshimoto 二条良基
Ni Tsan 倪瓚
Nōami 能阿弥
nyogen zammai 如幻三昧
nyoraizō 如來藏
Ōei 応永
Ōnin 応仁
Ōuchi Morimi 大内盛見
Ou-yang Hsiu 歐陽修
pa 跋
Pan Ku 班固
pen-chüeh 本覺
P'eng-lai Shan 逢逨山
p'ing-ch'ang hsin 平常心
Pi-yen lu 碧巖錄
Po Chü-I 白居易
P'u-chi 普寂
Pu-hua 普化
pu-li mo-tzu 不立文字
Pu-tai 布袋
Ranshitsu mankō 懶室漫稿
Ranshitsushū 懶室集
renga 連歌
Rikkyoku-an 栗棘庵
rinen 離念
Rokuon'in 鹿苑院
Ryōgenshū 了幻集
Ryūshū Shūtaku 竜湫周澤
Ryūzan Tokken 竜山德見
sabi 寂
Saeki Kiyoyasu 佐伯清泰

Saigyō 西行
san-chien ta-chien shih-chieh 三千大千世思
Sanjūrokkasen 三十六歌仙
sankyō itchi 三教一致
san-shu 三疏
sansuiga 山水画
San-t'i shih 三體詩
Seiin Shunjō 西胤俊承
Sekiho 績甫
Sen no Rikyū 千利休
Sesshū Tōyō 雪舟等陽
Sesson Yūbai 雪村友梅
shan 山
shashutsu 写出
shen 神
Shen-hsiu 神秀
shen-hui 神會
Shen Kua 沈括
shen-miao 神妙
Shen Tso-pin 沈作賓
shen-t'ung san-mei 神通三昧
shen-yu 神遊
shiban 詩板
shigajiku 詩画軸
shih 是
Shih Ching 詩經
Shih-jen Yü-hsieh 詩人玉屑
Shih-te 拾得
shih-yin 市隱
shih-yi-t'u 詩意圖
shiizu 詩意図
shijiku 詩軸
shikai 詩会
shin 心
shin 真
Shinchi Kakushin 心地覺心
shinga 心画
Shinkei 心敬
Shitan 思堪
shin'yō 新樣
shō 性
Shōbōgenzō 正法眠藏
shōen 莊園
Shōfuku-ji 聖福寺
shoin 書院
Shōkai Reigen 性海靈見
Shokenkō 蕉堅稿
shoki 書記
shosaizu 書斎図
Shoshitsu Tsūryō 少室通量
Shōtetsu 正徹
Shōyōroku 從容録
shozan 諸山
Shūbun 周文
shugo daimyō 守護大名
Shūhō Myōchō 宗峰妙超
Shūkan Dōsen 秋澗道泉
Shun'oku Myōha 春屋妙葩
shūshin 修心
sōbetsuzu 送別図
sōdō 僧堂
Sōdō Tokuhō 草堂得芳
Sōen Ōsei 宗遠応世
Sōgi 宗祇
Sokuan Reichi 足庵靈知
sokushin 即心
Sŏn 禅
sōroku 僧録
Sōrō shiwa 滄浪詩話
Sōtō 曹洞
ssu 私
Ssu-ma Ch'eng-chen 司馬承禎
Ssu-ma Kuang 司馬光
ssu-tuan 四端
su 俗
Sugyōroku 宗鏡録
Sung Lien 宋濂
Sung Ti 宋迪
Su Shih (Tung-po) 蘇軾(東坡)
Ta-cheng ch'i-hsin lun 大乘起信論
ta-chien 大千
Ta-fo-ting ching 大佛頂經
Ta-hsiu Cheng-nien 大休正念

Ta-hui Tsung-kao 大慧宗杲
Taihaku oshō goroku 太白和尚語録
Taihaku Shingen 太白真玄
Taishin Sōi 太清宗渭
Ta-mei Fa-ch'ang 大梅法常
T'ang Hou 湯垕
T'an-luan 曇鸞
tao 道
Tao Ch'ien 道潛
T'ao Ch'ien 陶潛
tao-wen hsüeh 道問學
Tao-wu Yüan-chih 道吾圓智
tatchū 塔頭
te ch'i i 得其意
Tesshū Tokusai 鐵舟德濟
te yu hsin 得于(於)心
t'i 體
t'ien-chi 天機
t'ien-chih 天質
t'ien-hsin 天心
t'ien-hsing 天性
t'ien-li 天理
Tien-mu Chung-feng ho-sheng kuang-lu 天目中峰和尚廣録
t'i-hua shih 題畫詩
ting 定
tokonoma 床の間
Ts'ang-lang shih-hua 滄浪詩話
tsao-hua 造化
Tsao-tung 曹洞
tsao-wu-che 造物者
Tsung-mi 宗密
Tsung Ping 宗炳
tsun te-hsing 尊德性
Tu 杜
Tu Fu 杜甫
T'u-hui pao-chien 圖繪寶鑑
Tung-ling Yung-hsing 東陵永璵
Tung-shan K'ung ho-sheng wai-chi 東山空和尚外集
Tung-shan Liang-chieh 洞山良价
Tung-shan wai-chi 東山外集
Tung-wei-tzu chi 東維子集
Ūe Gukei 右慧愚溪
Unmon-an 雲門庵
ushin 有心
utaawase 歌合
uta no kai 歌の会
wabi 侘
waka 和歌
wakan renku 和漢連句
Wang Ch'i 王琦
Wang Hsi-chih 王羲之
Wang Fu 王紱
Wang K'ang-chu 王康琚
Wang Meng 王蒙
Wang Pi 王弼
Wang Shen 王詵
Wang Wei 王維
wan-hu ch'üan-yüan 萬斛泉源
watō 話頭
wei 偽
wei-fa 未發
wen 文
wen-jen 文人
Wen T'ung 文同
wen-tzu Ch'an 文字禪
wo 我
wu 物
wu 無
wu-ai 無礙
Wu-an P'u-ning 無庵普寧
Wu Chen 吳鎮
Wu Chi 吳集
Wu-chun Shih-fan 無準師範
wu-hsin 無心
Wu-hsüeh Tsu-yüan 無學祖元
Wu-men Hui-k'ai 無門惠開
Wu-men kuan 無門關
wu-nien 無念
wu-sheng shih 無聲詩
wu-wo 物我
Yamana Tokohiro 山名時熙
Yang-ch'i 楊岐

yang-hsin 養心
Yang Hsiung 揚雄
Yang Su 梁需
Yang Wan-li 楊萬里
Yang Wei-chen 楊維楨
Yao Kuang-hsiao (Tao-yen) 姚廣孝(道衍)
Yao Shih 姚式
Yao T'ing-mei 姚廷美
Yeh Sung (Tzu-yu) 鄭崇(子遊)
Yen Yü 嚴羽
yen-yü san-mei 言語三昧
Yōgi 楊岐
you 有
yu 遊
Yüan-chüeh ching 圓覺經
Yuan Hao-wen 元好問
Yüan-wu Ko-ch'in 圓悟克勤
yuge 遊戲(戲)
yuge zanmai 遊戲三昧
yu-hsi 遊戲(戲)
yu-hsi san-mei 遊戲三昧
yü-i 寓意
yü-lu 語錄
yung 用
Yun-ku 雲谷
Yun-men Wen-yen 雲門文偃
yu-sheng hua 有聲畫
yūsha 友社
Yūzan Shisai 友山士偲
za 坐
Zeami 世阿彌
Zekkai Chūshin 絕海中津
Zen 禪
Zengi gemonshū 禅儀外文集
Zenkizu 禅機図
zōsu 藏主

Selected Bibliography

Unless otherwise indicated, the place of publication for English-language books is New York, and the place of publication for Japanese-language books is Tokyo.

PRIMARY SOURCES

The Blue Cliff Record. Trans. Thomas and J. C. Cleary. 3 vols. Boulder, CO: Shambala, 1977.

Buddhist Wisdom Books, Containing the Diamond Sutra and the Heart Sutra. Trans. Edward Conze. Harper & Row, 1972 (orig. pub. by George Allen & Unwin, Ltd., 1958).

Chan, Wing-tsit, trans. *A Source Book in Chinese Philosophy*. Princeton, NJ: Princeton University Press, 1963.

Ch'en Yu-i. *Ch'en Yu-i chi*. Ed. and annotated by Wu Shu-yin and Chin Te-hou. Beijing: Chung-hua Shu-chu, 1982.

Ching-sou Chü-chien. *Pei-chien Chü-chien Ch'an-shih yü-lu*. *Z*, 2.26, 1 (vol. 601), p. 64b–84b.

Chou Pi, comp. *Santaishi*. Trans. Murakami Tetsumi. Chūgoku kotensen, vol. 16. 2 vols. Asahi Shinbunsha, 1966.

Chu Hsi. *Shisho shūchū*. Shushigaku taikei 7. Ed. Suzuki Yūjirō et al. 2 vols. Mintoku Shuppansha, 1974.

Chu Hsi and Lu Tsu-ch'ien, comps. *Reflection on Things at Hand: The Neo-Confucian Anthology Compiled by Chu Hsi and Lu Tsu-ch'ien*. Trans. Wing-tsit Chan. New York: Columbia University Press, 1967.

Chuang-tzu. *Chuang-tzu, the Seven Inner Chapters: and Other Writings from the Book "Chuang-tzu."* Trans. A. C. Graham. London: Allen & Unwin, 1981.

———. *The Complete Works of Chuang Tzu*. Trans. Burton Watson. Columbia University Press, 1968.

———. *Sōshi*. Chūgoku kotensen, 8. Trans. Fukunaga Mitsuji. 3 vols. Mainichi Shinbunsha, 1966.

Chūgoku senjutsu kyōten, ichi: Engakukyō. Bukkyō kyōtensen, 13. Trans. Yanagida Seizan. Tsukuma Shobō, 1987.

Chūhō En'i. *Chūhō oshō goroku*. 1885 manuscript copy of undated Tenryū-ji text. Shiryō Hensanjo, Tokyo University.

———. *Ranshitsu mankō*. *GBZ*, 3:2501–2630.

Chung-feng Ming-pen. *T'ien-mu Chung-feng Ho-shang Kuang-lu*. Woodblock print edition with 1387 preface and supplementary commentary. Zen Bunka Kenkyūjo, Hanazono University.

Colas, Alain. "Gozan no shisō." *Furansu no bungaku* 13 (1983): 19–59; 15 (1985): 47–79; 17 (1987): 33–72; 18 (1988): 69–109; 19 (1989): 1–51.

Confucius. *The Analects*. Trans. D. C. Lau. Penguin Books, 1979.

———. *Confucius: Confucian Analects, The Great Learning, and the Doctrine of the Mean*. Trans. James Legge. Dover Publications, 1971 (1893).

Early Chinese Texts on Painting. Comp. and ed. Susan Bush and Hsio-yen Shih. Cambridge, MA: Harvard University Press, 1985.

Eihei Dōgen. "Dōgen's 'Shōbōgenzō sansuikyō.'" Trans. Carl Bielefeldt. In *The Mountain Spirit*. Ed. Michael Charles Tobias and Harold Drasdo. Woodstock, NY: Overlook Press, 1979, pp. 37–49.

Fujita Tsuneo, comp. "Muromachi gasanshū." *Kōkan bijutsu shiryō*, vol. 2. Kamakura: Kōkan bijutsu shiryō kankōkai, 1985, pp. 155–222.

Gidō Shūshin. *Kūge nichiyō kufū ryakushū*. Ed. Tsuji Zennosuke. Taiyōsha, 1939.

———. *Kūgeshū*. *GBZ*, 2:1327–1897.

———. *Kunchū kūge nichiyō kufū ryakushū—Chusei Zensō no seikatsu to bungaku*. Trans. Kageki Hideo. Kyoto: Shibunkaku, 1982.

———. "Poetry and Prose of Gidō Shūshin." Trans. Bruce E. Carpenter. *Teizukayama Daigaku kiyō* 24 (1987): 18–76.

———, comp. *Jūkan Jōwa ruijū soen renpōshū Shinsenjōwashū*, Dainihon Bukkyō Zensho, ed. Bussho kankōkai, Bussho kankōkai, 1912.

Gozan bungakushū Edo kanshishū. Nihon koten bungaku taikei, 89. Ed. Yamagishi Tokuhei. Iwanami Shoten, 1966.

Gozan shisō. Nihon no Zen goroku 8. Trans. Tamamura Takeji. Kōdansha, 1978.

GBS. *Gozan bungaku shinshū*. Ed. Tamamura Takeji. 6 vols. Tokyo Daigaku Shuppankai, 1967-72.

GBZ. *Gozan bungaku zenshū*. Ed. Kamimura Kankō. 5 vols. Shokabō Shoten, 1906.

Han-shan. *Cold Mountain: 100 poems by the T'ang poet Han-shan*. Trans. Burton Watson. New York: Columbia University Press, 1970 (1962).

———. *Kanzan*. Trans. Iriya Yoshitaka. Chūgoku shijin senshū, 5. Iwanami shoten, 1958.

The Holy Teaching of Vimalakīrti. Trans. Robert A. F. Thurman. University Park, PA: The Pennsylvania State University Press, 1976.

Huang-po Hsi-yun. *Denshin Hōyō, Enryōroku*. Zen no goroku, 8. Trans. Iriya Yoshitaka. Tsukuma Shobō, 1969.

Iriya Yoshitaka, trans. *Gozan bungakushū*. Shin Nihon koten bungaku taikei, vol. 48. Iwanami Shoten, 1990.

Ishikawa Jun, et al., eds. *Kō Kōbō, Gei San, Ō Mō, Go Chin*. Bunjinga suihen. Chūō Kōronsha, 1985.

———, et al., eds. *Tō Gen, Kyo Nen*. Bunjinga suihen 2. Chūō Kōronsha, 1985.

Josetsu, Shūbun, San'ami. SBT 6. Ed. Matsushita Takaaki. Kodansha, 1978.

Kamimura Kankō. "Sekikarōzu san kaidai," *Kokka* 319 (1916): 196–204.

Kaō, Mokuan, Minchō. SBT 5. Ed. Tanaka Ichimatsu. Kōdansha, 1978.

Kiyō Hōshū. *Funi Ikō*. *GBZ*, 3:2877–3027.

Kobun Shinpō. Shinshaku kanbun taikei, 16. Ed. Hoshikawa Kiyotaka. Meiji Shoin, 1963.

Liao-an (Nan-t'ang) Ch'ing-yü. *Liao-an ho-sheng yü-lu*. *Z*, 2.6.4 (vol. 635), pp. 291a–396a.

Mencius. *Mencius*. Trans. D. C. Lau. Harmondsworth, UK: Penguin Books, 1970.

Musō Soseki. *Dream Conversations: On Buddhism and Zen*. Trans. Thomas Cleary. Boston, MA: Shambala, 1996.

———. *Musō Soseki kokushi goroku*. Trans. Yanagida Seizan. Gendai goyaku Zen no koten, 4. Kōronsha, 1983.

Nijō Yoshimoto. *Jūmon Saihisshō*, in *Rengaronshū Haironshū*. Nihon kokubungaku taikei, vol. 66. Ed. Kidō Saizō and Imoto Nōichi. Iwanami shoten, 1961, pp. 107–118.

Ou-yang Hsiu. *Ou-yang Hsiu ch'uan-chi*. Taipei: Shih-chieh shu-chu, 1961.

———. *Ou-yang Wen-chung-kung chi, SPTK*.

Owen, Stephen. *Readings in Chinese Literary Thought*. Harvard-Yenching Institute Monograph Series, 30. Cambridge, MA: Council on East Asian Studies, Harvard University, 1992.

Perfection of Wisdom in Eight Thousand Lines and Its Verse Summary. Trans. Edward Conze. Bolinas, CA: Four Seasons Foundation, 1973.

Pi-yen lu. Comp. Yüan-wu K'o-ch'in. T, 48, pp. 139–226.

The Platform Sutra of the Sixth Patriarch: The Text of the Tun-huang Manuscript with Translation, Introduction, and Notes. Trans. Philip Yampolsky. New York: Columbia University Press, 1966.

Pollack, David. *Zen Poems of the Five Mountains*. American Academy of Religion Studies in Religion, 37. Decauter, GA: The Crossroad Publishing Company and Scholars Press, 1985.

Santaishi. Trans. Marakami Tetsumi. Chūgoku kotensen 16. Asahi Shinbunsha, 1966. 3 vols.

Shih-ch'i Hsin-yüeh. *Shih-ch'i Ho-sheng Yü-lu*. *Z*, 2.28.1 (vol. 611), pp. 22b–79b.

———. *A Tune beyond the Clouds: Zen Teachings from Old China*. Trans. J. C. Cleary. Berkeley, CA: Asian Humanities Press, 1990.

Shinkei. *Sasamegoto*, in *Rengaronshū Haironshū*. Nihon Koten Bungaku Taikei, vol. 66. Ed. Kidō Saizō and Imoto Nōichi. Iwanami Shoten, 1961, pp. 119–204.

Shōtetsu. *Conversations with Shōtetsu.* Trans. Robert H. Brower and intro. Steven D. Carter. Ann Arbor: Center for Japanese Studies, University of Michigan, 1992.

Su Shih. *Chi-chu fen-lei Tung-p'o hsien-sheng shih. SPTK.*

———. *So Shoku.* Trans. Ogawa Tamaki. Chugoku shijinsen, 6. Rev. ed. Iwanami Shoten, 1983.

———. *So Toba shishū.* Trans. Ogawa Tamaki and Yamamoto Kazuyoshi. 5 vols. Tsukuma Shobō, 1983–.

———. *Tung-p'o Ch'uan-chi. SPPY.*

SPPY. Ssu-pu pei-yao. Comp. Kao Yeh-hou et al. Shanghai: Chung-hua Shu-chu, 1927–31.

SPTK. Ssu-pu ts'ung-k'an. Comp. Chang Yuan-chi, et al. Shanghai: Han-fen-lou, 1919–36.

T. Taishō Shinshū Daizōkyō. Ed. Takakusu Junjirō et al. Society for the Publication of the Taishō Edition of the Tripitaka, 1924–32.

Taihaku Shingen. *Gabi ashūshū. GBZ,* 3:2217–66.

———. *Taihaku oshō goroku.* Undated manuscript. National Diet Library.

Tamamura Takeji. *Gozan shisō.* Nihon no Zen goroku, 8. Kōdansha, 1978.

Tamamura Takeji et al., eds. *Nihon Kōsō iboku.* Vol. 1. Mainichi Shinbunsha, 1970.

Thurman, Robert. *The Holy Teaching of Vimalakīrti: A Mahayana Scripture.* University Park: Pennsylvania State University Press, 1976.

Ury, Marian. *Poems of the Five Mountains: An Introduction to the Literature of the Zen Monasteries.* Ann Arbor: Center for Japanese Studies, University of Michigan, 1992.

Wang Meng. *Huang-ho Shan-ch'iao shih-chao,* in *Yüan-li Ssu-hua-chia Shih-chiao-chi.*

Watson, Burton. *The Columbia Book of Chinese Poetry: From Early Times to the Thirteenth Century.* New York: Columbia University Press, 1984.

Wu Chen. *Mei-tao-jen i-mo,* in *Mei-shu Ts'ung-shu.* Comp Huang Pin-hung and Teng Shih. Taipei: I-wen, 1963. Third series, vol. 4, pp. 12–61.

Zekkai Chūshin. *Shōkenkō. GBZ,* 2:1899–1956.

———. *Shōkenkō: Zenchu.* Trans. Kageki Hideo. Pub. Kageki Hideo, 1977.

Z. Dainihon Zokuzōkyō (also *Manji Zokuzōkyō*). Ed. Nakano Tatsue. Kyoto: Zōkyō Shoin, 1905–12.

ZGS. Zenrin gasan: Chūsei suibokuga o yomu Ed. Shimada Shūjirō and Iriya Yoshitaka. Mainichi Shinbunsha, 1987.

SECONDARY SOURCES

Ajia no naka no Nihonshi. Ed. Arano Hironori, Ishii Masatoshi, and Murai Shōsuke. 6 vols. Tokyo Daigaku Shuppankai, 1992.

Akamatsu Toshihide and Philip Yampolsky. "Muromachi Zen and the Gozan System." In *Japan in the Muromachi Age*. Ed. John W. Hall and Toyoda Takeshi. Berkeley: University of California Press, 1977, pp. 313–30.

Akazawa Eiji. "Ōei shigajiku kenkyū." *Tokyo Gakugei Daigaku kenkyu hōkoku* 11 (1960): 17–32; 12 (1961): 21–31; 14 (1963): 13–19.

———. "Shijiku to shigajiku—Ōei shigajiku joron." *Bijutsushi* 40 (1961): 105–18.

App, Urs. "Reference Works for Chan Research: A Selected Annotated Survey." *Cahiers d'Extreme-Asie* 7 (1993–94): 357–409.

Asakura Hisashi. *Zenrin no bungaku*. Seibundō shuppan, 1985.

———. "Zenrin ni okeru shikai no yōsō—Shōkoku-ji." *Chūsei bungei*. Sōsho bekkan 3: 235–57, and 50 (Oct. 1972): 19–40.

Barnhardt, Richard. "Yao Yen-ch'ing, T'ing-mei, of Wu-hsing." *Artibus Asiae* 39 (1977): 105–23.

Berling, Judith A. *The Syncretic Religion of Lin Chao-en*. New York: Columbia University Press, 1980.

Bielefeldt, Carl. "Filling the Zen-shū: Notes on the Jisshū yōdōki." *Cahiers d'Extrême Asie* 7 (1993–94): 221–48.

———. "No-Mind and Sudden Awakening: Thoughts on the Soteriology of a Kamakura Zen Text." In *Paths to Liberation: The Mārga and Its Transformation in Buddhist Thought*. Ed. Robert C. Buswell Jr. and Robert M. Gimello. Honolulu: University of Hawaii Press, 1992, pp. 475–505.

Bol, Peter. "Chao Ping-wen (1159–1232): Foundation for Literati Learning." In *China under Jurchen Rule: Essays on Chin Intellectual and Cultural History*. Ed. Hoyt Tillman and Stephen West. Albany: State University of New York Press, 1995, pp. 115–44.

———. "Culture and the Way in Eleventh Century China." Ph.D. dissertation, Princeton University, 1982.

———. *"This Culture of Ours": Intellectual Transition in T'ang and Sung China*. Stanford, CA: Stanford University Press, 1992.

Brown, Claudia. "Some Aspects of Late Yüan Patronage in Suchou." In *Artists and Patrons: Some Social and Economic Aspects of Painting*. Ed. Chu-tsing Li. Seattle: University of Washington Press, 1989, pp. 101–10.

Bush, Susan. *The Chinese Literati on Painting: Su Shih (1037–1101) to Tung Ch'i-ch'ang (1555–1636)*. Harvard-Yenching Institute Studies, 27. Cambridge, MA: Harvard University Press, 1971.

Buswell, Robert. "The 'Short-Cut' Approach to *K'an-hua* Meditation: The Evolution of a Practical Subitism in Chinese Ch'an Buddhist." In *Sudden and Gradual: Approaches to Enlightenment in Chinese Buddhist Thought*. Ed. Peter N. Gregory. Honolulu: University of Hawaii Press, 1983, pp. 321–77.

———. *Zen Monastic Experience: Buddhist Practice in Contemporary Korea*. Princeton, NJ: Princeton University Press, 1992.

Cahill, James. *The Lyric Journey: Poetic Painting in China and Japan*. Cambridge, MA: Harvard University Press, 1996.

———. "Wu Chen: A Chinese Landscapist and Bamboo Painter of the Fourteenth Century." Ph.D. dissertation, University of Michigan, 1958.

Chappell, David W. "Hermeneutical Phases in Chinese Buddhism." In *Buddhist Hermeneutics*. Ed. Donald S. Lopez Jr. Kuroda Institute Studies in East Asian Buddhism, 6. Honolulu: University of Hawaii Press, 1988, pp. 175–206.

Chaves, Jonathan. *Mei Yao-ch'en and the Development of Early Sung Poetry*. Columbia University Press, 1976.

Chisaka Takashi. "Gozan bungaku e no michi—joron." *Seiwa* 14 (1977.3): 25–42.

———. "Gozan bungaku e no michi—jūyon seiki no gozan ni okeru shisōteki tokuchō o megutte." *Seiwa* 15(1978.3): 23–57.

Collcutt, Martin. *Five Mountains: The Rinzai Zen Monastic Institution in Medieval Japan*. Cambridge, MA: Council on East Asian Studies, Harvard University, 1981.

———. "Zen and the Gozan." In *Cambridge History of Japan*, vol. 3, Medieval Japan. Ed. Kozo Yamamura. Cambridge: Cambridge University Press, 1990, pp. 583–651.

Ebine Toshio. "Kan no sekai no seiritsu to tenkai." *Suibokuga to Chūsei emaki*. Nihon bijutsu zenshū, 12. Kōdansha, 1993, pp. 146–53.

———. "Sōen Ōseihitsu Byakue Kannonzu." *Kobijutsu* 53 (July 1977): 89–96.

———. "Suibokuga—Mokuan kara Minchō e." *Nihon no bijutsu* 333 (1994): 1–98.

Edwards, Richard. "Ūe Gukei—Fourteenth Century Ink Painter." *Ars Orientalis* 7 (1968): 169–78.

Egan, Ronald. *The Literary Works of Ou-yang Hsiu (1007–72)*. Cambridge: Cambridge University Press, 1984.

———. "Ou-yang Hsiu and Su Shih on Calligraphy." *Harvard Journal of Asiatic Studies* 41.2 (1989): 365-419.

———. "Poems on Paintings: Su Shih and Huang T'ing-chien." *Harvard Journal of Asiatic Studies* 43.2 (Dec. 1983): 413–51.

Faure, Bernard. *Rhetoric of Immediacy: A Cultural Critique of Chan/Zen Buddhism*. Princeton, NJ: Princeton University Press, 1991.

Fontein, Jan and Money Hickman. *Zen Painting and Calligraphy*. Boston, MA: Museum of Fine Arts, 1970.

Foulk, T. Griffith and Robert H. Sharf. "On the Ritual Use of Ch'an Portraiture in Medieval China." *Cahiers d'Extrême Asie* 7 (1993–94): 149–219.

———. "Japanese Views of Zen Institutions in Sung China." In *Creating the World of Zen: The Transmission of Sung Dynasty Ch'an in East Asia*. Eds. John McRae and Albert Welter. Fo Kuang Shan Buddhist Studies Series, forthcoming.

Frankl, Herbert. "The Plum Tree in Chinese Poetry." *Asiatische Studien* 6 (1952): 88–115.

Fu, Shen. "A Landscape by Yang Wei-chen." *National Palace Museum Quarterly* 8.4 (1973): 1–13.

Fujioka Daisetsu. "Zen'in uchi ni okeru Tōhanshū ni tsuite—toku ni Muromachi bakufu no zaisei to kanrenshite." *Nihon rekishi* 145: 19–28.

Fujishima Tateki. "Genchō Bukkyō no ichiyēsō—Chūhō Minhon o meguru kojitachi." *Ōtani gakuhō* 57.3 (Nov. 1977): 14–26.

Fuller, Michael A. "Pursuing the Complete Bamboo in the Breast: Reflections on a Classical Chinese Image for Immediacy." *Harvard Journal of Asiatic Studies* 53.1 (1993): 5–23.

Gimello, Robert M. "Apophatic and Kataphatic Discourse in Mahayana: A Chinese View." *Philosophy East and West* 26.2 (1976): 117–36.

———. "Mārga and Culture: Learning, Letters, and Liberation in Northern Sung Ch'an." In Robert E. Buswell Jr. and Robert M. Gimello, *Paths to Liberation: The Mārga and Its Transformation in Buddhist Thought.* Honolulu: University of Hawaii Press, 1992, pp. 371–437.

Gomez, Luis O. "From the Extraordinary to the Ordinary: Images of the Bodhisattva in East Asia." In Luis O. Gomes, ed., *The Christ and the Bodhisattva.* Albany: State University of New York, 1987, pp. 141–93.

Grant, Beata. *Mount Lu Revisited: Buddhism in the Life and Writings of Su Shih.* Honolulu: University of Hawaii Press, 1994.

Gregory, Peter N. *Tsung-mi and the Sinification of Buddhism.* Princeton, NJ: Princeton University Press, 1991.

———. "What Happened to the 'Perfect Teaching'? Another Look at Hua-yen Buddhist Hermeneutics." In *Buddhist Hermeneutics*. Ed. Donald S. Lopez Jr. Kuroda Institute Studies in East Asian Buddhism, 6. Honolulu: University of Hawaii Press, 1988, pp. 207–30.

Haga Kōshirō. *Chūsei Zenrin no gakumon oyobi bungaku ni kansuru kenkyū.* Shibunkaku Shuppan, 1981 (orig. pub., Nihon Gakujutsu Shinkōkai, 1956).

———. "Zensō no bungakukan no hensen." *Nihon koten bungaku taikei geppō* 2.23 (Feb. 1965): 6–8.

Hightower, James Robert. *The Poetry of T'ao Ch'ien.* Oxford: Clarendon Press, 1970.

Horikawa Kishi. "'Daiji hakkeishi ni tsuite." *Kokugo to Kokubungaku* 67.6 (1990): 30–43.

Hoshiyama Shin'ya. "Gyokuen Bompō ni tsuite." *Geijutsugaku kenkyū* 2 (1976): 33–57.

Hsieh, Evelyn Ding-hwa. "Yüan-wu K'o-ch'in's (1063–1135) Teaching of Ch'an *Kung-an* Practice: A Transition from the Literary Study of Ch'an *Kung-an* to the Practical *K'an-hua* Ch'an." *Journal of the International Association of Buddhist Studies* 17.1 (1994): 66–95.

Hyers, Conrad. *Zen and the Comic Spirit*. Philadelphia: The Westminster Press, 1974.

Ichikawa Mototarō. *Nihon Jukyōshi*. Vol. 3. Chūsei hen. Tōa Gakujutsu Kenkyūkai, 1992.

Ide Shōsuke. "Manzai-ji no Ikō Tokukenzō." *Bukkyō Bijutsu* 166 (May 1986): 50–64.

Ikeda, Hisako. "Ashikaga Yoshomochi hitsu *Hoteizu*." *De Arute* 8 (1992).

Imaeda Aishin. "Chūsei Bukkyō no tenkai (sono ni)." In *Nihon Bukkyōshi II, Chūseihen*. Ed. Akamatsu Toshihide. Kyoto: Hōzōkan, 1967, pp. 153–221.

———. *Chusei Zenshūshi no kenkyū*. Tokyo Daigaku Shuppankai, 1970.

Imaizumi Yoshio. *Tōgo Seiwa: Muromachi bunka sunbyō*. Yoshikawa Kōbunkan, 1993.

Iriya Yoshitaka. "Chinese Poetry and Zen." *Eastern Buddhist* 6.1 (May 1973): 54–67.

———. "Kidō no geju o yomu tame ni." In *Daitoku-ji bokuseki zenshū*. Ed. Marouka Muneo. Mainichi Shinbunsha, 1984, p. 249–51.

———. *Kyūdō to etsuraku: Chūgoku no Zen to shi*. Iwanami shoten, 1983.

Iriya Yoshitaka and Koga Hidehiko, eds. *Zengo jiten*. Kyoto: Tanaka Shuji, 1991.

Ishida, Hou-mei Sung. "Early Ming Painters in Nanking and the Formation of the Wu School." *Ars Orientalis* 17 (1987): 73–115.

Itō Setsuko. "The Muse In Competition: Uta-awase through the Ages." *Monumenta Nipponica* 37.2 (1982): 201–22.

Japan: The Shaping of Daimyo Culture. Ed. Yoshiaki Shimizu. Washington, DC: National Gallery of Art, 1988.

Japanese Ink Paintings from American Collections: The Muromachi Period, An Exhibition in Honor of Shūjirō Shimada. Eds. Yoshiaki Shimizu and Ann Yonemura. Princeton, NJ: The Art Museum, Princeton University, 1976.

Josetsu, Shūbun. Nihon bijutsu kaiga zenshū, 2. Ed. Matsushita Takaaki. Shūeisha, 1979.

Josetsu, Shūbun, San'ami. Suiboku bijutsu taikei, 6. Eds. Matsushita Takaaki and Tamamura Takeji. Kōdansha, 1978.

Kageki Hideo. *Chūsei Zenrin shishi*. Tsukuma Shoin, 1994.

———. *Gozan shishi no kenkyū*. Kasama Shoin, 1979.

Kanazawa Hiroshi. *Japanese Ink Painting: Early Zen Masterpieces*. Trans. Barbard Ford. Kodansha International and Shibundo, 1979.

———. *Muromachi kaiga*. Nihon no bijutsu, 207. Shibundō, 1983.

Kaō, Mokuan, Minchō. Suiboku bijutsu taikei rō. Ed. Tanaka Ichimatsu. Kodansha, 1978.

Kawase Kazuma. *Gozanban no kenkyū*. 2 vols. The Antiquarian Booksellers Association of Japan, 1970.

Kawazoe Shōji. "Japan and East Asia." In *The Cambridge History of Japan*, vol. 3. Ed. Kozo Yamamura. Cambridge: Cambridge University Press, 1990, pp. 396–445.

Kitamura Sawakichi. *Gozan bungaku shikō*. Fuzanbō, 1941.

Kō Kōbō, Gei San, Ō Mō, Go Chin. Bunjinga Suihen 3. Ed. Ishikawa Jun et al. Chūōkōronsha, 1985.

Konishi Jin'ichi. "Michi and Medieval Writing." In *Principles of Japanese Classical Writing*. Ed. Earl Miner. Princeton, NJ: Princeton University Press, 1985, pp. 181–208.

———. *Michi: Chūsei no rinen*. Kōdansha, 1975.

Kumagai Nobuo. "Ōei nenkan no shigajiku: Toku ni sono sansuiga no hatten ni okeru ichi ni kanshite." *Bijutsu kenkyu* 4 (1932): 122–28.

Kusumoto Fumio. *Nihon Chūsei Zenrin no Jugaku*. Busshorin, 1992.

LaFleur, William. "Saigyō and the Buddhist Value of Nature." *History of Religions* 13.2 (1973): 93–128 and 13.3 (1974): 227–48.

Liscomb, Kathlyn. "Wang Fu's Contribution to the Formation of a New Painting Style in the Ming Dynasty." *Artibus Asiae* 48 (1987): 39–78.

Lynn, Richard John. "The Sudden and the Gradual in Chinese Poetry Criticism: An Examination of the Ch'an-Poetry Analogy." In *Sudden and Gradual: Approaches to Enlightenment in Chinese Thought*. Ed. Peter N. Gregory. Honolulu: University of Hawaii Press, 1987, pp. 381–427.

McRae, John. *The Northern School and the Formation of Early Ch'an Buddhism*. Kuroda Institute Studies in East Asian Buddhism, vol. 3. Honolulu: University of Hawaii Press, 1986.

Malenfer, Valérie Marie. "'Dream Journey over the Xiao and Xiang': Scholar-Amateur Landscape Painting in Southern Song China (1127–1279)." Ph.D. dissertation, Harvard University, 1990.

Matsushita Takaaki. "Shigajiku ni tsuite." In idem, *Nihon suibokuga ronshū*. Chūō Kōron Bijutsu Shuppan, 1983, pp. 84–92.

Mostow, Joshua. "Painted Poems, Forgotten Words: Poem Pictures and Classical Japanese Literature." *Monumenta Nipponica* 47 (1992).

Murai Shōsuke. *Ajia no naka no chūsei Nihon*. Azekura Shobō, 1988.

———. *Higashi Ajia ōkan: Kanshi to gaikō*. Asahi Shinbunsha, 1995.

Nagatomi Masatoshi. "Mānasa pratyakṣa: A Conundrum in the Buddhist Pramāṇa System." In *Sanskrit and Indian Studies: Essays in Honor of Daniel H. H. Ingalls*. Ed. Masatoshi Nagatomi et al. Boston: D. Reidel, 1983, pp. 243–60.

Nambokuchō, Muromachi, Momoyama. Shodo zenshū, 8. Ed. Shimonaka Kunihiko. Heibonsha, 1966.

Nanami Hiroakira. "Musō Soseki no geju to shisō—'yūsha' no genkei o chūshin to shite." *Nihon bungaku* 28.7 (July 1979): 53–63.

Nihon kōsō iboku. Ed. Mainichi Shinbunsha Juyō Bunkazai Iinkai. 3 vols. Mainichi Shinbunsha, 1970.

Nishimura Tokihike. *Nihon Sōgakushi*. Osaka: Sugimoto Ryōkodō, 1909.

Nishio Kenryū. "Genchō ni okeru Chūhō Minhon to sono dōzoku." *Zengaku kenkyū* 64 (Nov. 1985): 31–56.

———. "Muromachi bakufu gaikō ni okeru gozansō—Zekkai Chūshin o chūshin ni." *Nihon rekishi* 537 (1993): 35–54.

Nivison, David. "Protest against Convention and Conventions of Protest." In *Confucianism and Chinese Civilization*. Ed. Arthur F. Wright. Stanford, CA: Stanford University Press, 1975, pp. 227–52.

O'Flaherty, Wendy. *Dreams Illusion and Other Realities*. Chicago: University of Chicago Press, 1984.

Ogisu Jundō. "Chūsei bungaku michi no shinka to kotei—Shōtetsu, Shinkei kara Sōgi e." *Kokugo to Kokubungaku* (1947): 20–30.

———. "Mujun Shiban to Kidō Chigu." *Zenbunka* 56 (Mar. 1970): 30–40.

———. "Nihon Chūsei Zenshisō no tenkai." In *Zen to Nihon bunka no shōmondai*. Ed. Ogisu Jundō. Kyoto: Heiraku-ji Shoten, 1969.

Ōnishi Hiroshi. "Hyōnenzu to Hyōtan no Jujutsusei." In *Uri to ryōda*. Ima wa Mukashi Mukashi wa Ima, 1. Fukuinkan shoten, 1989.

———. "Sesshū shiryō o yomu." *Nihon bijutsu kōgei* 448–475 (Jan. 1976 to Apr. 1978).

Ōta Takahiko. "Muromachi jidai ni okeru kaiga hihyō ni tsuite—Masaki Bijutsukanzō bokubaizu no daishi o chūshin to shite." In *Geijutsu no riron to rekishi*. Ed. Kyoto Daigaku Bigaku Bijutsushigaku kenkyūkai. Kyoto: Shibunkaku, 1989, pp. 76–85.

———. "Muromachi jidai no bokubai—Motsugaihitsu En'ira hassō daishi 'bokubaizu' no shiteki icchi." *Nihon koten no chōbo*. Ōfūsha, 1990.

Owen, Stephen. *The Great Age of Chinese Poetry: The High T'ang*. New Haven, CT: Yale University Press, 1981.

Parker, Joseph D. "Attaining Landscapes in the Mind: Nature Poetry and Painting in Gozan Zen." *Monumenta Nipponica* 52.2 (Summer, 1997): 235–57.

———. "Contested Orthodoxies in Five Mountains Zen Buddhism." In *Religions of Japan in Practice*. Ed. George Tanabe, Jr. Princeton, NJ: Princeton University Press, 1998.

———. "The Hermit at Court: Reclusion in Early Fifteenth Century Japanese Zen Buddhism." *Journal of Japanese Studies* 21.1 (1995): 103–20.

———. "Historicizing Gender Representations: Zen Buddhist Nuns from Thirteenth-Century Japan." Unpublished manuscript.

———. "The Religious Meaning of Poetic Practice in Nijō Yoshimoto's Poetics." Unpublished manuscript.

———. "'Scribbling without End': Chinese Zen Monks' Views of Textual and Artistic Study in Kamakura Japan." Unpublished manuscript.

———. "Writing Cultural Practice Past and Present: Orthodoxy and Literary Practice in the Transmission of Sung Chinese Ch'an Buddhism to Japan." In *Creating the World of Zen: The Transmission of Sung Dynasty Ch'an in East Asia*. Eds. John McRae and Albert Welter. Fo Kuang Shan Buddhist Studies Series, forthcoming.

Pollack, David. *The Fracture of Meaning: Japan's Synthesis of China from the Eighth through the Eighteenth Centuries*. Princeton, NJ: Princeton University Press, 1986.

———. "Literature as Game in the T'ang." In *Legend, Lore, and Religion in China*. Ed. Sarah Allan and Alvin P. Cohen. San Francisco: Chinese Materials Center, 1979, pp. 205–24.

Rosenfield, John M. "The Unity of the Three Creeds: A Theme in Japanese Ink Painting of the Fifteenth Century." In *Japan in the Muromachi Age*. Ed. John Whitney Hall and Toyoda Takeshi. Berkeley: University of California Press, 1977, pp. 205–25.

Ruch, Barbara. "The Other Side of Culture in Medieval Japan." In *Cambridge History of Japan*. vol. 3. Medieval Japan. Ed. Kozo Yamamura. Cambridge: Cambridge University Press, 1990, 500–43.

Sasaki Tomoko. "Kamakura zaiju no Gidō Shūshin." *Nihon bungaku* 29.11 (1980): 12–28.

Satō Dōshin, "Kaiga to gengo (1): 'Ga' to kanji" and "Kaiga to gengo (2): Gago to risō no sekaikan." *Bijutsu kenkyū* 353 (1992): 17–33 and 357 (1993): 21–33.

Shimada Shūjirō. "Gozan bungaku to Muromachi kaiga." In *Gozan no gakugei*. Ed. Okazaki Hisashi. Daitokyū Kinen Bunko, 1985, pp. 65–100.

———. "Motsugai no bokubai." *Kokka* 770 (May 1956): 148–56.

———. "Muromachi jidai no shigajiku ni tsuite." *ZGS*, 10–31.

———. "Shigajiku no shosaizu ni tsuite." *Nihon shogaku shinkō iinkai kenkyū hōkoku* 4 (1943): 138–45.

———. *Shimada Shūjirō chosakushū: Chūgoku kaigashi kenkyū*. Chūō kōronsha, 1993.

———. *Shimada Shūjirō chosakushū: Nihon kaigashi kenkyū*. Chūō kōronsha, 1987.

———. "Shūbunkei sansuiga ni kansuru ni, san no mondai." In *Zaigai Nihon no shihō*. Ed. Shimada Shūjirō. Gakushū kenkyūsha, 1968.

Shimao Arata. *Hyōnenzu—Hyōtan namazu no ikonorojii*. E wa kataru, 5. Heibonsha, 1995.

———. "Hyōnenzu no kenkyū—Daigaku Shūsū no jo ni mirareru 'shin'yō' o chūshin to shite." *Bijutsu kenkyū* 335 (Mar. 1986): 24–38.

———. "Shoki shigajiku no yōsō—*Kūgeshū* ni mieru *Unjuzu* shigajiku o chūshin to shite." *Bijutsushi* 114 (May 1983): 98–110.

Shimizu, Yoshiaki. "Problems of Moku'an Rei'en (?–1323–1345)." Ph.D. dissertation, Princeton University, 1974.

———. "Zenke no shigajiku ni okeru ga to san no mondai." *Suibokuga to chūsei emaki*. Nihon bijutsu zenshū, 12. Kōdansha, 1993, pp. 162–69.

———, ed. *Japan: The Shaping of Daimyo Culture*. Washington, DC: National Gallery of Art, 1988.

Stanley-Baker, Richard. "Some Proposals Concerning the Transmission to Muromachi Japan of Styles Associated with Painters from Chekiang of the Late

Yüan and Early Ming: With Particular Reference to the Styles Favored in the Hung-chih Academy." In *Suzuki Kei sensei kanreki kinen: Chūgoku kaigashi ronkō*. Ed. Suzuki Kei Sensei Kanreki Kinenkai. Yoshikawa Kōbunkan, 1981, pp. 71–96.

Steadman, John M. *The Myth of Asia*. Simon and Schuster, 1969.

Stein, Rolf A. *The World in Miniature: Container Gardens and Dwellings in Far Eastern Religious Thought*. Trans. Phyllis Brooks. Stanford, CA: Stanford University Press, 1990.

Sueki Hiroyuki, "'Hekiganroku' no chūshakusho ni tsuite." *Matsugaoka bunko kenkyū nenpyō* 7 (1993): 23–54.

Sugihara Takuya. "Gidō Shūshin no Dojakukenki ni tsuite." *Kamakura* 55 (1987): 39–57.

Suzuki Hiroyuki. "Ōkansuru kaiga—jūgo seiki kanji bunkaken no naka no 'karae' no igi." *Bijutsu kenkyū* 361 (1995): 1–23.

Tamamura Takeji. "Daikyū Shōnen bokuseki 'sekihashi gejikujo' ni tsuite." In idem, *Nihon Zenshū shironshū*. Vol. 1. Kyoto: Shibunkaku, pp. 1121–35.

———. *Gozan bungaku*. Rev. ed. Shibundō, 1966.

———. "Gozan sōrin no tatchū ni tsuite." In idem, *Nihon Zenshūshi ronshū*. Vol. 1. Shibunkaku, 1976, pp. 197–243.

———. *Gozan Zenrin shūhazu*. Kyoto: Shibunkaku, 1985.

———. *Gozan Zensō denki shūsei*. Kōdansha, 1983.

———. "Nihon Zensō no tōkai sangaku kankei o hyōjisuru shūhazu." In idem, *Nihon Zenshūshi ronshū*. Vol. 3. Shibunkaku, 1976, pp. 151–71.

———. "Nihonsō no gunsanshita Sōmatsu Gensho Chūgoku Zenrin no shōeka." In idem, *Nihon Zenshūshi ronshū*. Vol. 2. Shibunkaku, 1976, pp. 779–85.

Tayama Hōnan. *Zenrin bokuseki shūi*. 1977.

Tillman, Hoyt C. "A New Direction in Confucian Scholarship: Approaches to Examining the Differences between Neo-Confucianism and Tao-hsüeh." *Philosophy East and West* 42 (1992): 455–74.

Tō Gen, Kyo Nen. Bunjinga suihen, 2. Ed. Ishikawa Jun et. al. Chūō Kōronsha, 1985.

Tu Wei-ming. "'Inner Experience': The Basis of Creativity in Neo-Confucian Thinking." In Tu Wei-ming, *Humanity and Self-Cultivation: Essays in Confucian Thought*. Berkeley: Asian Humanities Press, 1979, pp. 102–20.

Yanagida Seizan. *Zen no jidai: Yōsai, Musō, Daitō, Hakuin*. Tsukuma Shobō, 1987.

Yonemura, Ann and Yoshiaki Shimizu, eds. *Japanese Ink Paintings from American Collections: The Muromachi Period, an Exhibition in Honor of Shūjirō Shimada*. Princeton, NJ: The Art Museum, Princeton University, 1976.

Yu, Chun-fang. "Ch'an Education in the Sung: Ideals and Procedures," in *Neo-Confucian Education: The Formative Stage*. Ed. John W. Chaffee and William T. de Bary. Berkeley, CA: University of California Press, 1989, pp. 57–104.

———. "Chung-feng Ming-pen and Ch'an Buddhism in the Yuan." In *Yüan Thought: Chinese Thought and Religion under the Mongols*. Ed. Hok-lam Chan and Wm. Theodore de Bary. Columbia University Press, 1982, pp. 419–78.

"Zenshū denrai kankei shiryō." In *Zen to bijutsu: kenkyū happyō to zadankai*. Bukkyō bijutsu kenkyū Ueno kinen zaidan jōsei kenkyūkai hōkokusho. 10 (Mar. 1983): 21–48.

Zensō to bokuseki—Shōichi Kokushi o megutte. Nara National Museum, 1986.

Zürcher, Erik. *The Buddhist Conquest of China: The Spread and Adaptation of Buddhism in Early Medieval China*. 2 vols. Leiden: E. J. Brill, 1959.

Index

Note: Italic folios refer to paintings that are illustrated. For terms found throughout the text, such as Kitayama or Five Mountains, index entries are given only to their description in the introduction.